HOW THE WEST STOLE DEMOCRACY FROM THE ARABS

The Syrian Congress of 1920 and the Destruction of its Historic Liberal-Islamic Alliance

ELIZABETH F. THOMPSON

Grove Press
New York

Published simultaneously in Canada
Printed in the United States of America

Text Design by Norman Tuttle of Alpha Design & Composition
This book was set in 11.75-pt.Dante MT with ITC New Baskerville
by Alpha Design & Composition of Pittsfield, NH

First Grove Atlantic hardcover edition: April 2020
First Grove Atlantic paperback edition: September 2021

Library of Congress Cataloging-in-Publication data is available for this title.

ISBN 978-0-8021-4860-5
eISBN 978-0-8021-4821-6

Grove Press
an imprint of Grove Atlantic
154 West 14th Street
New York, NY 10011

Distributed by Publishers Group West

groveatlantic.com

21 22 23 24   10 9 8 7 6 5 4 3 2 1

For all Syrians

Contents

Photo Credits

Photos 1.1 (Public Executions 1916), 1.2 (Wartime famine), 1.4 (Sharif Hussein), 8.1 (Rashid Rida), 9.3 (coronation postcard), 11.3 (Qassab), 14.3 (Wilson plaque), 15.1 (Damascus in flames), 15.3 (Shahbander), 16.2 (Banna): Courtesy of Wikimedia Commons, photographers unknown.

Photo 1.3 (Georges-Picot): Reproduced from *L'Illustration*, no. 3908, January 26, 1918.

Photos 2.1 (Arab troops), 2.3 (Damascus street), 3.4 (Faisal Victoria Hotel): Courtesy of the Imperial War Museum.

Photo 2.2 (T.E. Lawrence): Photographed by Lowell Thomas, 1919.

Photos 3.1 (Faisal), 5.3 (big four), 12.4 (Curzon): Courtesy of the George Grantham Bain Collection, Library of Congress Prints and Photographs Division; LC-USZ62-55640; LC-DIG-ggbain-29038, photographed by Edward Jackson; LC-DIG-ggbain-35223.

Photo 3.2 (Deraa Station): Courtesy of Nigel Tout, September 12, 2000.

Photos 3.3 (Allenby), 7.3 (Crane): Courtesy of the Library of Congress Prints and Photographs Division, Underwood and Underwood; 1921, LG-DIG-anrc-14227; 1920, LC-USZ62-35870.

Photo 4.1 (Faisal in Aleppo): Courtesy of Fonds Iconographique, Service Historique de l'Armee de Terre at Vincennes, Paris.

Photos 4.2 (Rikabi), 8.4 (Atassi), 9.1 (Faisal's coronation), 10.2 (Yusuf), 10.3 (Abid), 13.1 (Azmeh): Courtesy of the Sami Moubayed Archive.

Photos 4.3 (Umayyad Mosque), 7.4 (King Crane Commission): Courtesy of SALT Research, Ali Saim Ülgen Archive.

Photos 5.1 (Haidar), 16.3 (Deraa protest): Courtesy of Getty; Hulton Archive; AFP PHOTO / YOUTUBE.

Photos 5.2 (Abd al-Hadi), 11.4 (Darwazeh), 14.1 (Syro-Palestinian Congress): Courtesy of the Institute for Palestine Studies; photographer unknown, 1931; photographer unknown, ca. 1932; photographer unknown, 1921.

Photo 5.4 (American map): Courtesy of the Library of Congress Manuscripts Division, Papers of Tasker H. Bliss, box 354.

Photos 6.1 (Wilson), 6.3 (Rustum and Faisal): Reproduced from *L'Illustration*, no. 3960, January 25, 1919; cover; p. 87.

Photo 6.2 (Lighthouse): Reproduced from Al-Manar, December 2, 1918; cover.

Photo 6.4 (Bliss): Courtesy of American University of Beirut, Jafet Library Archives and Special Collections.

Photo 6.5 (De Caix): Courtesy of Archive du Ministère des Affaires Étrangères, Série G, Image no. A007860, passport photo 1915.

Photos 7.1 (Faisal's welcome), 10.1 ("The Initial Law of the United States of Syria," 1919): Courtesy of Oberlin College Archives.

Photos 7.2 (Mandatory Wives), 13.2 (Gourard): Courtesy of the Library of Congress Prints and Photographs Division; CAI-Rogers, no. 252; LC-USZ62-122341, photographer unknown, ca. 1923.

Photos 8.2 (Nationalist demonstration), 11.2 (Hoyek), 12.1 (San Remo), 12.2 (Millerand), 12.3 (Cachin): Courtesy of Bibliotheque nationale de France, département Estampes et photographie.

Photo 8.3 (snowy Damascus): Original postcard postmarked 1923, published by Ed Angell, Beyrouth et Damas.

Photos 9.2 (Cousse), 9.4 (Independence Map): Reproduced from *Dhikra Istiqlal Suriya* (Damascus: Sioufi Ikhwan, 1920), reprinted in Cairo by Matba`at Taha Ibrahim wa Yusuf Barladi.

Photo 10.4 (Marjeh Square): Courtesy of Matson Photograph Collection, Library of Congress Prints and Photographs Division, LC-DIG-matpc-11717.

Photo 11.1 (Arslan): Courtesy of Hassan Eltaher, ©eltaher.org.

Photo 11.5 (Fatat meeting): Courtesy of Izzat Darwazeh, grandson of Congress secretary Izzat Darwazeh.

Photo 13.3 (French army): Reproduced from *L'Illustration* on the family website of Gen. Mariano Goybet: http://goybet.e-monsite.com/pages/prise-de-damas-en -1920-par-le-general-goybet-presse-du-monde-et-reportage-de-l-illustration.html.

Photo 14.2 (Rappard): Courtesy of United Nations Archives at Geneva.

Photo 15.2 (Syrian Revolt): Courtesy of *Le Petit Journal*, November 29, 1925, cover, "Un contre Dix: l'Héroisme de nos Troupe en Syrie".

Photo 16.1 (Faisal Iraq): Courtesy of Matson Photograph Collection, Library of Congress Prints and Photographs Division, LC-DIG-matpc-16055.

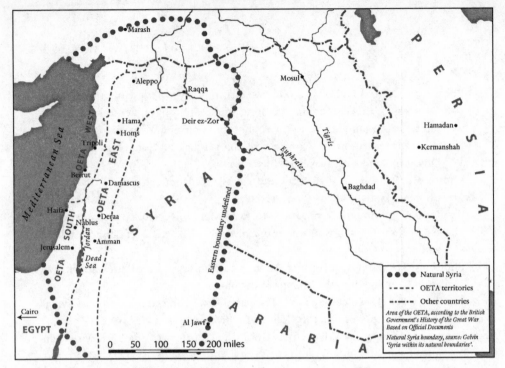

Territorial Claims in 1919. Prince Faisal claimed the territory of "Bilad al-Sham," also known as "Greater" or "Natural" Syria, in his presentation to the Supreme Council of the Paris Peace Conference. Meanwhile, the Entente armies had occupied the entire territory and divided it into zones of Occupied Enemy Territory.

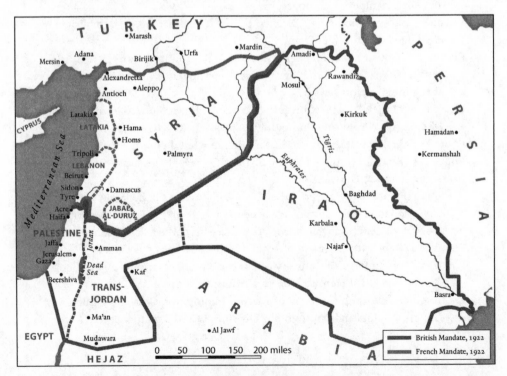

Territorial Claims in 1922. The regions of Greater Syria were officially partitioned and apportioned to Britain and France by the League of Nations Council in July 1922.

Preface

On March 8, 1920, the Syrian Congress issued its Declaration of Independence in the name of the largely Arabic-speaking peoples living in Greater Syria, comprising today's states of Lebanon, Syria, Jordan, Palestine, and Israel. During World War I, the Syrian Arabs joined the Allies in fighting against the Ottoman military dictatorship. At war's end, they embraced "Dr. [Woodrow] Wilson's lofty principles of freedom for great and small nations alike, their independence based on equal rights, and the renunciation of the politics of conquest and colonialism."[1] The Congress had already begun drafting a constitution for a democratic, parliamentary monarchy. Syria could then take its place in "civilized international society" alongside Poland, Czechoslovakia, and other nation-states carved from the Russian, Austrian, and Ottoman empires defeated in World War I.

Scholars and politicians remember Wilson's famous Fourteen Points that declared the goals of the Great War, but most have forgotten Syria's pivotal role in the effort to fulfill the American president's vision of a new world order. Aside from disputes over how to punish Germany, plans for Syria provoked the bitterest fights among the statesmen who gathered at the Paris Peace Conference in 1919.

Wilson had arrived in Paris as a messianic prophet of peace after four years of carnage. He promised to sweep away the international system that had thrown the world into war in 1914. In place of imperial rivalry and diplomatic intrigue, a League of Nations would manage relations of states under a new regime of international law. "The day of conquest and aggrandizement is gone by; so is also the day of secret covenants," Wilson had declared. "[We demand] that the world be made fit and safe to live in; and particularly be made safe for every peace-loving nation which, like our own, wishes to live its own life, determine its own institutions, be assured of justice and fair dealing by other peoples of the world."[2]

Middle Eastern, Asian, and African peoples embraced Wilson's vision to end the colonial era and ensure rule by consent of the governed. But Wilson had to overcome stiff resistance from the leaders of the victorious Entente, who commanded the British, French, Italian, and Japanese empires. In order to get them to support the League of Nations, he had to make distasteful compromises, like agreeing to the French occupation of Germany, a British protectorate in Egypt, and Japan's occupation of the Chinese Shandong Peninsula.

But in the case of Syria, Wilson stood his ground, insisting on Syrians' right to self-determination. In the summer of 1919, he had sent the famous King-Crane Commission to poll Syrians on their political aspirations. Syrians submitted hundreds of petitions reminding the Entente leaders that they had fought as allies alongside them, and helped to defeat the Ottomans. Syrians had participated in parliamentary government under the Ottomans; they now considered themselves a nation deserving of sovereignty.

But Wilson suffered a stroke late in 1919. The United States would never join the League he had created. Just months after the Declaration of Independence, Syrians were stripped of both their sovereignty and their democracy. In direct contravention of the League covenant and Wilson's Fourteen Points, France and Britain forcibly occupied Greater Syria, partitioning it between them into the states of Lebanon, Syria, Palestine, and Jordan. They justified the use of force through the League of Nations itself, by declaring the occupations temporary "mandates," periods of tutelage for peoples not ready to rule themselves. In the end, the Great Powers at the Paris Peace Conference treated their Arab allies worse than their German enemies, imposing terms suffered only by peoples who had been colonized before the war. Syrians experienced firsthand what one legal scholar has called the "sordid origin of international law as a derivative of a colonial order" that continues to reinforce, rather than uproot, the inequality of rights among nations.[3]

Syrians' bitter disillusion was shared across continents. The text of the Syrian Declaration of Independence had been published in an Arabic magazine read from Morocco to India and had been recited in the French Chamber of Deputies in Paris. Reports of the Declaration were also published in the Syrian diaspora's newspapers across the Americas, as well as in the major dailies of New York, London, and Paris.[4] The defeat of Syria sounded the death knell of postwar justice. The Paris Peace Conference's reactionary efforts to restore the pre-1914 world order infamously provoked a second world war and decades of anticolonial revolt. "The most durable of these post-imperial conflicts proved to be those that haunted the Arab lands once ruled by the Ottomans," one European historian recently remarked.[5]

Anti-European revolts roiled Syria, Palestine, and Iraq in the 1920s and 1930s. As a famous book title put it, the Allies had imposed on the Middle East *A Peace to End All Peace*.[6] At stake, however, was not simply a dispute over the control of territory. Under the League of Nations mandate system, the democratic sinews of governance broke. Arab liberals who stood up to European imperialists in 1920 were discredited by their defeat, jailed, and exiled. The French and British states were colonial in all but name. Under militarized regimes of surveillance, parliaments held little or no power. With no venue for legal opposition, political leadership passed to those who employed violence in their resistance. By the time the British and French evacuated after World War II, power in the post-Ottoman Arab world had passed to antiliberal army officers, landowners, and religious populists.

The story recounted in these pages—of how Europeans stole Arab democracy and expelled Syria from the so-called civilized world—has never before been told in English. British and American historians have tended to focus on the war years and on the British officer T. E. Lawrence, known—notably in the epic movie—as "Lawrence of Arabia." Arab historians have placed Lawrence in a more realistic perspective, as a secondary advisor to Prince Faisal, commander of the Northern Arab Army in the Arab Revolt against the Ottoman

Empire. In both versions, however, the story typically ends when the British military takes control of Greater Syria in October 1918.[7] Faisal is usually portrayed as an honest but weak leader, and the Syrian Arab Kingdom as doomed to fall because Syrians unrealistically resisted the decisions of the Paris Peace Conference.[8]

More recently, historians have begun to use Arabic-language documents to compose a more nuanced picture of this political moment in Syria.[9] But they still tell the story as one of national martyrdom, not of democracy denied.[10] Only four books, all in Arabic, have until now focused on the deliberations of the Syrian Arab Congress and the drafting of a constitution, which were in fact the primary focus of political activity in Damascus in 1918–1920. The Congress produced a 147-article constitution modeled on its Ottoman predecessor with modifications inspired by American federalism and checks and balances. Most notably, it reduced the monarch's power, disestablished Islam as the state religion, and granted equal rights to Muslims and non-Muslims alike.[11]

The historical neglect of the Syrian Congress and the 1920 constitution is not accidental. My research has revealed a deliberate effort by European politicians not only to destroy the Syrian Arab state but also to erase all evidence of its democracy. France and Britain suppressed a 1919 American poll of Syrians' political preferences, favoring self-rule under a constitutional monarchy. Instead, the French and British declared the Syrian Congress illegal and colluded to destroy the government in Damascus. Fearing that the nascent League of Nations might yet uphold Syrian independence, the French prime minister explicitly ordered his generals to destroy every trace of the Syrian Arab Kingdom's government. French troops consequently ransacked the offices of the Congress and Faisal's palace. Since then, Syrian historians have searched, to no avail, for an original copy of the constitution, which is known to have been in France's possession as late as August 1920.

French and British diplomats used the League of Nations to justify the occupation and to silence the protests of Syrian Arabs. They enlisted willing journalists to deploy propaganda about Arabs as incapable of self-rule, ignorant of modern liberal values, and hotheaded

"Through brilliant scholarship and engaging prose, Thompson pieces together the Arab constitutional order that European imperialism shattered in the aftermath of World War I. "
—Eugene Rogan, author of *The Fall of the Ottomans: The Great War in the Middle East* and *The Arabs: A History*

"*How the West Stole Democracy from the Arabs* should be required reading for policymakers and pundits who promote the lie that Arabs require western invasions to impose democracy. It proves that the West, far from promoting democracy in the Middle East, strangled it at birth. This excellent and enlightening book ranks with Margaret Macmillan's award-winning *Paris 1919: Six Months That Changed the World* as a ground-breaking work of both thorough scholarship and fine writing."
—Charles Glass, former ABC News Chief Middle East Correspondent and author of *Tribes with Flags: A Journey Curtailed* and *They Fought Alone: The True Story of the Starr Brothers, British Secret Agents in Nazi-Occupied France*

"There are historical periods that seem full of possibilities for those who experience them; only in retrospect—when those possibilities have been foreclosed—do outcomes seem clear and inevitable. Harnessing meticulous research to careful analysis; moving among international diplomacy, personal interactions, and local politics, Thompson expertly argues that after World War I, the fate of Ottoman Arab lands was not merely contested but that radically different outcomes for independence, constitutional government, and liberal arrangements were very live possibilities, far more so than is generally remembered."
—Nathan J. Brown, Professor of Political Science and International Affairs at George Washington University

"In a book sure to interest students of Middle Eastern history, particularly in the 20th century, Thompson fashions an original, authoritative study, laying out the process of the "theft" of Syrian democracy . . . Bitter lessons from the past unearthed and expertly reexamined." —*Kirkus Reviews*

"That the interests of great powers override the voices of small nations is an unremarkable observation in diplomatic history, yet reading Thompson's account of the circumstances in one particular context, and knowing the consequences that followed, is enough to make you feel outraged once again." —*Washington Independent Review of Books*

Praise for *How the West Stole Democracy from the Arabs*
A Literary Hub "Most Anticipated Book of 2020"

"Elisabeth Thompson's illuminating n *Democracy from the Arabs*, breaks new gr efforts of Syria's shortlived National Co tutionalism and Islam . . . [It] succeeds and the lost potential, of this aborted moment of self-rule.

—*New York Review of Books*

"Elizabeth Thompson has successfully combined her mastery of the immensely complex relationship between the Middle East and the West during World War I with her capacity for excellent storytelling and explains better than ever before how the dreams of those who supported the new leaders clashed with the know-how of seasoned colonialists who appropriated lands and imposed political systems that defeated democracy for more than a century since. It is an essential read."

—Leila Fawaz, Issam M. Fares Professor of Lebanese and Eastern Mediterranean Studies, Tufts University and author of *A Land of Aching Hearts*

"At the end of World War One the Arabs tried to create a constitutional democracy in Syria. Had this succeeded, the country—and the region—might be in a much better way today. But France and Britain conspired to destroy it. Elizabeth F. Thompson has brilliantly recreated this fateful turning point in twentieth century Middle Eastern history. I thought I knew this story well. But the new details she reveals in this riveting account often left me open-mouthed."

—James Barr, author of *Lords of the Desert: The Battle Between the United States and Great Britain for Supremacy in the Modern Middle East* and *A Line in the Sand: The Anglo-French Struggle for the Middle East, 1914-1948*

"Elizabeth Thompson, in a sweeping and magisterial argument, demonstrates that the perpetual hand-wringing in London, Paris and Washington over the lack of democracy in the Arab World is sort of like Jack the Ripper complaining about the high murder rate. Her situating of radical Islam in the betrayals at Versailles and San Remo is breath-taking in its moral clarity."

—Juan Cole, Richard P. Mitchell Collegiate Professor of History, University of Michigan

British Officers and Statesmen

T. E. Lawrence (1888–1935) Born in Tremadog (Wales), he worked on the British intelligence staff in the Arab Bureau at Cairo before joining Prince Faisal in the Arab Revolt. He advised Faisal during the Paris Peace Conference but soon became disillusioned. Withdrawing from politics, he wrote his famous account of the Arab Revolt, *Seven Pillars of Wisdom*.

General Edmund Allenby (1861–1936) Born in Nottinghamshire, England, he commanded the British Egyptian Expeditionary Forces, based in Cairo. Allenby liberated Jerusalem in December 1917 and supported Faisal in the capture of Damascus in late September 1918. Sympathetic to Syrian independence, Allenby was forced to defer to the Foreign Office in favor of France.

Prime Minister David Lloyd George (1863–1945) Born near Manchester, England, he took over the War Cabinet in 1916, at the depth of the Great War, and rallied the British to victory. An evangelical Christian, Lloyd George took great pride in conquering the Holy Land. After the war, he used his prestige to expand Britain's control over Iraq's oil fields.

George Nathaniel Curzon (Lord Curzon, 1859–1925) Born in Kedleston, England, to an aristocratic family, he served as viceroy of India before the Great War, and as foreign minister from 1919 to 1924. An imperialist of the nineteenth-century school, Curzon demonstrated little interest in or favor toward the Wilsonian vision of a new world order.

French Officers and Statesmen

Premier Georges Clemenceau (1841–1929) Born in the Vendée, France, he was known as the "Tiger" for his aggressive republicanism and vigorous command during the Great War in 1917–1918. An anti-imperialist, he attempted to strike a modest compromise on French claims to Syria. But pressure from France's colonial lobby and from Lloyd George would force him to sacrifice those ideals.

Robert de Caix (1869–1970) Born in Paris to an old aristocratic family, he became a leading journalist and pundit for the return of French provinces lost to Germany. De Caix was also a leader of the colonial lobby, which advocated the expansion of France's empire as a reward for victory in the Great War. He was the anti-Lawrence of France, an outsider to the foreign ministry who campaigned tirelessly for the occupation of Syria.

General Henri Gouraud (1867–1946) Born in Paris to a family of medical doctors, he pursued a military career in the French colonies of West Africa and Morocco. As a general in the Great War, he fought at Gallipoli and Champagne before becoming high commissioner at Beirut in 1919. He would direct the conquest of Syria and occupation of Damascus in July 1920.

Premier Alexandre Millerand (1859–1943) Born in Paris, Millerand made his early political career as a Radical Socialist who defended workers' rights. Before the Great War, his views became more conservative and he gravitated toward the colonial lobby. Millerand became prime minister and then president in 1920, after Clemenceau's fall from power.

Note on Nomenclature, Spelling, and Transliteration

In rendering foreign names and terms into English, I have endeavored to balance accessibility for the general reader with the needs of specialists. I have followed a simplified system of transliteration from the Arabic to the Latin alphabet that is used in the *International Journal of Middle East Studies*. In the main text, I have dropped virtually all diacritical marks; however, in the notes I retain the letter `ayn and the hamza for clarity. Generally, I have chosen place names that were used by local people in the post–World War I era: "Ottoman Empire" rather than Turkey, and "Constantinople" instead of Istanbul. When particular spellings are popular among English-speakers, I have chosen them over the phonetically correct transliteration: "Beirut," rather than Bayrut and "Damascus" rather than Dimashq. When names are known by multiple spellings, I have chosen one for consistency: I use "Prince Faisal" throughout, except in quotations from authors who have spelled his name variously as Faysal, Fayssal, Feisul, and Faissal. In notes and citations, however, I have added diacritical marks and reverted to phonetic transliteration in order to facilitate researchers' effort to locate the materials in library and archive catalogs.

Abbreviations Used for
Archival Sources

Bodleian Library	Special Collections, Bodleian Libraries at Weston Library, Oxford
Library of Congress	Manuscript Division and/or Prints and Photographs Division, Library of Congress, Washington, DC
LN-Geneva	League of Nations Archive, Geneva
MAE-Courneuve	French Ministry of Foreign Affairs archive at La Courneuve
MAE-Nantes	French Ministry of Foreign Affairs archive at Nantes, Beyrouth series on the French mandate in Syria and Lebanon
St. Antony	Middle East Centre Archive at St. Antony's College, Oxford
SHAT-Vincennes	French Historical Service of the Army in Vincennes
TNA-London	The National Archives of the United Kingdom in London

PART I

An Arab State
in Syria

Chapter 1

Damascus:
Enter the Prince

Monday, September 30, 1918. Night fell in Deraa, a small town at a major railway junction sixty miles south of Damascus. "How wonderful to be happy," wrote Rustum Haidar in his diary. Haidar was personal assistant to Prince Faisal, leader of the Northern Arab Army, which had waged armed revolt against the Ottoman Empire for more than two years. The wartime Ottoman regime's desperate measures had combined with the Allies' blockade to starve and brutalize Syrians. That was why, earlier that day, the people of Deraa had cheered the Arab army's arrival.[1]

Haidar had just come from a meeting with Faisal at the local train station. The two-story stone structure stood in lonely vigil along the tracks of the Hijaz Railway, which stretched 820 miles south to the holy city of Medina. The revolt had followed those tracks northward from its starting point, in Arabia, in June 1916.

Outside the station, darkness shrouded the grim underside of victory. Wounded soldiers of the retreating Ottoman army groaned in alleyways. The dead lay strewn across the land, incompletely buried. Abandoned horses roamed the town. Desperate peasants, starved in the last years of the Great War, had plundered the Serail, the governor's palace, and ripped off its wooden doors and window frames for fuel. The Serail's forlorn shell symbolized the end of the Ottoman Turks' four-hundred-year rule in this land.

Inside the station, the two men lit scented candles to ward off malaria-carrying mosquitoes, and took stock of their situation. Faisal spoke with the hard accent of his homeland in the Arabian Peninsula. At age thirty-five, he had the lean look of a desert warrior, with a neatly trimmed goatee. Only thirty years old, Haidar had the shorter and broader build of Mediterranean peoples. He looked at Faisal with intense, deep-set eyes and spoke with the soft lilt of his hometown near Mount Lebanon. A scholar, not a soldier, Haidar had attended a top college in Istanbul and studied political administration in Paris. He spent the war as principal of elite schools in Jerusalem and Damascus. Faisal was a sharif, a Sunni descendant of the Prophet Muhammad, and third son of Hussein, king of the Hijaz and caretaker of the holy city of Mecca. Haidar came from a prominent family of the opposing Islamic sect, Shiism. Despite the long history of conflict between Sunnis and Shiites, the two men bonded in their mission to claim an independent Arab state from the wreckage of the Ottoman Empire.

The revolt sprang from Arabs' discontent with the rule of the Young Turks, who had betrayed the hopes for local autonomy, democracy, and rule of law that had been raised in the 1908 Ottoman constitutional revolution. The Young Turks' 1912 coup had effectively suspended the constitution. They had purged the government and reorganized the military to privilege Turks over Arabs. Early in World War I, even as many Arab soldiers fought on the side of the Turks in the victorious battle at Gallipoli, the Ottoman governor of Syria had executed a dozen prominent Arab leaders and exiled many more on suspicion of treason for their earlier political dissent.

Within his family, Faisal remained the most loyal to the empire and especially to the Ottoman sultan who also reigned as the caliph, or spiritual leader, of Sunni Muslims. Faisal had grown up in Istanbul and served in the parliament at the outset of the war. He considered the Ottomans the best protection against Europeans' long-standing desire to partition and colonize the empire, as they had already done in Egypt and the Arabic-speaking countries of North Africa. Ottoman defeats early in the war, at Basra in Iraq and at the Suez Canal in Egypt, cast doubt on that protection.

Even though Arabs were fighting in the Ottoman army, the Young Turks worried that Arab politicians might waver in their loyalty. When Faisal's father learned of a Turkish plot to remove him from power, he chose Faisal, his most pro-Ottoman son, as his envoy to Istanbul. What Faisal saw on his trip in the spring of 1915 broke his faith. He arrived in Istanbul just as two hundred Armenian leaders were arrested; from his train windows he saw the first mass deportations of poor Armenians. Stopping at Damascus, he learned of similar arrests among Arab leaders. The Ottoman commander in the city, Jemal Pasha, greeted him coldly. Faisal secretly joined the Fatat nationalist organization that Rustum Haidar belonged to, and met the men who were now poised, in 1918, to build a Syrian state: General Ali Rida al-Rikabi, also known as Rida Pasha al-Rikabi and General Yasin al-Hashimi both assured him of military support; Dr. Ahmad Qadri and Dr. Abd al-Rahman Shahbandar pledged political support. In June 1915, Faisal carried the Damascus Protocol back to his father. It set the terms of a potential alliance with Entente powers against the Ottomans, primarily the promise of an independent Arab state stretching from Anatolia to the Gulf and Red Sea.[2]

On the basis of support in Damascus, Faisal's father, Sharif Hussein, opened negotiations with the British high commissioner in Egypt in the summer of 1915. The British, who were then fighting a losing battle against the Ottomans at Gallipoli, desperately sought a prominent Muslim ally to wage a counter-jihad. They feared that the millions of Muslims under their rule, in Egypt and India and beyond, might otherwise rebel. But it was a risky move to rebel against the Ottoman caliph in wartime. Hussein could do so only by justifying the revolt as a means to defend the sovereignty of the Arabs and Islam. He therefore proposed to High Commissioner Henry McMahon in Cairo that Britain promise the Arabs an independent state covering the territory of Greater Syria, Iraq, and the Arabian Peninsula. In October 1915 McMahon responded in the affirmative, with the exception of territories along the Syrian-Lebanese coast claimed by the French and in southern Iraq and along the Persian Gulf occupied by the British and their clients. Hussein rejected French claims and insisted that the Iraqi lands be evacuated after the war. The alliance was sealed in March 1916, but the vague wording of McMahon's promises, unknown to Faisal in 1918, would haunt British-Arab negotiations at war's end.[3]

The Arabs launched the revolt after Jemal Pasha ordered a second round of hangings of prominent Arabs, conducted in the main squares of Beirut and Damascus on May 6, 1916. By then, food shortages had already begun to starve the Syrian population. Jemal Pasha deported five thousand Syrian families to exile in Anatolia and transferred all Arab troops from the region. The Arab Revolt could no longer depend on internal Syrian support. The British alliance was now critical to its success. On June 10, 1916, Hussein launched the revolt with the conquest of Mecca. Arab forces moved northward and by the following summer liberated the key Red Sea port of Aqaba. The British spy T. E. Lawrence, who met Faisal in October 1916, masterminded the sabotage of the Hijaz Railway, crippling Ottoman troop movements. Faisal proved to be Hussein's most militarily skilled son. His Northern Arab Army battled through today's Jordan in coordination with the British-led Egyptian Expeditionary Forces, which conquered Jerusalem in December 1917. On the eve of the final push toward Damascus, Faisal commanded 8,000 regular troops and 4,000 irregulars, fighting alongside 69,000 troops under the British general Allenby, facing 34,000 Ottoman troops. By then, Faisal's Northern Arab Army consisted of mainly Syrian soldiers and tribal units. Hijazi tribes who had launched the revolt two years earlier remained in the south as local Syrians deserted the retreating Ottoman army to join Faisal. Syrian-Arab troops played a critical role in disrupting the Ottoman communications hub at Deraa, disabling 25,000 enemy soldiers, and diverting Ottoman troops from British forces' advance along the coast. General Allenby sent Faisal a thankful note crediting his Arab army as a key factor in the Allies' success.[4]

Rustum Haidar had been the revolt's contact behind Ottoman lines. In August 1918, as Ottoman fortunes sank, he and other Fatat members escaped Damascus to join Faisal's army for the final push. The day before the Arab army entered Deraa, Faisal and Haidar had raised the Arab flag at nearby Busra, an ancient Roman town built on dark volcanic rock. The flag had three horizontal stripes—green, black, and white—representing the three ancient Arab caliphates. A red triangle represented the Hashemite dynasty of Faisal and his father. Busra's support was crucial because the town controlled food supplies and roads needed for the march to Damascus.

At the same time, the approaching forces sent an open letter to the city's Ottoman commander, announcing that they had come in judgment against the Young Turk regime that had heedlessly dragged their subjects into the Great War on Germany's side in 1914. The Arab Revolt would avenge the victims of their war crimes. The letter read as follows:

> God protect humanity from you and your Genghis-like evils.
> You destroyed the houses of the orphans with the intention
> of doing good and cut down the trees to burn in your trains
> which carry the sons of the country to destruction and death.
> You declared your unjustifiable war legal and you shattered the
> city of the Muslims [Mecca] and borrowed millions for your
> own benefit and burdened the people whom you did not even
> consult about the war and [who] had no will for it.[5]

The Arabs' triumph now lay within reach. The next day, the army would enter Damascus.[6] But, now, at the eleventh hour, a new obstacle arose. Faisal and Haidar heard rumors that the British aimed to reach Damascus first and place it under their own military command. Britain's leaders appeared to have conflicting policies. Whereas in 1915 they had promised the Arabs an independent state simply for joining the Allies, the previous summer they had altered that promise: the Arabs would command only the territory that they themselves directly liberated from the Ottomans. It was therefore vital that the Arabs reach Damascus first, Haidar advised Faisal. Everything hinged on speed.

General Edmund Allenby, commander of Britain's Egyptian Expeditionary Force, ordered his troops (mostly Australians) to move in on Damascus from the coast. British airplanes dropped leaflets warning the Turks that their ally Bulgaria had just surrendered. General Liman von Sanders, the German-Ottoman commander in Syria, ordered a full evacuation northward to Aleppo.[7] That very night, September 30, the last Ottoman train pulled out of Damascus under a rain of rebel bullets fired from roofs and balconies. The last to depart were German soldiers, who exploded stockpiles of ammunition.

From a ridge overlooking the city, a British intelligence officer named T. E. Lawrence watched the geysers of flame and bursting shells. "The roar and reverberation of the explosions kept us all awake," he recalled.[8] Lawrence, also just thirty years old, had fought alongside the Arabs for almost two years. How many nights he and Faisal had talked of this moment! As the sun rose, he descended toward the fabled city with Faisal's chief of staff, Nuri al-Said, a former Ottoman officer from Iraq. Peasants were already tilling their fields. "The silent gardens stood blurred green with river mist, in whose setting shimmered the city, beautiful as ever, like a pearl in the morning sun."[9]

The cool Barada River had watered Damascus and its surrounding orchards since ancient times. At the heart of the city towered the seventh-century Umayyad Mosque, built on the site of a former Roman temple and church. Next to the mosque was the tomb of Saladin, who defeated the Crusaders five hundred years later. Since then, the faithful had gathered every year outside the mosque to launch the pilgrimage to Mecca. Damascus was already a center of religious faith and learning when the Ottomans conquered it in 1516. It was now also a center of the modern Arab cultural renaissance. Losing Damascus broke the Ottomans' four-hundred-year hold on the eastern Arab world.

On the morning of October 1, the Arab army entered Damascus from its southern borders. Hundreds of soldiers marched through the Midan neighborhood of grain merchants and rural migrants toward city center, passing buildings festooned with the striped Arab flags.[10] "By the thousands, people gathered on the side of the road . . . clapping, calling, and singing and ululating and tossing flowers. Rose water showered upon us," a soldier wrote in his diary. "My tears poured down and my heart nearly stopped beating."[11] "Many were crying, a few cheered faintly, some bolder ones cried out our names: but mostly they looked and looked, joy shining in their eyes," Lawrence later wrote.[12] "Pandemonium reigned," recalled William Yale, an American intelligence agent who witnessed the scene. "We were invited into people's homes and had wine and sweetmeats pushed upon us. It was a wild, hectic day, the like of which a man is fortunate to experience but once in a lifetime."[13]

Behind all the smiling faces, however, lurked fear and anxiety. Many Damascenes had not slept the night before, fearing that the Germans might torch the city before leaving. They also feared the wild-looking Bedouin in the Arab army, who were known to plunder. The city had been without streetlights since 1917, when the cash-strapped Ottomans had shut down its electric plant.[14]

In the previous two weeks, Damascus had descended into chaos. The police department shut down. Most of the city's ruling elite, who usually provided additional security, were absent, either dead or in exile. Only the prominent Jaza'iri family had stepped into the void. At the request of the departing governor, they deployed their private militia to patrol the streets. They then proclaimed a Syrian Arab state under the authority of Faisal and his father, Sharif Hussein of Mecca. They even raised atop the Ottoman Serail an Arab flag, which they claimed to have carried from Mecca on Faisal's orders.[15]

This was not, in fact, the official plan. Faisal had commanded the revolt's agents in Damascus to form the Arab government immediately upon the Turks' departure. Other leaders of the revolt were suspicious of the Jaza'iris because the family had long been clients of France, which had designs on Syria. These leaders believed the Jaza'iri brothers aimed to grab power for themselves.

"We couldn't tolerate this situation," recalled Dr. Ahmad Qadri, a close associate of Rustum Haidar.[16] On October 1, he and Lawrence expelled the Jaza'iris from the Serail. One of the brothers was killed. That night, in response, the family unleashed hundreds of their militiamen onto Damascus streets and made violent speeches against Faisal.[17] The Northern Arab Army crushed them in a few swift street battles that night, claiming control of the city. But the incident portended future resistance by old city notables against the government of the young rebels.

William Yale, the American agent, obtained a copy of a new Arabic newspaper published that same day to proclaim independence. "Hail to these O Arab arms that spread peace and cheerfulness in these unhappy countries, which oppression and persecution have destroyed and laid waste," read its lead editorial. It pledged loyalty to Sharif Hussein, king of Syria and the Hijaz. "O Arabs. This is your Independence, watch over it. This is your flag, love it. This is your King, establish him."[18]

Yale, a burly thirty-one-year-old related to the founder of the university bearing his name, was not enthusiastic about Sharif Hussein, and he was suspicious of Faisal. He had come to the Middle East before the war as an employee of Standard Oil. During the war, he worked as an agent for the US State Department, and he had spent the previous two years reporting on Syrian affairs from Cairo, where he picked up an attitude of suspicion toward Muslims from British agents like T. E. Lawrence (on frequent leaves from the battlefield), from Lebanese Christians, and from Zionists. He knew only a smattering of Arabic.[19] In his reports to Washington, Yale cautioned against taking Syrian Muslims' praise for Wilson and their desire for a constitutional government at face value. He offered Orientalist warnings about Muslim tendencies toward dictatorship, chaos, and contempt for non-Muslims. Beneath Turkish tyranny, only the American Syrian Protestant College at Beirut had promoted tolerance and national unity among Muslims and Christians, Yale claimed, basing this observation only on hearsay from Cairo sources.[20] The reports Yale filed from Syria that fall were bound to influence the American peace delegation in ways that Prince Faisal and Rustum Haidar would deplore.

The next day, October 2—even as German generals officially informed their government that they had lost the war—Arab forces worked to establish order in Damascus. They restored electricity, organized police patrols against looting by Bedouin soldiers, and cleared streets of corpses and army debris. Shipments of food from Haifa and army depots soon arrived.[21] The Turks had even abandoned their wounded soldiers at the military hospital. Lawrence helped to bury those who had died.[22]

Faisal also telegraphed news of the conquest across Syria. Local nationalists immediately raised Arab flags in in the major inland cities —Homs, Hama, and Aleppo—and on the coast in Beirut, Tripoli, and Latakia. Each flag staked a claim to Arab rule against European colonial ambitions.[23]

The Arabs followed plans that had been drawn up weeks earlier by leaders of Fatat, the secret nationalist organization. Haidar and Qadri had founded Fatat before the war, when they were students in Paris. During the war they had expanded Fatat's network with branches in most Syrian cities. Faisal had joined the organization in 1915, during a visit to Damascus. It was the alliance between Fatat and Faisal, the combination of urban political expertise with tribal military power, that had shaped the Arab Revolt.

On October 2, Qadri organized the cleaning and decorating of Damascus streets in preparation for Faisal's triumphal entry. While these preparations were under way, Faisal and Haidar bided their time, visiting villages south of the city to secure the loyalty of local leaders. They waited anxiously for news about the entry of Arab troops. Had they reached Damascus first, or had the British outrun them? Faisal worried because he had learned of a secret agreement Britain had signed with France, dividing Arab territories between the two nations. While the agreement was said to have allocated autonomous territory to the Arabs, France had never publicly acknowledged Britain's promise to Faisal's father of full independence. It was imperative that the Arab army stake its claim.

To Faisal's relief, Druze leaders living near Deraa reported news that the Arab army had indeed beaten the British to Damascus. In fact, they boasted, their own Druze troops, who had recently joined Faisal's army, were the first to enter the city.[24] Faisal chose not to dispute the point. Druze support for the revolt was fragile. The Druze were a tight-knit tribal community that followed a secretive sect within Islam. Although they spoke Arabic, they did not fully identify with Arab nationalism. Faisal therefore responded by congratulating the Druze elders whose sons had helped to conquer Damascus. "There is no difference between us," he proclaimed. "The important thing is to enter Damascus." Then Faisal sent Haidar ahead to organize a triumphant parade.

The Arab Claim to Syria

On October 3, 1918, Faisal marched into Damascus on horseback at the head of a procession organized to display the Arab Revolt's broad and local support. Nuri al-Said, a native of Baghdad, followed close behind with other elite Iraqi officers who hoped to establish an independent

Iraqi state in confederation with Syria. Next came Rustum Haidar, representing coastal Lebanon, in a carriage with two Damascenes: General Ali Rida al-Rikabi and Dr. Ahmad Qadri. Rikabi was a highly decorated, middle-aged officer; Qadri was a medical doctor, barely twenty-five years old. During the war, both al-Rikabi and Qadri had worked as Fatat agents inside Syria, behind Turkish lines. Next came tribes from Greater Syria—the Howeitat, Rowala, and Druze—followed by hundreds of ordinary soldiers, mostly from Greater Syria, marching on foot. Troops from the Arabian Peninsula, who had launched the revolt two years earlier, had by then returned home.[25]

"Their numbers were huge, more than a thousand," an Arab army officer recalled. "It was an amazing sight."[26] Faisal's straight-backed figure, adorned with a lightly patterned headdress and dark cloak, stood out amid a sea of fezzes and turbans. Photographs show a few women in the crowd that cheered the procession.[27]

Suddenly, a red Mercedes-Benz pulled up alongside Faisal on the parade route. Behind the wheel was Major Hubert Young, who had served as the Northern Arab Army's supplies officer. The flashy car had been captured from German officers. Young informed the prince that he had been summoned to the headquarters of General Edmund Allenby, commander in chief of British forces in Syria, at the Victoria Hotel in the city's center.

Faisal was startled. He explained that the parade was meant to end at the Serail, where a reception of prominent notables awaited him. No, Young said, General Allenby insisted that Faisal meet him first. The prince consented, but he refused to ride in the Mercedes. Instead, he and Nuri al-Said galloped ahead beneath the Arab flags draped from rooftops and balconies while Young followed. "I drove in splendor for some distance, embarrassed by the plaudits of the crowd, who naturally took me for the hero of the hour."[28]

They reached Marjeh Square, the political heart of Damascus, minutes later. Situated just outside the old city's walls, Marjeh was lined with hotels, cafés, theaters (including the city's first movie theater), the police station, city hall, and the governor's imperial Serail. To deter looters, a gallows had been erected in front of city hall.[29] At that same spot, on May 6, 1916, the Ottomans had hanged Arab nationalists from the city's most respected families.³⁰ Faisal paused to honor the martyrs, then crossed to the nearby Victoria Hotel. Nuri al-Said and Major Young entered with him.

With Lawrence at his side, Allenby had watched Faisal's arrival, amid the joyous throng, from the balcony of his room. As soon as the prince entered, Lawrence translated a telegram from London for him: the Foreign Office officially recognized the Arabs as Allied belligerents, thereby guaranteeing them a seat at the coming peace talks.

"Faisal, smiling through the tears which the welcome of his people had forced from him, put it [the telegram] aside to thank the Commander-in-Chief for the trust which had made him and his movement," Lawrence wrote. "They were a strange contrast: Feisal, large-eyed, colourless, and worn, like a fine dagger; Allenby, gigantic and red and merry."³¹

Faisal and Allenby were meeting for the first time, after weeks of coordinating with one another on parallel battlefronts. They now had to arrange temporary administration of the occupied territory, until a final settlement after the war's end. According to Major Young, Allenby informed the prince that he would remain the general's subordinate, as a military officer with the rank of lieutenant general. Faisal would report to Allenby through his liaison in Damascus and chief political officer. He was not to dabble in civil affairs. None of this surprised Faisal.

But then came the bombshells: Faisal would also report to a French liaison, soon to be appointed. And his Arab administration would extend only to the Syrian hinterland, not to the Lebanese or Palestinian coast.³² Faisal was an even-tempered man, rarely given to anger. "I have never seen a more patient person in my life," Fa'iz El-Ghussein wrote.³³ But the prince showed his anger now. "Faisal objected very strongly," recalled a witness to the scene. He swore that the Arabs would never accept French supervision, nor would he ever meet with a French liaison. Allenby calmed Faisal by promising that the French military governor at Beirut would not meddle in Arab politics.³⁴

What Allenby did not tell Faisal was that on September 30, the British and French had formally confirmed their commitment to the 1916 Sykes-Picot Agreement. Drawn up secretly in Paris, the agreement granted direct rule to France over the Syrian-Lebanese coast and in southeastern Turkey and to Britain in Iraq from Baghdad south. Palestine was to be an international zone. The agreement provided only for a semi-independent Arab state restricted to the hinterland and split between French and British zones of influence.[35] The British had made these promises to France at a low point in World War I, when the French worried that while they concentrated their troops on the Western Front, British troops on the Ottoman front stood to gain colonial territory. By promising France territorial gains, the Sykes-Picot Agreement bolstered the alliance. But it violated the promise of a large, completely independent Arab state that Britain had made in 1915 to Faisal's father. The British high commissioner in Egypt, Sir Henry McMahon, had made the promise to Sharif Hussein in exchange for Arab support in defeating the Ottomans.

Faisal's hope that Britain would honor the promises made to his father was deeply shaken. But now was not the moment to challenge Allenby. His people were waiting outside to celebrate. The prince swallowed his disappointment and rushed to the reception at the Serail. "When he arrived, cheers rose up," Haidar wrote that night. "Everyone threw himself on Faisal's hands [trying to kiss them], rejoicing. . . . People pushed through the door." Government officials, tribal and religious chiefs, and city notables greeted the prince. The mufti of Damascus pledged allegiance to Faisal and to his father, Sharif Hussein. Like the other notables gathered at the Serail, the mufti had until recently supported the Ottomans. He had also, Haidar noted, signed a wartime fatwa ordering Faisal's assassination.

Faisal understood that he had to win the support of these conservative Damascene notables, who would jealously guard their local influence against inclusion in an Arab national state ruled by younger men like himself. As he stood up to speak, he found comfort in the faces of Arab nationalists whom he had met on visits to Damascus.[36] He thanked everyone for the warm welcome, then explained that Syria's revival could be accomplished only by "uniting our hearts and tongues, and standing shoulder to shoulder." The war was not yet done, and Syria was not yet fully won, he reminded them: "We need to expel the Turks from Aleppo, to beyond the Taurus Mountains!"[37]

After the reception, Faisal attended a banquet hosted by General Allenby. He then met individually with the city's notables and religious leaders, who appeared to welcome his vision of Arab unity.[38] Although Faisal's day had begun with disappointment at Allenby's announcement that Britain intended to limit his power, it ended with hope that the Damascene elite would support his rule.

Before going to bed that night, Faisal ordered Rustum Haidar to depart immediately for Beirut to raise the Hashemite flag and establish Arab rule there. The prince had no intention of heeding Allenby's warning to leave the coast to the French. By establishing facts on the ground, the Arabs might force the British to keep their promises. Haidar packed his bags and hit the road before daybreak.

T. E. Lawrence also took his leave on the morning of October 4. He and Faisal had grown to be close friends in the previous two years. They addressed each other as "dear friend" and "brother" in their letters. Faisal might have expected Lawrence to stay on, to help build the state. Why Lawrence decided he would not remain is unclear. It may have been shock—or perhaps even guilt—over Allenby's orders to Faisal that prompted him to leave so suddenly. Lawrence had heard reports of the Sykes-Picot Agreement in the spring of 1917. But like Faisal, he had hoped the Arabs' valor would shame Allenby into granting them their due. As soon as Faisal had left the Victoria Hotel, Lawrence spoke personally to General Allenby. Expressing his disappointment that Britain would honor French claims, he requested permission to return to England immediately. Allenby reluctantly granted it.

During a stopover in Cairo, Lawrence told a fellow officer from the Arab Revolt that he had left because he was exhausted. "As we hoped we got to Damascus, and there I had to leave the Arabs—it is a pity to go, and it would have been unwise to stay. I feel like a man who has suddenly dropped a heavy load—one's back hurts when one tries to walk straight," he wrote. "We were an odd little set, and we have, I expect, changed history in the near East. I wonder how the Powers will let the Arabs get on."[39]

However, Lawrence's actions upon arrival in London suggest he was on a mission of damage control. He scheduled multiple meetings with British officials to discuss methods for blocking French rule over the Arab state.[40] In a secret report submitted to the British cabinet, Lawrence credited Faisal and his father with loyalty and courage as war allies. He warned that the Arabs were strong enough to resist European occupation. "Faisal requires to be sovereign in his own dominions," Lawrence advised. "His assets in Syria are not small. He controls most of the good corn land and the four industrial towns. He has 80% of the Moslems (including all the fighting men) on his side, all the Ansariya [Alawis], all the Jews." He also predicted that the Arabs would contest the validity of the secret Sykes-Picot Agreement at the peace conference. Lawrence did not trust any effort by Lloyd George's cabinet to amend Sykes–Picot; the Arabs would be secure and satisfied only with the full independence promised to Faisal's father, Sharif Hussein, and promised by the American president Wood-row Wilson in his speeches on transparent diplomacy and rights to self-determination. "For this reason," Lawrence concluded, "I would suggest no second edition of the Sykes-Picot Treaty be produced."[41]

On October 5, Faisal made another move to establish facts on the ground, with a public proclamation of Syrian independence. He there-fore published a leaflet reproducing his speech to the notables, and he distributed it across Syria. "I thank all Syrians for the sympathy, affection and cordial reception they accorded our victorious armies," the leaflet began. It proclaimed that the new state would be an "abso-lutely independent, constitutional Arab government for all of Syria in the name of Sharif Hussein." The leaflet also announced that General Ali Rida al-Rikabi would act as governor over a temporary military administration, until a formal government was organized.[42]

This proclamation violated Allenby's orders that Faisal remain a military commander only. The prince clearly spoke as the authority on matters of civilian rule.[43] He also addressed his proclamation to all Syrians, with no explicit limit to the territory he controlled in the Damascus hinterland. In the common parlance of the time, "Syria" referred to territories of six Ottoman provinces that comprise today's Syria, Lebanon, Jordan, and Israel/Palestine. More than 3.5 million people lived there in 1914, out of about 20 million total in the Otto-man Empire.[44] Faisal and other Arabs viewed this "Greater Syria" as an optimal national unit. It was naturally bounded by desert in the east and south, the Mediterranean in the west, and the Taurus Mountains to the north. Its people all spoke the same dialect of Arabic and shared family networks across major cities, along lines of trade linking inland grain centers with ports on the Mediterranean and the Red Sea. To partition the territory, as the Europeans' secret treaties intended, would truncate the land, harm livelihoods, and split families.

In the same spirit of defiance, Faisal sent Nuri al-Said, chief of the Arab army, north to claim Aleppo from the Turks before the British could. He sent another Fatat member as governor in Beirut, where newspapers published Faisal's proclamation of an independent Syrian state. Alarmed at the news, a French envoy sent a dispatch to Paris, urging the immediate deployment of French troops to Beirut. "The Sharifians [as the French called Faisal's army] are trying to establish a *fait accompli* against us," he warned.[45]

Meanwhile, Faisal and his military governor, Rikabi, quietly appointed Fatat loyalists to top posts in Damascus: army chief of staff, police chief, civilian governor of Damascus, president of the top court of appeal, and governor of Aleppo. Contrary to British portrayals of Faisal as a naive desert warrior, he ruled in accordance with the program he and the Fatat organization had been developing since 1915. Highly educated and experienced politicians within the Fatat organization now served as his principal advisors.[46]

Faisal's opponents, especially pro-French Maronite Christians in Mount Lebanon, portrayed his regime as foreign, led by Bedouin from the distant Arabian Peninsula. (This image was replicated decades later in the movie *Lawrence of Arabia*.) Actually, Faisal ruled through an administration staffed by soldiers and bureaucrats from Greater Syria (including modern Syria, Lebanon, Jordan, and Palestine/Israel). These men would play a central role in events over the next two years. They included not just Rikabi, Haidar, and Qadri, but also Kamil al-Qassab, a Muslim cleric, and Faris al-Khoury, a Christian politician, both from Damascus; Riad al-Solh, a young lawyer from Lebanon; and Izzat Darwazeh, a veteran Ottoman bureaucrat from Nablus, in Palestine.[47] Faisal's father, Sharif Hussein of Mecca, had no influence on politics within Syria.

The Arab regime's next clash with Allenby came within a week. Haidar and Faisal's appointed governor had been delighted to discover that Beirut's mayor had already raised the Arab flag. They also ensured that the flag flew in nearby Baabda, the capital of Mount Lebanon.[48] But shortly after the governor's arrival, French troops landed at Beirut and demanded that he vacate the Serail. He refused, insisting that he represented the will of the people, in keeping with President Woodrow Wilson's promise of self-determination, and maintaining that he would not vacate his post without a direct order from Faisal.[49] To resolve the conflict, France called on the British to use their superior military force and influence. On October 9, General Allenby sent a British officer to the Serail to oust the Arab governor and take down the flag.[50]

Outraged, Faisal resigned his position as lieutenant general, protesting that the flag represented the self-determination of the Arab people. "Divine justice and the nobility of mankind will not accept such an action. I demand that the stain upon that flag be obliterated and that people of Beyrouth should attain their wishes."[51]

Allenby, who was headquartered in Jerusalem, traveled personally to Damascus to reassure the prince that the French military governor was temporary, though he apparently had no authority to make such a guarantee, as revealed in a report he quickly filed in London: "I gave the Amir Faisal an official assurance that whatever measures might be taken during the period of military administration they were purely provisional and could not be allowed to prejudice the final settlement by the peace conference, at which no doubt the Arabs would have a representative," Allenby wrote. "I reminded the Amir that the Allies were in honour bound to endeavor to reach a settlement in accordance with the wishes of the peoples concerned."[52]

Arab's suspicions were raised again only days later, when Allenby produced a map dividing Syria into three military zones. It severed the Lebanese coast from Faisal's jurisdiction in the hinterland, leaving Syria landlocked. It also transferred the Bekaa Valley, traditionally part of the Ottoman province of Damascus, to the French zone. The map undercut Faisal's credibility as an independent Arab ruler, before the public and before the peace conference, where final boundaries would be set. If the British enforced this boundary, Faisal warned Allenby, "my position will become impossible."[53]

Fearing armed revolt, Allenby capitulated. He ordered the French military governor at Beirut not to cross the Lebanese mountains into the Bekaa Valley, which would for now revert to the control of Damascus. Nor should the French raise their flag at Beirut, in a gesture to reassure Arabs that sovereignty on the coast would be decided only at Paris. Allenby further appeased Faisal by granting him full civil and military control over Arab affairs in his territory, with a population of 1.5 million. Now designated OET-East (Occupied Enemy Territory, Eastern Zone), Faisal's domain stretched from Aleppo south to Aqaba and the Red Sea and east to Deir ez-Zor. From Beirut, France would rule the OET-West, stretching along the Mediterranean coast from today's northern Israel to Turkey. And from Jerusalem, the British would rule OET-South, encompassing today's Israel and Palestine. Allenby salved concerns of both the French and the Arabs about the boundaries by assuring them that these were temporary, to be settled later at a peace conference.

The armistice was, however, still weeks away. Even as Allenby and Faisal negotiated, Nuri al-Said and the Arab army continued to march northward, in parallel with the British Desert Mounted Corps, to oust the Ottomans completely from Syria. The Arabs occupied the city of Homs on October 14, and Hama five days later. As Ottoman forces fled north into Anatolia, their Arab personnel defected in droves. Many officers and hundreds of ordinary soldiers joined the Arab army. With his ranks swelling, Nuri al-Said set out for Aleppo.[54]

Shortly before midnight on October 24, the Arab army occupied Aleppo's medieval citadel. Nuri established his headquarters at the famous Baron Hotel, a popular lodging for European travelers on the Orient Express. Two days later, the British marched into the city, welcomed by a "wild" demonstration of popular enthusiasm.[55] The Ottoman army, led by the future Turkish president Mustafa Kemal, retreated over the Taurus Mountains. Much to Britain's discomfort, the Arabs publicly claimed Aleppo, once a major trade crossroads of the Ottoman Empire, as the northernmost city in their emergent Kingdom of Syria.

Within days, the Ottoman sultan's government signed an armistice. On October 31, 1918, war on the Ottoman front came to an end.

Chapter 2

Aleppo: A Government
and Justice for All

"The Arab nation has suffered during the Turkish regime atrocities
that none but God knows," a Beirut newspaper declared on October 2.
"It had no alternative but to abide patiently, waiting for deliverance
until its cries reached the throne of God crying for deliverance from
pain, from misery, and from hunger, and finally God answered its
cries and supplications."[1]

Many others also welcomed Faisal and the Arab government as
heroes delivering the nation from the gates of hell. The peoples of
Greater Syria had been traumatized by four years of total war, which
blurred the line between battlefield and home front, civil and military rule, more than in any European country.[2] The Ottoman state
recruited virtually every able-bodied man and requisitioned every
healthy horse and farm animal, chopped down forests, and confiscated food stocks across the empire. No family was left untouched by
deprivation and death. During the summer of 1918, food ran short in
Damascus after Arab rebels captured Druze grain stores near Deraa.
Food completely disappeared in September, when retreating Germans
set fire to food depots.[3] In the four years of war, up to half a million
people, or one in six, died of starvation and related diseases in Greater
Syria. Parents had laid their emaciated children down to die at the
door of the Umayyad Mosque in Damascus. Corpses had become a
common sight on streets.

"The thief of illness managed to steal the souls of the people. The Angel of Death rolled up his sleeves and he prevailed in his work, over-burdening the mortuaries and committees organized to bury the dead," wrote the Greek Orthodox patriarch of Damascus on October 11, 1918. The patriarch enumerated the Turks' wartime injustices: they had raised taxes on people with no resources; they had drafted the elderly and ill and then cast them to all corners of the empire without even a loaf of bread; and they had profited on the black market instead of regulating prices of food. "It would have been worse, but for God's merciful intervention to limit suffering," he wrote. "No doubt the government's injustice to the people will bring God's wrath upon the aggressors [Turks]."[4]

The Syrian countryside was just as desperate. As the Arab army marched north, it crossed a burned-out land. Once-rich farmland lay fallow in ruins. Farmers had no tools or livestock—all had been requisitioned during the war. Many men who had once worked the fields never returned from the front.

Arab leaders knew that they had to bring relief quickly, or they too might suffer the people's wrath. Their opponents—supporters of the Jaza'iris and Maronite Catholics loyal to France—already blamed delays in food shipments on the Arabs' destruction of railways and bridges. They also blamed the Allies for the outbreak of epidemics—soldiers brought malaria, typhus, and the Spanish flu with them.

The new government also felt pressure from Europeans, who would judge Arabs' fitness for independence on its performance. The Arabs must build "a sound and reliable administration in Damascus," advised General Allenby's chief political officer, in order "to have something tangible to show at the Peace Conference."[5] The Arab state would also have to prove that it represented all Syrian people, in order to claim the right of national self-determination.

Faisal therefore devoted his first month in Damascus to constructing an apparatus of social relief and to persuading political leaders that his government would bring justice, reversing the evils of the Young Turks' wartime regime. The Young Turks' commander in Syria, Jamal Pasha, had hanged prominent citizens and exiled entire families of the political elite to repress dissent. Arabs in the army were treated as second-class citizens, and non-Muslims were forced into harsh and humiliating labor brigades that built railways, chopped down forests to fuel military transport, and cleaned garbage and corpses from the streets. Syrians blamed Jamal Pasha for the food shortage, amid rumors of sumptuous parties and late-night debauchery among his officer elite. Many, especially Arab Christians, feared they might face annihilation, as the Armenians living north of Syria did. Despair drove some women into prostitution and others to commit suicide. By war's end, even the soldiers were starving.[6]

Memories of mass trauma would not fade quickly, but Faisal's Arab regime promised to restore the dignity of citizens and the rule of law. Faisal drew support from liberals who had opposed the Young Turk dictatorship as a betrayal of the 1908 Ottoman constitutional revolution. Arabs had joined crowds in Istanbul and Aleppo, Beirut and Jaffa, Damascus and Jerusalem, to celebrate the revolution. They had run candidates in the fall elections. Sixty-seven Arabs had entered the Ottoman parliament that year.[7]

Arab, Armenian, Kurdish, Greek, and Turkish deputies united in 1909 to adopt constitutional amendments that ensured parliamentary control over the Ottoman sultan, equal rights of citizens, and freedom of the press and of association. Dozens of newspapers and magazines were published. Workers joined unions. Women formed associations to demand education and fairer marriage laws.

But the euphoria of 1908 dimmed as the clouds of war gathered. Italy invaded the Ottoman province of Tripoli, Libya, in 1911, and an alliance of Balkan states attacked the empire the following year. Hard-liners tied to the Ottoman military overwhelmed their liberal opponents. When Arab deputies lobbied for greater autonomy in their provinces, the Young Turk regime opposed them. The Turkish ruling class reasserted primacy in politics with a program to centralize government in Istanbul. Arabs suffered retribution during the Great War. Now, victory in 1918 offered hope of restoring the constitutional government that had been lost. Unlike Turkish nationalists organizing to the north in Anatolia, Faisal, Fatat, and the majority of Arab politicians favored a return to ideal of pluralism, tolerance, and liberal democracy in Greater Syria.

Deliverance for a Traumatized Society

The prospects for peace were grim in October 1918. In both Syria and Europe, suffering and shortages continued long after the armistice of November 11. World War I was a total war, a battle won only by exhausting the enemy's entire society—draining it of resources needed to fight and feed its population. The Ottoman Empire collapsed alongside both the Austro-Hungarian and Russian empires. In the vacuum they left, deprivation, disease, and disorder fueled new rounds of violence. Another four million Europeans died in postwar revolts, civil wars, and revolutions.[8]

After World War II, the massive Marshall Plan salved wartime suffering and launched economic recovery among defeated nations. There was no such effort after World War I. It would take Syrians a full decade to restore their economy to 1914 production levels. The old world was dead, but as Faisal worked to set up his new state, the new world order was hardly visible.

By the end of October, Damascus had begun to function again. A new police force patrolled the streets. Streetlights shone at night and the trolleys began running. Regular food shipments filled city markets. To redress postwar inflation and black-market corruption, the government established the Local Resources Board to regulate supplies and prices.[9]

But as winter loomed, the Arab state ran short on relief for the 1.5 million living in OET-East. The Ottomans had absconded with that year's harvest tax revenues. The French, who controlled the coast and the ports, refused to share the customs duties they collected. Faisal was therefore forced to seek subsidies from Britain, but regular monthly payments would not begin until April 1919.[10] British control of Syria's purse strings and France's hoarding of moneys to provide its own aid on the coast were both serious political threats.

By the summer of 1919, Faisal's administration had restored the basic functions of government, employing thirteen thousand civil servants.[11] Most worked in the army; the rest were employed by four civilian departments: Interior, Education, Justice, and Finance. A council of state, appointed by Faisal, oversaw the entire civil administration.

To finance it, the council collected taxes and confiscated land that had been royal property under the Ottomans. Faisal retained personal control of his palace budget, which he spent mostly on publicity, through grants to charities, newspapers, and Arab cultural clubs.[12]

Each civilian department struggled to meet the needs of a traumatized population on a meager budget. The Interior Department's public health service, for example, immediately confronted the outbreak of the Spanish flu that circled the globe in 1918 and 1919. The illness raged through the region in November, a month marked by cold rains.[13] Ordinary Syrians suffered without medical care, because the country's dozen public hospitals remained understaffed. Continued food shortages weakened resistance to disease. In the southern region of Salt, seven thousand people died of starvation and its related diseases during the winter after the armistice.[14]

Even though Faisal promoted education as a top priority, public schools would not resume classes fully until the fall of 1919. With great effort, however, the Education Department reopened the medical school and law school, both closed since the start of the war.[15] Dr. Ahmad Qadri, the Fatat leader who also served as Faisal's personal physician, was a member of the founding medical faculty. These schools formed the kernel of the future Damascus University.

The Finance Department employed a staff of 140 under the direction of an experienced Ottoman-era bureaucrat. With the help of British auditors, it established regular budgets and even reviewed Faisal's personal expenses. The department also managed the agricultural bank and land registry, crucial to restoring farm production. However, its efforts to assess property taxes were handicapped by the fact that the Ottomans had carried all land records back to Istanbul.[16]

The Justice Department suffered the most crippling staff shortages: judges were among the 80 percent of officials who had chosen to retreat with the Ottoman army. Consequently, overburdened and undertrained judges ran the state's thirty-six tribunals, five courts of appeal, and highest court of cassation. Response to public criticism was slow; it would be years before the law school could supply needed expertise. Yet, despite these handicaps, the legal system managed to overcome an outbreak of crime and banditry after the Ottomans' retreat and to restore law and order.[17]

Despite dire social need, the bulk of the state budget went to the military. This decision reflected the territory's political reality: Only the threat of armed revolt seemed to convince General Allenby to permit Arab self-rule. Only the building of a regular army was likely to secure Arabs' full independence.

The state also utilized the military to build popular support. Many Ottoman veterans in Syria felt a lingering loyalty to the sultan, which posed a threat to Arab independence. Faisal responded with persuasion rather than repression. He granted them amnesty and traveled to Aleppo, Homs, Tripoli, and Beirut to recruit them for service in the Arab state. In Tripoli, for example, Faisal took up residence in the mufti's home and then summoned Captain Fawzi al-Qawuqji, who had fought with the Ottomans until their final retreat. "I do not criticize, nor do I condemn any soldier who stayed with the Turkish army," Faisal said. "The fate of this country, of which you are a part, has been put in our hands and I call upon you to serve it." Captain Qawuqji joined the Syrian army "with joy and satisfaction" and helped to write its first training manuals.[18]

Faisal appointed another Ottoman veteran, General Yasin al-Hashimi, as commander in chief. A native of Iraq, Hashimi launched a campaign to recruit local Syrians, whom he trained in a new academy at Damascus. Despite low salaries and French opposition, the army enlisted seven thousand men by September 1919.[19]

But government jobs were not enough. Across Syria, people still lacked jobs and food, as one American Red Cross worker observed in the summer of 1919. "During the winter that lies ahead of us there will be an appalling number of families in great distress," she wrote. "They are without houses, without bedding, without a change of clothing, without a single cooking utensil, and have absolutely no resources with which to procure the barest necessities." The summer's warmth provided only temporary respite. "They cannot hold out much longer. Death is ahead, but they face it bravely, without complaint."[20]

Opponents blamed Syria's prolonged suffering on Faisal's incompetence; however, the Arab state performed no worse than other postwar regimes. In eastern Europe, societies were still devastated a year after the armistice. Their states also struggled to establish boundaries, mint new currency, and repair roads and railroads amid ongoing civil strife.[21]

In the former Ottoman Empire, however, the political stakes were higher. The Allies at least recognized the sovereignty of the German, Polish, and Czech states in the fall of 1918. By contrast, the Allies directly threatened to occupy Ottoman successor states on the pretext that they were incapable of self-rule. In Istanbul, as in Syria, food ran short in the winter of 1918–1919. Many households were headed by widows. The lucky men who returned from the front and found government jobs often went months unpaid. Even so, the French prime minister demanded that the Ottoman government reimburse the cost of France's occupying troops. Greek banks lent Ottoman Greeks funds to purchase property from financially strapped Muslim Turks. The British forced the sultan, a virtual political prisoner, to agree to severe armistice terms. Meanwhile, British and French troops openly embraced Greeks and Armenians who called for an end to Turkish rule.[22]

The Plan to Establish Democracy

Prince Faisal and Rustum Haidar, as well as Turkish politicians in Istanbul, knew that the Allies planned to partition the Ottoman Empire into sectarian zones, in order to protect Greeks and Armenians in Anatolia and to create a Jewish homeland in Palestine and a Christian enclave in Lebanon. A year earlier, the Balfour Declaration promising Zionists a Palestinian home, and the Sykes-Picot accord that divided Syria and Iraq between France and Britain, had been publicized in newspapers.

In response, Faisal and his advisors strategized to restore trust and unity among religious communities and so unite Syrians around a common Arab identity against Europeans' partition plans. Faisal concluded his October 5 proclamation of a constitutional Arab state with an oath to Christian and Jewish religious leaders linking their rights with social progress and Arab independence: "Everyone should know that our Arab government has been established on the principles of justice and equality. It will treat alike all those who speak Arabic, regardless of sect or religion, and not discriminate in its laws between Muslim, Christian, and Jew. . . . It will aim at improving their condition and achieving diplomatic status among civilized nations."[23]

Faisal also paid personal visits to Christian leaders in Damascus, offering them subsidies. The Greek Orthodox patriarch desperately needed the funds for refugee relief. In gratitude, he held a Mass in Faisal's honor and sent a letter to Orthodox bishops around Syria, urging them to support the new Arab state. Prince Faisal was an instrument of God, he wrote, sent to rescue Syrians from the injustice of Ottoman rule.[24]

However, some Christians viewed Faisal as a descendant of the Prophet who intended to restore Muslim dominance. They heeded the call of the Maronite Church (an affiliate of the Catholic Church in Rome) to embrace France as their protector. At first, the Greek Catholic patriarch of Damascus also favored France, fearing that if Faisal's bid for independence failed, local Christians would be blamed and massacred. But within the year all Christian patriarchs in Damascus pledged loyalty to the Arab prince.[25]

Faisal also found support on the coast from some Greek Orthodox and a few prominent Maronites, including the president of the Lebanese Administrative Council, Habib al-Sa`ad.[26] A Greek Orthodox newspaper in Beirut, *Tongue of the Arabs*, had hailed the arrival of Arab rule on October 2 in the very terms Faisal preached. "Today the nation is enjoying what she yearned for, the longing desire of returning to her former grandeur," it proclaimed. "The Arab nation is today not a Mohammedan nation, but a national one around which move Muslims, Christians, and Jews."[27]

A high-ranking Maronite priest, Habib Istifan, welcomed Faisal's representatives in Beirut. Istifan had personally taken the confessions of men condemned to death by Jamal Pasha. Now, at war's end, he stood on the balcony of the Serail before a huge crowd. He recited a poem hailing a new era of Arab freedom. Istafan warned Christians not to welcome the French, who would only bring new tyranny upon them.[28]

Democratic inclusion was not merely a strategy devised in response to British and French policy. It was rooted in the common experience of Faisal and Fatat members before the war.[29] Rustum Haidar and Ahmad Qadri had been students in Istanbul at the time of the 1908 constitutional revolution. It inspired them to found the Fatat organization. Back then, they had envisioned Arab political and cultural revival within the Ottoman Empire. But early in the war they had shifted their goals to establishing an Arab democracy independent of the dictatorial Young Turks.

Riad al-Solh, another Fatat member active in Syria, had no doubt that Syrian Arabs were ready for democracy. At age fourteen he had attended the Ottoman parliament's opening session, on December 17, 1908. His father had just been elected as a deputy from Beirut. Sultan Abdulhamid II addressed the gathered deputies, reminding them that Ottoman schools had prepared them for democracy. "The level of ability of the various classes of my people [has] been raised, thanks to the spread of instruction," he declared. I have therefore "proclaimed the constitution anew without hesitation."[30] Months later, Solh enrolled in Istanbul Law School along with other future members of Fatat. He met Faisal in 1915 at a secret Fatat meeting in Damascus.[31]

Faisal had himself served in parliament on the eve of war, in 1912–1914. Like Riad al-Solh, he had lived in Istanbul as a child and spoke Turkish fluently. In November 1908, the new revolutionary government appointed his father the sharif (or prince) of Mecca. Faisal had joined his father there to organize and subdue rebellious tribes in the Hijaz province surrounding the holy cities of Mecca and Medina. But four years later, in 1912, he returned to Istanbul as his father's representative in parliament. In light of the growing tyranny of the Young Turks, he sympathized with the Arab Congress convened by Fatat in Paris in 1913. The congress demanded that the Ottoman government grant equal rights to Arabs and greater autonomy to the Syrian provinces.[32] The outbreak of war a year later dashed Arab hopes for reform.

This experience shaped Faisal's plan for postwar Syria, drawn up in nighttime meetings during the revolt. Now, he had to publicize the plan to the Syrian people.

On November 4, 1918, Prince Faisal left Damascus on a fifteen-day automobile tour of northern Syria. He made his first stop in Zahle, a largely Christian city located forty miles northwest of Damascus, in the Bekaa Valley. Next, he visited nearby Baalbek, Rustum Haidar's predominantly Muslim hometown, famous for its Roman ruins and a strategically important railway junction. The royal motorcade proceeded northeast toward Homs and Hama. People gathered along the road to show support and gratitude to the prince, as Dr. Qadri recalled.[33] In Hama, locals honored Faisal with a pledge of four thousand gold coins to support the city's schools.

Aleppo, the region's largest city, had once ranked among the top Ottoman cities. It lay on the old trade route that connected Asia to Anatolia, and so its cuisine featured more spices than that of Damascus. Before the war, its population topped 100,000, with nearly 25 percent non-Muslims and non-Arabs. The city's busy commercial and government middle class had fully embraced the liberal ideals of the 1908 constitutional revolution. The American consul commented on the atmosphere of tolerance around that time: "Moslems, Christians and Jews mingled together, with brotherly feeling, and strong men of all sects wept with joy," he reported. Staff officers led soldiers in an oath to "swear on the Koran to defend the constitution."[34]

During the nineteenth century, Aleppo had produced a prominent Arab philosopher, Abd al-Rahman al-Kawakibi, whose thoughts on Islamic democracy influenced an entire generation of Arab reformers. Kawakibi published a newspaper that promoted equal rights for Armenians, Christians, and Jews. Sultan Abdulhamid's government repeatedly censored it. When a hostile governor finally arrested Kawakibi, crowds of supporters rallied to free him. Upon his release, and in fear of another arrest, Kawakibi fled to Egypt in 1900. In Cairo, he published the book that made him famous, *The Nature of Despotism*. It argued that tyranny violated Islamic teachings and that tyrants were responsible for Muslim nations' weakness in the face of Europe. The truest expression of Islamic politics was democracy, Kawakibi claimed, as long as it was based on the brotherhood and unity of Arabs regardless of religion.[35]

But as Faisal approached Aleppo in early November 1918, he worried about how his proposal for an Arab democracy would be received. The city was alien to Faisal and to most Fatat members. Owing to Ottoman wartime censorship, few Aleppines had even heard of the Arab Revolt. And while Faisal could expect some support for a constitutional monarchy, he also knew that the city's Muslim elite still identified strongly with the Turks and the Ottoman caliph. In contrast to the fully Arabized cities to the south, Aleppo lay in the transition zone between Arabic-speaking Syria, Kurdish highlands to the north and east, and Turkish and Armenian regions to the north and west.

Aleppo's non-Arab population was also much larger. Thousands of Turks, many tied to the defeated empire, still lived in the city. And the Armenian population had ballooned with the arrival of thousands of wartime refugees. Beginning in 1915, the Young Turks had driven the Armenians out of their ancient homeland with the intent to annihilate their presence in Anatolia. The word "genocide" was later coined to describe their mass expulsion, which resulted in an estimated one million dead. Tens of thousands of Armenian survivors now huddled in and around Aleppo, living in squalid camps, spreading disease, and competing for still meager food supplies.[36]

Faisal was sensitive to the Armenians' needs. He had himself witnessed Armenians being marched from their homes in May 1915, while he was traveling from Istanbul to Damascus. His personal secretary, Fa'iz El-Ghussein, had published a book on atrocities he had witnessed in the city of Diyarbekir, not far from Aleppo.[37] Since 1917, as the Arab army moved north into Syria, Faisal had provided support for Armenians because, as his father said, "they are the protected people of the Muslims." He donated camels, food, and armed protection to rescue squads that shuttled survivors from Anatolia to safety in Syria.[38] At Damascus, Faisal found more than six thousand destitute Armenian survivors. Thousands more were drifting from villages into other Syrian cities. The prince granted Armenians free travel on trains and better shelter in the city. Many Syrian Muslims shared his generosity, as evidenced by newspapers' sympathetic appeals. But the new government did not have the resources to feed them. By November, for example, reports of hunger among Hama's large community of Armenians grew alarming. In the first months of Arab rule, before foreign aid arrived, many Armenian men and women had lost the poorly paid jobs with the Ottoman army that had kept their children alive.[39]

In Aleppo, however, Armenians posed a political problem for Faisal. The city bore the weight of the highest concentration of Armenian refugees in Syria. While many of them intended to return home to Anatolia, their continued presence in the city ignited sectarian tension. Muslims resented what they viewed as unfair competition for food and jobs. At the same time, the French took up the Armenian issue as part of their general appeal for Christian loyalty in the region. Foreign propagandists had stigmatized all Muslims as responsible for the murder of Christians, unfairly casting blame on Arabs.

To Faisal's relief, women, men, and children turned out to welcome him to Aleppo on November 6, 1918. "Cries of joy and ululation rose up to the sky, as the roses and white flowers tossed to the Prince filled streets," Qadri recalled. Faisal immediately set to work. He met with Nuri al-Said and installed a loyal nationalist as military governor as first steps in organizing a government and building ties of affection and trust.

On November 11, Faisal gave a historic speech at Aleppo's new Arab Club, which his regime had opened to promote Arab culture in the city. It was an auspicious occasion: local notables had organized the meeting as a show of loyalty and the audience liked the speech, Qadri recalled.[40]

"There is no doubt, gentlemen, that you expect great deeds from us," Faisal began. "Since Aleppo is at the edge of Arab territory, its people were untouched by our revolt against the Turks." Faisal dismissed Turkish rumors that his father had sold Muslim lands to the West: such a betrayal was unthinkable for a family descended from the Prophet Muhammad: "We rebelled for no other reason than to avenge the righteous and to aid the oppressed," the prince declared. "When the Turks sounded the trumpet of war, they committed deeds repugnant to humanity. . . . My father saw that the Turkish government acted neither to advance religion nor to benefit the country. Instead, it proclaimed a holy war in alliance with the Germans. Its aim was to take revenge on the races under its rule, including the Arabs." That was the reason Sharif Hussein made an agreement with the Allies, Faisal explained. "He believed they would stand up for the weak, restore the rights of oppressed peoples, help us expel the Turks, and return to us, the Arabs, what the Turks had stolen."[41]

Faisal emphasized that he was no foreigner. Nor would he challenge the privileges of Aleppo's elite. "I am an Arab and I have no privilege over any other Arab, not even by the weight of an atom," he vowed, in reference to a verse in the Qur'an. Unlike secularized nationalists, Faisal spoke a language rich in religious references.

The prince dismissed worry about the presence of European troops in the city. "I, in the name of all Arabs, inform my brothers in the Grey City [Aleppo] that the Western governments, especially England and France, have done us a great favor and given us tremendous support." Only with their help would Arabs be able to expel the Turks and so to punish them for the atrocities they had committed. "The Arabs will never forget what they have done for us, for as long as we exist on Earth," Faisal vowed.

Faisal then waved a document triumphantly before his audience, as proof that Europeans did not intend to colonize the Arabs. "I will now read to you a telegram that came to me three days ago," he declared, "in order to let all citizens understand that we have not sold the country and will never sell it." Faisal then read the text of the November 8 Anglo-French declaration on Allied war goals:

> The aim of France and Great Britain in carrying on in the
> Near East the war let loose by Germany's ambition is the
> complete and final liberation of the peoples so long oppressed
> by the Turks and the establishment of governments and
> administrations deriving their authority from the initiative and
> the free choice of the native populations.[42]

The telegram was of "great historical importance," Faisal promised. It appeared to confirm Britain's promises of independence made to his father, Sharif Hussein, in 1915. Such proof was crucial to Faisal's political stature. Many Muslims, including some in his audience that day in Aleppo, had considered the Arab Revolt a heresy for waging war against the Ottoman caliph.

Faisal knew that future of his rule required the withdrawal of foreign troops from Syrian soil. Otherwise, Syrians would have every right to accuse his family of selling out. On the basis of this promised independence, he sought to recruit Aleppines to help build the new Arab state. "Countries cannot live amid chaos," Faisal continued. "I urge my Arab brothers, whatever their religion, to grasp the reins of unity and mutual understanding, to spread knowledge and to form a government that will make us proud," he said. "If we behave as the Turks did, God forbid, we will be expelled from the country just as they were. But if we rise to our duty, then history will record our deeds with the ink of glory."

Faisal closed his speech with a revolutionary statement. In order to succeed, he said, the new state must rest on a loyalty above religion, to include all Arabs. "I repeat what I have said everywhere, that the Arabs were Arabs before Moses and Jesus and Muhammad and that religions command us to pursue truth and brotherhood on Earth. Therefore, anyone who sows division among Muslims, Christians, and Jews is not an Arab."[43]

This was a radical break with Ottoman political tradition. For five hundred years, the Ottoman sultan had ruled with the title of caliph, successor to the Prophet Muhammad. In that capacity, every Ottoman sultan pledged to protect all Sunni Muslims and to uphold the rule of Islamic law. Even the revolutionaries of 1908 had dared not challenge the religious foundation of the state. Muslims remained first-class citizens despite the Ottoman constitution's promise of equality among all citizens. In a sense, Faisal was fulfilling the spirit of that revolution now, by disavowing the primacy of Muslim over non-Muslim.[44]

Faisal's statement was also a daring challenge to his own father. Sharif Hussein had waged the Arab Revolt against the secularist Young Turks, who routinely violated Islamic law and waged a false "jihad," in alliance with infidel Germans. Only the Arabs, the original Muslims, could now restore the Islamic caliphate. Because Sharif Hussein's family had guarded Islam's most holy cities for centuries, he could declare the revolt based on his Islamic authority.[45]

Faisal's break with his father reflected political calculation. He knew that many Syrians opposed Sharif Hussein's pretensions to rule their land. They had heard that he ruled in Mecca as an autocrat, employing brutal corporal punishments long rejected by the Ottomans. Faisal was using his speech to demonstrate to Syrians in the city farthest from Mecca and least sympathetic to the Arab Revolt that he was enacting a formal break with his father. He intended to build a state in Syria separate from (but allied with) Hussein's Arabian kingdom.[46]

However, Faisal's call to equality also challenged Aleppo's notables, whose status was built on Ottoman social hierarchy. Because of their loyalty to the Ottoman caliph, many had colluded with Ottoman officials during the war, despite the state's persecution of non-Muslims.[47]

Faisal therefore offered a new political bargain. Aleppines would enter into a new community, defined not by loyalty to the Ottoman dynasty but rather by mutual respect among Arabs. It would revive Arab glory after six hundred years of Ottoman humiliation. He reminded Aleppines that the Ottomans had treated Arabs as second-class soldiers and citizens, despite Syrians' wartime sacrifices.[48] It was now time to abandon old social hierarchies that had long stifled social development. It was time to embrace modern progress. Faisal argued, offering himself as an example of the new national spirit: "I ask my brothers to consider me as a servant of their country," he said. "I will not relent in promoting justice and resisting injustice, and in doing everything I can to raise the status of the Arabs." He assured the notables that they would retain their prestige by serving Aleppo in public office. Teachers, policemen, and city administrators were in honorable professions. "People do every kind of job in their homes. We even find the man of the house sweeping the floors with his own hands. He does not regard this as a dishonor."[49]

Faisal closed his speech with an appeal to recruit teachers. "Aleppo is empty of schools. I wish for it a future as glorious in knowledge as its past," he said, in reference to the great scholar Kawakibi. "God grant us success in the service of the country and in our efforts for mankind. May the nation enjoy a life of comfort and peace!"[50]

Looking to Woodrow Wilson

Faisal's liberalism was not merely the product of naive nostalgia for the lost, prewar world. While he and his Fatat advisors looked back to the 1908 constitutional revolution, they also looked forward, to reviving a post-Ottoman Arab civilization inspired by universal political values common to all civilization.

Rustum Haidar, for example, not only had studied law at the Sorbonne in Paris but was familiar with the leading political textbook of the day, President Woodrow Wilson's *The State: Elements of Historical and Practical Politics*.[51] Constitutional democracy, according to Wilson, was the pinnacle of modern political development. Of particular interest to Syrian Arabs was Wilson's contention that democracy was no cookie-cutter system; it had to be rooted in the specific conditions of each country. The presidential and decentralized form of government in the United States, for example, responded to its peculiar political circumstances. Arab nationalists took an interest in American federalism as a model that might resolve competing demands for pan-Arab unity and local autonomy.[52]

William Yale, the American agent, remarked on the Arabs' admiration for Wilson in a report he filed from Beirut on November 9, 1918. Muslim notables in Syria had already heard of Wilson's promise of self-determination, Yale wrote, quoting a letter sent by Muslims of Beirut to the White House: "We most respectfully appeal to you in the spirit of that historic address of yours pronounced at the tomb of [George] Washington, and the democratic spirit of the Americans, to prevent the imposing upon us of any government which is not of our choosing."

While Yale praised Faisal's proclamation of a government established on principles of justice and equality among all religions, he warned the State Department that the Syrians were "incapable of administering" Damascus without British help. He also noted that Maronite Christians of the coast "unanimously opposed the Cherifian

[Sharifian] government" and "fear a massacre." Enlightened Muslims therefore opposed Faisal's "Cherifian" government, he claimed.[53] Yale had not yet, apparently, learned of Faisal's political break with his father, Sharif Hussein. Nor was he familiar with the liberal views of Faisal's Fatat advisors.

The Syrian Arab government's call for liberalism was indeed unusual in the postwar era. To its members, the Great War had not discredited liberalism, only damaged it. They sought to restore the plural society that the Young Turks had destroyed. By contrast, many in Europe—Czechs, Poles, Hungarians, and Greeks—sought peace by establishing homogeneous nation-states. They, like Syria's neighbors, embraced an ethno-nationalist vision of self-determination. In the winter of 1918–1919, Turkish nationalists organized to expel more Christians from Anatolia, to make it completely Muslim; the Maronite Church lobbied France to make Lebanon a Christian state; Zionist Jews worked to realize the promise of the British foreign minister, Arthur J. Balfour, for a Jewish homeland in Palestine.

Recent scholarship suggests that the Arabs understood self-determination in the same way that Woodrow Wilson did: not as a command to create states for each distinct nationality, but rather as a deliberative process wherein peoples could decide for themselves how they would like to be governed. Wilson's private understanding of the term "self-determination" permitted the kind of pluralistic, liberal society that existed in the United States and that the Arabs in Syria sought to establish in late 1918.[54]

Prince Faisal and Rustum Haidar understood the magnitude of the challenge they faced in building a political revolution in a war-ravaged society. They knew they needed time, trust, and support. Faisal wrote to his father seeking funds for reconstruction. "Otherwise I cannot establish a proper government," he warned.[55] He planned to remain in Aleppo for several weeks in order to establish a sound administration. He would need many months to establish the fait accompli in Syria, against the ambitions of France and Britain.

The prince was therefore disappointed to receive from his father not funds but instead a summons to travel to Paris for the peace talks. Sharif Hussein's telegram arrived on November 11, the very day of

Faisal's speech. He begged his father to send one of his brothers to Paris in his place, but Sharif Hussein refused. Faisal found little consolation in his father's promise to send the inexperienced Zaid, Faisal's younger brother, to serve as a temporary caretaker in Damascus.[56]

On November 14, 1918, Faisal reluctantly departed Aleppo, heading for Beirut to board a ship for France. As he passed through the French-controlled coastal region, crowds of supporters greeted him. In Tripoli, leaders swore their loyalty to Syria and formally designated Faisal—not the French—as their representative at the peace talks. Faisal arrived in Beirut with Rustum Haidar and Ahmad Qadri at his side, and with three truckloads of wheat for the poor. In violation of a French ban on demonstrations, Beirut's mayor led two thousand citizens to greet them. Young men pulled Faisal's carriage through the streets toward Beirut's central Burj Square as the crowds chanted, "We accept only you as our king!"[57]

Feeling reassured, Faisal wrote to his father from Beirut, boasting that 80 to 90 percent of Syrians supported the Arab state. He lamented that most Maronite Catholics in Lebanon remained loyal to the French.[58] Faisal also wrote to General Allenby, reminding him that the Allies' November 8 declaration promised a government according to popular consent. A poll should be taken, preferably supervised by a neutral power like the United States, he advised.

But Faisal also complained that he was leaving Syria "at this critical time" against his will. The new French high commissioner had just arrived in Beirut—and he was none other than the coauthor of the detested 1916 Sykes-Picot Agreement, François Georges-Picot. Picot was a wily adversary who would exploit Syria while it was still weak. Faisal believed that he could defend Syrian sovereignty best by staying in place and establishing firm foundations for the Arab state. One of his brothers could just as well conduct negotiations at Paris. "Please assist this young kingdom with men and money," he begged his father.[59]

Despite his anxiety about travel, Faisal also saw hope in Paris. President Wilson was to attend the peace conference personally. Like Haidar, Faisal had read the American president's speeches that had been translated and published in Egyptian newspapers.

They were already familiar with Wilson's famous Fourteen Points, war goals enumerated in the president's speech to the US Congress on January 8, 1918, and officially accepted by the Allies. Point Five called for "a free, open-minded, and absolutely impartial adjustment of all colonial claims," in which questions of sovereignty would be decided by giving the interests of the populations concerned "equal weight" with those of the potential colonial power. Point Twelve promised "secure sovereignty" for the Turks and "an absolutely unmolested opportunity for autonomous development" for other nationalities under Ottoman rule.

Turks, like Arabs, believed that Wilson could hold the Allies' ambitions in check. In Istanbul, already occupied by Allied troops, journalists formed the Wilsonian Principles League to seek American support.

And so Faisal boarded HMS *Gloucester* on November 22 with hope that Arab independence could be achieved two thousand miles away, in Paris. With him traveled a team of trusted advisors: Rustum Haidar, his chief of cabinet; Nuri al-Said, his aide-de-camp; Fa'iz El-Ghussein, his secretary, Dr. Ahmad Qadri, his physician; and Tahsin Qadri, his bodyguard.

What Faisal could not know was that Yale's November 9 report portrayed him as a liberal-minded but weak man "surrounded by clever, shrewe [*sic*] and unscrupulous politicians." Syrians supported his government only out of blind and pious loyalty to Faisal's reactionary father, Yale advised. Employing Orientalist stereotypes, Yale warned that Syria was a country of Muslim fanatics. "The small body of enlightened and educated Moslems cannot resist such a wave of popular and religious feeling," Yale warned. "A Cherifian [Sharifian] Government would mean the ruin of all hope of progress in their country."[60]

Yale did not mention that some leading Christians also spoke in hopeful terms about Wilson.[61] Ominously, Yale cautioned against distributing Wilson's speeches in Syria, because the French would regard them as hostile propaganda.[62] His report reflected the sectarian tensions surrounding the Syrian question even before the peace conference opened. It also matched the views of Yale's boss, Secretary of State Robert Lansing, who was skeptical about Wilson's call for national self-determination.

Faisal made a fateful choice to seek sovereignty at Paris rather than stake a claim on Syrian soil. He did so not just because he was pushed by a domineering father but also because he was pulled by the euphoric messianism that became known as the Wilsonian Moment.[63]

Chapter 3

Cairo: A Sheikh Prays to an American President

As Faisal's ship steamed out of Beirut, Rashid Rida set to work in his office, located 350 miles to the southwest, on Darb El-Jamamiz Street in Cairo, Egypt. He intended to declare public support for Faisal's mission in the December issue of his magazine, *The Lighthouse*. Like Faisal, Rida was a descendant of the Prophet. Unlike the prince, Rida was a native of Syria, born in Qalamun, a coastal village outside Tripoli (now in Lebanon). He was not a soldier but rather a prominent Islamic scholar, the student and heir of a famous Islamic reformer, Muhammad Abduh, former mufti of Egypt. Rida was a sheikh of the modern age, a cleric who led Muslims not in prayer in a single mosque, but in the pages of his magazine. Now in its twenty-first year of publication, *The Lighthouse* was read from Morocco to Indonesia by pious modernists who sought to free their religion from stale tradition.[1]

Rida had followed Faisal's actions with interest.[2] At age fifty-five, he was a leader of Cairo's Syrian community, comprising 35,000 expatriates and refugees. Rida had moved to Egypt in 1897 to escape Ottoman censorship and to study with Abduh. A heavyset man of medium height, he had a handsome, close-shaven face with intense brown eyes. He preferred to dress in striped, floor-length tunics with an outer robe, and he always carried his mustard-yellow prayer beads. Rida wore a white turban in the Egyptian style, but still preferred Syrian cooking. And although he frequented the offices of the powerful, he continued to ride the tram in second class. Mechanically inclined, he personally managed and repaired his printing press. Rida was so devoted to his life's work that he married late. In 1918, he and his wife Su'ad, also from Tripoli, were parents to two toddlers.[3]

In *The Lighthouse,* Rida wrote not only for religious scholars but also for the educated elite. His message—repeated in articles on religion, society and politics—was that Islam was a supple, scientific, and moderate faith. Its core principles could free modern Muslims and guide them toward a more prosperous life. Contrary to claims of European imperialists, Rida maintained that Muslims need not discard their faith in order to participate in the modern world.

With his international prestige, Rida did not shrink from angering the traditional clerics at Cairo's preeminent Islamic university, al-Azhar. He condemned their narrow learning and superstitions. Nor did Rida fear to criticize politicians. He preached that Islamic principles and virtues could flourish only in free societies. British colonialism in Egypt corrupted Muslims, as did tyranny of all kinds. Rida had welcomed the 1908 constitutional revolution in the Ottoman Empire for its promise to limit the sultan's power, and he condemned the Young Turks' military despotism.

Sentenced to death in absentia by the Young Turks in 1915 for alleged intrigue with the British, Rida in fact alienated the British in Egypt as well. He did not trust the promises of independence made to Sharif Hussein, and in a 1916 pilgrimage to Mecca, he distributed Arabist leaflets warning pilgrims against French ambitions in Syria. Upon his return to Cairo, the British warned Rida to stay out of politics or face exile. In July 1918, Rida personally delivered a letter of protest to the American consul in Cairo, appealing to President Wilson to protect Arabs from British colonial aims. For Rida, political sovereignty was the bedrock of social justice.[4]

In his October 1918 issue of *The Lighthouse,* Rida attributed the Ottoman Turks' defeat to their "national fanaticism." But he was skeptical that Faisal and his father were true liberators. They appeared to rely too much on the British, whose duplicity Rida had observed closely in Egypt. "Had the Turks decided to leave Syria to its people, or rather to sell it to the Allies . . . as spoils of war?" he asked.[5] Rida's magazine became the public platform for Syrians who demanded full independence in the face of the Allies' maneuvers at the Paris Peace Conference.

The Syrian Union Party's Constitutional Program

Rida had been politically active before and during the war as a member of the Decentralization Party, founded by exiles from the Young Turk regime. Allied with Fatat and the goals of the 1913 Arab Congress at Paris, they had advocated for Arab autonomy within the Ottoman Empire. Now, with the empire's defeat, exiles in Egypt reorganized the Syrian Union Party (SUP). Of the party's twenty leading members, half were natives of coastal Syria, mainly from Beirut and Mount Lebanon. The others were mostly Syrians from Damascus, Aleppo, and Homs; two leading members were from Jaffa and Jerusalem in Palestine. They were journalists, merchants, scholars, lawyers, and doctors. The party advocated unity of Syrians across religious and regional lines in an independent state covering all of Greater Syria, from Aleppo in the north to Jerusalem, Gaza, and Aqaba in the south, and to Deir ez-Zor in the east. A federal state would govern through locally elected provincial councils, and the rights of minorities would be protected.[6]

In early December, as Faisal arrived in Paris, the SUP elected Rida as vice president and Michel Lutfallah as president. Lutfallah, a tall man with a handlebar mustache, came from a Greek Orthodox family in Beirut that had made a fortune in Egyptian cotton plantations and banking; they had been especially successful in their partnership with Sharif Hussein in Jeddah. Lutfallah had supported the Arab Revolt and now provided the funds needed to build the Syrian Union Party and to send emissaries to Paris and Syria.

Also prominent in the SUP was Dr. Abd al-Rahman Shahbandar, from Damascus. Fifteen years younger than Rida, he had attended the American medical school in Beirut. In 1916, when Jamal Pasha rounded up Arab nationalists, Shahbandar abandoned his clinic in Damascus and fled to Cairo. With his light-colored eyes, strong chin, three-piece suits, and fluent English, he fit in socially with the British officials at the Arab Bureau, where T. E. Lawrence had worked. The British eagerly pumped him for information about Syria. Rida held ambivalent feelings toward Shahbandar: he was suspicious of the doctor's secularism and British ties but also trusted him as a fellow member of the Decentralization Party.

In Cairo's Syrian circles, Rida was known as an uncompromising advocate of full independence, against Shahbandar, who accepted cooperation with Britain. They had fought bitterly over the issue earlier in the year, after the Bolsheviks raided the deposed tsar's offices and publicized the secret Sykes-Picot Agreement. In light of this evidence, Rida argued that Shahbandar was naive to believe British promises. Nationalists in India, whom he had met on a visit before the war, knew the British far better than the Arabs did, and distrusted them completely.[7] Only with full sovereignty, Rida insisted, would Syrian Muslims and Arabs be able to build a truly free and just government.

One of Rida's closest supporters was a fourth member of the SUP, Sheikh Kamil al-Qassab. A native of Homs, north of Damascus, Qassab belonged to Rida's generation. He had come to Cairo at the same time as Rida to study with Abduh at Azhar University. Unlike Rida, he had returned home to Syria, to open a popular school in Damascus. Qassab joined Fatat and earned a reputation for his spirited activism and firebrand sermons. Early in the war, he served the Arab cause by traveling between Syria and Egypt on the pretext of religious and educational missions. Qassab and Rida met with Dr. Shahbandar frequently during the war. The doctor persuaded them that Faisal was not as ignorant or feckless as his enemies portrayed him. By the war's end, Qassab had decided to join the Arab Revolt.

By the time Faisal entered Damascus in October 1918, Rida, Lutfallah, Qassab, and Shahbandar had reluctantly decided to engage with his new Arab government. They still worried about his ties to the British. While they waited for permission to return home, they discussed strategy for the upcoming peace conference, held debates on the nature of the new Syrian state, and brokered meetings with other Syrian exile groups in Cairo and the Americas.

Syrian exiles rallied to Faisal's call for support in the diaspora for his mission to Paris. Egypt-based Syrians knew Faisal from visits conducted late in the war to his desert headquarters. Faisal's October call for a constitutional state protecting minorities was probably inspired by such contacts. Faris Nimr, the Syrian, Greek Orthodox editor of the widely read newspaper *Mokattam* in Cairo, had engaged Faisal in discussions in early 1918 about founding an independent state on a constitutional basis. If need be, he told one of Faisal's advisors in April 1918, he would accept temporary American tutelage after the war. Nimr had once favored British protection for a Syrian state, but in late 1918 he grew frustrated with British censorship and restrictions on travel. Fluent in English, having attended the American Syrian Protestant College in Beirut as a young man, Nimr shared his views with the American agent William Yale.[8]

In anticipation of the peace settlement, SUP leaders decided to draft a constitution for Syria. Not only would a constitution impress the leaders of the peace conference with the Syrians' capacity for self-rule, it would also unite Syrians and help them to forge compromises. The movement's leaders—Haidar and Faisal, Shahbandar and Rida—had read enough about European politics to understand that the Allies would judge the worthiness of all the peoples who emerged from the defunct Russian, Austro-Hungarian, and Ottoman empires. Only those peoples deemed "civilized" and "modern" enough would be recognized as capable of self-government. In 1918, modern government meant constitutional government.

Rida and another member drew up draft articles of the Syrian Constitution in mid-December. They asserted Syria's full independence under the protection of a future League of Nations. Rida opposed proposals for a secular republic, fearful of drawing the ire of Sharif Hussein. He did agree, so as to ease concerns of non-Muslims, that religious affairs and laws should be placed under the authority of religious clerics, not the state. Shahbandar warned the SUP that Syria's government must take a form acceptable to the proposed League of Nations. Most important, Shahbandar argued, it must exclude Muslim hard-liners and include more Christians. His proposals sparked negotiations with Lebanese Christian groups and debate on the role of religion in the future government, a debate that would not be resolved for more than a year. To ensure broad support, the SUP reached out to Christian-dominated Syrian parties.[9]

To draw the support of local leaders and ethnic groups, the constitution also called for a decentralized, or federal, government that granted autonomy to provinces. Like members of Fatat, several SUP leaders were familiar with the American constitution and its federal structure. Nimr and other SUP members had, like Shahbandar, attended Syrian Protestant College (soon to be renamed the American University of Beirut).[10] Over the coming weeks, a constitution for the "United States of Syria" took shape, with the addition of articles calling for a civil, democratic, constitutional monarchy with Faisal as king, and for the equality of all Syrians before the law. As Faisal had proclaimed, Damascus would be the capital and Arabic would be the official language.[11]

Outside the SUP's secret meetings, Rida had to be careful in public. Like Nimr, Rida had grown suspicious of the British, despite their early support for the Arab Revolt. The British feared Rida's criticism of their policies and had threatened him with exile unless he stayed out of politics. At that very moment, the British denied visas to Egyptian nationalists who wished to attend the Paris Peace Conference. They also denied travel visas to Syrians like Rida, who wished to bring aid and a political message to liberated Syria. Rida worried about his relatives in Qalamun, where people were still in dire need of food and clothing.[12]

As a consequence, Rida had to edit the new issue of *The Lighthouse* so as to circumvent the censors. He would cloak his anticolonialism with praise for the Allies and the peace conference and he would focus on the Americans as beacons of impartial justice and freedom.

A Muslim Cleric Looks to America

And so it was that as Faisal crossed the Mediterranean toward France, Rashid Rida decided to dedicate the December issue of *The Lighthouse* to Woodrow Wilson and the United States as God's instruments of justice. "In the name of God, the Merciful, praise the Powerful One who acts with Wisdom in the world," Rida began, in his introduction to the issue.

> Among the greatest examples [of God's justice] is that God saved Europe from the German aggression against her . . . by the hand of the great Nation least prepared for war, the Power farthest from seeking sovereignty over other nations or from ambition against other countries. That Nation is the United States of America. It tipped the balance of power in favor of the Allies, more with its moral strength than with its troops and matériel. Indeed, its president (Dr. Wilson) has called to build peace among nations on the basis of his proposed principles of truth and universal justice.

Those who violated God's truth by waging unjust war had now been punished, Rida declared. With quotations from the Qur'an, he explained that God's peace could not be established by further aggression. "Any nation that does not spread justice is doomed to destruction," he wrote. "The only peace in the world exists in equality and justice and by abandoning the politics of conspiracy, hypocrisy, and secret treaties."

Wilson understood God's justice when he demanded that peoples be granted independence under governments of their own choosing, and that a League of Nations be established to arbitrate disputes, Rida continued. "Truly, the only good comes with freedom. This what the President [Wilson] called on all warring factions to do."

Rida buttressed his anticolonial message with a threat. Those who undermined Wilson's program were the "greater criminals," he warned, prophetically. He urged his readers to heed the lessons of the Qur'an and history, lest they suffer again from abuses of power. Following the president's program was a moral duty, Rida concluded "There is no salvation without that. If you don't do it, you will produce war [*fitna*] on Earth, massive corruption, revolutions, and widespread evil."[13]

Rida then presented extended excerpts from four speeches Wilson gave in 1918, including the president's December 2 announcement that he would travel to Paris to secure the peace based on the Allies' acceptance of his Fourteen Points. He offered his own commentary on

Wilson's September 27 speech in New York City, in which Wilson had expanded on the president's vision of a League of Nations "composed of all countries to prevent the outbreak of another great war." Wilson insisted on the peace that the "mass of men" had fought for—not in "statesmen's terms" involving territorial swaps and divisions of power, but rather "in terms of broad-visioned justice and mercy and peace and the satisfaction of those deep-seated longings of oppressed and distracted men and women and enslaved peoples."[14]

Faris Nimr's newspaper, *Mokattam*, had praised the speech for its proclamation that "the interests of the weakest in Creation are as sacred as those of the powerful," Rida noted. Nimr's editorial declared Wilson's speech a "prophecy" based on principles shared by all revealed religions. It concluded, "The small nations in all regions of the world raise their hands, praying to God to prolong the life of Wilson and to grant him the strength needed to realize his hopes. Wilson's name will be inscribed on the pages of the hearts of the oppressed men and women and the enslaved nations that he seeks to comfort."

Rida thought Nimr had not gone far enough: Wilson did not simply agree with the wisdom of revealed religion; he spoke the word of God. "*Mokattam* was right to say that President Wilson is the one who proposed these principles of truth and justice. But he is not the first to call for them. For God [*Allah*] had done so." He then cited verses of the Qur'an on impartial and universal justice that is fair and not vengeful. Just as France was rightly demanding to take back land occupied by Germany, so too should other peoples regain their land from Britain and France. Rida's meaning was indirect, but clear: he was calling for Britain and France to withdraw from the Arab lands they had occupied late in the war.

Rida closed with a warning: the Qur'an had shown that politicians adorn themselves in public with high ideals while pursuing their selfish ends in private. "Everyone knows this, although it pleases us to see all the Allied nations praise and support Wilson today."[15] He drove home his point by publishing the contradictory promises of the French and British, in secret to one another in the Sykes-Picot Agreement, and in public, in the declaration of November 8, 1918, read out by Faisal in Aleppo.

In terms unimaginable a century later, the most famous Islamic scholar of the day praised a devout, Protestant, American president as an instrument of God's will. Rida was not alone in taking such a view. The Wilsonian Moment, as historians have come to call it, inspired similar hopes among many in Egypt. Syrian émigrés across the political spectrum appealed to American envoys for protection against partition and occupation. Egyptian nationalists hoped the United States might force Britain to evacuate their country after thirty-six years of occupation. Like the Syrians, they flooded the American embassy with petitions and filled daily newspaper columns with praise for Wilson.[16]

A Revolutionary Moment: President Wilson and Arab Aspirations

Arabs were not the only people who saw the Paris Peace Conference as a historic moment of liberation. When Wilson arrived on the Continent on December 13, 1918, thousands upon thousands flooded the streets of European capitals to greet him. Many more sent him blessings and appeals by mail, from as far away as China and India.

By December 1918, "the Fourteen Points had acquired the status of sacred text, and the word 'Wilson' was now becoming something more than simply the name of a president." Wilson had become the world's "moral authority," the only leader who could speak to both rich and poor of all nations, declared Romain Rolland, a French writer, pacifist, and winner of the 1915 Nobel Prize for literature.[17] The old order that had led to total war and more than ten million dead was gone. The new order was to be forged, whether on Wilson's liberal model, or on Lenin's Bolshevik model. While different peoples read different futures into Wilson's words, all seemed possible.

The year 1919 promised to be a time of world revolution. Wilson became a charismatic prophet alongside Lenin, whose promises of self-determination and socialist justice had inspired revolution a year earlier in Russia. Already, in November 1919, the Germans had overturned their monarchy in favor of the Weimar Republic, and Marxists in Munich planned to proclaim a socialist state. Talk of revolution spread across the lands of the defeated Habsburg Empire, in opposition to the entire social edifice of monarchy. While Czech nationalists proclaimed democracy, Hungarians embraced Bolshevism to build a communist movement. More moderate socialists prevailed to the north, in Finland.[18] Even in the United States, W. E. B. Du Bois saw hope for a revolution in race relations.

Wilson was not himself the revolutionary type. He shunned political violence and sudden change in favor of gradualism. He was a man of the pragmatic and progressive school of politics, which believed that citizens must formulate local solutions to local problems. He likewise intended the Fourteen Points as manifesto for a new era of international relations that would unfold through discourse and debate, not force.

The Fourteen Points set out new principles of public diplomacy and popular participation against the old politics of secret treaties. The League of Nations would regulate international relations through the enforcement of law, through courts and common defense, not with gunboats. Wilson refused to lay out a strict plan for the League: to be effective it would have to evolve organically, through cooperation and experiment. After a disastrous intervention in the Mexican Revolution, he no longer believed that democracy could be imposed from the outside. Later in the twentieth century, American politicians would incorrectly assert either that Wilson had planned to spread democracy by force of arms, or that his vision of world democracy cloaked imperialist aims. In fact, it was built on a sustained engagement with progressives and pacifists. His vision challenged the foreign policy of Republicans like Theodore Roosevelt, a vigorous advocate of foreign intervention and American expansion.[19]

Most compelling to Syrians and Egyptians was Point Five of Wilson's Fourteen Points, proposing the "free, open-minded, and absolutely impartial adjustment of all colonial claims." It stipulated that "the interests of the populations concerned must have equal weight with the equitable claims of the government whose title is to be determined." Wilson had penned the language himself; it did not appear in earlier drafts by his staff. He knew Point Five challenged the imperial order of the day, and he worried about the Allies' reaction. But he resisted suggestions to omit it.[20]

Likewise, Wilson drafted Point Twelve with the aim of preempting the partition of the Ottoman Empire among European Allies. He also aimed to free Ottoman peoples from paying war debts to Germany, thereby eliminating German influence in the region. Wilson rejected his advisors' recommendation of protection of Arabs by "civilized" nations, meaning some form of European control. "The Turkish portion of the present Ottoman Empire should be assured a secure sovereignty, but the other nationalities which are now under Turkish rule should be assured an undoubted security of life and an absolutely unmolested opportunity of autonomous development."[21]

Wilson intended to use Americans' contribution to war victory to overturn the international system built by Europe. Rather than compete in narrow self-interest, states would cede a bit of sovereignty to a League of Nations to support common interests and defense. Rather than assert a hierarchical order through military force, states would respect the rights of all nations under international law. The League of Nations would defend the integrity of "great and small states alike." In speeches throughout 1918 he expanded on his view that people's interests should be considered in the establishment of postwar governments and that their consent should be required.[22]

Out of his fundamental belief in participatory politics, Wilson refused to dictate to nations the meaning of the term "self-determination." He originally meant the term to mean self-government—the right of people to a voice in the political process, not the unilateral right to secede or declare independence. But Wilson's many admirers who filled the streets of Paris, London, and Rome in late 1918 brought their own understanding to his intent, seeing an agenda of liberation from the defunct Russian, Austro-Hungarian, and Ottoman empires. Wilson did not correct them. This meant, as one historian recently put it, that even the basic definition of sovereignty was open to negotiation in 1919.[23]

Syrian Arabs joined in this transnational imagining of the possibilities for a postwar world. Rida, for example, was correct to see in Wilson a concept of international justice based in religion. Wilson's proposal for a covenant among nations, binding them to a League of Nations, was founded partly in the Presbyterian ideas taught by his own father, a minister. Christianity prepared the ground for the emergence of international law by fostering a community based on moral standards, civilization, and brotherhood. Any nation could join the community if it recognized common principles of right. It was this vision that led Wilson to choose as his first secretary of state William Jennings Bryan, a Christian pacifist.

But like Rida, Wilson practiced a living faith and shunned dogma. In the years leading up to World War I, Wilson turned "covenant" into a political idea by drawing on Progressive thinkers of the day, like William James and John Dewey. They extended their ideas about an ethical, communitarian republic to envision a new, non-imperialist role for the United States in international affairs. In their view, individuals exercised their fullest freedom through cooperation with others. Likewise, love of one's own country did not necessitate hatred toward other countries; rather, it ought to inspire an international public spirit.[24]

Not all historians have recognized the fluidity and potential for radical change in 1919. Prominent English-language historians have dismissed Arab appeals to Wilson for postwar independence as based on a misunderstanding. Like Secretary of State Robert Lansing, they have portrayed self-determination as a "calamity" and the "dream of an idealist unaware of the dangers." In their telling, Wilson never showed interest in Syria and gave Arabs only false hopes that complicated a peace process actually governed by old-fashioned Great Power politics. Colonized and stateless peoples from outside Europe were "a largely unintended but eager audience for Wilson's wartime rhetoric," another historian contended. They imagined Wilson as a champion of their case, when in fact he had "no intention of entertaining the claims for self-determination of dependent peoples" outside Europe.[25]

In fact, the record of Wilson's actions on Syria suggests otherwise. Several witnesses reported that aboard the ship to Europe in December 1918 Wilson thought about the Middle East. He and his assistants were disturbed by the secret treaties that aimed to split the Ottoman Empire among victorious Allies. "They are making it [the Middle

East] a breeding place for future war." Aboard the *George Washington*, Wilson strategized to secure freedom for peoples once governed by the defeated Central Powers—in Europe and the Middle East—by awarding trusteeship to a third power with no interest in colonization, ideally a Scandinavian country.[26] General Tasker H. Bliss, chief of staff during the war, objected to "carving up the world arbitrarily." After arriving in Europe, Wilson and his advisors continued to discuss the 1916 Sykes-Picot Agreement to divide Syria between the British and French: "Could we not agree that the secret pacts of the Powers must be thrown in the waste paper basket?" proposed another staff member of the American peace delegation.[27]

Counterrevolutionary Forces against Wilson and the Arabs

The revolutionary potential of Wilson's vision was certainly apparent to his opponents. In the United States, Wilson confronted a jingoistic press and a political leadership that saw the war as a step toward American imperial expansion. They were loath to cede sovereignty to a League of Nations or to grant rights and self-determination to small nations. At their head were formidable Republican leaders like former President Theodore Roosevelt and Senator Henry Cabot Lodge. In the summer of 1918, Roosevelt waged a public campaign to repudiate the Fourteen Points. In November, the Republican Party won control of Congress, weakening Wilson's political hand before he crossed the Atlantic. As soon as Wilson's ship docked in France, Roosevelt cabled to the British foreign secretary, Arthur Balfour, to assure him that the Republican Party supported his preference for a weak League of Nations that would not interfere with imperial aims.[28]

In Europe, Britain and France commanded colonial empires built on the denial of consent of the governed. As Rida correctly predicted, the two nations paid lip service to the Fourteen Points, but schemed behind the scenes to expand their empires into the Middle East.

The British prime minister Lloyd George was "a Liberal turned land-grabber," according to Margaret MacMillan, his great-granddaughter. "Like Napoleon, he was intoxicated by the possibilities of the Middle East."[29] In the dark days of defeat in 1917, he boosted Britons' morale by occupying Baghdad and conquering Jerusalem as a Christmas present.[30] "Rightly or wrongly, these two great events have added more to the prestige of Britain throughout the world than almost any event in the whole course of the war," he had declared to Parliament.[31] A month earlier, Balfour had publicly promised Britain's support for a Jewish homeland in Palestine. By 1918, Lloyd George sought even greater imperial rewards for Britain's costly war effort: oil fields in northern Iraq, permanent rule over Egypt and Palestine, and complete control of the Arabian and Red seas.

Syrian Arabs in Egypt had witnessed clear signs of British counter-revolution in November 1918. Barely a week after Britain and France issued their declaration of intent to liberate Arabs in Syria and Iraq, a delegation of Egyptian nationalists visited the high commissioner in Cairo. He dismissed their request for permission to travel to the peace conference. On the basis of Wilson's principles, the Egyptians complained, they had as much right as Faisal to go to Paris. At precisely the moment when Rida composed his magazine issue praising Wilson, the Egyptians formed the popular Wafd (Delegation) Party, to rally the people for independence.[32]

In London, however, domestic pressures threatened to curb imperial ambitions. Soldiers were desperate to return home. Funds were needed to support widows and to treat the wounded. Food and basic supplies were still short. Lloyd George could not be sure of the resources to finance expansion in the Middle East. T. E. Lawrence had exploited this situation in his meeting at the Foreign Office on October 28, when he had argued that the Arabs had earned a right to self-rule and that Sykes-Picot was an unworkable "folly." He also found willing ears at the War Office, which issued a formal memo recommending that Sykes-Picot be discarded. Britain must heed "the wave of democratic feeling which has passed over the world," the memo said, and accept "the principle, so loudly voiced by President Wilson, of popular determination."[33]

Syrian Arabs might have had reason to expect more justice from the French. France had suffered more than England in war losses. And the French prime minister was Georges Clemenceau, a dyed-in-the-wool republican who hung portraits of revolutionary heroes on his walls. He was also a lifelong opponent of France's colonial empire. Nicknamed the Tiger, the octogenarian Clemenceau had rallied soldiers in the trenches of northern France to fight not for empire, but for revenge against the Germans. He remembered the day, a half century earlier, when the kaiser's army had occupied the northeastern French provinces of Alsace and Lorraine in 1870. As a district mayor of Paris, he had personally resisted the German siege of France's capital city. Clemenceau's primary aim at the peace conference was to secure the return of the lost provinces and to ensure that Germany could never invade France again.

But Lloyd George's Middle Eastern ambitions had energized Clemenceau's political enemies in France's colonial lobby. Foreign minister Stephen Pichon was astonished to learn, in late October, that the British had unilaterally orchestrated the Ottoman armistice without waiting for their French allies to arrive in Constantinople. Meanwhile, General Allenby violated the 1916 Sykes-Picot Agreement when he granted Faisal civilian powers in Syria. It had been a humiliation for Pichon to ask British officers to lower the Arab flag at Beirut. Out of anger and suspicion, Pichon had ensured that the wording of the November 8 declaration was vague enough to permit France to pursue its claims under the Sykes-Picot accord.[34]

The leader of the French colonial lobby was a man who was destined to play a decisive role in Syria's future: Robert de Caix. A bit younger than Clemenceau, he had been raised on stories of the 1870 siege of Paris. Being from an aristocratic family, however, de Caix did not look for national redemption in republican terms of empowering average citizens, as Clemenceau did. Since the 1890s, he had used his voice as a prominent journalist to call for restoration of France's prestige through the expansion of the colonial empire. By 1914, he had helped to expand the colonial lobby to include France's leading businessmen and a formidable number of deputies in the parliament. A bitter Anglophobe, de Caix now flooded the Parisian press with stories about France's historical claim to Syria, going back to the Crusades. Public opinion would not permit Britain to humiliate France in the wake of victory.[35]

On November 26, 1918, Faisal felt the influence of the colonial lobby when his ship docked at Marseille. Balfour had neglected to inform the French of his arrival. Faisal was not given the full honors as representative of his father, a head of state; rather, he was greeted by a retired diplomat and a mid-level military officer who had served in Arabia. On orders from Paris, they were to delay the prince's trip to London, where Clemenceau was headed for a tête-à-tête with Lloyd George. So they escorted Faisal on a ten-day tour of French battlefields. Faisal's frustration was somewhat eased at Strasbourg, the principal city of recaptured Alsace (and now the seat of the European parliament). In a formal, but cold and rainy, military ceremony, General Henri Gouraud awarded the Croix de la Légion d'Honneur to Faisal, as commander of the Northern Arab Army and loyal ally of the Entente. The two men would meet again a year later, when Gouraud was appointed France's high commissioner of Syria.

Finally, on December 7, French president Raymond Poincaré invited Faisal to a meeting at the Élysée Palace in Paris. Two days later, after a brief lunch meeting with foreign minister Stephen Pichon, Faisal hurried to cross the Channel to London. He was delighted to find the friendly face of T. E. Lawrence there to greet him at the port.[36]

Faisal missed the triumphant arrival of Woodrow Wilson, whose reception in France was far more welcoming than his had been. On December 14, the American president was met at the train station personally by both President Poincaré and Premier Clemenceau. More than a million spectators cheered Wilson as he waved his top hat from an open carriage that passed the Arc de Triomphe and rode up the Champs-Élysées, festooned with American flags.[37] Faisal may have missed Wilson, the man. But the prince soon became an integral player in the fight for Wilson, the ideal of world peace.

PART II

A Chilly Peace
at Paris

CHAPTER 4

Wooing Woodrow Wilson

On a wintry evening in December 1918, Rustum Haidar looked out a window of the palatial Carlton Hotel in London. He mused about how his life had turned upside down when he met Prince Faisal. A former schoolmaster and history teacher, he was now on a diplomatic mission with life-and-death consequences for his country. Neither he nor Faisal spoke English, and yet all their hope lay in this strange anglophone world.

"London is not like Paris in its holidays. Smiles and happiness in Paris, chill in England," Haidar wrote in his diary. Lonely, he had taken a walk through the British capital that Christmas day. It had only deepened his gloom. Christmas was happier before the war, T. E. Lawrence had explained.

Londoners' mood brightened the next day, when President Wilson arrived. The American president was touring Europe before the peace conference began. People lined the streets to cheer his motorcade, which passed the Carlton Hotel on its way to Buckingham Palace.

"I saw Wilson in a royal carriage, sitting to the right of George V, King of England and Emperor of India," Haidar wrote. "He is a man of the people, not distinguished from the people in the crowds around him. What made him sit next to a King, a man from the common people, son of a Protestant preacher, instilling lofty Christian principles in the minds of people of the world, making them love their oppressed brothers and sisters?"

Haidar had been schooled in the ideals of the French Revolution while studying at the Sorbonne. But now he turned to Americans to champion the Rights of Man. Their president had promised rights even to small nations. "Will Wilson be able to do this?" he asked himself. "In the eyes of oppressed nations, Wilson is the awaited messiah."[1]

Faisal may have agreed with Haidar, but he played along with the royal pageantry. After a cool reception in France, he had come to secure British support before the conference. At the palace, King George bestowed war honors on him. Even through an interpreter, Faisal impressed the court with his dignified manner, his rich musical voice, and his wit. When he walked in the royal gardens, often wearing a frock coat rather than robes, he blended well into aristocratic society. At five feet, ten inches tall, he cut a graceful and dignified figure.[2]

For the previous two weeks, he and Haidar had attended numerous elegant dinners with British officials. Ever so politely, their hosts warned that Britain would never sacrifice its friendship with France for Syria. The road to independence ran through Paris, they advised.

Faisal's anxiety peaked on December 28, in a meeting with Lord Curzon. The former viceroy of India, Curzon now played a prominent role in British foreign policy. When Faisal asked for Britain's commitment to Arab independence, Curzon equivocated: "We will go to the conference and demand as much as we can."[3]

Alarmed, Faisal, Lawrence, and Haidar drafted a formal memorandum outlining Arab desires, which was received positively by several officials in the British Foreign Office, who thought it reasonable and modest. But the memo had little impact on the one man who controlled British policy in Syria, Lloyd George.[4]

Faisal also wrote a letter to his brother Zaid in Damascus, ordering him to begin building Arab defenses. He advised Zaid to buy military equipment, send a contingent to Egypt to learn to drive armored tanks, and order the army to expand Syria's border north of Aleppo. Force might become necessary, should the British and French revert to their prewar colonial ambitions and not respect Arab rights. In the meantime, he confided to his brother, he would cultivate the one power that seemed not to play the old imperial game: "We have channeled all our ambitions into winning over the Americans."[5]

Pre-Conference Maneuvering, in Public and in Secret

On January 9, 1919, after more dinners and teas, Faisal and Haidar finally left London for Paris. Their train traversed the frigid, ravaged countryside of northern France, the now silent Western Front. Haidar was nervous: "It is possible that Wilson might strike with an iron bar," he wrote in his diary, "and so rescue small nations from the misery that engulfs them due to Great Power ambition. But many difficulties stand in the way."[6]

They arrived back in Paris the next day and headed to the Hotel Continental, a stone's throw from the Louvre. There they met Haidar's old friend Awni Abd al-Hadi, who, in their month's absence, had organized a private wing of the hotel into the Arab delegation's headquarters.

Abd al-Hadi recalled his surprise in December when he opened the door of his Left Bank apartment to find Rustum Haidar with Dr. Ahmad Qadri.[7] They had not seen one another in four years. The trio were the original founders of the Fatat nationalist organization. While Haidar and Qadri had returned to Syria, Abd al-Hadi had still been in France completing his degree in August 1914 when the war broke out. Unable to travel, he had spent the war years working as a journalist and translator. With a broad forehead and dark locks, he had the intense look of Edgar Allan Poe.

The Hotel Continental was an opulent edifice situated on the Seine's Right Bank, in a swanky section of Paris that Abd al-Hadi rarely frequented. There, he was awed to meet Prince Faisal, the legendary hero of the Arab Revolt. Faisal dispensed with ceremony and immediately asked Abd al-Hadi to brief him on French politics. The Parisian press, Abd al-Hadi warned him, had already convinced the French public that Arabs were backward, and that France should therefore colonize Syria.

"Faisal stopped me and said he thought the French view might be changed, since the Arabs had fought with them for their independence," Abd al-Hadi recalled. "I told his Highness that France is incapable of changing the colonial policy she has followed for decades. The reason is that France is short of men . . . while her [German] neighbor's population grows."[8] Abd al-Hadi referred to the fact that France had to rely on colonial troops to defeat the Germans. That fact had tempered the anticolonialism even of Premier Georges Clemenceau.

What the Syrian delegates did not know was that Clemenceau and British Prime Minister Lloyd George had already rigged the diplomatic game against them. The French and British leaders had met secretly at the French embassy in London on December 1, before Wilson's arrival. In defiance of the first of his Fourteen Points, which banned secret treaties in favor of transparency, they had quietly cut a deal to carve victors' spoils from the defeated Ottoman Empire. (T. E. Lawrence probably suspected such a deal, which was why he had followed Faisal to Paris.)

Lloyd George promised Clemenceau to honor the secret 1916 Sykes-Picot Agreement, but with a few modifications. Specifically, he proposed that the northern city of Mosul be added to the former Ottoman provinces of Baghdad and Basra, which Britain already occupied. The British suspected oil fields lay beneath Mosul, and they desperately needed petroleum. In addition, Lloyd George proposed that Britain retain rule of Palestine, even though the Sykes-Picot Agreement had designated it an international zone. Britain had to keep its promise made by Balfour to support Zionists in building a Jewish national home there.

Clemenceau was not terribly concerned with the Arab territories; Germany worried him much more. However, the Parisian press was filled with outrage that Britain might gain all the spoils of war in the Middle East. So, he responded to Lloyd George's proposal by demanding a quid pro quo—if Britain got to occupy Iraq and Palestine, France must colonize Lebanon and Syria. He also demanded a portion of the petroleum produced in Mosul, since France, too, had run dangerously short of oil during the war. The Great War had

begun with cavalry but ended with the victory of the internal com-
bustion engine, driving tanks, ships, and airplanes. The deal struck
on December 1, 1918, launched the politics of petroleum that still
governs international affairs in the Middle East.[9]

However, the deal also contradicted the Anglo-French declaration
of November 7, 1918, which promised to help Arabs establish "native
governments" freely chosen by themselves.[10] In his Aleppo speech
Faisal had hailed that declaration because it appeared to affirm Britain's 1915 promise to his father of an independent Arab state, alongside
the 1917 promise to Zionists. As Faisal met with his advisors at the
Hotel Continental, he also assumed that the peace conference would
proceed according to Wilson's spirit of open covenants.

The double-dealing by Clemenceau and Lloyd George was driven
first by their need for oil, but second by their need to satisfy public opinion in France and Britain. The crowds that turned out to
welcome Wilson also demanded revenge and reward for wartime
suffering. Thousands of French citizens sent letters to President
Wilson demanding that he punish the Germans.[11] Likewise, Lloyd
George had won reelection in December by promising to "make the
Germans pay."[12] French and British citizens also demanded tangible
gains for their millions dead. Their rulers, with bankrupted treasur-
ies, could offer them only conquered territory. A year earlier, Lloyd
George had presented the occupation of Jerusalem as a Christmas
gift to the British people. Clemenceau knew that his own citizens
would demand equal gains.

Faisal, too, appreciated the new power of public opinion. At previous European conferences—in 1815 at Vienna and in 1878 at Berlin—
aristocrats had met in secret to rearrange the world map. Now they
staged ceremonies and press conferences for their citizens. The Arabs
could never win a diplomatic game played behind the closed doors of
Parisian salons. So Faisal and his advisors strategized to insist publicly
on President Wilson's call for consent of the governed. They encouraged Syrian-American groups from across the Atlantic to send petitions
to the White House, demanding independence. Proof of popular support might convince President Wilson to send a commission of inquiry
to Syria, and so undercut France's sentimental claims of historical ties.

Faisal also strategized to win over the French public. Following T. E. Lawrence's advice, he deliberately wore ornate Arab robes and a headdress. The costume won him much notice in the press and, if Haidar was to be believed, much admiration from Parisian ladies. A certain Comtesse de Kellermann invited Faisal regularly to lunch and introduced him to high society.[13] He and Haidar also made public appearances at the theater and the opulent Paris Opéra.

As the drama of peacemaking unfolded, the Arab presence disrupted the Great Powers' script. As Wilson had feared when he penned Point Five a year earlier, "colonialism was the third rail of world politics."[14] While negotiations over peoples already colonized—as in Germany's former colonies or the British protectorate in Egypt—proceeded smoothly, the proposal to assert colonial rule over their Arab allies who had been sovereign citizens of the Ottoman Empire produced fireworks matched only by the fight over German reparations. In public, Wilson maintained cordial relations with the British and French negotiators. But behind closed doors he demonstrated a willingness to shock and stun racialists intent on imperial gains.

A Chilly Opening of the Paris Peace Conference

Upon his arrival in Paris, Faisal secured an appointment with Clemenceau. Known as the Father of Victory, the French premier simultaneously served as war minister . And so Faisal met him at the war ministry on the morning of January 11, accompanied by Abd al-Hadi.[15]

They entered Clemenceau's dark, cluttered office and quickly discerned that the premier was preoccupied by domestic problems. His citizens were freezing this winter, in need of fuel and food. Five million soldiers would soon be demobilized; all needed jobs.[16] Most of all, Clemenceau needed to heal France's wounded soul. It was a "mournful victory" for the French, who had suffered four years of German occupation and more than 1.3 million deaths. Only six months earlier, the German army had approached close enough to bombard Paris with its huge Emperor William gun. That morning, Clemenceau planned sweet revenge. He would open the peace conference on January 18, the same date when forty-eight years earlier the Germans had impudently crowned William I their emperor at the Palace of Versailles. The 1919 peace settlement would reverse that humiliation.[17]

So, Clemenceau kept his meeting with Faisal short. He greeted the prince cordially and assured him vaguely that the French government would help to liberate the Arabs, as promised in the November 7 declaration. Ever hopeful, Faisal wrote enthusiastically to his brother Zaid about meeting "the great Frenchman." More cynical, Haidar confided his doubts about Clemenceau to his diary: "What did he really intend for the Arabs?"[18]

Faisal's good mood faded a few days later, when he approached the French foreign ministry about attending the peace conference. He met Jean Gout, assistant director for Asian affairs. An unkempt bureaucrat who wore a monocle, Gout responded rudely. There was no place at the peace table for the Arabs, he declared. The Hijaz was not on the published list of states represented at the conference. Faisal panicked and sent his men across Paris to search for T. E. Lawrence.

That night, Haidar couldn't sleep. Nor could Faisal. At two in the morning, Lawrence arrived to find the prince wandering the hotel corridors. The next afternoon, less than twenty-four hours before the opening ceremony, the Englishman reappeared bearing good news: Balfour had secured French approval for two conference seats to represent King Hussein of the Hijaz. Faisal would have to represent his father, because Syria had not yet been recognized as an independent state. "The Arabs will attend!" the prince announced jubilantly.[19]

The Paris Peace Conference formally opened the next day, January 18. Shortly before three o'clock, President Wilson arrived at the Quai d'Orsay, the French foreign ministry, in a large automobile. Lifting his hat with a smile to the crowd, he was greeted by a band of trumpets and kettledrums.[20] Rain poured down, but people cheered anyway. As more delegates arrived, they filed into the Clock Room, named for the ornate timepiece embedded in a huge marble fireplace. Red draperies and massive crystal chandeliers also warmed the room. Beneath the clock sat Clemenceau, with Wilson and Lloyd George beside him. Faisal greeted the French and British foreign ministers,

Pichon and Balfour. Then he and Haidar took their assigned seats at the U-shaped table, between delegates from Guatemala and Liberia.[21]

French president Raymond Poincaré welcomed the assembly of "governments and free peoples" and urged them to seek "nothing but justice," meaning reparation for victimized peoples and "punishment of the guilty." He thereby launched France's first salvo of the peace conference—to define its mission narrowly, as a military settlement in Europe.

Wilson parried Poincaré's thrust first by nominating Clemenceau as conference president, and then by redefining the event's mission. It was right that the nations meet in Paris, Wilson began, because "some of the most tragic sufferings of the war" occurred in France. It was also right, he continued, because Paris was a world capital, and this was an unprecedented global event. "This is the supreme conference in the history of mankind," Wilson said. "More nations are represented here than were ever represented at such a conference before; the fortunes of all peoples are involved." For Wilson, the conference's mission must go beyond military affairs, to enact the global reform of international relations.

Clemenceau's acceptance speech was vaguely conciliatory. The conference, he promised, would not only repair the war's material devastation, but also accomplish "the nobler and higher reparation" to free people from militarism, grief, and terror. "Everything must yield to the necessity of a closer and closer union among the peoples who have taken part in this great war. The League of Nations is here. It is in yourselves; it is for you to make it live."[22]

Haidar's diary entry that day made no mention of these pretensions. "Oppressive atmosphere," he jotted down, irked at how western Europeans dominated the proceedings. They talked of punishing the German Kaiser Wilhelm, but made no mention of Ottoman war criminals. There was no talk, either, of the rights of small nations.

The Arabs believed their claims should be treated on a par with those of peoples liberated from the Austro-Hungarian Empire. Like Faisal, eastern European leaders had made their way to Paris that winter to propose new nation-states. Some, like Czech leader Tomáš Masaryk, had already won international recognition for their countries. Poland had declared independence on November 11, even as two rivals battled for control of the country. In the closing weeks of 1918, South Slavs had convened an assembly to found the Kingdom of Yugoslavia. And Romanians proclaimed a new Greater Romania after annexing Transylvania from defeated Hungary.

But it became clear that guns—not rights—determined the status of nations at Paris. Eastern Europeans won seats at the conference table by creating facts on the ground with rump armies.[23] The Arabs had little hope of matching their firepower: British and French occupiers blunted their efforts to expand the Arab army. Other peoples of the defeated Ottoman Empire—Turks, Armenians, and Kurds—were also absent from the table, as were most African colonies, even those that had supplied thousands of soldiers to the Allied armies.

The French press claimed that Syria was not worthy to join the Poles and Czechs in statehood, Faisal complained in a letter to his father the day after the conference opening. "They tell people that Arabs are backward, not civilized."[24] Although the Hijaz was technically a sovereign state, its Arab subjects were deemed an inferior race deserving of colonization.

The Hijaz delegation soon realized that Syrian Arab claims to independence threatened European colonial rule elsewhere. How could France let Faisal speak when North African Arabs, who had fought in French trenches, were denied a voice? Likewise, the British had blocked an Egyptian delegation from traveling to Paris, even though more than one million Egyptians had served the war effort as forced labor. Balfour had facetiously claimed that Saad Zaghlul, the Egyptian nationalist leader and former cabinet minister, was a Bolshevik paid by Moscow to wage jihad.[25]

In this atmosphere, Faisal's embrace of the Americans was a desperate and revolutionary act. Some historians would later argue that it was a foolish one. President Wilson was leading the world into "uncharted territory" by calling for a peace without annexations and for the right of peoples to choose their own rulers. French and British diplomats regarded Wilson's proposals not only as a threat to empire, but also as an unwelcome complication to an already difficult peacemaking agenda.[26] Moreover, the Americans were not yet strong enough to change the rules of the imperial game. Wilson had lost control of the US Congress in the November elections, and he did not yet understand how to wield American financial power to his advantage. Past historians of the peace conference have argued therefore that Faisal's best shot would have been to strike a compromise with Clemenceau for a limited form of French influence in Syria.[27]

However, these historians neglect the fluidity of events in January 1919. They view the conference with retrospective knowledge of the outcome and primarily through the lens of documents left by European officials. They do not appreciate the perspective of those who experienced the game as it unfolded. Faisal acted with the same determination as the hundreds of other delegates who flocked to Paris that winter to make their voices heard and their claims felt. The conference was not just about a few men in a room. It was a revolution occurring in the minds of people across the city and the globe. The Poles and Czechs had already won recognition of their states. So, in the spirit of the euphoric Bolshevik takeover of Saint Petersburg a year earlier, the delegates from small, oppressed nations came to turn the world upside down at Paris. At the opening ceremony on January 18, even staid President Wilson proclaimed it the "supreme conference in the history of mankind."

Mass enthusiasm for Wilson made a transformation of the international system seem plausible. Socialists across Europe hailed Wilson for his promise of economic justice, and as a liberal alternative to the Bolsheviks. Women approached Wilson to advocate for their participation at the conference and for suffrage at home. Likewise, non-Europeans actively worked against the efforts of the Great Powers to sideline them. To these groups, it appeared principled—not foolish—to harness Wilson's immense popularity in the winter of 1918–1919 to their projects for a new world order based on equality, rights, and law.[28]

In this atmosphere, Faisal thought it was reasonable to choose risk over compromise. He and his advisors had good reason to trust the American president. Like Haidar, they admired Wilson's textbook, *The State,* and the promise it made that all peoples could establish a democratic government suited to their needs.[29] They therefore adopted the strategy of holding Wilson to his famous Fourteen Points speech, especially to Point Five's call for "a free, open-minded and absolutely impartial adjustment of all colonial claims," and Point Twelve's guarantee of "autonomous development" for non-Turkish peoples of the Ottoman Empire.[30]

Wooing the American Delegation

Two days after the Clock Room ceremony, on January 20, Faisal and Lawrence attended a private dinner with the American peace delegation. The prince charmed the Americans. "His face was one of the most attractive I have ever seen, beautifully shaped, with clear, dark eyes that struck us all as being those of a man who, although he has been facing constant danger for many years, retains an irresistible sense of humor," recalled James Shotwell, a Columbia University professor. "This descendant of Mohammed was cracking jokes all evening, in the midst of his most serious argument for the Arab cause."[31]

"This is a remarkable man, really. I am a convert," wrote William Westermann, a professor of ancient history from the University of Wisconsin.[32] The very next day, Westermann told President Wilson about Faisal's proposal for sending a commission of inquiry to Syria. Even Secretary of State Robert Lansing gushed with praise for Faisal: "No one could look at the Emir Feisul without the instinctive feeling that here was a man whom nature had chosen to be a leader of men, a man who was worthy to be a leader of men."[33]

Barriers to meeting the president, however, were high. The American offices were located at the Hôtel de Crillon, around the corner from the Hotel Continental, and were deluged with telegrams and appeals from around the world; sentries turned supplicants away at the door. Wilson met only a select few visitors on weekday evenings at his residence, a mile north at the Murat Palace, which was donated by an aristocratic family. On January 12, T. E. Lawrence used his fame and a British contact to approach General Tasker H. Bliss, the American delegate to the Supreme War Council, with an invitation to dinner at the Majestic Hotel, where the British delegation resided. The general declined.[34]

Lawrence managed to secure a meeting with Wilson's gatekeeper, Stephen Bonsal. Bonsal listened to Faisal and Lawrence make their case, but decided that their rhetoric was too radical for the president. Faisal reassured him that the Arabs had no intentions of jihad. "Our allegiance to the West demonstrated that this was not a war against our religion but a war to safeguard it, and so the Holy War cry of the Turks came to nothing," he said. He begged Bonsal not to listen to "those who say that we should be discriminated against because we, the Arabs, are a wild, unruly people incapable of self-government." Faisal then continued: "I am confident that even the least fortunate of our race are as able to assume this task as were the Greeks and the Serbs and the Bulgars but a few decades ago."[35]

Access to President Wilson at Murat Palace was finally won thanks to an American rabbi, Stephen Wise. Wise was a prominent Jewish-American leader; a supporter of President Wilson; and a friend of Louis Brandeis, a Supreme Court justice and Zionist advocate. He was also a progressive. Wise headed the Free Synagogue in New York City, supported labor unions, and had participated in the 1909 founding of the National Association for the Advancement of Colored People. He supported the League of Nations, home rule for the Irish, and the cause of Jews oppressed under the Russian and Austro-Hungarian empires. He therefore viewed Zionism as a democratic and progressive cause and had come to Europe to ensure that poor eastern European and Russian Jews would find security in their own homeland in Palestine. Wise himself had been born in Budapest.[36]

Faisal had met Wise a few weeks earlier, at a London banquet held in the prince's honor by Lord Rothschild. Their conversation that evening was one of many discussions that Faisal and Lawrence held with Zionists on prospects for the coexistence of Arabs and Jews in Palestine. Before leaving London, Faisal had signed a memorandum of understanding with the British Zionist leader Chaim Weizmann. It welcomed Jewish immigration to Palestine—considered part of Syria—on condition that the Jews live within an independent Arab state.[37] This was a honeymoon period, when peace between Jews and Arabs in Palestine appeared possible. In exchange for Faisal's signature on the memorandum, Zionists offered to promote Arab independence. As he signed, Faisal added a postscript asserting that he would consider the memorandum void should the Arabs not obtain their own state.

In this atmosphere of mutual support, Wise eagerly offered to help with Faisal's appeal to Wilson. He had already arranged such a meeting for his friend Tomáš Masaryk, president of Czechoslovakia. Wilson had recognized Czech independence after that meeting; might he do the same for the Arabs? After all, Wilson's Tenth Point promised the peoples of Austria-Hungary the same "autonomous development" that his Twelfth Point promised to Ottoman peoples.

On January 15, Wise wrote to Wilson, urging the president to schedule a meeting. "I rejoice to think that Prince Feisul and Colonel Lawrence are to have the privilege of discussing with you the aspirations for freedom of the Prince's people who have done so much to free the Near East from Ottoman rule."[38] A few days later, Faisal received the cherished invitation to meet the president "in accordance with a memorandum sent him by Rabbi Stephen F. Wise." He was scheduled to meet Wilson at 5:45 on Thursday evening, January 23, between Wilson's appointments with the Swiss president and George Davis Herron, a leader of the American social gospel movement and wartime spy.

The tall windows of Murat Palace glowed brightly as Faisal and Lawrence turned onto Rue Monceau. The two men stepped into a Victorian-style salon decorated with portraits of French aristocrats. Wilson greeted them with a fatigued air. The president had just turned sixty-two years old, and looked it. The conference had barely begun and he was already overworking, against his doctor's orders. He had spent an exhausting day of debate with Allied leaders about demobilizing their armies. Wilson had lost his former playfulness because of the stress of dual battles that fall—fighting the war to its end and a brutal midterm election campaign. Republicans had won control of Congress. Bitter but defiant, the isolated president sought redemption in Europe. He had closeted himself during his transatlantic voyage, immersed in his work, and had traveled across France, Italy, and England to rally enthusiastic crowds to his vision of peace.[39]

Faisal understood immediately, as they took their seats at Murat Palace, that Wilson was not focused on Arab affairs. The president feared that popular pressure to demobilize armies would weaken the peace conference's ability to enforce its terms. Earlier that day, when Lloyd George had tried to shift discussion to colonial matters, Wilson had refused. Europe was the key to world peace, he had insisted.[40]

Wilson politely reassured the prince that he would uphold his peace principles, but he refused to discuss specifics. Don't worry about what you read in the newspapers, he advised. Ominously, as Faisal and Lawrence headed to the door, Wilson asked whether the prince had consulted French politicians about his ambitions in Syria. Later that night, Faisal briefed Haidar and Abd al-Hadi. He was "quite unhappy because he did not obtain a firm word from the President," Haidar recalled.[41]

Wilson left no record of the meeting in his papers; however, documents from late January suggest that Faisal had received extraordinary treatment. Wilson's policy was to avoid meeting heads of state altogether. He also routinely rebuffed requests for appointments from Armenian and other national leaders. Wilson showed concern for Ottoman peoples by ensuring food shipments. The administration's director of food relief, Herbert Hoover, appealed on January 27 against the effort of Republican Senate leader Henry Cabot Lodge to cut off food to Muslims. Wilson responded the very next day with a telegram arguing that all hungry peoples must be fed, since there was no way to separate Muslims from Christians.[42]

In addition to Rabbi Wise, other close friends of Wilson intervened for the Syrians. Most important was the arrival of Dr. Howard S. Bliss (no relation to General Tasker Bliss), president of the Syrian Protestant College in Beirut. Bliss was born on Mount Lebanon, the son of the college founder. A graduate of Amherst College and an ordained minister, he had transformed the college curriculum along the progressive, liberal lines that Wilson shared. As the son of a Presbyterian minister, Wilson sympathized with Bliss's educational mission. Bliss was also related by marriage to one of Wilson's oldest friends and most generous political supporters, Cleveland Dodge, who was president of the Syrian Protestant College's board of trustees in New York. Vice president of a mining and railroad conglomerate, Dodge had helped bankroll Wilson's 1916 presidential campaign. During the war, Wilson had supported the efforts of Dodge and Bliss to distribute relief to Armenian and Syrian refugees. Dodge had urged Wilson not to declare war on the Ottoman Empire, for fear of endangering relief efforts.

By January 27, Howard Bliss was meeting with the American delegation to invite an American fact-finding committee to Syria. He firmly supported Wilson and Faisal on the need to discover Syrians' views on their future government. Bliss took a more benign view of Syrians than did William Yale, who also arrived in Paris to join the delegation staff. Bliss, who had lived most of his life in the region, regarded Syrians as intelligent but inexperienced, in need of counsel from a neutral power. Yale, by contrast, continued to advance his less developed views on the need to control violence-prone Muslims. "The races of the Orient are unfit and unprepared for self-government," he advised. "The Orientals do not understand what liberty and justice mean."[43] While Wilson met personally with Bliss, there is no indication that he ever met Yale or read his reports. Yale would eventually forge friendships with the French colonial lobby.

Charles R. Crane, another financial backer of Wilson with interests in the Middle East, arrived in Paris in early February. Crane was the globe-trotting heir to a Chicago plumbing fortune who had personal acquaintances with heads of state in Russia, eastern Europe, and Asia. He supported American colleges in Constantinople and Beirut. Crane, too, was an ardent opponent of the secret treaties and a supporter of Wilson's vision of a new world order.

Crane and Wise both served on the board of a charity that petitioned Wilson on January 31 to protect weaker peoples and to resist the partition of Syria as called for by the Sykes-Picot accord. The American Committee for Relief in the Near East (ACRNE) was "alarmed" that the Near East might be carved into zones of influence, wrote director James Barton. "This would be a complete surrender of the American ideal" and would endorse the principle of might as right. The ACRNE urged Wilson to ensure that representatives of a "disinterested" power be assigned as mandatories in post-Ottoman territories, and only on a temporary basis.[44]

These friends emboldened Wilson, as the glow of welcoming crowds faded and negotiations moved behind closed doors. The business of designing the League and settling borders now fell to the Council of Ten, also known as the Supreme Council, which included two delegates from each of the five Entente powers: the United States, Britain, France, Italy, and Japan.

A "minority of one" in his anti-imperialism, Wilson was ready for a fight. As a prominent historian put it, "the quarrel over colonies collided with the League of Nations with perhaps greater force than any other issue at the peace conference."[45]

Chapter 5

The Covenant and
the Colonial Color Line

On January 24, the day after his meeting with Wilson, Faisal's mood darkened further. His nemesis, Jean Gout, appeared at the Hotel Continental. Gout was the foreign ministry official who had tried to block Faisal's attendance at the conference, until Balfour stepped in. As a member of the French colonial lobby, Gout commanded a staff that filed reports on Faisal warning of his ambition to build "an enormous Arab empire" and characterizing his supporters as demagogues and Muslim fanatics.[1]

To Faisal's surprise, Gout stayed for two hours. Haidar took notes on the conversation, which revealed the rhetorical weapons of the colonial lobby. "France wanted to lay her hands on Syria under any guise—as a protector, mandatory, advisor," Haidar recalled. "But the Prince demonstrated a sharp intelligence that unnerved Gout."[2]

Gout opened with a legal argument, claiming that Faisal had no standing to represent Syria. He then played the sectarian card. After the Armenian massacre, he contended, no Christian could trust a Muslim ruler. France had a duty to protect Syria's Christians. Faisal responded by invoking Wilson's principle of consent of the governed. Syrians should be polled on whom they desired as their ruler. No matter how the people decided, Faisal would always welcome French advice.

"France's interest in Syria is well known, and we confirm it. But you must guarantee us our independence," Faisal declared.

"France does not want to own Syria, or protect it. She just wants to organize it," Gout responded.

"What do you mean by organize? How long would it last? England said the same thing in Egypt [in 1882] and she is still there," Faisal pointed out.

Gout again insisted that France must protect the rights of the Christian minority. Faisal resented the apparent double standard. "Why did the Powers permit Romanians to form Romania? Aren't there minorities of another race there? As for us, we have no minority, because all of us are Arabs," Faisal argued. "The Syrian nation is no less prepared to rule itself than other nations," he continued. "Don't they have the right to decide on their destiny? They fought and carried the burden of war, as everyone knows."

Gout shifted ground. Syria was too weak to govern itself, he remarked. Since Britain and France had "conquered" it (here, he was ignoring the Arab Revolt's role) they should rule it. Faisal insisted that Arabs be respected as allies, just as the Romanians and Serbs were. France must not invade an ally by force. Any French protectorate must be established only by Syria's request.

In parting, Gout promised that France would not partition Syria, nor interfere in its government, as long as Britain did not. For his cooperation, Faisal would reap rewards. "It would please the French nation that a great man like you, both a reformer and a modernizer, like your Highness, would be at the head of the Syrian state," Gout said.

Faisal rightly suspected that the Frenchman's promises were hollow. That same day, January 24, Gout filed a report opposing any change in the 1916 Sykes-Picot accord. It predicted that independent Syria would oppress Christians just as the Ottoman Turks had done and warned that Faisal's Arab nationalism threatened France's rule in North Africa. With no reference to Wilsonian ideals of self-determination, Gout's report focused on the fact that Britain had violated the 1916 accord to grab the lion's share of Arab lands.[3]

The French lobby may have been deceptive, but it was not paranoid. It was responding to Britain's ambitious expansion in the Middle East. The British army had marched north from Baghdad to capture Mosul after the November 11 armistice. At that very moment, British naval intelligence issued warnings to keep the French and Americans out of the oil field there. "The security of this country and of the British Empire is dependent on oil," the lobby's reports advised.[4] In coming months, Iraqi oil would prove dearer to Lloyd George than promises he had made about Syria.

Meanwhile, rival wings of the British colonial apparatus—the India Office and the Egyptian high commission—competed to claim rule across the territory between them without the consent of the governed. The India Office refused any negotiation with Iraqis on self-rule even as the high commissioner imported additional troops from Palestine to quell nationalist demonstrations in Cairo. While Faisal negotiated in Paris, his father faced attacks near Mecca from the tribal army of Abdulaziz ibn Saud, who was backed by the India Office.

What piqued Gout's ire with regard to Syria was that British officials masked their land grab in the Middle East by manipulating the Arabs and Americans to focus on the injustice of French claims.[5] British duplicity provoked even the anticolonial Clemenceau. "Lloyd George had achieved what the colonialists could not," remarked a historian. "He had persuaded Clemenceau that the Middle East mattered."[6]

Faisal's Presentation to the Supreme Council

On January 29, Faisal submitted a formal memorandum to the Council of Ten (the Supreme Council) stating his claim to rule Syria—not as a representative of the Hijaz. As "commander of the Syrian revolt," he wrote, "I base my claims on the principles enunciated by President Wilson." He quoted Wilson's Mount Vernon speech of July 4, 1918, which guaranteed "the settlement of every question, whether of territory, of sovereignty, of economic arrangement, or of political arrangement upon the basis of the free acceptance of that settlement by the people immediately concerned."[7]

Faisal's memo was not an essay in naive idealism. It displayed a sure grasp of political realities. For example, Faisal demanded independence only for Syria, conceding that global interests might demand that Palestine and Iraq be ruled temporarily under foreign mandate.

And he acknowledged that Syrians, because they were more advanced than Arabs of the Hijaz, should not be ruled from Mecca.

Faisal also adopted the language of nation and race prevalent at the conference, wherein only homogeneous and "white" races were considered capable of independent rule and constitutional democracy.[8] He opened with a description of the Arab homeland as inhabited by close relatives of the same "Semitic race." (Prevailing racial theories, popularized in Arabic, classified Semites as white.) To further boost the image of Syria as a homogeneous nation, he claimed that 99 percent of the population spoke the same language, Arabic. And he assured the conference that because Arabs and Jews were both Semites, they would have no basic conflict with one another. Faisal's memo reflected the consensus of Arab intellectuals who since before the war had spilled much ink regarding Arabs' whiteness and civilization.[9]

For days, the Arab delegation waited for a response from the Supreme Council. Haidar and Abd al-Hadi met delegates from Romania and Serbia to discover how other small Allied nations made their claims. Faisal consented to an interview with the editor of a French newspaper to popularize Syrian claims. Haidar attended a play about Louis Pasteur, whom he praised as a true humanitarian.

Finally, word came on February 5 in the form of a summons: the Supreme Council requested that the Hijaz delegation present its case the following day.[10] In frenzied excitement, Haidar and the staff worked until four in the morning to draft Faisal's statement. Mark Sykes, coauthor of the infamous 1916 treaty, and T. E. Lawrence arrived to offer advice.

"From time to time the Prince came to listen to us read what we wrote. Sometimes he approved what we said. Sometimes he added an idea of his own. At midnight he went to bed. But I am not sure if he slept that night because he was so anxious," Haidar recalled.[11] At seven thirty the next morning, Faisal summoned Haidar for more changes: for the time being they must set aside claims to include Palestine in Syria, despite Zionist promises in the memorandum he had signed earlier in the month. Faisal feared alienating Americans who were advocating for a Jewish homeland. Sykes also counseled them to omit details of Lebanon's status, since Lebanese Catholics (Maronites) feared becoming a minority under Muslims.[12] Faisal should keep the focus on the Syrian hinterland that he now governed.

At 2:40 p.m. on Thursday, February 6, Faisal, Haidar, Abd al-Hadi, and Lawrence exited through the iron scrollwork of the Hotel Continental's entrance. A snowstorm had blown in.[13] They descended the staircase to their car and drove past snow-covered German guns scattered in the Place de la Concorde. Crossing a bridge over the Seine, they arrived at the Quai d'Orsay.

"We entered a big hall and met Lloyd George. Then Clemenceau came and Pichon and Wilson," Haidar recalled. Then he saw the dreaded Jean Gout take a seat next to Clemenceau. Wilson and the Americans sat at the head of the conference table, with Italian, Japanese, and British officials ranged on its sides. Faisal, dressed in a white robe with a scimitar belted at his side, circled the room shaking the delegates' hands. He then took his place in the center. The room fell silent and Clemenceau announced, "The floor belongs to Prince Faisal."

Faisal stood up and began to speak in Arabic, pausing at intervals for Lawrence to read a prepared English translation. "I am happy to be here at this conference which includes the greatest men of the most powerful nations. And I believe that this high court will grant justice to the Arab countries as they defend their natural rights," he began.

Faisal's voice rose and fell with emotion as he recited the major points of his January 29 memo: (1) The Arabs were a civilized people who had sacrificed their blood to help defeat the Central Powers. (2) Arabs killed in battle deserved recognition of the independent state that they fought for. (3) Most Syrians supported his government: within days of his entry into Damascus, patriots had raised the Arab flag in numerous cities. (4) Religious differences were inconsequential: members of all creeds had cooperated in the Arab army to free their country, and interfaith cooperation continued in the civil service. Should the members of the Supreme Council have any lingering doubts about popular consent, Faisal invited them to send a committee of inquiry to poll Syrian Arabs.[14]

The audience was spellbound, Haidar remarked. Listeners were fascinated by the sound of Faisal's Arabic and attentive to Lawrence's translation. President Wilson frequently nodded his approval, as did the Italian prime minster, Vittorio Orlando. Lloyd George smiled. The French, however, frowned throughout.[15] Clemenceau made no comment after Faisal finished. Lloyd George asked for more detail on the Arabs' military contribution. At Gout's prodding, Pichon asked, "Didn't the French do anything in the East?" Faisal replied, with a touch of sarcasm, "Yes. France sent four 60 mm guns and two old 80 mm guns. We will thank France for that as long as we live."

Wilson indicated that the Council favored placing the Arabs under a temporary form of external tutelage, called a mandate, until they were ready for self-rule. Would all Arabs prefer to be placed under one mandatory power, or several? he asked. "It depends on the opinion of the people, for they have the right to determine their future," Faisal replied. Wilson pressed harder: "But I am asking your opinion." Placing his trust in the American president, he replied candidly, "I prefer not to split up the territory and I demand independence."

The ice broken, Faisal closed with an emotional appeal. "My nation has a great civilization. When my nation was civilized, the nations you represent were still barbaric and savage. I ask you not to demean this nation that has truly served civilization."

Exhilarated and exhausted, Faisal and Haidar left the room. They heard later that Wilson appreciated Faisal's message and supported the commission of inquiry. Lawrence's sources told him, however, that the Americans might still impose a limited form of guardianship on Syria.

Despite this reassurance, Faisal panicked when he heard that the Supreme Council had invited his archrival, Shukri Ghanem, to speak the following week, on February 13. Ghanem was Gout's protégé, head of the pro-French Syrian Central Committee. Faisal asked to attend the session, but his request was denied.

His anxiety eased when he learned that Dr. Howard Bliss, president of the Syrian Protestant College in Beirut, would also speak that day. Bliss had earned a heroic reputation among Arabs for keeping the college open and feeding the poor during the war. While he was not free of missionary zeal, his reforms made the college a more welcoming place for Muslim students than its French counterpart in

Beirut, St. Joseph University. Several Syrian nationalists had attended it. Even Rashid Rida, the publisher of the progressive magazine *The Lighthouse,* applauded the college's contribution to Muslims' education. Most important to Faisal, Bliss was a personal friend of Wilson. The two men had already held a meeting in Paris and exchanged multiple notes on Syrian independence.[16]

On February 13, Bliss spoke about Syrian Arabs with both affection and condescension. "They are intelligent, able, hospitable and lovable," he said, but they also exhibited the "defects of a long-oppressed race—timidity, love of flattery, indirectness." Faisal would regret to hear that Bliss had supported a mandate, while assuring the Council that Syrians "will grow into capacity for self-determination and independence." Sweeter to Faisal's ears was Bliss's insistence that the Council respect Syrians' right to choose their government. "I therefore plead," Bliss said, that the commission of inquiry requested by Prince Faisal be sent out "as soon as possible."

Shukri Ghanem followed Bliss's presentation. An expatriate French citizen who had lived in Paris for thirty years, he spoke for more than two hours. Syrians were not Arabs, Ghanem claimed, and they should not be ruled by a dynasty from the Hijaz. Faisal intended to impose a Muslim theocracy over Syria's many minorities, he contended.[17] Faisal and Haidar learned with satisfaction that Ghanem's speech flopped: Wilson had paced the room out of boredom and Clemenceau supposedly scolded Pichon for letting Ghanem speak.

Hope was renewed.

The League of Nations Covenant

The very next day, February 14, Haidar and Faisal returned to the Clock Room to hear Wilson present the draft covenant of the League of Nations.

"In order to promote international cooperation and to secure international peace by accepting obligations not to resort to war, by prescription of just, honorable relations between nations, by the firm establishment of the understandings of international law, as the actual rule of conduct among governments," Wilson began, "the Powers signatory to this Covenant adopt this constitution of the League of Nations."

"It was a great moment in history," the president's wife Edith recalled. "He stood there—tall, calm and powerful in his argument—I seemed to see the people of all depressed countries—men, women and little children—crowding round and waiting on his words." Others, less attached to the president, thought the reading dull, until they realized they were hearing a global manifesto.[18]

Wilson read each article of the covenant, detailing how the League would establish a permanent secretariat, a general member council, and an executive council dominated by Great Powers. The League would impose binding rules on reducing stockpiles of armaments, enforce sanctions against countries that threatened war, and establish a world court to adjudicate international disputes.

Faisal and Haidar pricked up their ears at Article Nineteen, "Control of Colonies and Territories." It provided for the tutelage of peoples recently liberated from states defeated in the war—and contained the language that Haidar and Faisal longed to hear: "Certain communities of people recently liberated from the Turkish Empire have reached a stage of development where their existence as independent nations can be provisionally recognized, subject to the rendering of administrative advice and assistance by a mandatory power until such time as they are able to stand alone. The wishes of these communities must be the principal consideration in the selection of the mandatory power."[19]

Even more auspicious was the speech of a French delegate, the eminent statesman and pacifist Léon Bourgeois. He hailed the covenant's promise for small nations: "In the view of just people, there are no small and no great states. All are, and all will be, equal before the principle of international justice."[20] Bourgeois and Wilson cooperated on the League subcommittee to ensure that small states would serve on the League executive council as a bulwark against imperialist ambitions of the Great Powers.[21]

In the discussion following the formal speeches, Haidar commented on Article Nineteen. "There is a word in the text which seems to me rather vague—the word 'Mandate,'" he said in French. "And yet on the interpretation of that word will depend the future of all the nations which, till today, have been oppressed by tyrants." He urged that the covenant explicitly guarantee Arabs the freedom to choose their mandatory power untrammeled by the secret Sykes-Picot accord. "This agreement concluded without [the people's] assent should of full right be pronounced null and void." Clemenceau quickly called the session to a close.[22]

"My speech was a bombshell," Haidar later wrote. "The next day Lawrence told me my speech was good, that it had good effect. . . . Nuri [Said] and Awni [Abd al-Hadi] came to shake my hand, smiling."[23]

Euphoria passed, and the Hijaz delegation soon sank into a month-long limbo. Wilson and Lloyd George returned home for a month to tend to domestic politics. Mark Sykes died suddenly on February 17, a victim of the influenza pandemic. Two days later, an anarchist shot Clemenceau. The old Tiger miraculously survived.

Faisal took to his bed with a cough and fever. He feared tuberculosis. On February 20, he wrote his father a reassuring letter. But the very next day he called Haidar to his room in a panic. They talked at length about French ambitions in Syria. Why do the French ignore the fact that the majority don't want them? Faisal asked. Why do the French stubbornly support the Maronite Church? "Is it because we are Muslims, or what?"[24]

At this time, Faisal began to set aside his Arab robes in favor of a black tunic and trousers. Outdoors he wore a long King Albert coat.[25] Emphasizing his Arab culture had been a gamble. While it had attracted public notice, it had also invited Europeans to regard him as an exotic and medieval Oriental out of the *Arabian Nights* stories. The newspaper *Le Figaro* recounted his reception at the Paris city hall by comparing his headdress to that of "the Egyptian Sphinx."[26]

To the European eye, Faisal's robes may have signaled a lack of modernity, making him unfit as a member of the League of Nations. The problem was partly intellectual: most people considered modernity as synonymous with European culture. The problem was also political: Faisal's status as a descendant of the Prophet Muhammad linked him by religion to the Turks and to their war crimes against Christians and the annihilation of the Armenians. He learned this when a February 28 riot in Aleppo resulted in fifty Armenians dead.

Faisal understood that the city suffered deep social stress from persistent food shortages and disease, both aggravated by the presence of thousands of Armenian refugees. But the French press reported that the massacre was committed by Arab agents of the Turks and that only France could protect Christians from ongoing violence. Press linkage of Arabs to Turks undercut Faisal's effort to insert Syria into the family of civilized nations. In response to the Aleppo riot, Foreign Minister Pichon pressured Clemenceau to postpone meetings with Faisal.[27]

Haidar and Faisal could only guess what prejudices, secret understandings, and chance remarks might determine their fate. As Gout had revealed, the French foreign ministry routinely justified its claim to rule Syria by invoking the need to protect the Christian minority from the fanatic Muslims. Even Americans like Howard Bliss spoke in Orientalist stereotypes. Secretary of State Lansing noted in his memoir, "Of the many prominent representatives in Paris . . . there was none more striking in appearance than this prince from the Sacred City, where the mysteries of Islam were so long guarded from Christendom by the deserts of Arabia and the fanaticism of the followers of the Prophet."[28]

The tendency to conflate all Muslims into one exotic and inferior race was not new, but it was especially dangerous in the wake of the Armenian genocide. Fa'iz El-Ghusein, Faisal's secretary, had warned of the danger in the 1918 English translation of his *Martyred Armenia*. "I have published this pamphlet in order to refute beforehand inventions and slanders against the faith of Islam and against Moslems generally," he wrote. The Young Turks murdered Armenians not out of Islamic jihad but out of "nationalist fanaticism," he argued. Even if some Armenians rebelled, "it does not justify the annihilation of the whole people, men and women, old men and children, in a way which revolts all humanity and more especially Islam and the whole body of Moslems."[29]

Haidar and Faisal drew comfort from the few in Paris who respected their culture. Among them was the novelist Anatole France, who paid frequent visits to the Syrian leaders. He told them of a French poem that bemoaned the lack of Arab cultural influence in Europe. It described how Charles Martel had perpetuated barbarism in Europe when he defeated the Arabs at Poitiers in 711. Other friends included the Duchess of Clermont-Tonnere, a leftist, lesbian writer close to Marcel Proust. She served them an Eastern-style lunch of grilled meat and dates and spoke passionately of her travels to Syria.[30]

Faisal had even accepted the Duchess's offer to stay at her "château." According to Awni Abd al-Hadi, staying there enabled the Arab prince to build a network among the French aristocracy. Every morning, Abd al-Hadi met Faisal there to teach him French. He read French books about great political reformers. "Faisal was intelligent," Abd al-Hadi recalled, "even though he continued to follow his father's bad advice." Indeed, Sharif Hussein continued to send letters from distant Mecca, blindly insisting that Faisal follow Britain's advice. He had no understanding of the political intrigue at Paris. Despite his effort to separate Syria from Arabia at the Supreme Council, Faisal felt a lingering filial duty to heed his father's directives.[31]

Abd al-Hadi and Haidar directed the delegation's business from their rooms at the Hotel Continental. Abd al-Hadi responded to setbacks at Paris with pugnacity, devising new political strategies. Haidar, the romantic, sank into disillusion. He was deeply offended by the racial discrimination he faced in Paris. He had lived there for years as a student, spoke the language fluently, and had embraced the republicanism that Clemenceau embodied. His diary entries in late February reflect his disenchantment. As he waited for the Council's decision, Haidar began writing about the Russian Revolution. Everyone in Paris talked about its influence in Germany and eastern Europe. "I have come to like Bolshevism," he wrote, saying this was because it advanced the principle of equality.[32]

The Arabs and the Problem of the Color Line

Transcripts of Supreme Council meetings held in January and February reveal the tension between the Allies' liberal ideals of inclusion, freedom, and equality and their prejudices that reflected the imperial age. Lloyd George, Clemenceau, Wilson, and Orlando, known as the

"Big Four," had built their careers on the democratization of domestic politics at the turn of the century. They had won office by opposing privilege and tyranny. But they were also older, white men (at age fifty-six, Lloyd George was the youngest) whose instincts were rooted in nineteenth-century norms and institutions. They freely invoked white racial superiority in their discussions about non-European territories, including usage of the "n-word."[33]

Surprisingly, the participant most scorned for his racism at home—Woodrow Wilson, who had permitted the segregation of federal government offices in Washington DC—proved to be the most ardent opponent of racially justified colonialism. Wilson lobbied hard for a mandate system that could not be hijacked by colonial powers. He was supported by Tasker H. Bliss, the elderly general with a drooping mustache, who was also a member of the Supreme War Council. Although Bliss had declined T. E. Lawrence's dinner invitation, he quietly opened a file on the Arab states with an original map of the Sykes-Picot Agreement and Faisal's memorandums on Arab desires in Syria. As a member also of the American peace delegation, Bliss reviewed a draft of the League covenant. He was a staunch advocate of Wilson's peace plan against the hawkish and imperialist factions in the British and French peace delegations.

To blunt imperialist subversion of the League's principles, Bliss and Wilson believed that only small, disinterested states should take on the mandates in countries seeking political autonomy. Small states would not be tempted by colonial exploitation as the Great Powers would. To that end, at a January 27 meeting of the Supreme Council, Wilson proposed that the League maintain a fund to cover expenses of mandate administration. That would enable small states without abundant resources to accept the role of mandatory. Lloyd George, angrily interrupting before Wilson could finish this proposal, insisted that he must consult his own staff before further discussion of the point. Wilson's proposal effectively died.[34]

The two leaders locked horns again on January 30. Lloyd George united the British Empire delegation around a proposal to assign three types of mandates, depending on the population's level of development. Syria would be an "A" mandate, requiring the least administrative advice for the shortest period, while South West Africa and Germany's former Pacific Island colonies would be "C" mandates, remaining much longer under heavier European tutelage. "B" mandates would be zones like Palestine, where potential conflict necessitated a strong mandatory hand. Wilson stonewalled. He insisted that these were matters for the League to decide, once it was established. Lloyd George exploded, complaining that he was "filled with despair." Clemenceau chimed in, mocking Wilson for wanting to write a "constitution for the whole world."

Wilson responded so bitterly that he later asked to have his rude language expunged from the minutes. He condemned the Council's blatant colonialism, vowing that "the world would not permit the parceling out among the Great Powers of the helpless countries conquered from Germany." He also expressed outrage at an article in the *Daily Mail*—based on leaks from Australian prime minister Billy Hughes—that claimed Britain's solid imperial interests were being sacrificed to Wilson's vague ideals. Hughes and his counterparts in South Africa had advocated outright annexation of German colonies.[35] At that point, the South African prime minister broke in to say reassuringly that he shared Wilson's higher ideals and that the meeting should not "stop at small things." Embarrassed by his own outburst, Wilson accepted the conciliatory gesture.

At day's end, Wilson agreed, provisionally, to the system of A-B-C mandates on the condition that the League have the final authority in assigning the mandatories. The Council therefore resolved to sever non-Turkish territories from the Ottoman Empire and confer them as a "sacred trust of civilization" on the League. The resolution noted that Ottoman territories like Syria were developed enough to allow their existence as independent nations to be "provisionally recognized," subject to the administrative advice of a mandatory power. Syrian opinion had to be a "principal consideration" in choosing the mandatory. The Council would let the League resolve the outstanding legal question of where sovereignty should reside under a mandate—with the people or with the mandatory.[36]

Wilson was willing to barter much in order to win what he considered the holy grail, approval for the League of Nations. The League was the key to revolutionizing the world order, and to eventually abolishing colonialism. Once the League was established, Wilson reasoned, then the compromises might be undone through the proper deliberation of members.

The president waged battle for the League with the knowledge that its principle of universal rights had broad support in the Allied countries, if not among their prime ministers. Progressive reformers and pacifists across Europe and the United States had promoted the League for years. By guaranteeing basic rights to nations and providing mechanisms to arbitrate disputes and impose collective security, they had hoped to avert the Great War that finally broke out in 1914.[37]

Wilson envisioned the League of Nations as more than a world policeman; he saw it as a world parliament. A "global community of politically commensurable individuals would become the effective lawgiver on the most vital issues of international law—war and peace," he declared.[38] Upon entering the war, the Wilson administration explicitly waged battle not just for Americans' and Europeans' liberty, but for "the liberties of all other peoples as well." It therefore sent copies of his speeches beyond Europe to Asia, Africa, and Latin America.[39]

"Men have never before realized," Wilson proclaimed at Buckingham Palace in December, "how little difference there was between right and justice in one latitude and in another, under one sovereignty and another."[40]

While Wilson's original vision was universal, it was steadily narrowed and racialized during the negotiation process. On January 30, he effectively accepted the racist logic of the mandate system's three-tiered structure. Indeed, he had insisted that no Europeans (meaning no whites) should come under mandates. Despite Haidar's February 14 criticism of the mandate's vague definition, the covenant's final draft simply defined it as a form of "tutelage" and a "trust of civilization" wherein "advanced nations" guided "peoples not yet able to stand by themselves under the strenuous conditions of the modern world."[41]

In a last-ditch maneuver to prevent the colonial carve-up of Ottoman lands, Wilson proposed sending American troops to help garrison the territory. But his secretary of war responded that the public would want to send troops only to Christian lands like Armenia, not to Turkey or Mesopotamia. Faisal was outraged to learn a few days later, on February 9, that the Supreme War Council had decided to send French troops to Syria. Two days later, Wilson invited Howard Bliss to testify personally before the Council of Ten. On the same day, he authorized an allotment of $5,000 from the defense budget to finance the cost of a commission to Syria.[42]

Wilson failed in his battle against imperial expansion because few negotiators in Paris accepted his radical attempt to shift the basis of international law from states to individual and popular rights. Most of the Supreme Council—and Wilson's own staff, including his secretary of state Robert Lansing—insisted on the old model of national sovereignty. They therefore insisted that sovereignty must lie with the mandatory power chosen by the League. Without commitment to Wilson's revolutionary shift of sovereignty to the individual, the mandates could become fig leaves for old-fashioned colonialism.[43]

Wilson did not at first perceive his defeat. He was less troubled by the ambiguities in his vision and in his compromises than his critics were. Like his favorite political philosopher, Edmund Burke, he was a believer in the deliberative process. Patient negotiation, followed by trial and error, would produce more organic and sustainable change than the rapid overthrow of regimes.[44] Wilson viewed the vaguely defined mandate not as a betrayal of principle but rather as a practical step forward. He believed that the "permanent processes" of the League would eventually work out the kinks.[45] Only after he left Paris would it become clear that he had let the foxes run the chicken coop.

A second flaw in the bargains struck over the mandate system was the assumption of a racial hierarchy. Wilson was ultimately as blind to racial injustice as his opponents on the Supreme Council. His liberalism, like that of many progressives in the United States, was based on the belief that only like-minded, worthy—and white—citizens could create a modern political community; it therefore justified the exclusion of those deemed irrational or ill-educated.[46] Wilson had only lately come to accept women's suffrage and the possibility that Mexican revolutionaries might be democrats. He still adhered to the belief that nonwhites were inferior and dangerous to the harmony of political community. This made him vulnerable to colonialists' arguments about the need to subordinate non-Europeans in the new world order.

Wilson's international racial posture was rooted in domestic politics. Within United States territories, Hawaiians and "inferior Spanish races" of New Mexico were deemed incapable of self-government. Wilson had himself employed the concept of self-determination not to liberate blacks, but rather to protect states' rights against federal intervention to enforce racial equality.[47] In logic mirroring that of the mandate system, American progressives like Wilson embraced Booker T. Washington's program of racial segregation as step toward the advancement of Negroes. They rejected the views of W. E. B. Du Bois, leader of the NAACP, who opposed segregation. In Du Bois's view, only through integration could American society move toward racial equilibrium.

In his 1903 *Souls of Black Folk,* Du Bois had famously declared that the problem of the twentieth century was "the problem of the color line."[48] In the past, there had been a spectrum of racial identities, he argued. But now, under Jim Crow laws, racial politics had narrowed, demarcating a strict line separating white Europeans from all others. Du Bois recognized a similar pattern at work in 1919 Paris. He feared the extension of the "color line" across the globe, under the guise of the League of Nations. That is why he had come to Paris.

Wilson's government had denied Du Bois permission to participate in the peace conference, so he had traveled to Paris instead on a journalist's visa. As soon as he set foot in Paris, Du Bois found he was being followed by American secret agents. And when he tried to hold an alternative, Pan-African Congress, the Americans did everything they could to block it.[49]

In a curious twist of history, Clemenceau sympathized with Du Bois's cause. In 1865, when Wilson was a boy playing baseball in the American South, Clemenceau arrived in New York City as a political exile from the monarchy of Louis Napoleon. He carried with him a copy of Alexis de Tocqueville's *Democracy in America.* Clemenceau took an intense interest in Reconstruction and its cause of racial equality. In historical importance, he felt that it compared to the

French Revolution. As a correspondent for the French paper *Le Temps*, Clemenceau championed the Republican US Congress as representative of the people's justice, against the efforts of President Johnson and the Supreme Court to block equal rights for African Americans. "We are threatened," he warned his French readers, "with seeing the nullification of all the measures taken by Congress to do justice to the blacks in the ex-Confederate states." In a veiled reference to the reactionary French aristocracy, he condemned the plantation elite of Wilson's home state, Virginia, for resisting Reconstruction's project of establishing the common humanity and equal rights of all races.[50]

Clemenceau's interest in American politics continued long after he returned to France in 1870 with an American wife. Since then, he had grown into an elderly statesman and come to view Africans in French colonies as cannon fodder in the French army. But his republican ideals lingered enough for him to decide—against American wishes—to accept the petition of a French deputy from Senegal to permit the Pan-African Congress in February 1919. The deputy, Blaise Diagne, had after all helped to recruit soldiers during the war. The French prime minister thus undermined the first Southern Democrat elected president of the United States by blurring the racial "color line" in Paris.[51]

Du Bois and Diagne convened the Pan-African Congress across the Seine at the Grand Hotel from February 19 to 21. Fifty-seven delegates attended, including several from the American-occupied territories of Santo Domingo and Haiti. They, too, demanded self-government and the League of Nations' protection of their rights. The conference drew little publicity, and Du Bois lamented that the "new religion" of whiteness prevailed in the new world order.[52]

The allocation of mandates had in fact followed the logic of Du Bois's color line. Before the conference opened, Italian prime minister Orlando, eyeing territory adjacent to Italy, had floated the possibility of mandates in formerly Austrian territories. Jan Smuts, the foreign minister of South Africa, supported him. Lloyd George had sent Smuts to investigate eastern and central European affairs. Smuts proposed that an arm of the League, perhaps under the mandate system, oversee international relations among the emergent states there. The League would act as a substitute for the old imperial governments, and so adjudicate disputes among the small ethnic states. Wilson rejected the idea out of hand. There would be no mandates in Europe, he declared.[53]

Equal rights for small nations were implicitly sacrificed to the persistent logic of a racial hierarchy. White peoples of Europe were deemed a priori capable of self-government. No effort was ever made to evaluate their ability to rule themselves, despite the administrative, legal, and political chaos that prevailed across Polish, Czech, Ukrainian, Hungarian, and Balkan lands. By contrast, Africans, Asians, and Pacific peoples were a priori deemed incapable of self-government and automatically assigned to B and C mandates.

Arabs occupied an ambiguous place on the legal boundaries of race. Like Italians and Greeks, they were sometimes considered white, sometimes not, by various governments. In the landmark case of *Dow v. United States*, a high court ruled definitively in 1915 that Syrians were white. The case concerned a Syrian immigrant who had been denied citizenship by lower courts, which ruled that he belonged to Asian "yellow" races barred under naturalization law. The *Dow* decision determined that Syrians were white because they were Semites, a group regarded by racial theorists as white. A book in Arabic quickly spread word that Syrians could gain American citizenship as whites.[54] Faisal referred directly to the case when he emphasized Arabs as Semites at the Supreme Council.

However, two years after that case, American politicians advocated declaring war on the Ottoman Empire to save "subject races," including Syrians and Armenians, from the "barbaric" Turks. Leading figures like former president Theodore Roosevelt demanded the expulsion of Turks from Europe, meaning the civilized world. In this debate, Roosevelt and Secretary of State Robert Lansing, among others, implicitly cast Syrians into a human category less civilized and less capable of self-rule than whites. This paved the way for Syrians and other Ottoman Arabs to be considered in the same group as peoples of the former German colonies in Africa and the Pacific in need of mandatory rule. Wilson finally refused to declare war on the Ottomans, following the advice of friends like Charles Crane, who sought to protect American relief operations and schools in Constantinople and Beirut.[55]

Wilson therefore stood up for Syrian self-determination in 1919 on contradictory terms, in the belief that Syrians were simultaneously white and a weak race in need of white tutelage. Members of the American peace delegation like Robert Lansing and William Yale did not accept Syrian whiteness. Nor did Wilson's supporters back in the United States. In February 1919, a former member of Wilson's own war propaganda staff published a racist cartoon in the *New York Herald* captioned "His mandatory wives—oh, Sam!" It showed Uncle Sam leaving an "International Matrimonial Bureau" with several wives on his arm, including a grossly caricatured African woman and an Arab woman wearing a face veil. The cartoon played to an American public that feared racial mixing in the era of Jim Crow segregation laws. In the minds of the *Herald's* readers, Arabs belonged to the same category as Africans.[56]

Syrians' claim to national sovereignty as Arabs further blurred their racial standing. On the one hand, the French army segregated North African Arabs from French soldiers in an effort to maintain white superiority. On the other hand, Arabs were able to mix with Europeans in civilian life, as Haidar and Abd al-Hadi had done at the Sorbonne. This permitted people to imagine social equality.[57] Anxiety about racial status may explain why Faisal repeatedly compared Arabs to Bulgarians and Czechs. It may also explain why Arabs declined invitations to the Pan-African Congress. It was an open secret at Paris that rights were for whites.

The secret that equal rights were intended only for white states was exposed to the public in April. Back in early February, Japan had quietly proposed to the Supreme Council that the League covenant include a clause affirming racial equality among nations. Japan was the only "nonwhite" Great Power in the victorious Entente alliance. The Japanese public pressured their delegates in Paris to insist on racial equality. As a people with a constitutional government and a modern army, the Japanese resented laws in Australia, the United States, and elsewhere that still barred their entry along with that of other "yellow" races.

Wilson at first welcomed the equality clause as an expression of the League spirit. But his own staff counseled against it. Lansing had already dismissed a Chinese demand for legal equality with Europeans. Colonel House foresaw difficulties with white Allies. British Dominion delegates flatly rejected the clause because they feared a deluge of Asian immigrants to their countries. Balfour dismissed equality as a discredited eighteenth-century ideal. He simply did not believe that "a man in Central Africa was created equal to a European."[58]

The February 14 draft of the League covenant that Faisal and Haidar heard did not, therefore, contain robust language about racial equality. Convinced that he must avoid last-minute complications, Wilson had omitted the Japanese proposal.

In late March and early April 1919, the Japanese renewed their campaign with a revised clause calling for the equality of nations rather than races. Czech, Greek, Chinese, Italian, and French delegates supported it as "an indisputable principle of justice." The British and their dominions opposed the clause, for fear that it might ignite colonial revolts in Ireland, Africa, and Asia. Wilson feared they might turn against the League entirely. His advisors warned that the clause might also threaten racial hierarchies inside the United States.[59]

Wilson also had personal reasons to withdraw support for the racial equality clause. He feared his party's loss of white voters' support in the 1920 presidential election. Wilson had won reelection in 1916 by a narrow margin, against a Republican opponent backed by the immensely popular Theodore Roosevelt. He owed his margin of victory to racial gerrymandering in the Southern states and to anti-Asian sentiment in California, where many white voters opposed continued Japanese immigration. As with the mandate question, Wilson decided to avoid controversy. He withdrew his support for a vote on the clause. The Japanese delegates were humiliated and outraged.[60]

The perpetuation of racial discrimination in the new postwar order disappointed people around the world.[61] European leaders who gathered at the Quai d'Orsay in 1919 likely did not foresee the full consequences of their endorsement of racial exclusion. They acted on the assumption that prewar hierarchies could be restored. Only years later would the consequences of this miscalculation become clear.

Through April, Faisal's delegation still retained hope that Syrians might fall on the "right" side of the color line at Paris. On February 14, Wilson had sent Faisal a personal note assuring him, "I am deeply interested in the whole Arabian question and have been giving it very close and thoughtful attention." Arabic newspapers continued to praise Wilson in expectation of equality under international law.[62]

But darker currents surfaced in French papers, which remained critical of the League and, increasingly, of Wilson. Abd al-Hadi wrote an angry letter to the pro-colonial *Journal des Débats,* complaining about its double standard. Why did the paper support Italians' demand for a poll in Fiume, but reject Arabs' demand for a poll in Syria? "They take two different approaches to solving the issues in Fiume and Syria on the choice of future government," he wrote. "It is hard to understand by what human logic they reached such a supposition to grant one a referendum and not the other."[63]

Behind diplomatic doors, those darker currents stirred controversy within American ranks. In Wilson's monthlong absence from Paris, Colonel House was wooed by Balfour and Clemenceau to rush punitive settlements on Germany that the president opposed. House effectively bartered away the leverage Wilson might have had against British and French ambitions in the Middle East. In order to win support for his League agenda Wilson had planned to use his veto power over proposals to punish Germany with harsh terms.[64]

In early March, despite Wilson's efforts to promote the need for a more cooperative world order, thirty-seven Senate Republicans lodged an objection to the League covenant out of concern that it infringed on American sovereignty. Their leader, Senator Henry Cabot Lodge, actually accused Wilson of following the politics of Leon Trotsky, the Bolshevik leader. Lodge specifically opposed the covenant's promise of collective security, which he claimed would oblige the American army to fight wars for every small nation on earth. The prospect that Republicans might succeed in defeating the League covenant in the Senate emboldened British and French hard-liners, who also preferred the old-fashioned politics—and who certainly did not want the United States to defend small nations.[65]

Charles Crane, the Chicago millionaire, rushed to defend Wilson's program to the skeptical Secretary of State Lansing, who had remained in Paris. Republicans might think that Wilson was too idealistic, Crane argued to Lansing on March 10, but "the necessity of the League of Nations is so apparent, when the facts are known, it seems impossible that it can be defeated."[66]

But Lansing remained hostile to the League's foreign entanglements. He also considered Wilson's revolutionary ideas on popular sovereignty in international affairs sentimental and vainglorious. "It did not seem essential for the United States to become the guardian of any of the peoples of the Near East," he later wrote. Following old norms of international law, Lansing insisted that sovereignty over the territories had already passed to the occupying powers and that the League would be too weak to assert its sovereignty over them.[67] These were precisely the views of Wilson's British and French opponents.

"I am alarmed at the way in which the old order of the world is reasserting itself consciously and unconsciously. The rights of Syria and similar countries are in danger," Howard Bliss wrote to Wilson that same day, March 10. Bliss had met with both Lansing and House, but they had not taken his concerns seriously. He urged the president to return from Washington quickly, so that promises of government by consent would not be brushed aside like "scraps of paper," a reference to the Belgian neutrality treaty that the invading German army had disregarded in 1914. Britain had joined the war to defend the authority of treaties. Bliss was warning Wilson that just as little Belgium had unleashed the war as a defense of international law, so little Syria was the key to establishing a postwar order based on international law. The point was a poignant one for Wilson: the Paris bar association had just commended him for promoting rule of law against rule of force.[68]

"No self-respecting man could face the people of Syria without shame, if a government is imposed upon them before they have been consulted. Syria is a little country but a big principle is involved in the settlement of its political future," Bliss warned.

Chapter 6

A Sip of Champagne, with a Sour Aftertaste

President Wilson returned to Paris determined to defend the League of Nations and uphold Syrians' right to determine their own future. He had to prevent a full slide into collusion with European imperialism. It was a point of honor with American popular opinion, which supported Wilson against his Republican opponents in the Senate: many supporters worried about the compromises already evident in the League covenant. Wilson decided he would seek to relax League rules on collective security but hold the line on the principle of popular sovereignty. Upon his arrival on March 14, however, he found the British and French eager to shift the conversation from the League to the German settlement. When France proposed a permanent annexation of German territory, Wilson balked. He insisted that Germans, like all peoples, still had the right to popular consent.[1]

The breakthrough on Syria came on March 20, as the first crocuses popped up along the muddy sidewalks of Paris.[2] Lloyd George convened a private meeting at his apartment on Rue Nitot, just south of the Arc de Triomphe. Peace talks were now being conducted by the Big Four: Wilson, Lloyd George, Clemenceau, and Orlando. They also shifted from hotels and the Quai d'Orsay of central Paris to private villas on the city's extreme west end. Wilson took up a new residence on the Place des États-Unis, just around the corner from Lloyd George. Clemenceau lived a mile away on Rue Franklin, near the Seine. And the Hijaz delegation moved to a villa a twenty-minute walk away on the Avenue du Bois de Boulogne (now Avenue Foch).

The Powers huddled in the privacy of this neighborhood to hammer out peace terms for Germany. But the Syria question immediately intruded, threatening compromises that had been agreed to on other matters. Clemenceau pushed for the French occupation of all of Syria; Lloyd George pushed back, insisting on Arab autonomy in the hinterland. With the intent of settling the Syria issue for good, Lloyd George summoned the French foreign minister, Stephen Pichon, and the British military commander in Syria, General Edmund Allenby, to Rue Nitot.[3]

The March 20 meeting immediately exploded into argument. Pichon opened by summarizing the 1916 Sykes-Picot Agreement, revised and confirmed in the deal struck between Clemenceau and Lloyd George on December 1: in exchange for Britain's occupation of Iraq, including Mosul, France would occupy all of Syria. Pichon then recalled France's historical ties to Syria. The French had opened schools for fifty thousand children, in addition to building hospitals and railroads. They would not relinquish their right to rule it.

Lloyd George reminded Pichon that the 1916 agreement granted France direct rule only on the coast. The Syrian hinterland was to remain autonomous within a sphere of French influence. Pichon insisted that a mandate was precisely the form of indirect rule that the treaty called for. Lloyd George countered that a mandate must not invalidate Britain's prior promise to Faisal's father, the sharif of Mecca, for an independent Arab state. Pichon dismissed that promise because it did not bind the French. The French, like Faisal, had received copies of the correspondence documenting the promise from the British only weeks before.

Wilson cut in, exasperated. The secret 1916 agreement was no longer valid, he argued, because one of its signatories, Russia, had withdrawn. Moreover, the United States was "indifferent" to rival European claims on Syria, because it insisted upon the principle of consent of the governed. The main issue in question, he said as he turned to General Allenby, was how Syrians would respond if France took the mandate. Allenby predicted that this would spark a "huge war," fueled by the "strongest possible opposition by the whole of the Moslems and especially by the Arabs." Even Christians had protested to Allenby against French rule.

The president proposed to send a neutral commission to Syria to ascertain public opinion on a "scientific basis." Clemenceau agreed in principle, as long as the commission also polled British-occupied Palestine and Mesopotamia and other Ottoman territories. Lloyd George tentatively agreed. Balfour, however, opposed the commission on the pretext that it would delay a peace settlement too long. In the end, the Big Four agreed to let Wilson draw up the terms for an inter-Allied commission. The president left the meeting, "cursing everybody and everything . . . disgusted with the whole business."[4]

At seven o'clock that evening, Lawrence delivered the good news to the villa on the Avenue du Bois de Boulogne. In celebration, it is said, Faisal drank champagne for the first time in his life.[5] "I cannot find words in which to show our gratitude to you," the prince wrote to Wilson on March 24. "I would esteem it the greatest honour if you could find time, in the midst of your many engagements, to give me an opportunity of thanking you personally."[6]

Wilson had indeed expended considerable political capital to uphold the right of self-determination in Syria—because it was the heart and soul of the League. He had not, however, gone so far as to demand Syrian independence, which would only have undermined his project to convince imperialist France and Britain to approve the League. Wilson's pragmatic motives are underscored by his consent to the continuation of the British protectorate in Egypt. Lloyd George had presented it as the price of cooperation on the Syrian commission of inquiry.[7] Preventing the new and unilateral occupation of Syria served fundamental principles of the world order; by contrast, challenging the fait accompli of Britain's thirty-seven-year-old occupation did not serve his objectives.

The Intervention of Robert de Caix

Faisal planned his immediate departure for Damascus to prepare for the visit of the Inter-Allied Commission. But the intoxication of joy quickly dissipated. Once again, Jean Gout appeared at his door. Gout advised the prince to stay in Paris a bit longer to tie up loose ends. Faisal reluctantly agreed.

Days passed with no word of a meeting. The only reaction from the French was public attacks on the Inter-Allied Commission, printed in Parisian newspapers. They were planted there by the colonial lobby, which was aghast at the prospect of polling Syrians. Clemenceau apparently had not been aware that such a poll would certainly reveal overwhelming hostility to French rule.[8]

Haidar had come to recognize the larger stakes of the Syrian question. "The nations at the present time need to safeguard the principle that all nations have gathered around . . . in support of the 'rights of humanity,'" he wrote in his diary on March 29. Would the Paris Peace Conference stifle revolution, as the Congress of Vienna had done a century before? "Did the world spend all its money, shed all this blood, so that nations can be ruled against their free will?"[9]

The Big Four had in the meantime quietly approved the commission, on two conditions. First, it would poll Arabs in British-occupied territories as well. Second, independence would not be offered as an option in the poll. The commission's inquiry would be based on the January 30 mandates resolution. It had determined that Arabs should fall under an "A" mandate, which would render "administrative advice and assistance" because Arabs were "not yet ready to stand by themselves under the strenuous conditions of the modern world." The commission would therefore poll local opinion on two questions only: boundaries of the future mandates and choice of mandatory power.[10]

Wilson personally chose his trusted friend Charles Crane to head the American section of the Inter-Allied Commission. Crane had served as Wilson's special envoy to Russia during the war and acted as his eyes and ears in Paris. Cochair of the American section would be Henry Churchill King, president of Oberlin College and a well-respected liberal. He was then conducting humanitarian work in Germany for the Young Men's Christian Association (YMCA). Three technical advisors were quickly chosen from the American peace delegation: Albert Lybyer, a historian of the Ottoman Empire who had briefly taught at Robert College in Istanbul; George Montgomery, a journalist and Congregationalist minister who was fluent in Turkish, having been raised by missionaries in eastern Anatolia; and none other than William Yale, the young, broad-shouldered oilman and intelligence agent who had been reporting on Syria since 1917.

As March turned to April, however, relations among the Big Four again soured, delaying the appointment of British and French members of the commission. As they sparred over German reparations and Italy's claim to rule Fiume, the spirit of compromise dissipated. Conflict reached such a pitch that on April 6 Wilson issued an ultimatum. Unless the Big Four backed down from annexations that would undermine the Fourteen Points, he would open the negotiations to the full plenary nations, or simply sail home. (Orlando would actually quit later in the month.) The threat did its magic. Negotiations continued even while the American president fell ill and was confined to bed for a week.[11]

Faisal had still received no response to his note to Wilson. Finally, he received an invitation to an April 9 reception at the Wilson residence. It was a rainy afternoon, and the president, still recovering, did not attend. Faisal spoke with Lloyd George, who advised him that the "old man," Clemenceau, knew nothing about Syria, and that it would be a good idea to meet him before leaving Paris. What Lloyd George did not tell Faisal was that he was having second thoughts about sending the Inter-Allied Commission, fearing it would threaten British rule in Mesopotamia. That fear lay behind his advice that Faisal strike a deal with Clemenceau now, settling the Syrian question without the commission.[12]

Faisal met personally with Clemenceau for the first time since January on Sunday, April 13, again in his cluttered war ministry office. They were to have to a private tête-à-tête, without interference from the foreign ministry. The colonial lobby was alarmed to discover that this conversation had taken place. Clemenceau left no official written record, but Awni Abd al-Hadi, who acted as translator that day, took notes. The transcript, published years later, no doubt inspired Arab nationalists to agree with T. S. Eliot's words, "April is the cruellest month."[13]

Clemenceau greeted Faisal with assurances that France sought only to help Syria sustain its freedom and independence, not to colonize it. "And I want you to know, Your Excellency, that I am an enemy of colonialism and that I have battled against colonialism for fifty years."

Faisal assured the French premier that he had faith in his altruistic intentions. But, he explained, Clemenceau was an octogenarian surrounded by colonial wolves: "I fear that someone else might take over as prime minister of France, and he will not be the same as you, an enemy of colonialism."

Clemenceau brushed away Faisal's fear. The French government was not seeking another colony. But the people would not let another country break France's bonds of friendship with Syria either. France must be the power that advised Syrians. "Therefore, they ask to replace British troops in Syria with French troops."

"No, no, Mr. President. Syria has no need for foreign troops to protect it," Faisal insisted. Should Syria ever need an ally for its defense, however, it would not hesitate to ask France for help.

Clemenceau insisted that France could not withdraw its troops now. "It would look like her soldiers had retreated from the battlefront," he explained. "All France needs there is a small number of troops."

Faisal suggested that they postpone the discussion for now, until after the Inter-Allied Commission polled Syrians on their preferences. On that note, the prince took his leave of the premier.[14]

Faisal did not yet know it, but the April 13 conversation would prove to be the best offer Syrians would ever receive.[15] Clemenceau had defined the French mandate in its most limited, Wilsonian terms, as the administration of advice to a provisionally independent Syria. His main concern in April 1919 was to earn American support for imposing strong peace terms on Germany.[16]

However, Clemenceau could not ignore the colonial lobby. His was a lonely voice against expanding the empire, and he feared a backlash in the French parliament. On the right, colonialists deployed a powerful press campaign against him. On the left, Clemenceau had long ago lost the support of League defenders like French delegate Léon Bourgeois, since he had scorned them as pacifists during the war. The Father of Victory wanted to stay in office long enough to accomplish the peace treaty. He therefore dared not grant Syria full independence.[17]

Faisal ignored the realities of French politics because he fully expected the Inter-Allied Commission's inquiry to support him.[18] Meetings with Wilson's top advisor, Colonel House, encouraged Faisal to believe that the commission would soon depart. House had even hinted that the Americans might consider taking the mandate if the Syrians were united in support of it. To Faisal's mind, it was time to bring their diplomatic victory home.

What Faisal did not reckon on was the indomitable perseverance of Robert de Caix, who had weaseled his way into becoming Clemenceau's new advisor on Syria. An austere man with a pince-nez and a short, pointed beard, de Caix was a powerful leader of the colonial lobby. He considered Wilsonism an "epidemic" and the concept of a limited mandate anathema. Even as Faisal met with Clemenceau, de Caix was currying favor with the American delegation. He and Georges-Picot socialized, in particular, with William Yale. De Caix actually warned the Americans that French forces would need to be on the ground in Syria in order to stop Faisal when "he started to hang people opposed to him."[19]

De Caix also managed to preempt any written commitment by Clemenceau based on the April 13 conversation. Acting as the premier's representative, he drafted a letter that accorded recognition not of independence, but only of Syria's *right* to independence. Haidar and Abd al-Hadi immediately recognized the letter as a ruse to convince them to accept a mandate. When they submitted a note rejecting the draft, de Caix rejected their blunt language as "a monument of insolence." Here was the language of colonial exclusion. In de Caix's mind, Arabs did not have the right to speak to the French as equals.[20]

Faisal was forced to leave Paris without a written guarantee. He would have to place all his bets on the Inter-Allied Commission. On April 21, he paid the premier a farewell visit. Clemenceau reassured Faisal that they agreed in principle. He even apologized for delegating matters to de Caix, explaining that he himself was preoccupied with questions regarding Germany.[21]

That evening, Haidar and Abd al-Hadi accompanied Faisal to his train at the Gare de Lyon. Faisal asked them to stay in Paris and negotiate a deal based on Clemenceau's terms—recognition of independence in exchange for Syria's promise to rely exclusively on French aid and advice. Also gathered on the platform to bid the prince farewell were Gout, Picot, de Caix, and T. E. Lawrence. As Faisal's train pulled away, Lawrence took the Frenchmen aside in quiet conversation. "I have come to doubt the politics of this young Englishman," Haidar confided to his diary that night.[22]

Faisal made a stop in Rome, where he was feted by the king of Italy and received by the pope, and then arrived in Beirut on April 30. He had come full circle since November. Having exhausted diplomatic efforts, he now turned back to the Syrian people to claim their sovereignty. The prince therefore planned elections for an Arab congress, to welcome the commission and to write a constitution. By insisting on sending the commission of inquiry, Woodrow Wilson had unwittingly launched a remarkable experiment in democracy at Damascus.

PART III

Syria's Declaration of Independence

Chapter 7

The Syrian Congress and the American Commission

Prince Faisal's ship docked in Beirut on April 30, 1919, to the cheers of a welcoming crowd. In a speech at the Great Mosque, he greeted both Christians and Muslims as "brothers in the love for our country." He urged them to "unite yourselves so that Europe will know that Syria wants to live in independence."

The following day, Faisal paid visits to city hall and the American Syrian Protestant College, issuing a formal call for Syrians to mobilize. In Paris, he announced, "The independence of your country was agreed to in principle." Syrians now had to turn principle into reality. The four Great Powers were sending a commission to inquire into Syrian desires and to meet "the temporary General Syrian Congress which will soon convene," he promised. "You must prove to them that you are worthy of independence and capable of managing your own affairs . . . that you are a people who will sacrifice everything you hold dear for the most honorable of goals, independence."[1]

En route to Damascus, crowds cheered Faisal at every train stop. "LONG LIVE ARAB INDEPENDENCE!" and "LONG LIVE THE PRINCE!" their banners declared. The people were so eager to greet him that the train was delayed twenty to thirty minutes at each stop, a Beirut paper reported. Among the many supporters who joined Faisal on the train were the mayor of Beirut and Habib Istifan, the Maronite priest who had welcomed the prince's envoys to Beirut with an eloquent speech the previous October.[2]

Hours before his arrival in Damascus on May 3, men, women, and children lined the streets of the capital and gathered on rooftops. "I saw the nation's heart beat as if an electric spark ran through her body," wrote a reporter for the government's official paper, *The Capital.* "Without a doubt, the Arab nation's celebration today was unprecedented in this country's history."[3]

Two days later, Faisal assembled delegates from across Syria at the Serail in central Damascus to reassure them of his achievements and to enlist their support before the Inter-Allied Commission arrived. "My words will be of historic significance with regard to the past and future of the new Arab nation," he began. Faisal reminded the delegates that he and Syrians were united in a legitimate political movement—contrary to Europeans' ignorant view that Arabs were uncivilized Bedouin and that he himself was a foreigner. Syrians were the moral heart of the Arab movement that inspired Arabs of the Hijaz to rebel. "So we see that the glory is to be shared by all, thank God," he said. "I went therefore to claim *our* due at the Conference which was meeting at Paris," he said [emphasis added.] "I pleaded for a Syria within her natural borders. I said that the Syrians want their country to be independent without any partner." The other Arab regions, Iraq and Arabia, asked for their own independent states.

Now, Faisal continued, Syrians must present their demands directly to the Inter-Allied Commission. "They will ask you to express yourselves in any way you please, for the nations today do not want to govern other peoples except with their consent." Representatives should now be chosen. "The leaders of the Revolt acted without consulting the people simply because time did not permit it," he explained. Would the notables assembled here formally elect him as their leader, to establish his authority under international law?

"Yes!" roared the crowd with applause.

"Do you want us to continue our work or not?"

The crowed again yelled, "Continue."

The speech was a huge success. Delegates from the Hawran region around Deraa, from the Druze community, and from Palestine stood up to give Faisal their oath of loyalty. They were followed by patriarchs of Syria's many religious sects—Roman and Syrian Catholic,

Orthodox, Nestorian, Jewish—and by urban leaders from Baalbek, Homs, Hama, Aleppo, Sidon, Amman, Latakia, Salt, and Mount Lebanon. The archbishop of the Armenian refugees, speaking in Turkish, thanked the Arabs for their support during the war. "Our history will inscribe the name of the Arabs in gold ink. I bless you and thank you."

Faisal pledged to respect the wishes of minority groups and to treat all citizens alike, regardless of religion. He urged all Syrians to build a community of trust and common purpose, for their own good and to reassure the Great Powers that they were a united nation. "Let us protect the great and the small among us, our neighbors, and those who seek refuge with us." In conclusion, he warned: "There will be no independence for you unless you maintain order and do as the one to whom you have given your support [Faisal] says."[4]

Faisal's appeals in the first week of May 1919 set in motion a process of mass popular mobilization that had never been seen before in Syria. The official newspaper, *The Capital*, reinforced his appeal with articles written by members of the Fatat party. They hailed the arrival of "Arab democracy" and the future "United States of Arabia," and they explained the political meaning of terms such as "parties," "socialism," "equality," and "workers' strikes." Given his reading of Woodrow Wilson's *The State*, Rustum Haidar would have appreciated *The Capital*'s analysis of Faisal's proposed regime: "The difference between the American government and the Arab government will be this: The first is a constitutional republic, the latter will be a constitutional monarchy."[5]

Faisal was so successful that he soon lost control of the movement he unleashed. In coming months, as the struggle for independence intensified, Syrians also organized autonomous movements to claim democratic rights against his royal prerogative.

Convening the General Syrian Congress

In anticipation of the Inter-Allied Commission's arrival, Governor Ali Rida al-Rikabi called for elections across Greater Syria to choose delegates for the new Congress. He based the elections on Ottoman electoral law, but decided to skip the first stage of the customary two-stage election process in order to save time. Electors chosen in the last Ottoman election (1913) should convene in their districts to choose their Congress deputies. In early June, electors in the East Zone met publicly to cast their votes. However, France and Britain blocked elections in the Western (Lebanon) and Southern (Palestine) zones, and would later claim, on that basis, that the Congress was not legitimately elected. However, electors in the French and British zones managed to meet in secret and choose their representatives to the Congress. In general, they reappointed deputies who had been elected to the former Ottoman parliament.[6]

The election campaign in Damascus was a passionate affair. In late May, city streets exploded with political excitement. On one side were the wealthiest of the city's notables, Fawzi Pasha al-Azm and Abd al-Rahman al-Yusuf, pro-Ottoman conservatives who had opposed Faisal's father, Sharif Hussein, and the Arab Revolt. In Faisal's government, they saw young politicians, many from outside Damascus, who intended to diminish the conservatives' traditional influence. They waged hostile campaigns against nationalists. In response, hard-line nationalists staged protests and distributed pamphlets with titles like "Autonomy or Death." They also spread rumors of Christian and Jewish plots against Syria. Fatat's candidates played a moderating role, countering both the conservatives and the extremists with liberal promises.[7]

When nationalist protests shut local government offices down, General Allenby, who remained the supreme military commander of Syria, grew alarmed. Faisal defended the electoral process. He explained to Allenby that the Syrians had "decided among themselves to ask for their national rights and defend their national being with all the powers they have of legal means." If they were forced to submit to a mandate, he warned, there would be bloodshed.[8]

In the end, the conservatives emerged victorious. They captured fourteen of the sixteen seats for Damascus. Only two nationalist deputies were elected from the capital: Fa'iz al-Shihabi and Fawzi al-Bakri, an advisor to Faisal and cofounder of Fatat along with Rustum Haidar, Ahmad Qadri, and Awni Abd al-Hadi.

In the first week of June, the elected deputies made their way toward Damascus. A certification committee verified their identity and their right to represent their respective districts. Forty percent of the eighty-nine deputies who arrived came from the four major towns of inland Syria: Damascus, Homs, Hama, and Aleppo. As in Damascus, most of them were from conservative landowning families.[9]

Only eighty-seven of the 120 delegates actually appeared, however. Many of the thirty-three empty seats belonged to dissenting districts like Mount Lebanon, where the Maronite Church called for a Christian Lebanon, separate from Syria. Districts belonging to the Alawi minority of coastal Syria and the Druze minority south of Damascus were governed by tribal leaders who defended their autonomy from Damascus.

European and Syrian critics would later challenge the Congress's legitimacy because of these irregularities in procedure and representation. Historians have since shown, however, that the gaps were due only partly, and perhaps minimally, to nationalist efforts to exclude minorities. Many of the representatives in Lebanon and Palestine had not appeared was that the French and the British had thrown up travel barriers. French agents had also toured the dissenting Druze and Alawi districts, distributing funds and favors to dissuade delegates from attending the Congress. Like the Maronites, Zionist leaders boycotted the election because they desired a state separate from the Damascus government.[10]

The General Syrian Congress convened for the first time on June 7 at the Arab Club, located near the Hijaz Railway Station. The club, established by Rikabi to promote cultural revival, had become a popular political center. Faisal offered a formal welcome, with a speech on the origins of the Inter-Allied Commission in Wilson's Fourteen Points. He then charged the Congress with three tasks: (1) to represent the nation before the commission; (2) to enact a constitution that preserved minority rights; and (3) to prove to the world that the Arab nation deserved to be free. Faisal conceived of the General Syrian Congress as a temporary advisory body, a constituent assembly. Just as Faisal was still, technically, a military commander of occupied territory, so the Congress was not a formal parliament.

The Congress quickly demonstrated it would be no lapdog of Faisal's Fatat movement. Most deputies were conservative notables, wealthy landowners, tribal chiefs, and religious patriarchs who had been favored under the Ottoman regime. Only fourteen deputies were members of Fatat. As the first president of Congress, the deputies elected Fawzi Pasha al-Azm, an aging aristocratic landowner and Ottoman loyalist. Abd al-Rahman al-Yusuf, one of Syria's wealthiest men, was chosen as vice president. Yusuf was of Kurdish, not Arab, descent. Within a year, he would lead a faction to reassert Damascene control of the government, against the participation of Faisal and Arabs from across Greater Syria, and especially against their democratic agenda.[11]

Though socially conservative, most deputies favored Syria's political independence. And much to Faisal's satisfaction, the Congress included a disproportionately high number of Christians, mostly elected from the Syrian interior, as well as a Jewish deputy from Damascus. Also much to Fatat's satisfaction, Izzat Darwazeh, the deputy from Nablus, Palestine, was elected Congress secretary. Darwazeh had joined Fatat during the war, while working as a post office director in Beirut. He was a highly intelligent but self-taught man of humble origins. With a burly build and a bushy black mustache, he was a natural politician, with abundant energy and formidable organizational skills. Even though he had arrived in Damascus only recently, he had already made many friends.

Darwazeh met Faisal for the first time at a tense Fatat meeting convened to set strategy for the Inter-Allied Commission's visit. Faisal, who was less confident of Allied support than he pretended to be in public, proposed that Fatat indicate to the commission that it supported a British mandate. Faisal had deep suspicions of the French, and he thought the British would respect Syrian sovereignty. Darwazeh, leader of the opposition, was called on to reply. He was at first intimidated, he wrote in his memoir. But he stood up to make a forceful case that Fatat demand full independence—against the rules laid out by the Supreme Council. The British had betrayed the Arabs already, he argued, when they signed the Sykes-Picot Agreement to split Syria with France. They could not be trusted again.

Faisal, disconcerted by such a strong retort from a lowly civil servant, turned to his guard, Tahsin Qadri, the brother of Dr. Ahmad

Qadri. "Where did this guy come from?" he asked discreetly, in Turkish.[12] The prince soon discovered that Darwazeh had mustered support from leading politicians in Damascus, who helped organize street demonstrations against a British mandate, forcing Faisal to back down.[13] It was the beginning of the prince's education in democracy.

Supporting Darwazeh's opposition were leaders of the Syrian Union Party, established six months earlier in Cairo. Since winter, the SUP had distributed leaflets in Damascus and elsewhere. These promoted the SUP program, demanding complete unity and full independence for Greater Syria, and a government built on "democratic principles of decentralization" that would grant provinces autonomy under their own elected councils, and on civil law. Only matters of family and personal status were to be covered by religious law. The SUP was the force calling for a "new civil constitution."[14]

While the British denied Rida permission to travel, they had permitted three SUP leaders to return to Damascus in time for the Congress: Kamil al-Qassab, the populist Muslim preacher; Michel Lutfallah, the Greek Orthodox banker; and Abd al-Rahman Shahbandar, the medical doctor. They carried with them strong opposition to the British, based on what they had witnessed of the Egyptian Revolution that spring. The British had arrested and exiled the popular nationalist leader Saad Zaghlul because he persisted in demanding to attend the Paris Peace Conference. After Zaghlul's arrest, students had sparked large popular demonstrations. In defiance of curfews, Muslims and Christians, men and women, marched under banners of the Crescent and Cross, proclaiming national unity and independence. British troops responded with gunfire. In April, General Allenby—whom Syrians had trusted to support their liberation—was called to Cairo to quash the revolution.

By June 1919, Rida had also lost faith in the British. Not only had they denied the rights of Egyptians, but they had also shown cruel indifference toward the fate of the Syrians. Since the November armistice, Rida had tried to send food and clothing to his family and village. Qalamun had been hit hard by famine and disease during the war. But British border agents held up the shipment. As of June, the food and clothing had still not arrived in Qalamun.[15]

Rida followed the events in Syria with concern. In the June issue of *The Lighthouse*, he warned Syrians that they were bickering over minor issues, unaware that France and Britain were busy carving up their land as colonies. "It is bewildering for an outsider to see how divided these supposedly intelligent Syrians are regarding the fate of their land," he wrote. Syrians were still strangers to the Allies, and far too trusting, Rida worried. "The call for foreign protection spreads among them disguised with the word "aid," he wrote. "Because they think it represents merely financial aid, they believe it will not threaten their independence."[16]

He was desperate to counsel Faisal and to join the new Syrian Congress. But the British were loath to let activists return to Damascus. Lutfallah had managed to return to Lebanon on the pretext of inspecting charity operations. Qassab and Shahbandar gained permission to return home to Damascus only after promising to avoid politics. As soon as they arrived, they broke their promise and opened a branch of the Syrian Union Party. The SUP quickly became the backbone of opposition to Faisal's tendency to compromise on full independence. Qassab had supported Darwazeh at the Fatat meeting when the latter confronted Faisal. And it was at an SUP banquet that Faisal had been forced to publicly proclaim his support for full independence.

At the end of June, the Congress finally gathered to debate how to present Syrian views to the King-Crane Commission, as the American section of the Inter-Allied Commission came to be called. In a marathon session, delegates reached a consensus on what would be known as the Damascus Program.[17] It opened,

> We the undersigned members of the General Syrian
> Congress, meeting in Damascus on Wednesday July 2nd 1919,
> made up of representatives from the three Zones, viz., the
> Southern, Eastern, and Western, provided with credentials
> and authorizations by the inhabitants of our various districts
> Moslems, Christians, and Jews, have agreed upon the following
> statement of the desires of the people of the country who
> have elected us to present them to the American section of the
> International Commission."[18]

Congress unanimously adopted four resolutions, following the SUP's program. The resolutions also recapped Faisal's argument that Syrians were as advanced as Europeans, in no need of a mandate:

1. "Complete political independence" for Greater Syria, from Anatolia to the Red Sea, from the Euphrates River to the Mediterranean.

2. A "democratic, civil, constitutional Monarchy on broad decentralization principles, safe-guarding the rights of minorities and that the King be our Emir Faisal."

3. "Considering the fact that the Arabs inhabiting the Syrian area are not naturally less gifted than other more advanced races and that they are by no means less developed than the Bulgarians, Serbians, Greeks and Romanians at the beginning of their independence, we protest against Article 22 of the Covenant of the League of Nations, placing us among nations in their middle stage of development which stand in need of a mandatory power."

4. "And desiring that our country should not fall a prey to colonization and believing that the American Nation is farthest from any thought of colonization and has no political ambition in our country we will seek the technical and economic assistance from the United States of America, provided that such assistance does not exceed 20 years."

A fifth resolution was adopted with some dissent. It accepted Britain as a second choice, but only under strict limits set in point four: "In the event of America not finding herself in a position to accept our desire for assistance, we will seek this assistance from Great Britain."

In points six through ten of the Damascus Program, the Congress unanimously rejected partition of Greater Syria into the separate states of Palestine, Lebanon, and Syria. It also called for the annulment of European agreements imposed unilaterally, without popular consent: the Balfour Declaration by Britain to establish a Jewish home in Palestine and the Sykes-Picot accord dividing Greater Syria and Iraq between Britain and France.

In essence, a Congress dominated by social conservatives embraced Wilson's democratic revolution in the world order. The Damascus Program echoed demands of peoples across the non-European world in 1919.

Charles Crane and the American Commission

"He looked like a parrot," wrote British historian Arnold Toynbee, who recalled Charles R. Crane's "quizzical air" and insatiable curiosity.[19] Crane was a bit eccentric. A throwback to the nineteenth-century mold of aristocratic world traveler, he had organized expeditions to the North Pole and enjoyed tea with the Russian tsar. But he was also a passionate believer in Wilson's ideals. And he loved Middle Eastern culture. In his travels through the Ottoman Empire, he learned the Turkish jokes and stories featuring the beloved thirteenth-century comic figure Nasreddin Hoja. Before leaving Paris for Syria, Crane told one of those tales to cheer up President Wilson at a particularly low point in the negotiations:

> Nasreddin went out to the well one night to get some water, and looking into the well he saw the moon. "Great heavens," he said. "The moon has fallen into the well. I must get her out." With a long stick, Nasreddin poked into the water to dislodge the moon. Pulling hard, he slipped and fell on his back. Looking up, he saw the moon in the sky. "Well," he said, "that's a job well done."

"That is what we have been doing here at the peace conference," Wilson had laughed.[20]

Crane credited the "wonderful and inspiring" Howard Bliss with convincing Wilson to insist on sending the commission. Secretary of state Robert Lansing gave him a briefing based on the Supreme Council's March 25 agreement. The commission was to guide Syrians' "placement under mandatories" as a step toward independence, already encouraged by Britain and France in their November 1918 declaration.[21] Crane's experience on the commission would launch two decades of activism on behalf of Syrians.

While Crane was the commission's social diplomat, his cochair Henry King played the role of scholar and director. As a theologian, King embraced Wilson's vision of a new international order based on Christian values.[22] In April, as the Americans waited for the British and

French to choose their commissioners, King worked at the American delegation's office in the Hôtel de Crillon, conducting interviews, collecting books, and consulting maps of the region.[23]

Yale, meanwhile, socialized with the French. Not a supporter of Wilson's principles on consulting the people, he focused on the need for diplomatic compromise. High Commissioner François Georges-Picot warned Yale that "we are at the twelfth hour." He employed the same apocalyptic and sectarian language that Gout and de Caix used. A French mandate must be assigned quickly or the "Islamic movement" would take over in Syria, Picot predicted. The commission might prove to be a fatal delay, he argued, reminding Yale that Armenians had already been massacred at Aleppo in the February riots.[24] De Caix and Picot stalled the commission by setting preconditions for the mission, first demanding that partition boundaries be set, then insisting that a final assignment of mandates be made in Paris before the Syrians were polled.

Wilson nearly canceled the commission, not just because of French maneuvering. American Zionist leaders also objected to it, fearing that a poll of Arabs would "cheat the Jewry of Palestine." But General Allenby in Egypt and Colonel House warned him that Syria would explode in violence if he did so. Admiral Mark L. Bristol, the American commissioner in Constantinople, also supported the commission. Wilson was also touched by a departing note from Faisal on April 20, assuring him that the commission would find in Syria "a country united in its love and gratitude to America."[25] As Wilson gave the go-ahead, the British finally appointed their commissioners, with Sir Henry McMahon, author of the 1915 promises to Sharif Hussein, as chair, and the historian Toynbee as secretary.

On May 1, King and Crane submitted a memo to Wilson stating that the partition of the Ottoman Empire represented the ultimate test of the Allies' war aims. They proposed that the disinterested United States take the lead, by accepting mandates in Constantinople and Armenia (but not in Syria, as Faisal had proposed). They warned that the selfish division of spoils—and the imposition of mandates by force—would spark violence, stain America's reputation, and threaten the entire postwar order. "It would also go far to convince men of independent judgement all over the world . . . that the aims of the Allies had become as selfish and ruthless as those of the Germans had been."[26]

Their worst fears soon materialized. Frustrated by Wilson's rejection of secret treaties, the Italians took matters into their own hands. They landed troops in southern Anatolia to claim their share of territory promised during the war. In response, the Greeks dispatched their troops to claim their allotment against Italy. Upon landing at the port of Smyrna on May 15, Greek troops killed more than three hundred stunned Turks. Unaware that Wilson had joined Lloyd George in support of the Greek invasion, the American commissioners despaired.[27]

On May 21 and 22, the fiercest conflict yet over the fate of Syria flared in the Supreme Council. Worse than any disagreement regarding Germany, the issue threatened to cause a split among the Allies. Lloyd George arrived at the meeting worried that the entire Muslim world—and especially the many Muslims in India—was upset by the turmoil in the Ottoman Empire. To calm the Muslims, he proposed a revised mandate plan, allocating more territory to the Turkish state and establishing American mandates in Constantinople and Armenia. The additional Turkish territory would be taken from areas previously assigned to France.

Clemenceau exploded in anger, accusing Lloyd George of breaking his promises yet again. First, he had excluded the French from setting terms of the armistice in November. Then, in December, he had promised to withdraw from Syria in exchange for Mosul. But British troops still remained there. Now, he dared to redraw the map of Anatolia to cut territory promised to France. At the end of a long list of British insults and perfidy, Clemenceau announced,

> I am the least colonial of all the French. I cannot be accused, in that respect, of excessive ambition. But if this decision is taken, I will not do what my Italian colleagues did. I will not quit the Conference, but I will quit the Government.

All of the bile stored up since the end of the war now spilled out. Lloyd George retorted that more British soldiers than French had died in Syria, and that France therefore had no right to claim the Arab interior zone. He had done all he could for France, and he demanded an apology.

Clemenceau refused. If Britain had moved its troops to Europe, he said, rather than use them to claim more territory for its empire, the war would have ended sooner. "I will not continue to engage with you, in any fashion, on this part of the world if mutual agreements are not upheld," he concluded.

Lloyd George refused to back down. He even threatened to cancel France's portion of Mosul oil promised on December 1. "If France does not send commissioners to Syria, then neither will we. I will accept the decision of the American commissioners."[28]

Again, as in March, Wilson cut in to say that he "had never been able to see by what right France and Great Britain gave this country away to anyone." That same day, May 22, the president received a telegram from Faisal, "anxiously awaiting the arrival of the Commission." Earlier in the week, Rustum Haidar had come to the Hôtel de Crillon to remind Colonel House, Wilson's advisor, that Wilson had given Faisal his word of honor that the commission would go to Syria. Wilson invited King and Crane to lunch and ordered them to depart alone. They would file a report personally with him. Wilson promised that no permanent settlement on the mandates would be made without their report. And so, the Inter-Allied Commission became the American, or King-Crane, Commission.[29]

Faisal had a premonition of trouble when François Georges-Picot reappeared in Beirut. The prince considered the high commissioner a virtual war criminal. During the war Picot had left in the French embassy incriminating papers that exposed Arab nationalists' political relations with the French. The Ottoman military governor had arrested and hanged a number of the men named in the documents. Now, in the weeks before the American commissioners arrived, Picot paid Faisal multiple visits, trying to persuade him to support a French mandate.[30] Faisal at first discussed only the lightest terms, as suggested by Clemenceau in April. But Picot pushed harder for the deployment of French troops and advisors in the hinterland. When Faisal balked, Picot scolded him for publicly disavowing the Sykes-Picot Agreement. Syrians could not abrogate an international treaty, he told Faisal. Faisal retorted that he honored Wilson's principle that all secret treaties should be outlawed. The international commission was a sham, Picot replied through his envoy.[31]

To make matters worse for Faisal, news arrived from Mecca that his brother Zaid had been defeated in a battle by Abdulaziz ibn Saud, the charismatic leader of a tribal faction from Riyadh that Britain's India Office championed. Ibn Saud had already occupied the eastern half of the Arabian Peninsula and now threatened Faisal's family homeland in the western, Hijaz region. Arab tribes began to defect from Faisal's father, Sharif Hussein, to the Saudis. That meant fewer troops for Syria's defense against the French. It also meant playing a weaker hand at the diplomatic tables in Paris.[32] So much now depended on the Americans.

On May 25, Crane departed for Syria by way of Bulgaria, where he met friends like King Vladimir Tsanoff; and Constantinople, where he spoke at the graduation exercises of a girls' school he funded.[33] The Ottoman capital had been thrown into an uproar by the Greek invasion. Greek-speaking residents of the city publicly unfurled Greek flags in joy. Muslim Turks, in response, staged a huge demonstration at the Blue Mosque, with banners that read "WILSON'S 12TH POINT," promising Turkish independence.

After the demonstration, Crane met one of its main speakers, Halide Edib, a graduate of the American School for Girls. She had served in Syria during the war, running an orphanage near Beirut. Edib wished Crane and the commission well: "I hope your visit to Syria will help their poor cause."[34]

The remaining four American commissioners arrived at Constantinople on June 4. The group set sail three days later and arrived at Jaffa, in southern Syria, or Palestine, on June 10. Yale took the lead in setting their itinerary but was soon frustrated by Crane's tendency to wander off schedule to meet old friends and attend musical concerts. Their relations worsened as their political differences became more apparent, especially over Zionism and France. Despite these tensions, the commissioners visited a dozen towns, where they interviewed Muslims, Christians, and Jews about the region's political future. They were pleased to encounter much enthusiasm and affection for the United States.[35]

The King-Crane Commission Visits

Crane hurried to arrive in Damascus by June 25, in time to witness the Night of Power. He had heard that the city's celebration of the holiday was "astounding." It marked the night, near the end of the fasting month of Ramadan, when the Prophet Muhammad received his first revelation. The gates of heaven were said to open, and Muslims gathered in mosques all night to pray for forgiveness, as the musical prayers of muezzins floated across rooftops.

Syrians also hoped that political doors would open with the commission's arrival. In desperation, Faisal had written to President Wilson on June 22, seeking reassurance that the commission's report would be taken seriously: "I and all the Syrian people believe you are the most outstanding man in the world, and that you will not permit the Syrian people to air their opinions only to shame them."[36]

On June 26, the commission began its work. Crane appeared at a meeting at the Damascus Palace Hotel wearing a white, wide-brimmed hat that matched his white goatee. With his fluent English, Abd al-Rahman Shahbandar of the SUP became Crane's translator, host, and, by the end of the visit, friend.

They began with interviews of Prince Faisal and top religious officials, who demanded a "civil democratic government," not an Islamic regime. Syria was ready for self-rule, they insisted. Only if necessary would they accept a mandate, and then only an American mandate, "because America loves humanity, entered the war on behalf of oppressed nations, will not colonize, and is very rich."[37]

Over the next three days, the commission interviewed Greek Orthodox, Catholic, and Jewish patriarchs; Druze leaders; members of the royal Jaza'iri family, who had lost their bid for power in October; and government officials. The commissioners were much impressed with the Damascus police chief, Gabriel Haddad. A graduate of Syrian Protestant College in Beirut, he spoke English in the manner of a modern bureaucrat, and he allowed that some foreign guidance would help root out remnants of Ottoman corruption. Less impressive were leaders of Fatat's Independence Party, who rejected any talk of a mandate. The Commissioner's notes labeled them "extremist."

Faisal lavished royal favor upon his guests with elaborate meals and programs of nationalist songs. At a banquet marking the end of Ramadan, the men gathered in a garden patio, donned Bedouin costumes, and feasted on a huge platter of grilled meats, vegetables, and rice, while being entertained with Arabic music. Dinner on July 2 was served in the French style, featuring soup, fish, chicken with beans, meat stew with okra, grilled meats with potato, pastry, ice cream, fruit, and coffee.[38]

Faisal's own presentation was "superb," the commissioners noted. He spoke in the name of 300,000 Syrians who had signed an affidavit authorizing him to represent them. They shared a "fear of colonization and division of their country" and a "desire for liberty and independence," he claimed. Faisal urged the Americans to reject the double standard at Paris: Balkan peoples had been granted independence without any prior inquiry, even though they were no more advanced than the Syrians. In closing, Faisal had warned that France's occupation of the coast had "engendered hatred" and stifled both culture and industry.[39]

In the afternoon on Thursday, July 3, 1919, a twenty-one-member congressional delegation presented the Damascus Program to the commission. The Congress president, Fawzi Pasha al-Azm; and the chair of its constitutional committee, Hashim al-Atassi of Homs, led the delegation. Atassi and Izzat Darwazeh presented the "Basic Law of the United States of Syria," based on the SUP's draft constitution. Faisal would be king, ruling through a bicameral legislature in a federal-style "democratic monarchy." The central government would rule through nine states, each with its own elected council. Freedom of speech and association, and the right to public education and to equality under the law would be guaranteed.[40]

The Congress impressed several commissioners. Lybyer, the Ottoman historian, compared its constitution to the Americans', because both called for the "separation of church and state." He considered Faisal an "outstanding figure capable of rendering the greatest service for world peace." Lybyer also cabled to Paris that Faisal was "the heart of the Moslem world with enormous prestige and popularity, confirmed believer in the Anglo-Saxon race, great lover of Christianity."[41]

King agreed, concluding that Faisal was "a broad and open-minded man," fit to rule Syria.[42]

At the end of the Syrian visit, Crane cabled President Wilson directly to report that the Syrians were ready to build their own state: they were "sober, industrious, intelligent," with a strong culture based on "the rich and beautiful Arabic language" and both Christian and Muslim faith.[43]

These three commissioners warned the president that imposing a French mandate on Syria "would precipitate warfare."[44] They were convinced that the Muslim majority in Syria favored independence. Christian minorities held mixed views, with those in Mount Lebanon solidly in favor of a French mandate.

Most remarkable to Crane were the petitions by women. At Damascus, Nazik al-Abid, the daughter of a former Ottoman official, led a group of Muslim women to appear before the commission. To stress their modernity and their trust in the Americans, the women removed their veils as they pleaded for independence. Crane was impressed by Abid's argument and command of English (Abid had attended an American school while exiled in Izmir). In Beirut, another group of Muslim women appealed for an American mandate. They lamented that the West saw Arab women as playthings or slaves in harems, when in fact they were educated and, since the war, had entered public affairs.

"The sight of thousands dying homeless has inspired us to strive for better things for our people," their petition stated. "Realizing that all we have suffered has been the result of subjugation . . . we crave for ourselves not merely independence of existence, but the right and opportunity to a development which will assure us a place among the responsible nations of the world." They asked for independence under a constitutional government led by Prince Faisal, with guidance from the nation "most worthy of being followed and most in accord with our own," the United States.[45]

William Yale, the young oilman, opposed these conclusions in a separate letter to the American delegation. His views formed in Paris had only been confirmed upon the visit, he wrote. In deference to the strength of French and Zionist claims, the only realistic course was to divide Greater Syria into three sectarian states: Christian Lebanon, Muslim Syria, and the Jewish homeland in Palestine. The British would be able to repress by force any Muslim and Christian opposition to Zionism in Palestine. Yale dismissed the many petitions demanding a secular, national, unified Greater Syria as the work of Faisal's propaganda, not a reflection of popular sentiment.[46]

As evidence of this claim, Yale and other critics pointed to the similarity in wording among many petitions supporting a unified Syrian government. King, Crane, and Lybyer, by contrast, judged the petitions to be representative, despite efforts of French, British, and Arab officials to influence them. Historians have since judged the similarity as typical of petitions in any modern political movement, whether in Syria or Europe. These historians agree with King and Crane that the petitions did reflect popular opinion. They regard the orchestrated petition campaign as evidence that Syrian politicians had mastered the techniques of publicity and propaganda that were being used against them by the French.[47]

Like a Moon in the Pond:
The Fate of the Report

The commissioners wrapped up their research with visits to Tripoli, where French police suppressed a crowd that followed them in the streets; and to Aleppo, where they visited an Armenian refugee camp. In late July they began drafting their report in Constantinople. They had collected 1,863 petitions. Of these, more than 80 percent demanded the unity of Syria, Palestine, and Lebanon. More than 70 percent demanded full independence, with no mandate, and 72 percent opposed the Zionist program. Nearly 60 percent of all the petitions—including those from Christians—supported the Damascus Program for a "democratic, non-centralized, constitutional kingdom." Because the Big Four had ruled out full independence as an option, the commission recommended a limited American mandate to reorganize administration, root out corruption, and provide economic support.[48]

The report's conclusion largely endorsed the Damascus Program and flew in the face of the Sykes-Picot Agreement and the Balfour Declaration. It recommended a brief, restricted mandate that would ensure rule of law and the rights of minorities until the government was stable. The commission found no evidence of pan-Islamism or intent to found a theocracy. "Syria offers an excellent opportunity to establish a state where members of the three great monotheistic religions can live together in harmony," the report concluded. "Since now the majority declare for nationalism, independent of religion, it is necessary only to hold them to this view through mandatory control until they have established the method and practice of it."

Second, the report recommended that the unity of Greater Syria be preserved, with substantial autonomy for Christian-dominated Mount Lebanon. The Congress, it pointed out, had even discussed granting half of the parliamentary seats to Arab Muslims, and half to all minorities. Syria's diverse people had coexisted under the Ottomans, and they would thrive together under a modern state. Third, Faisal should be made head of the state because the Congress nominated him, because he was a good leader, and because there was no clear alternative. Fourth, in light of overwhelming negative opinion, the commissioners recommended, "with a deep sense of sympathy for the Jewish cause," that limits be placed on Zionist settlement and on the size of the Jewish home. Palestine should be included in Greater Syria, not segregated into a separate Jewish state. The holy sites should be placed under an international, interreligious commission, including Jews and guaranteed by the League of Nations. As for the choice of mandatory, the majority of those petitioned rejected France and preferred the United States. The commissioners concluded that the Americans should take on the sacred trust.[49]

Yale appended to the report a dissenting opinion, upholding the division of Syria according to the Sykes-Picot and Balfour plans. He dismissed the Syrians' personal testimony, claiming that their democratic rhetoric was merely a mask for theocratic ambition. Like Robert de Caix, whom he had befriended in Paris, Yale regarded Faisal as too weak to "break religion's hold" on intolerant Muslims. "Christians should be protected from Muslim oppression" by a foreign power, he concluded. Montgomery concurred with Yale's view.[50] A recent review of the commission's procedures concludes that its majority—Crane, King, and Lybyer—represented Syrians' majority opinion fairly and accurately.[51]

The majority report spoke an inconvenient truth, too late. By the time King and Crane reached Damascus, the Big Four had agreed to sign the Versailles treaty, including the League of Nations covenant, on June 28, 1919, five years to the date after a Serbian nationalist had assassinated the Austrian archduke and set the wheels of war in motion. French premier Clemenceau planned to humiliate the Germans with a ceremony in the Hall of Mirrors at the Palace of Versailles, where Wilhelm I had been crowned emperor in 1871. When the King-Crane Commission had sailed to Palestine, Paris had been buzzing with rumor and recrimination over the treaty's terms. Its 433 articles imposed harsh terms of peace on the Germans, including loss of territory, disarmament, punitive reparations payments, and a clause declaring them guilty of starting the war. Leaders of the new Weimar Republic were angry. They had overthrown the kaiser in late 1918 in the hope that they would obtain more moderate peace terms, based on Wilson's Fourteen Points.

Though symbolic, the date of June 28 was problematic for the Arabs. Awni Abd al-Hadi—Faisal's advisor during the peace conference who had remained in Paris with the Hijaz delegation—protested that the treaty violated the peace terms promised by the Fourteen Points. He lobbied vigorously against including the unrevised League covenant in the treaty. Article 22 still designated Syrians and other Ottoman peoples as in need of a mandate. But the American delegates pointed out that the covenant did not name a mandatory for Syria and that the ultimate decision on mandates would be made by the League. Once the League was established, they reassured him, the offending clauses could be revised.[52]

And so, on June 28, Abd al-Hadi had reluctantly joined Wilson, Clemenceau, Lloyd George, and a host of other officials at Versailles to sign the first of five peace treaties ending World War I.

The next day, President Wilson and the American delegation's Middle East advisor, William Westermann, set sail for home aboard SS *George Washington*. Westermann was not confident about revising the Syrian mandate. He was sure that they had signed Syria over to France. That evening, he recorded a prescient entry in his diary:

> If France gets Syria there will be war, a long tedious and costly one. After about two years France will win, by force of superior modern equipment. She will have but little joy of her conquest. The net result will be another bit of poison, which will rot the Near East until the distant day when the Arabs and all the East shall definitely discard the unjustified assumption of Westerners embodied in the formula of the "white man's burden."[53]

Despite these deep concerns, the president forgot all about Syria as soon as he arrived home. He devoted the summer to a fight against leading senators to get the treaty ratified.

On August 30, Crane cabled to his friend Wilson, urging him to publish the commission's report immediately. If the report was ignored, war might break out, he predicted: "The flouting of the doctrine of no annexations will horrify millions of people whose only trust now is in America and in you." While in Paris, Crane had seen the angry newspaper articles published by de Caix, which attacked the British stance on Syria. Other articles contained innuendos about the bias of the King-Crane Commission. And rumors circulated in Paris that the French and British had resumed secret negotiations to permit France's occupation of Syria. Lloyd George faced pressure to withdraw British troops from Syria in order to quash revolts in Ireland, Egypt, Iraq, and India.[54] The imperial edifice, so dearly defended in the Great War, was in peril.

General Tasker H. Bliss shared Crane's fears. He had placed a copy of the King-Crane report in the files on the peace settlement with Turkey. Bliss had stayed in Paris to continue peace negotiations, in which he learned that Lloyd George proposed American mandates only in order to serve a British "landgrab." As he wrote to his wife on August 5,

> The British have seized Mesopotamia where they have found what is likely to be the largest oil deposit in the world. That is the reason they are abandoning the Caucasus and leaving the Armenians to be massacred. The French demand Syria because the British have taken Mesopotamia and the Italians and the Greeks now demand their share.

Bliss advised Wilson's secretary of war, Newton Baker, to refuse to sign a treaty regarding the Ottoman territories that obliged the United States to support such imperialist aims.[55]

Wilson did not heed these warnings, for he faced his own political peril. Negotiations with the Senate had gone badly in July. Republicans continued to reject articles in the League covenant on mutual defense as an infringement on American sovereignty. On September 3, Wilson took the treaty directly to the people, to convince them of the need to sacrifice a bit of sovereignty for world peace. He boarded a train at Union Station in Washington, DC, for an eight-thousand-mile tour of the United States.

Wilson's speeches, given to enthusiastic crowds across the continent, suggest that he had not, after all, forgotten his anticolonial principles. "The heart and center of this treaty is that it sets at liberty people all over Europe and in Asia who had hitherto been enslaved by powers which were not their rightful sovereigns and masters," Wilson declared at San Diego.[56] At Pueblo, Colorado, on September 25, he condemned colonial powers as enemies of peace. "The men who sat around that table in Paris knew that the time had come when the people were no longer going to consent to live under masters," he declared.[57]

Two days later, a copy of the King-Crane report finally arrived at the White House.[58] By then, Wilson had collapsed with exhaustion. Five days later he suffered a massive, crippling stroke. Without the president's consent, the report remained locked in a drawer.

Crane looked back with regret on the missed opportunity in Syria in the summer of 1919, remarking, "That part of the world opened up its mind and heart as it had never done before and will never do again."[59]

Chapter 8

A Democratic Uprising in Damascus

By the time Crane sent his cable warning Wilson on August 30, 1919, riots had already broken out in Damascus. Rumors flew that Britain had formally accepted a mandate in Palestine, thereby severing it from Syria. More rumors circulated that British troops would pull out of the Syrian hinterland, leaving it to France. Furious meetings convened nightly at the Arab Club.

"Syria has gained nothing from the American Commission but schism and distress of mind," complained a nationalist newspaper.[1] Ever since the King-Crane Commission's departure in July, Faisal had tried to return to Paris to capitalize on its report. But the British denied him a ship, and Allenby and Lawrence advised him to stay put. Finally, in early September, Faisal received a telegram summoning him to London for negotiations.

When Faisal arrived at 10 Downing Street on September 19, Lloyd George presented him with a fait accompli. On September 15, the prime minister had traveled to Paris to sign a deal with Clemenceau that echoed the terms of the Sykes-Picot accord: within two months, British troops would pull out of the Syrian interior, leaving the Arab army there under France's indirect control. France would maintain its army on the coast.[2] To no avail, T. E. Lawrence had published a warning in *The Times* of London that there could be no peace in the Middle East without respect for Arab opinion and for promises made to the Arabs. But Lloyd George was short of men and cash. He needed to transfer British troops from Syria to India, Egypt, and Ireland, where nationalist protests raged. He also planned to end Britain's monthly subsidies to the Syrian state. Faisal would have to seek financial aid from the French.

Faisal expressed shock at such "an unjust return to the policy of ambitious imperialism."[3] Even the Francophile William Yale condemned the "pernicious" pact.[4] News of it inspired Wilson's public attacks on colonialism during his speaking tour. In early October, after Wilson's stroke, a British visitor to Damascus remarked sadly that school children still sang a patriotic song praising the American president for laying down "the principles of freedom."[5]

Faisal remained in England for a month, until it became clear that Lloyd George had washed his hands of Syria. Rustum Haidar met Yale, who arrived in London late in September on an unauthorized, personal mission. Haidar was so angry, he confessed, that "at times he was possessed with a violent desire to throw bombs at Lloyd George and other British Imperialists." If the Americans didn't take action, Faisal vowed, he would lead armed resistance to French occupation. But Yale's efforts at mediation met a wall of resistance from British officials, who insisted that they had to honor their promises to France, not the Arabs. Only Lawrence and Allenby expressed interest in compromise. Yale responded with warnings that their aim to monopolize oil resources in Mesopotamia would spark conflict with the United States.[6]

The editor of *The Times* told Yale that he had suppressed publication of a letter from T. E. Lawrence regretting his celebrated role in the Arab Revolt. But the editor agreed to print Yale's proposal for a solution to "the Arab Problem" anonymously. It called for respect of British interests in Mesopotamia and of France's interests in Syria, but under limited mandates. Just as Britain should permit an Arab government in Baghdad, so too should it support a "practically independent state" under a popularly elected government for Arabs in Syria. France would maintain direct rule in Lebanon, as promised by the Sykes-Picot Agreement, and Britain would control Palestine and organize a Jewish home, as Yale had advised in his dissent to the King-Crane report.[7] Privately, however, Faisal advised Yale that the proposal would be a hard sell to the Syrian Congress, which would object to partitioning Greater Syria under multiple powers.

Back in Paris, General Bliss and the American peace delegation accepted Yale's unofficial report in silence. Colonel House wanted to fold up the tent and send the delegation home. The president's stroke and Republican senators' vocal opposition to the Versailles treaty had drastically weakened their negotiating position.

In mid-October, Faisal abandoned his effort to change Lloyd George's mind and reluctantly followed Yale across the Channel to seek an audience with Clemenceau. He ordered Prince Zaid to place the Syrian army on high alert for any movement of French troops from the coast.

Clemenceau had no intention of sending troops until after the French elections in the next month. But he quietly kept the pressure on Lloyd George. In an October 10 note to the British prime minister, he too demanded parity of terms in Syria and Mesopotamia, but in language different from Yale's: just as France did not interfere with British politics in the Mesopotamia zone, so Britain should not interfere with France's relations with Arabs in Syria.[8] Meanwhile, Foreign Minister Pichon was busy behind closed doors at the Quai d'Orsay, with plans to fully implement the 1916 accords. His first step would be to replace the feckless Picot with a military general as high commissioner.[9]

From Beirut, however, Picot telegraphed reports of militias forming in every major city of Syria.[10] The Syrian people were taking defense into their own hands.

Britain's betrayal of its promise to the Arabs was a turning point in Syrian politics. It weakened Faisal and set loose popular movements that tilted power toward the Congress he had created. While the Americans' support for Arab self-determination had dissolved into an empty gesture, their commission had actually laid the foundation for democracy.

Rashid Rida Comes to Syria

Rashid Rida was destined to play a leading role in Syria's democratic revolution. But he had no inkling of the recent turn of events on September 12, when he arrived at Cairo Station to board a Damascus-bound train. The British had finally granted him a visa, and he wanted to meet Faisal. The prince had impressed him by supporting the Damascus Program and asserting control over the civilian government against British orders. "With his kind and generous manner," Rida had informed his readers in June, the prince united Syrian factions to support him as king of an independent Syria.[11]

Before the train pulled out of the station, however, a friend arrived with news that Faisal had already departed for Europe. "This upset me very much, because meeting the prince at that time was the main reason I was traveling directly to Damascus, not Beirut or Tripoli," Rida wrote in his diary. With ticket already in hand and bags packed, he decided to go to anyway.[12] Rida's train pulled into Damascus's Hijaz Station shortly after midnight on Monday, September 15, the very day Lloyd George signed the evacuation agreement with Clemenceau.

Just shy of his fifty-fourth birthday, Rida was exhausted by the trip. He headed to the hotel closest to the train station, the same Victoria Hotel where General Allenby had first met Faisal a year earlier. Rida took the last vacant room, a small one on the first floor. There was no plumbing, so he washed up in a basin, said his prayers, and fell asleep. Dr. Shahbandar, his SUP colleague, came by later to offer medical advice for Rida's aching foot.

Word of Rida's arrival spread quickly. By morning, visitors were lining up at his door. Among the first was the military governor, Rida Pasha al-Rikabi. Rikabi had sent Rida a personal invitation to Damascus, he said. Rida responded that he had never received it. Perhaps the British had blocked that, too. The two men chatted easily and soon became trusted friends.

A Congress deputy from Aleppo, Ibrahim Hananu, offered Rida his own room at the Khawwam Hotel next door. It was a bigger room with more light and full plumbing. To Rida's satisfaction, the Khawwam also served ice water at lunch.[13]

The next day General Yasin al-Hashimi, the military chief of staff, arrived in his car—a luxury in a city with few automobiles. Hashimi and Rida drove out of the city to the residence of Prince Zaid, Faisal's younger brother and surrogate ruler during the elder prince's absence.

Rida and Hashimi dined alone that night to talk over the political situation.

Rida liked Hashimi because he too was a realist. A highly disciplined former Ottoman officer, Hashimi was dedicated to turning Faisal's Northern Arab Army into a modern fighting force. As soon as he learned of Britain's plan to evacuate Syria, he began organizing a volunteer militia to defend against any French threat. City leaders also organized militias in their neighborhoods. They commissioned their tailors to cut uniforms, which became a mark of social prestige in Damascus that fall.[14]

On the evening of Saturday, September 20, Rida joined Hashimi again, this time at a secret meeting to plan the resistance. Sheikh Kamil al-Qassab, Rida's old friend and fellow SUP member, was one of the speakers. The two men had bonded during the war. When Qassab was arrested while on a secret mission to Egypt for Fatat, Rida had bailed him out of jail. Qassab then spent two years in Mecca, but he too became disenchanted with Sharif Hussein's narrow views. In the months before the war's end, he had returned to Cairo and joined the SUP.[15] Now, Qassab was organizing his neighborhood in Damascus. He was the kind of charismatic leader who could unite the elite political class with the populace to ignite a revolution.

That night, Qassab, Rida, and Hashimi drew up a list of twenty-one Damascenes who might cooperate in the resistance. They planned to meet again the following night at Qassab's home for further strategizing. But the next day Hashimi was summoned to British headquarters in Palestine. The British had got wind of Hashimi's military plans and, because he was a native of Baghdad, they feared he might extend a Syrian revolt into Iraq. On September 21, Rida and Prince Zaid bade Hashimi farewell at the Hijaz train station.

The following day, Rida himself was summoned to British headquarters. An official there denied rumors that Britain had sold Syria to the French, showing him a telegram which stated that Arab troops would remain in control of the interior zone. But the telegram also noted that the Arab government must now depend on France for all assistance, including financial aid. "That is a clear implementation of the 1916 agreement," Rida responded.[16]

As tempers in the city rose, top officials sought Rida's counsel and support. Two days after his interview with the British, Rida dined with Governor Rikabi. "The military governor showed me great respect and even wanted to kiss my hand," Rida recalled. Over dinner, Rikabi offered Rida the post of minister of religious affairs in the Syrian government. In a personal visit to Rida's hotel, Prince Zaid repeated the offer on Faisal's behalf.

"Prince Zaid told me that the government is in great need of my help," Rida recalled. But he replied to Zaid that he had left his family in Cairo, and that he could not accept a post in a government in such disarray. Zaid persisted, admitting that "morals in al-Sham [Syria] are weak, and that men are easily scared. But if people like me [Rida] don't rise to the work of reform, who will?"[17]

To avoid the political pressure, Rida decided it was time to visit his family in Qalamun. On the morning of September 29, he paid his hotel bill of nine Egyptian pounds (Syria had still not established its own currency) and took the train to Beirut. Through the windows, he saw his homeland for the first time in many years. "The train passed through a beautiful valley, with a river running through it." As they crossed the mountains, the air turned wintry cold. Then they descended toward the coast, arriving in Beirut by evening. Rida completed his prayers at the station and found a pleasant waterfront hotel with good food.

Rida appreciated Beirut for its social progress: Muslims and Christians cooperated, and education was highly valued. He was pleased to find that the city's Muslim women had adopted a healthy middle way between tradition and progress. Many had gained an education. The women's club even invited Rida to give a lecture on women's status in Egypt. Rida filled his diary with descriptions of delicious meals shared with old friends. It was good to be home.[18]

Within days, however, Rida was pulled into politics. He gave lectures in mosques on the need for Muslims to unite in reviving their nation, especially by building schools. He listened to Muslim friends complain about France's high taxes and its preference for Christians in government posts. They expressed more hope for Faisal's government than Rida had. On October 7, Rida met High Commissioner Georges-Picot to complain that the French were treating Muslims unjustly. "I told him that even though people still talk of the Turkish atrocities—in which they killed people and made indecent assaults on women—they wish the Turks would come back, due to the [French] insults to their religion and complaints about how they are treated," he wrote.

Georges-Picot admitted mistakes and promised Rida that he would correct the abuses. In fact, the French received numerous complaints about the brusque condescension of colonial personnel transferred from North Africa. They treated Muslims in Syria as colonial subjects, not people worthy of provisional independence. Picot reassured Rida that France intended to encourage equal access to jobs for people of all religions and that he would be more considerate of Muslim feelings. He also promised that Arabic would remain Syria's official language and that only civilian advisors, not soldiers, would be posted in the Syrian interior. Picot would not guarantee that Syria would remain united under Faisal, however.[19]

After the pleasures of Beirut, home came as a shock. Rida surprised his brother Ibrahim Adham when he arrived in Qalamun on the night of October 12. The next morning, he woke to the grim aftermath of war. Conditions were far worse than what had been reported to Rida in Egypt. He and his brother took a sunrise walk along a road lined with orchards and fields that the family still owned. The lemon and orange crops had yielded half of what had been harvested the previous year. The people's spirit was broken. Relatives told Rida harrowing stories. "There remained in Qalamun only one-fourth of its people. Most of them died of hunger," Rida wrote in his diary. "It was so bad that some women had even eaten dead bodies."[20]

Rida spent the next two weeks trying to regain the title to the family mosque that the Turks had confiscated. His efforts landed him in jail. On October 28, he desperately needed to get to Beirut to file some paperwork. But he missed the last taxi. When he tried to board a ship heading to Beirut, police arrested him on suspicion of political subversion. "The policeman searched all my papers, including the seventh volume of the *Tafsir* [Rida's commentary on the Qur'an]. When I told him that it was just the index of a book, he replied that it might reveal some political content."

The police captain decided to refer the case to Beirut. Rida was thrown into a cell with a broken window. He was cold, with his clothing dampened by sweat. In the middle of the night, he was taken to Beirut. He saw his old friend, Rida al-Solh, from the car window. They had met ten years earlier in Constantinople. Solh posted Rida's bail. But Rida woke the next morning with a fever. A doctor diagnosed malaria. "You need to fire the police chief of Lebanon and Inspector Hanna, who humiliated me," Rida complained to Picot's aide.

The French not only fired the offending police officers but also astonished Rida with an offer of a teaching post that would enable him to oversee the affairs of Muslims. "Serving my country is a priority and a duty. I thank you for your concern," Rida responded. He had no interest in serving the French, so he gave them the same excuse that he had given in Damascus, that his family awaited him in Cairo.

"You know that Islam was the first to emphasize the principles of justice and equality—such that the caliph himself was on an equal footing with a common person, in terms of rights," he warned Picot's aide. "The Qur'an advised the Prophet not to be a tyrant."[21]

On November 21, Picot's successor as high commissioner, General Henri Gouraud, arrived in Beirut. The switch to a military high commissioner undercut Picot's assurances that France would stay out of the Syrian interior. Rida refused an invitation to attend Gouraud's official reception. As he headed back to Tripoli, he saw thousands of British cavalrymen, most of them Indian, on the road. The British evacuation had begun.[22]

Democracy Explodes in Damascus

The political fever had not died down in Damascus. Since September, local activists seized the initiative to build a grassroots resistance movement. By the time Gouraud arrived in late November, they wielded enough power to persuade the Syrian Congress to demand full independence, challenging leaders who sought compromise with France: Faisal, Zaid, and Governor Rikabi.

At the heart of the movement was Rashid Rida's old friend, Sheikh Kamil al-Qassab. The son of merchants from the Syrian city of Homs,

Qassab had studied with Rida's mentor, Mohammed Abduh, in Cairo and returned to Damascus to open a school before the war. Now, at age forty-six, he was a veteran of political organizing with Fatat and the new Syrian Union Party. He used his ties among the city's merchants, educators, and religious leaders to build support for independence. His flair for fiery oratory was a key to his rise as leader of the popular resistance.

Qassab lived in the old city of Damascus, where merchants' shops lined ancient, narrow streets surrounding the magnificent seventh-century Umayyad Mosque. The Umayyad dynasty had ruled a vast caliphate stretching from Iran to Spain. Behind austere gray walls, Damascenes still lived in Mediterranean-style homes encircling lush garden courtyards. The city's 240,000 residents lived in forty-eight distinct neighborhoods, tight-knit communities where people knew one another, and where old notable families commanded patronage networks. Christians and Jews lived throughout the city but clustered most in its eastern quarters. The city's important southern section, the Midan, stretched along the road to the rich farmlands of the Hawran. Large grain merchants built networks here, much like those of the landowning and trade elites in the old city. Both the old city and the Midan remained popular districts, distinct from the government center in Marjeh Square and from the new, elite northern neighborhoods of Salihiyya and Muhajirin, where Faisal's palace stood.

In early November 1919, each of the city's forty-eight neighborhoods elected representatives to a new coordinating council of resistance, called the Higher National Committee (HNC). It convened for the first time at the home of the mayor, a relative of Governor Rikabi, to establish bylaws and goals, chiefly to defend the country's unity and sovereignty and to revive the Arab national spirit. The bylaws set out transparent rules for election to the twenty-seven-member coordinating council, whose presidency rotated at each meeting.[23] In contrast to the Congress, dominated by notables, the HNC was a more populist and egalitarian organization. One-third of its members, were from the middle classes, including spice sellers, grain merchants, and mosque preachers. It met regularly at neighborhood branches to raise funds, organize demonstrations, and supervise military drills among youths.

As one of the HNC's leaders, Qassab delivered forceful speeches that attracted ordinary citizens of all types who were tired of post-war instability and poverty. The HNC was neither a militia nor an Islamist movement. Both Christian and Muslim leaders blessed the HNC and attended its meetings. To mobilize common people, members deployed a more populist rhetoric than elite nationalists did. "Remember the words of God: struggle and wage jihad," one leaflet declared. "Enough of your tolerance and inaction. They have lied to you, deceived you, betrayed you."[24]

National committees emerged in other Syrian cities as well. Branches were less democratic in structure than the HNC, and many of them focused primarily on military defense. The strongest militia was organized near Aleppo by Ibrahim Hananu, the Congress member who had given Rida his hotel room. His band of armed guerrillas grew to four hundred men. Syrians were inspired by Italian nationalists' occupation of Fiume in defiance of Paris policy, and by the Turkish nationalist movement that emerged just over the Syrian border in Anatolia. In late summer, Turks had organized their own national congresses under the leadership of Mustafa Kemal. They, too, openly rebelled against the Paris Peace Conference that had sent foreign troops to occupy their land.

The HNC in Damascus was unlike these other groups, however. While ordinary Syrians had in the past protested through local militias or through the personal factions of notables, they had not before organized into a formal political organization. Previously, only elites had founded political parties. In a departure from Ottoman times, the HNC launched a new era of mass politics.

The HNC emerged alongside, not against, elite political groups. It invited representatives from all other nationalist parties to attend its meetings. Individual members of Congress, the Fatah movement, and the Syrian Union Party often did so.

Qassab's colleagues in the Fatah movement, for example, issued the manifesto of the democratic uprising in late September in a leaflet titled "The First Call to Diplomatic Traitors in the Civilized World."[25] It condemned Western powers' betrayal of Syria and all other peoples excluded from rights at Paris. Signed only "Blood and Iron," it may have been written in the secret meeting that Rida, Hashimi, and Rikabi attended.

> O politicians! Open your eyes! You stoke a new Balkan volcano in Syria and the Arab lands. . . . You are ravenous wolves who proclaimed the liberation of peoples only to divide and devour them. . . . O Arab Nation! Look at how they have shown their devouring wolf teeth and mocked Wilson's principles. . . . So, come, grandsons of noble ancestors. Call Humanity to our aid to defend Righteousness. . . . We will rid Humanity of these ferocious beasts.

At about the same time, the Syrian Union Party sent a petition to Lloyd George in the name of an association of political and professional groups. It protested against the King-Crane recommendation of a mandate for Syria, and called for complete independence: "We demand that [the Allies] keep their promises and leave it to us to decide the future of our country." Shahbandar was among those who signed the petition for the SUP. The number of other groups whose members signed indicates the breadth of the resistance movement: Arab Independence Party, Intellectual Revival Committee, Syrian Alliance, Alliance for Iraq, Iraq Association, Syrian Congress, Palestine Revival Committee, Bekaa Committee, Syrian Youth Association, Philanthropic Association, High School Alumni Association, the Commercial Club, and the Jazira Association and Agricultural Association, as well as associations for journalists, editors, physicians, lawyers, teachers, and students.[26]

On the strength of this popular mobilization, the Syrian Congress reconvened without Faisal's authorization. Acting as the representative of the Syrian nation, it challenged Faisal's authority by claiming the right to intervene in foreign policy. On October 27, the Congress appointed its own commission of deputies to meet with foreign diplomats resident in Damascus. They intended to visit the embassies to explain that the September 15 evacuation accord violated popular opinion expressed to the King-Crane Commission.[27] Deputies also discussed the formation of a national army. Like the Italians, the Turks, and the Egyptians, Syrians must defend their land, a deputy declared.[28]

In November, Congress formally voted to reject the September 15 accord. The conservative Congress president, Fawzi Pasha al-Azm, issued a formal protest, cosigned by Congress secretary Izzat Darwazeh, against the accord, condemning it as a violation of popular will and Syrian sovereignty. In a separate petition, the new Arab Independence Party protested directly to French Foreign Minister Pichon that the September 15 accord violated Article 22 of the League of Nations covenant.[29] Congressional leaders, including Darwazeh and Ahmad Qadri, also openly endorsed the HNC's call to cut off negotiations with France. Negotiations, they reasoned, would only compromise the Syrian independence already provisionally recognized in Article 22.[30]

Public protest erupted again when Britain began withdrawing its troops. The largest demonstration up to that point filled the streets of Damascus on November 9. Coordinated by the HNC, an estimated fifteen thousand people marched peacefully, calling for Syrian unity and independence. Religious clerics, women, and even children sang patriotic songs as they marched. "Nothing like it has been seen in Syrian history," a journalist reported. In solidarity, Muslims marched alongside Christians, the poor alongside the rich. At the government offices, Governor Rikabi and Prince Zaid greeted the protesters to assure them of the country's future and deny rumors of a French invasion. Later, some youths marched in military formation to Faisal's royal residence, shouting "To war! To war!"[31]

"Revolution is at the gates!" Zaid cabled to Faisal on November 16. The next day, Qassab stirred more revolts with a speech condemning any limit on Syrian sovereignty.[32] "I cannot stop the revolution," Zaid again cabled to Faisal. "A French attack from . . . Lebanon has burned down a village. Refugees have come to Damascus."

The members of Governor Rikabi's cabinet tendered their resignations that same day, November 17. They had intercepted a secret British memo that redefined the new Syrian–Lebanese border according to the terms of the discredited 1916 Sykes-Picot Agreement. "Such a policy will lead to popular resentment and disorder," the cabinet's letter warned. "Given that the government does not represent the people, then it cannot be responsible for implementing this decision."[33] Ministers were angry that Faisal had violated democratic principles by not informing them of the new border. In fact, Faisal had not known about it. Zaid refused to accept their resignations.[34]

Popular revolt was further stirred by the arrival of General Gouraud, the new military face of the French occupation, on November 21.[35] In his first speech in Beirut, Gouraud recalled France's last occupation of the Holy Land during the Crusades, even as he reassured Syrians that Catholic France was also the Republic of France. As a child of the Revolution, he would bring liberty and progress to Syria.[36]

In following days, the Syrian Congress took up debate on declaring war against France. In an address to Congress, Prince Zaid publicly considered the merits of such a declaration. However, given Rikabi's advice on the weakness of the Syrian army, he ultimately decided against it.[37] Few welcomed Rikabi's call for calm on November 22, when he dismissed political fears of Congress. Syria's fate would be decided by diplomatic means in Paris, not by military means, he assured the deputies.[38]

Even as Rikabi spoke, the crisis took a darker turn. On the pretext of an invitation to tea, British officers kidnapped the Syrian army's chief of staff, General Yasin al-Hashimi, and spirited him to Palestine in an armored car. France had been demanding his arrest since September, when he had renewed calls for a military draft in Syria.[39] The British agreed that the Arab army must be kept too small to challenge their September 15 accord. Fearing that Hashimi intended to wage war over the Bekaa Valley, they acted in the last days of their military presence on Syrian soil.

The city's markets shut down in protest of Hashimi's capture. Militias and clubs organized mass demonstrations against the "unjust act" that violated their "most sacred rights." Kamil al-Qassab and the HNC marched to Prince Zaid's residence to deliver a petition condemning Hashimi's arrest. Qassam then convened a meeting of political elites. He gave a rousing speech and presented an oath rejecting any limits to national sovereignty. No one was permitted to leave without signing it.[40]

News from Washington intensified Syrians' alarm. A few days earlier, the Senate had voted to reject the Versailles treaty and American membership in the League of Nations. The vote was taken without any reference to the King-Crane report, which had not been released.[41]

Ironically, some senators voted against League membership because they feared it would enable colonial expansion. "When this league, this combination, is formed, four great powers will rule one half of the inhabitants of the globe as subject peoples—by force," Senator William Borah declared. "You must either give them independence, recognize their rights as nations to live their own life and to set up their own and form their own government, or deny them these things by force."[42]

Washington's cold shoulder was felt directly in Syria. American consuls, in advance of November's protests, evacuated their staffs' wives and children from Syria's inland towns to French-controlled Beirut. They sent urgent cables that expressed no sympathy for the Syrian resistance, warning of Arab violence. "[The] French are gradually using more force in punishing opposition," a November 7 cable reported. "The whole population is being worked up to a high pitch and the fear of the Christians is greatly increasing," the Aleppo consul reported. "The French apparently hope to awe natives by prestige of General Gouraud," an American source in Beirut reported on November 19. When the British kidnapped Chief of Staff Hashimi, the American consul blocked the Arab state's representative in Beirut from sending a protest telegram to Faisal.[43]

The sense of abandonment and diplomatic isolation prompted the Syrian Congress to take unilateral action. On November 24, the Congress voted to implement immediately the Damascus Program presented in July to the Americans. The resolution called for a constitutional government truly responsible to the people that would issue a declaration of independence for Greater Syria in all three zones.[44]

Zaid attempted to stall. On December 1, he assured Congress that Faisal would support the formation of a representative, constitutional government in the near future. But for now, order must be maintained so that Faisal could play the strongest hand at the peace conference.[45]

War parties on both sides aimed to undercut diplomacy. While Congress continued to call for military action, General Gouraud ordered French troops to occupy the Bekaa Valley and Baalbek, Rustum Haidar's hometown. The Haidar family organized militias of Fatat members in defense. When a mosque was vandalized in the Bekaa, protest once again flared up in Damascus.[46]

Fearing open revolt, Zaid dissolved the Congress on December 4.[47] Rikabi refused to send the army into the Bekaa Valley, considering it a futile move that could backfire and trigger a French invasion. An angry crowd surrounded his house chanting, "We have no confidence in you!" and "We instruct you to resign! We shall never consent to a foreign government!"

Zaid summoned Rikabi to the royal residence. After a sharp exchange, Rikabi resigned. To nationalists' joy, the prince appointed a Fatat member, Colonel Mustafa Ni`ma, in Rikabi's place. Zaid also appointed Yusuf al-Azmeh, the Arab delegate in Beirut, to replace Hashimi as war minister. Their new government immediately issued a compulsory draft law, requiring military service for all men aged twenty to forty.[48]

General Gouraud advised Premier Clemenceau to suspend negotiations with Faisal. Citing his long experience with Muslims in Africa, he argued that force was the only way to solve the Syria problem.[49] Gouraud's assistant, Robert de Caix, agreed. De Caix was furious at reports that Clemenceau had reopened negotiations with Faisal after he and Gouraud had departed Paris. He feared that the premier would upset plans approved by Foreign Minister Pichon to implement the long-deferred terms of the Sykes-Picot Agreement. He and Pichon intended to cement an alliance with Christians in Syria in order to limit Arab nationalists' influence there. That way, they would ensure France's continued dominance over the Muslim coasts of the Mediterranean world.[50]

Conclusion

In Paris, the American delegation packed its files and evacuated the Hôtel de Crillon. On December 9, its mission to the peace conference came to an end. As he stepped aboard the train, headed for the port of Brest, General Tasker Bliss kissed France's Marshal Foch on the cheek in a bittersweet farewell.[51]

Clemenceau, meanwhile, had indeed opened negotiations with Faisal. He drew on a tradition of French diplomacy that was different from the heavy-handed tactics favored by de Caix. Since the early centuries of Ottoman rule, France had formed bonds with the Sunni Muslim majority, not set the minorities against it. Likewise, Clemenceau intended to assert French interests through a united Syria ruled by Sunni Muslim urban elites. So he stepped in to avert war, ordering Gouraud to pull back from the Bekaa. "We have a clear interest in aggrandizing him and using him [Faisal]," Clemenceau wrote to Gouraud on the day the Americans left.[52]

Along the lines of their April discussions, Clemenceau again offered Faisal a minimal version of a mandate, much in Wilson's spirit of disinterested tutelage: French troops would remain outside the Syrian hinterland in deference to Arab sovereignty in a constitutional state. The high commissioner would maintain an office at Aleppo, but would enter Syria only by invitation of the Damascus government. In return, Syrians would promise to employ only French advisors and aides and accept Lebanon as an autonomous state. They initialed the secret accord on January 6, 1920.[53]

But nationalists at Damascus, now united politically under a new government, were in no mood for such a compromise. As word of the accord leaked to the press, they accused Faisal of treason. Although Faisal had called the Congress into being, it was clearly no longer an instrument of his political will.[54]

Faisal's response demonstrated a new political maturity. Back in June, Faisal had responded to his opposition by shutting down newspapers and scolding congressional deputies. Now, he judiciously advised Clemenceau that he would finalize the accord only after visiting Damascus to cultivate political support for it.

Faisal also sought to educate his own father in the new political realities. "I had been quite worried about political developments since the American commission left," he wrote to Sharif Hussein. Like his father, he had defended the British all summer. "But in the course of events I learned that we were wrong. I understood why they [the deputies] voted that way, given Britain's policy in Palestine and especially Iraq, and conditions in Egypt."

Faisal knew his father now supported the war party in Damascus. He shared his father's feelings. "Evil occurred and suspicion entered my heart," he confessed. "At times I got angry at the French, and thought they are the enemy." And then the Americans "departed from the political arena, which harmed us a lot. It was the major reason we fell into this trap."

But he insisted to Sharif Hussein that war was the wrong policy. Diplomacy was a better option than war with France, he argued, explaining, "God forbid if we were defeated. What would our situation be? The French armies would enter the four cities victoriously, after we had lost our youth, and after we had spent everything we have."[55]

As Faisal headed back to Damascus in mid-January, he confronted a political earthquake over the controversial Clemenceau accord. In the depths of an exceptionally chilly winter, his negotiations with Rida's SUP, Qassab's HNC, and leaders of the Syrian Congress would lead to the formal declaration of an independent, constitutional monarchy, established in defiance of the Allies, who had supposedly fought the Great War for democracy.

Chapter 9

Revolution at
the Quai d'Orsay

"I am in Algiers harbor," Robert de Caix wrote to his wife on January 12. "It is a magnificent city," he proclaimed. "Even if our work in Syria has every chance, neither you nor I will ever see Beirut in such a state."[1]

De Caix was rushing to Paris on the orders of General Henri Gouraud, high commissioner for Syria and Cilicia. The men had heard rumors that de Caix's mentor at the foreign ministry, Philippe Berthelot, was sabotaging French claims to Syria in negotiations with Prince Faisal. De Caix had jumped aboard the first ship out of Beirut that he could find, the *Buenos Aires*, which sailed to France by way of Algiers, the North African port that France had occupied almost ninety years earlier. He reached the ministry's offices of the Quai d'Orsay on Wednesday morning, January 14. He was too late. Faisal had already left Paris.

"I almost cried in rage upon seeing the treaty was signed," de Caix confessed.[2] Until that point, he and Gouraud had been certain that France would take Syria. De Caix's press campaign had compelled Britain to withdraw its troops. And the "epidemic of Wilsonism" had subsided with the American president's stroke.[3] Clemenceau had appointed General Gouraud as high commissioner, to the delight of conservative Catholics, who swept parliamentary elections. De Caix and Gouraud had immediately begun plans to undermine the Arab government. Before leaving for Beirut in November, Gouraud had lectured Faisal over lunch about the need to restore military order in Syria.[4]

However, within two weeks, just as the welcome ceremonies for Gouraud ended, distressing telegrams arrived in Beirut. They carried news about Berthelot's negotiations with the prince and reported that Clemenceau had even paid a friendly visit to Faisal's villa.[5] Now, as de Caix read the text of the accord on January 14, he concluded that the Tiger had been totally seduced by "Faisal's charms." The accord undid all of his and Gouraud's plans, with its promise of virtual independence for a united Syria under a constitutional regime.[6]

Furious, de Caix plotted his revenge. "I was forced, in meetings with those bigwigs in government, to spread the idea that Syrian realities demand that we tie ourselves as little as possible to Faisal and that we reverse much of what was begun," he told his wife.[7]

By mobilizing the colonialist networks that he had cultivated for twenty years, Robert de Caix would single-handedly reverse French diplomacy in the Middle East. For four centuries, it had been a standard of French policy to support the Sunni majority in the Ottoman Empire, and Clemenceau had honored that tradition. De Caix's Syria policy aimed to undermine Sunni influence by granting minorities autonomy and privileges. He also aimed to subvert Syrian popular will as expressed in the King-Crane report and defy Britain's promises to the Arabs. He would hijack Article 22 of the covenant of the League of Nations to support France's colonial aims.[8] The French mandate would be defined not in Wilsonian terms of limited guidance, but rather as the imposition, by force, of direct French rule.

A Revolution in Paris

De Caix's luck turned three days after he arrived in Paris. On January 17, a parliamentary caucus convened to cast a straw poll for a successor to President Raymond Poincaré, whose term was ending. Georges Clemenceau had announced his candidacy, but out of pride he refused to campaign openly. Consequently, few of his supporters attended the caucus, held at the Luxembourg Palace, seat of the French Senate. After all, Clemenceau's rival was a lightweight nobody named Paul

Deschanel, erstwhile president of the Chamber of Deputies, the lower house of the French parliament.[9]

Clemenceau did not know that his enemies were actively campaigning against him. At their head were President Poincaré himself and Marshal Foch, commander in chief of Allied forces. They resented Clemenceau's decision to end the war on November 11, 1918, rather than continue to occupy Germany. The Father of Victory had lost the peace, they claimed. They also campaigned on religious grounds. Deschanel was a Catholic and a darling of the many conservatives newly elected to the National Assembly. Clemenceau was a well-known atheist.

On January 17, 1920, the octogenarian Tiger finally lost his last battle. Deschanel tallied 408 votes in the straw poll, to Clemenceau's 389. The hall at the Luxembourg Palace emptied in silence.[10] The next day, the Assembly would meet formally to elect Deschanel as France's new president.

Shocked and humiliated, Clemenceau left Paris by automobile for Giverny, a village northwest of the capital, in Normandy. As the Assembly formally cast its vote, he ate his lunch in the famous yellow kitchen of his dear friend Claude Monet. The old painter consoled the old politician: "It was a question of dignity before which you, as savior of the country, could not and should not capitulate."[11]

The two men talked of Monet's latest masterpiece, a series of impressionistic murals of the water lilies in his pond. Monet had offered to donate them to the French state in honor of the war victory, and Clemenceau had gratefully accepted the gift. Publicly known as the Tiger, he nurtured a private passion for the arts. After years of art collecting, he had come to see cosmic meaning in Monet's work. In the painter's fury and the blended harmonies of his brushstrokes, Clemenceau saw the essence of life's eternal struggle: "The action on this battlefield is life itself, transposed luminously."[12] He would devote the next decade to installing Monet's famous water lily panels in their own dedicated museum in the Tuileries garden near the Louvre.

Clemenceau's fall came the day after the League of Nations Council met for the first time. The League had formally come into existence on January 10. The Council's gathering on the sixteenth in the Quai d'Orsay's Clock Room was but a sideshow to the parliamentary plots and maneuvers that preoccupied the French capital.

De Caix, meanwhile, lost no time in meeting both Deschanel and Poincaré. Both shared his anxiety about British gains at France's expense in the Middle East. On January 22, de Caix boasted to Gouraud that he had provoked a "palace revolution at the Quai d'Orsay."[13]

Compared with the bourgeois republican Clemenceau, Robert de Caix de Saint Aymour was an aristocratic reactionary. He presented a trim and nimble figure next to the Tiger's portly and ponderous physique. Although he looked like a banker, with his high collars, pince-nez, and goatee, de Caix wrote of France's glory with flamboyance and passion. The two men had one thing in common, however: their political attitudes had been formed in response to the German siege of Paris in 1871. While Clemenceau sought redemption by making French society strong, de Caix sought it by expanding France's overseas empire.

As an editor for the influential pro-colonial newsletter *Journal des Débats*, de Caix worked at the center of the colonial lobby, which by 1914 included two hundred members of the Chamber of Deputies. The fluid, loose structure of the French Third Republic permitted lobbyists easy access to high-level officials and to newspaper publishers, who assured the French public that the colonial civilizing mission was an altruistic and honorable endeavor. Well before the armistice, lobbyists had mapped out the French empire's postwar expansion into German and Ottoman territories in Africa and Asia.[14]

De Caix had written his first article on Syria in 1916, arguing that France must snatch it from Britain. "If we don't do it, it will be the Anglo-Egyptians," de Caix wrote. "We do not recommend the experience of 1882," when Britain beat France to the occupation of Egypt. Years later, de Caix confessed that he knew nothing about Syria at the time he wrote that first article.[15]

He was now in an opportune position to enlist the new premier, Alexandre Millerand, in overturning the Clemenceau accord. A member of the colonial lobby, Millerand had also worked alongside General Gouraud to establish French control over the recaptured provinces of Alsace-Lorraine.

Under de Caix's influence, Millerand replaced Berthelot with a man who knew little about Syria, Maurice Paléologue. "I felt embarrassed by it," de Caix admitted, because Berthelot had been his mentor at the Quai d'Orsay. But he did not hesitate to exploit widespread resentment of Berthelot as the éminence grise of foreign policy. De Caix publicly maligned Berthelot in the press as a traitor "seduced" by Faisal and positioned himself as the savior of French honor.[16]

Before returning to Beirut in early February, de Caix distributed a long memo at the Quai that soon became a revolutionary manifesto on Syria policy. He argued that Faisal did not represent Syrians, but rather was a "Sharifian"—a descendant of the Prophet aligned with the religious fanaticism of his father in Mecca. Sharifians, de Caix contended, sought to create a new caliphate to rule over other Arabs in Syria and Mesopotamia. Worse, they were Muslim theocrats who threatened France's Christian clients. "They systematically molest supporters of our country," he wrote. De Caix also claimed, tendentiously, that Faisal had been allied with Turkish nationalists, heirs to the fanatical Young Turks. In short, de Caix argued, the prince could not be trusted to compromise with a French mandate. He concluded that France should cut a deal with the British, giving them Mosul and Palestine in exchange for full control of Syria, rather than permit the creation of a powerful Arab state. "The very existence of a united Syria under Sharifian rule would constitute for us an obstacle and a danger," de Caix warned, referring specifically to French North Africa. "It will strengthen the kind of nationalist movements that the Wilsonian declarations have inspired across the world."

To better serve French interests, de Caix advised his fellow diplomats to split Syria into cantons and to grant autonomy to non-Muslims and Syrian notables who resented being ruled by Bedouin from Arabia. France should also cancel the January 6 accord's provision for a Syrian parliament, which he felt was an "absurdity" in a society "deprived of political or civic education." And finally, French advisors should not fall under Syrian control.[17]

As word of de Caix's revolution reached the Arab delegation office on Avenue du Bois de Boulogne, Rustum Haidar's grimmest predictions were confirmed. Haidar had only begrudgingly accepted the

January 6 accord. "No doubt Clemenceau wanted an agreement built on new principles. If the matter were simply between him and the Prince, it would have been done quickly," Haidar wrote. "But it was in the hands of imperialists like Berthelot and Gout. The actions of crusading colonialists like Gouraud and de Caix have great influence on the course of policy."[18]

Haidar saw clearly that the rules of the postwar game had changed. "America has washed her hands of the East and England has renounced any intervention in Syria," he remarked. "The Peace Conference has fallen into the hands of Britain and France."

By the time he attended the League of Nations Council session on January 16, Haidar had lost all faith in Wilson's liberal world order. "President [Léon] Bourgeois said it is based on justice and honor," he wrote. "It is based on spies, lies, and the power of force." The mandates were no longer a "sacred trust of civilization," Haidar understood. They had instead become an instrument of Europe's limitless colonial ambition in the Orient.

Haidar found solidarity with Muslim envoys from Algeria, Tunisia, India, and Turkey. They too viewed European diplomats as Christian crusaders who did not respect Muslim rights. "We are expecting a second war. Only Germany and Russia will save the Asian people," he wrote. On the day Clemenceau resigned, Haidar predicted that 1920 would "be a year built on the moans and cries of peoples."[19]

Massacre at Marash: France's Failure as Protector of Eastern Christians

De Caix returned to Beirut in early February. At the same time, Millerand sent a telegram to General Gouraud signaling an imminent change in policy. He ordered the high commissioner to enforce the terms of the January 6 accord strictly. If the Syrians failed to uphold their promises of keeping order and respecting the borders of the French zone, the accord could be canceled, just as Clemenceau had warned. Faisal must make Syrians respect the terms of the accord, Millerand warned: "If he is unable, we are authorized to take the measures needed to maintain order, defend the population, and secure our troops."[20]

As high commissioner of Syria and Cilicia, Gouraud had from the start posed as the protector of Christians in both regions. He had made no secret of his Catholic piety in his welcome speech on November 21, when he praised French troops as descendants of the Crusaders. Muslims had boycotted the occasion.[21] His closest advisors included Father Claudius Chanteur, a leading Jesuit at the French St. Joseph University in Beirut; Paul Huvelin, a colonial lobbyist from Lyon; and Monsignor Elias Hoyek, patriarch of the Maronite Church.

Gouraud and his inner circle characterized the conflict over the Bekaa Valley not as a mere political contest between the French and the Syrian governments, but as sectarian warfare. Clashes were reported as examples of age-old Muslim violence against Christians. They predicted a massacre if France did not occupy the hinterland.[22] Like them, de Caix raised the specter of Turkish-style annihilation of Christians in Syria. Faisal modeled his rule on the revolution of the Young Turks, he claimed: "Like them, he embraces nationalism as a mask for pan-Islamism."[23]

Crisis immediately threatened the new government's plan to exploit sectarian tensions and justify French rule as needed for the protection of Christians. It was in Cilicia, not Syria, that mass violence occurred. Located in Anatolia just over the Syrian border, Cilicia was a home- land for Armenians, which they had long shared with Turkish Mus- lims. In the months after the armistice, more than 200,000 Armenian survivors had streamed back to their villages and towns in Cilicia, many from Aleppo. When Gouraud toured Cilicia in December 1919, Armenians greeted him with cheers. France had taken control of the region after Britain's withdrawal that fall. But the French were short of troops, so they began to enlist Armenians in defense brigades. By January 1920, however, Armenians were begging for more military protection. Turkish nationalists, angered at the arming of Armenians, stepped up their attacks on multiple towns. Gouraud begged Paris for reinforcements. "Armenians are turning against us," he warned Millerand. Turkish nationalist leaflets promised to spread "holy war" to "all of Muslim Syria."[24]

On January 21, just days after the League of Nations' opening, Turkish residents in the town of Marash launched a revolt against their Armenian neighbors and the French garrison. Located three hundred miles north of Beirut, Marash had once belonged to the Ottoman province of Aleppo. More than twenty thousand Armenians had resettled there.[25] Aided by Mustafa Kemal's nationalist forces, the rebels set churches afire. "Comrades, war has begun. With the grace of God and in the spirit of the Prophet," the Turkish police chief proclaimed that day, "our country shall not be surrendered." Witnesses reported three thousand Christians killed in the next few days.[26]

Fighting continued in Marash until February 10, when French troops suddenly evacuated it, abandoning the Armenians to their fate. Witnesses of the massacre reported seeing stacks of dead bodies lying in the streets, covered with snow. Hundreds more died as they fled the town, caught in the same blizzard that blanketed Damascus that week.[27] Armenians blamed General Gouraud, but later reports revealed that it was a local official who had ordered the French withdrawal. Because of budget cuts, the Marash outpost had lacked radio equipment to communicate with Gouraud.[28]

An estimated seven thousand Armenians died at Marash. Rumors of twenty thousand dead spread at first. For Christians across the Middle East, the news revived the specter of genocide. For the Millerand government, the "Marash Affair" was a military embarrassment and a diplomatic disaster. The French had insisted on replacing British troops in Cilicia because the region had been promised to France under the Sykes-Picot accord. No such massacres had occurred under the British. The French suffered in part because their rule coincided with the rise of the Turkish nationalist movement. But their policy had also triggered Turkish anger. Short of troops, they had recruited Armenians into local militias. Turkish Muslims, fearful of Armenian revenge for the genocide, embraced sectarian propaganda calling for holy war to defend Islam.

"The French flag flies in every part of Anatolia. Isn't this a shame for you?" Mustafa Kemal proclaimed. "Brothers! Now is the time for patriotism and action. The Arab government itself relies on us. Their calls and their efforts make me proud. . . . You must be ready at any time for holy war." Another leaflet called the French "microbes of humanity" who "torture and destroy dear little Muhammads."[29]

Back in Paris, Haidar worried that Turkish nationalists threatened the tolerant, inclusive Syria that Faisal promised. Syrian dissidents, especially in pro-Turkish Aleppo, were joining Mustafa Kemal's movement in a common anticolonial cause. The rally to defend Islam would alienate Syrian Christians from the Damascus government.[30] Their sectarianism threatened Syrian democracy as much as the Maronite Church's did.

Reaffirming Dreams of a Christian State in Lebanon

Maronite Patriarch Elias Hoyek was a strong supporter of a French mandate over an independent Lebanon. He had lived through the wartime famine that killed more than 200,000 Lebanese, most of them Christian. Like the French, he blamed the Ottoman government's anti-Christian policies, as evidenced by the thousands of Armenian refugees in Lebanon.

A cold winter, a locust invasion, and the Ottoman army's diversion of food supplies to itself deprived poor villagers of food. The Allied blockade of Mediterranean ports prevented delivery of emergency rations.

Although the French had supported the blockade, they arrived in late 1918 promising to rescue Christians. Hoyek embraced the French as a means of ensuring the Maronite Church's domination of Mount Lebanon. The church denounced the Arab regime in Damascus just as it had discouraged participation in the Ottoman parliament during the 1908–1912 constitutional revolution. It had gained influence during the war, and now sought to marginalize secularized Christians who, through the mixed-sect Lebanese Administrative Council, had ruled Mount Lebanon before the war. Ordinary Maronites who had suffered unspeakable trauma during the war now sought security in the Maronite Church and in separation from Muslims. When the King-Crane Commission toured the mountain and coast, Maronites unanimously voiced support for a French mandate. A plurality of other Christians agreed with them, although most Greek Orthodox in the Western Zone supported the Damascus government.[31]

But now Hoyek began to doubt France's commitment to protecting Christians. On a visit to Paris in the fall, he had personally secured Clemenceau's promise of an independent Lebanon. But then Clemenceau turned around and ordered Gouraud to pull back from the Bekaa Valley, which was full of farmland that Maronites believed essential to a future Christian state. Hoyek accused Prince Faisal of fomenting sectarian war with his support of guerrilla attacks on the valley's pro-French Christian villages. Then, in January, Hoyek learned that Clemenceau had signed the January 6 accord. Despite the accord's assurance that Faisal would recognize the independence of Lebanon, Hoyek worried. Rumors reached him that Faisal had privately rejected Lebanese independence after returning to Damascus in mid-January. Hoyek knew that the accord did not designate the boundaries of Lebanon; nor did it define exactly what Lebanon's relationship to Syria would be.[32]

In late January, upon receiving news of Muslim-Turkish fighting in Cilicia, Hoyek finally decided to dispatch another delegation to Paris. To the annoyance of Haidar, a Shiite from Lebanon, the delegation claimed to represent the views of all Lebanese. Faisal had supported the guerrilla bands in the Bekaa and north of Aleppo as a means of pressuring the French. Critics would later claim that this strategy backfired because it stoked Muslim-Christian antagonism and provoked a more militant French attitude.

The Supreme Council Opens Debate on the Turkish Treaty

Meanwhile, in London, on February 12, the Supreme Council opened discussions on the Turkish peace treaty. The sessions were primarily devoted to the future state of Turkey promised by Woodrow Wilson in his Twelfth Point. A year earlier, the Council had agreed to sever the Arab territories from the Ottoman Empire. However, because European statesmen conventionally referred to the Ottoman Empire as the Turkish Empire, discussion spilled beyond the borders of Anatolia into matters concerning Syria.

While the Supreme Council first addressed issues concerning Turkish territory—permitting the Turks to remain in Constantinople and deciding on control of the Bosporus strait—they soon began outlining zones of economic influence across Anatolia and into Syria and Mesopotamia, following the template of the 1916 Sykes-Picot accord. France and Britain finally settled on the boundary between Syria and Palestine. Delegates expressed little enthusiasm for establishing an Armenian mandate, mainly owing to lack of military means to enforce it. Progress on other issues was slow, because Premier Millerand was called back to Paris frequently to deal with the crisis in Cilicia and a major railway strike in France.[33]

Events in Cilicia forced the London Conference to focus on Armenia, much to France's chagrin. When the first reports of the massacre arrived, Berthelot responded that France no longer planned to occupy Cilicia permanently. But on the morning of February 28, British foreign secretary Curzon interrupted the Supreme Council's negotiations to read aloud an urgent telegram reporting the latest casualty numbers from Marash. Lloyd George chastised the French, demanding to know "what steps the French Government proposes to take to restore the situation, to protect the Armenians who remained, and generally to uphold the prestige of the Allies."[34]

Millerand was stung by this second public insult lobbed by the British since the London Conference opened. The first had come when Curzon publicly told the British parliament that he regretted Clemenceau would not be at the negotiating table.[35] Millerand feared that the British prime minister had devised yet another devious strategy to gain diplomatic advantage. He ordered the Quai d'Orsay to obtain a precise account of events in Cilicia. A flurry of alarmist telegrams arrived on Gouraud's desk in the first days of March.

The Quai d'Orsay was in no mood to welcome the revolution that was climaxing in Damascus under a blanket of snow that February.

Chapter 10

The Prince, the Sheikh, and "The Day of Resurrection"

A rainstorm drenched Qalamun on the morning of Sunday, January 11, when Rashid Rida and his brother set out on a walk to Tripoli. The road turned muddy, so they stopped at the house of a friend, the city's former mufti. Because of his nationalist views, the French had expelled him from his office. Suddenly, a French messenger arrived with a note from General Gouraud: would Rida kindly attend the official welcome ceremony for Prince Faisal upon his arrival in Beirut on Wednesday?

After tending to his ongoing legal tangle over the mosque endowment, Rida set out for Beirut the next evening. The trip took six hours. Rain poured down and one of his car's tires blew out. He arrived near midnight. On January 14, Faisal disembarked at Beirut to enthusiastic crowds. General Gouraud hosted a reception and luncheon for the prince, attended by his top military brass as well as foreign consuls present in the city. Faisal assured Gouraud that the Clemenceau accord would open a new era of peaceful relations in Syria. Gouraud warned him that France would uphold the accord only if all guerrilla violence in the Bekaa ceased. The general sent a guardedly hopeful report back to Paris.[1]

The next morning, January 15, Rida arrived at the Damascus government's delegation in Beirut for a personal meeting with the prince. He had been waiting for this moment since September. Faisal arrived just before noon. "He welcomed me with much praise," Rida recalled.

The thirty-five-year-old prince and the fifty-four-year-old sheikh took an immediate liking to one another. Over the course of more than an hour they spoke frankly.[2] Faisal immediately confided to Rida the terms of the accord with Clemenceau. Since both America and Britain had abandoned Syria, there was no option but to strike a deal with France, he explained.

Rida warned that the French were laying a trap. Their advisors must not hold any administrative authority in the government, he advised. Syrians must be free to disagree with French advice. And the French must not be allowed to control the police or military. "Their control over security, for example, would allow them to rob the country of its freedom," Rida pointed out. "I cannot be free in my thoughts or opinions, or in advising my nation against their policy, if they can boot me out of the country for security reasons!"

"That is true," Faisal admitted. "But if we are united in the service of our country, we can protect ourselves against the dangers inherent in their authority." The only other option would be to wage war, Faisal reasoned, and he would not take responsibility for that: it was up to the people to choose between the accord and war.

Rida proposed to Faisal a third option. "If they would let you say at the Peace Conference that Article 22 of the Treaty recognizes the complete independence of Syria," Rida proposed, then Syria could act as a strong nation. It could choose its own advisors, not have France impose them. And Syria could "form a national government, elect deputies to the legislature, and enforce the laws."

International recognition of Syria's independence would also remove the threat of conquest, Rida argued. "The French Chamber of Deputies will not approve funding for a war of colonization, especially against a country that the peace conference had determined was independent." Rida demonstrated here familiarity with debates on Syria in the French Chamber of Deputies. Since the 1918 armistice, the socialist deputy Marcel Cachin had led a faction demanding respect for Syrian self-determination.[3]

Faisal parried that the colonial lobby would be likely to prevail over pacifists in the Chamber. "[France] feels the ecstasy of victory," he remarked. "She would consider an order to evacuate her army occupying Syria as an insult to her military honor."

Rida's counsel also suggests that he was acutely aware of the ambiguities of legal meaning in the League covenant that could either ensure Syria's freedom or seal its subjugation. Article 22 provided that "certain communities formerly belonging to the Turkish Empire have reached a stage of development where *their existence as independent nations can be provisionally recognized* subject to the rendering of administrative advice and assistance by a Mandatory" (emphasis added).[4] Article 22 left open to debate where sovereignty lay—with the nation, with the mandatory power, or with the League of Nations. Some theorists and policymakers interpreted "nations" to mean "states," meaning the Syrian state was essentially sovereign. Others, however, insisted that the article did not grant political sovereignty; as a mere nation, Syrians, like Zionist Jews in Palestine, could lay claim only to a homeland, not an independent state. They would remain under the sovereignty of the League (or the mandatory power ultimately designated by the League) until they proved their capacity to govern themselves and "to stand alone" in world affairs. Most radically, Balfour would insist in 1922 that mandates belonged to the conquering power, which accepted self-imposed limits to its rule. Given this disagreement, the League was bound to become a "laboratory of sovereignty," as one scholar put it. It would take years to define the terms of statehood in the postwar world order.[5]

In Rida's view, Syria must exploit this legal ambiguity. Its future depended on obtaining an official pronouncement in favor of the "state" interpretation of Article 22. That was the reasoning behind the Syrian Union Party's call to draft a constitution for presentation to the Paris Peace Conference. It would prove that Syrians were worthy of a state.[6]

Rida would later claim that he was the first to propose that Syria confront the Allies with the Declaration of Independence as a fait accompli. He was, in fact, only the herald that introduced the idea to the prince. The Syrian Congress had already adopted such a resolution on November 24 and deputies had repeated it to Faisal at an Arab Club meeting on January 22.[7]

Rida and other Syrian nationalists saw themselves as players in a global process of establishing a new regime of international law to govern the relations among states. At stake in the Syrian case were general principles that would shape the future of other nations as well. Since the nineteenth century, European statesmen and legal scholars had excluded non-Christians and non-Europeans from full membership in the family of sovereign nations. The Ottomans were deemed, until 1914, only marginal guests. But Wilson had opened the door to a universal regime of states' rights. The Syrians aimed to keep that door open and to walk through it.

Faisal and Rida said their good-byes over a formal lunch with two French officers, Colonel Antoine Toulat and Colonel Edouard Cousse. This would not be the last time the four would meet. Assigned as Faisal's liaisons to General Gouraud, Toulat and Cousse were destined to play an intimate role in the coming independence struggle. And unbeknownst to either Rida or Faisal, their January 15 meeting would launch an intense relationship for the next six months.[8]

The next day, just as Faisal departed on the Damascus Road, an ominous rainstorm broke. The prince worried about the reaction of Syrian nationalists to the accord. He knew they would reject the provisions granting control of foreign affairs and internal security to the French and granting independence to Lebanon. His plan was to persuade the cabinet that these terms were an interim step, not a capitulation.

Faisal's Return to Damascus

The largest demonstration yet in Damascus greeted Faisal upon his arrival on January 17. The Higher National Committee, led by Sheikh Kamil al-Qassab, had been planning it for weeks. Dr. Abd al-Rahman Shahbandar of the Syrian Union Party also played a prominent role at a general HNC meeting of delegates from throughout Syria.

Qassab claimed that more than 100,000 people marched. Widows and daughters of war martyrs led the procession, followed by clergy of all faiths, committees of national defense, political parties, notables, the municipal council, civilian and military employees, farmers, doctors, pharmacists, journalists, the Arab Clubs, the schools of law and medicine, teachers, merchants, artisans, guilds, and leaders of the city neighborhoods and nearby villages. They arrived at Marjeh Square with signs reading "The Arab Country Is Indivisible" and "Religion Is for God and the Country Is for All." Others demanded full independence and a national army. Faisal greeted the demonstrators in front of city hall, promising to heed the people's will. The crowd cheered when he proclaimed that he and the nation were fundamentally "in agreement for an independent, indivisible Syria."[9]

However, Faisal was not yet ready to cede authority to either the people or the Congress. At a large gathering at the Arab Club, he intervened in a debate between the Maronite priest Habib Istifan and Dr. Shahbandar. While Istifan pledged loyalty to Faisal, Shahbandar urged the assembly to recognize the government installed during Faisal's absence and to follow the example of the Egyptian nationalist revolution against Britain. Dr. Shahbandar, Faisal responded sharply, should stick to his own profession, medicine. The prince insisted that the current government was not an elected representative of the nation; it was merely a temporary, military administration. Since Syria was not yet recognized as a sovereign state, only he could represent the country, as a delegate of his sovereign father, Sharif Hussein. "I am the spirit of the movement," he declared. "I am the responsible person until a national assembly is elected, whereupon I shall relinquish my responsibilities and hand them over to the people."[10]

Faisal proceeded to dismiss the nationalist cabinet and restore Ali Rida al-Rikabi as head of government. He also supported the creation of a new conservative party to counterbalance the HNC. The Syrian National Party was led by anti-Fatat notables like the Congress vice president, Abd al-Rahman al-Yusuf, and Faisal's wartime generals, Nasib al-Bakri and Sharif Nasir. They favored compromise with France over what they viewed as certain defeat for a self-proclaimed independent state.[11]

But the prince could not turn back the political clock. Newspapers and Arab Club members publicly condemned the Clemenceau accord. Even Faisal's personal physician, Dr. Ahmad Qadri, gave a press conference against it.[12]

As a last resort Faisal called a meeting of Fatat leaders, but they too rejected the accord. Like Rida, they argued that it was a fig leaf for another French protectorate, as in Morocco and Tunisia. Faisal lost his temper and demanded that they file paper ballots to record their error for history. Then he called for elections for a new central committee. The new slate of Fatat leaders also voted against the prince.[13]

The Sheikh Joins the Prince

On a brief visit to Beirut in early February, Faisal sought out Rashid Rida for advice. Over dinner, the prince asked the sheikh to return with him to Damascus to act as a mediator with Fatat and other nationalist leaders. Faisal pointed out that Rida knew Qassab and Shahbandar personally and had influence within Syria's new Independence Party. But unlike those hotheads, Rida was a mature man of reason.[14]

The sheikh hesitated. He had already left his family for more than five months and had refused an offer to work for the Damascus government. He was also appalled at Faisal's naïveté. Faisal had foolishly trusted the British and now he appeared to be repeating the mistake with the French. But Rida also found Faisal an intelligent and eager student. In Faisal, Rida also recognized an opportunity to realize the Arab unity he had so long sought: If Syrians achieved independence, they might spark a revival across the Muslim world. So Rida agreed to Faisal's offer, with a caveat that he would be no yes-man.

Rida tied up his affairs in Beirut and took the train to Damascus on February 8, 1920. That very night, he met with his old friend Kamil al-Qassab to catch up on the local news.

The very next day, a snowstorm hit the capital, locking it down for three weeks.[15] The stretch of isolation proved to be a fertile period for political bargaining. Rida met Faisal nearly every day. In a fatherly manner, he dispensed the wisdom of age to the younger man. Rida also edited the prince's speeches and reviewed his correspondence with Lloyd George and Sharif Hussein. The two men discussed how Faisal had blindly followed his father's faith in the British, to no good end.

Rida also used his meetings at the royal residence to advance his ideas on building Arab strength through a league of states, based in

Mecca. He argued that the key to achieving political unity, internationally and within Syria, was to build cooperation from the ground up, not to impose unity from above by subduing the different parties. Rida drew his wisdom on democratic politics not from reading European or American textbooks but from his own experience in Ottoman politics. The Young Turks had betrayed the 1908 constitutional revolution by repressing opposition parties. Difference was natural, Rida explained to Faisal. In a righteous government, parties were free to debate and thereby minimize the harm in their differences by finding points of consensus.

To demonstrate his ideas, Rida invited the prince to a rally on February 9. As the wind blew drifts of snow, the city's elite gathered in tents warmed with carpets. Sheikh Kamil al-Qassab delivered "a long and eloquent speech" on how the nation would accept nothing short of absolute independence. Faisal gave a speech in response, in which he felt compelled to agree.

Rida advised Faisal to build solidarity through Islam. "We cannot establish Arab unity and restore the Arabs' glory and civilization without Islam," he contended. He also proposed ways of bridging differences among various Islamic sects. The prince was so enthusiastic that he asked Rida to move his family and magazine to Damascus. Rida assured Faisal that he would stay to build a righteous government based on the ideas of Islamic reformists.[16]

Rida firmly believed that Islam and democracy were not only compatible but also a necessary combination for ethical governance. His views were not universally popular, as he discovered when the dean of the newly founded law school invited him to give a lecture. Anticipating opposition, Dr. Ahmad Qadri, Faisal's personal physician, warned Rida not to deliver the speech. But when a secularist law professor objected to hosting a religious lecture in a state school, the dean overruled him. With Faisal in attendance, Rida gave his lecture, titled "Arab-Islamic Civilization and European Materialist Civilization." The prince liked the lecture and praised Rida for his mature views, Qadri later confided.[17]

In these crucial weeks of snowed-in consultation, Rida became a pivotal player in uniting Faisal and the Syrian Congress on a plan to declare independence. But it was not Rida who finally persuaded the prince to abandon negotiations with the French. Faisal realized the game was over when his own father, Sharif Hussein, published a personal attack on him and on the January 6 accord in a Cairo newspaper. An opposition paper in Damascus reprinted Sharif Hussein's demand for complete independence with no strings attached. The article launched a new round of public protest. Delegations arrived at Faisal's royal residence, demanding that he obey his father. The prince staunchly defended the need for the accord. On February 15, after Qassab gave a speech viciously attacking Faisal's policy, the HNC took a formal vote against the accord and against all compromise.[18]

Rida urged Faisal to reconcile with Qassab and Shahbandar. The nation's future depended on it, he warned. Faisal acquiesced and invited Qassab and Shahbandar to dinner at the royal residence the next evening, February 16. The three argued fiercely. Qassab insisted that the nation was ready to rise up en masse to claim independence. The time was ripe, since French forces had relocated from Syria to confront the Turkish nationalists in Cilicia. Faisal responded that the nation needed firm leadership, or else blood would run in the streets. No common ground was found. The dinner ended, however, with promises to keep their disagreement secret.

In desperation, Faisal cabled to Gouraud in Beirut pleading for a sign of French support for the terms of Arab independence promised in the January accord. "The people are waiting for actions by the French government in support of my efforts in this regard," he wrote. Their fears were heightened now, he explained, "since the publication of the message in which His Majesty my father advised me to demand independence for all the Arab regions."

But Faisal's effort to use his father's public warning as leverage with the French failed. Word of the royal rift had already leaked out. Colonel Cousse, the French liaison in Damascus, reported that it had revealed Faisal's weakness. Gouraud reported to Paris only that Faisal appeared incapable of upholding his promise, made on January 6, to maintain order in Syria. The staff in Paris agreed with Gouraud to make no more concessions to "extremists." They also agreed to reaffirm their advice to Faisal, that he should not return to Paris to finalize the accord until he could demonstrate solid political support for it.[19]

Faisal received no response from Gouraud until March 2. The general assured the prince that France did not intend to rule the East Zone directly, but that it would defend its position in Lebanon.[20] Faisal and Zaid held a last-ditch meeting at Rikabi's home in the hope of persuading several Fatat leaders. But the political pendulum in Damascus had swung toward an alliance for independence.[21]

The Case for Declaring Independence

In late February, even as he continued to meet Faisal, Rida attended Independence Party meetings on reconvening the Congress and drafting a declaration of independence. (The party was the public face of the secretive Fatat.) During several meetings held at Ali Rida al-Rikabi's home, a majority in the party agreed with Rashid Rida that the Congress must be established as the nation's representative—against Faisal's dynastic claims. Congress, not Faisal, would have to declare independence in the name of the people. As the snow began to melt in the last week of February, the Independence Party summoned its members from Lebanon and Palestine.[22]

Against minority proposals to hold new elections for Congress, Qadri and Shahbandar argued that Syria must declare independence immediately. The Congress could proceed legitimately based on the elections of June 1919. It must now exploit the window of opportunity that had opened with the transfer of French troops from Syria to Cilicia, where they were battling Turkish nationalists. Some party members objected that Syria's status had to be defined at the peace conference, in the treaty on the Ottoman Empire. The conference had only now opened discussions on the matter, after completing treaties with the other Central Powers since summer. But Qadri and Shahbandar insisted that Syria's right to provisional independence under Article 22 of the League covenant had already been ratified by France and Britain as part of the Treaty of Versailles, which had taken effect on January 20.[23]

Meanwhile, Izzat Darwazeh and others drafted a declaration of independence. At a subsequent party meeting, Rida proposed amendments to the draft. "He left out the most important of my proposals," Rida wrote, "which is to base independence on the natural right of the people to freedom and independence . . . and on the fact that Syrian Arabs and others rebelled successfully against the Turkish government." These points must be coupled with Syria's rights as defined by Article 22, he argued.

The palace was likely aware of these meetings, given that Rida requested copies of supporting legal documents from Awni Abd al-Hadi, who was Faisal's secretary and a leading member of Fatat. Abd al-Hadi had returned to Damascus with Faisal in January and had taken a personal interest in the plans for independence. He felt especially anxious because Britain had already claimed a mandate over Palestine, thereby separating his hometown, Nablus, from Syria. While Abd al-Hadi continued to lose weight, owing to anxiety, Rida eased his worries by indulging in the delicious cuisine of his homeland. In his diary, he noted he had gained four kilograms in February.[24]

On February 29 and March 1, the Independence Party opened debate on the role of Islam in the government. Until then, members had only vaguely talked of a constitutional monarchy with Faisal as its king and with Islam as its religion. Should the Syrian state have a top Islamic official, like the Ottoman Empire's Sheikh al-Islam? Should Islamic law be integrated into the regime? One side responded no, there was no need for a cabinet minister on Islamic affairs. The other side argued that a minister must govern Islamic courts and endowments. They asked Rida for his view.

The Syrian state would gain much prestige and support if it had an Islamic component, Rida argued. The caliphate had helped the Ottoman regime to survive, despite its military defeats, because millions of Muslims supported it. Second, Islam would strengthen Syria's confederation with Iraq and Arabia. The only bond uniting Arabs across the regions was their common religion. "Syria cannot remain as an independent kingdom unless it is united with other Arab countries surrounding it," he pointed out. Third, he said, most ordinary Muslims would consider a secular state unfamiliar and illegitimate. "They would overturn it in favor of a religious one at the first opportunity," Rida claimed. "Therefore, our Sharia should be the main source of needed legislation, even if the government is not Islamic." Rida proposed that the government include a minister for religious affairs as well as Islamic scholars on its staff. Such a state would not be a theocracy, he assured opponents. Nothing in Islamic law contradicted a civil state—only scholars of the strictest schools believed that there was any contradiction. The meeting disbanded without resolving the question.[25]

Faisal was by then convinced that he should reconvene the Congress. While critics later claimed Faisal was bullied by "extremists" into accepting the Declaration of Independence, the record of his sustained discussions with Rida and with party members suggests otherwise.[26] Faisal recognized that popular opposition to the French accord was overwhelming. He also recognized the legality of Syrian independence under international law. And he understood the need to establish an independent state as a fait accompli, given that the Americans were no longer arbiters against colonial aggression at Paris. In the end, Faisal was likely happy to hand responsibility for such a fateful decision to the Congress.[27]

The prince did, however, worry about his father's reaction. When a new flag was proposed, he insisted on pleasing his father by maintaining the stripes and red triangle of the Hijazi flag flown during the Arab Revolt. Party members agreed. The new Syrian flag would differ only by the addition of a white star inside the triangle.[28]

Drafting the Declaration

March blew in with a spring breeze. As the snow melted from mountain passes, Congress summoned its deputies from across Greater Syria. But Lebanese deputies worried that the French would block their travel. Rida volunteered to fetch them, unaware that the mission would keep him away for a critical five days. While in Beirut, he sought an appointment with General Gouraud, but instead met Robert de Caix, who said he was pleased to meet a famous scholar. Rida understood that the French were not pleased with his mission to summon Lebanese deputies to Damascus. Only later would he learn that de Caix was the mastermind behind France's plan to occupy and partition Syria. After meeting de Caix, he found that the deputies were extremely frightened to risk the trip to Damascus. It took several days to cajole them.[29]

While Rida was away, a quorum of deputies arrived in Damascus and convened on March 6. At three in the afternoon, the General Syrian Congress assembled at the Arab Club to elect a new leadership. Former president Fawzi Pasha al-Azm had died in November. The deputies elected Hashim al-Atassi of Homs, a former Ottoman district governor, as the new president. Darwazeh was pleased to be reelected as secretary.[30]

Faisal arrived at four o'clock. In keeping with Ottoman custom, which maintained that the monarch should not speak directly to parliament, Awni Abd al-Hadi, his secretary, read the prince's welcome speech to Congress:

> Gentlemen: As the time approaches for the final resolution of
> the Turkish question at the Peace Conference, I have decided
> to summon you again. At this critical moment, we must decide
> on the country's future according to the wishes of the people,
> who have entrusted you to represent them. President Wilson
> stated the following [war] goal at Mount Vernon, in his speech
> of 24 July 1918: "Every issue—whether political, economic, or
> international—must be settled on the basic principle of the free
> acceptance of the people directly concerned, not on material
> principles or interests that another nation or people requires to
> secure its external influence and policies."[31]

Following the mention of Woodrow Wilson, Faisal's address affirmed that sovereignty lies with the people and with Congress, as the people's representative. As a result, Congress had a right to declare Syrian independence based on Arabs' role in the war, on Allied declarations, and on the King-Crane poll. The declaration was not an act of revolt against the Paris Peace Conference, Faisal insisted. It merely restated what existed in fact: "We do not ask Europe to grant us what is not ours by right. We ask it to confirm the right that is granted to us as a living nation."[32]

Abd al-Hadi concluded Faisal's speech: "Gentlemen! Your task today is critical and your mission, great. Europe is watching us closely. She will decide either for or against us based on the political plan we adopt and the future actions we take. First and foremost, our new state, based on the patriotism of its noble citizens, must decide on its form and draft a constitution."[33]

Sheikh Kamil al-Qassab, Faisal's populist opponent, delivered the people's response to the throne. He was not shy before royalty. Qassab called on Syrians to declare independence under a civilian, representative, and democratic government. He nominated Faisal as Syria's first king, on condition that the constitution limit his power. To underscore the fact that sovereignty lay with the people, Qassab distributed his speech to the public in leaflets under the title "The Nation Dictates Its Will to the Syrian Congress."[34]

Rashid Rida's train pulled into the Hijaz Station at 4:35 in the afternoon on March 7. He paused to say his prayers and then hurried to the Arab Club, where Congress was still in session. Deputies were still discussing a response to Faisal's speech when he entered. Rida asked that the speech be read aloud again. Here, at the eleventh hour, deputies debated whether to include mention of Islam in the declaration. Non-Muslim deputies proposed that the declaration announce a secular government. Some Muslims agreed. Others argued that Islam should be declared the official religion of an Arab-Muslim government. After intense argument, Rida proposed a solution: not to mention the issue at all.

"If you declare it [the state] as non-religious, most Muslims would understand that it is an infidel government that doesn't abide by the rules of religion. That would make it illegitimate, to be neither obeyed or approved; rather, it would need to be toppled as soon as possible," Rida argued, recapitulating an argument he had made earlier to Faisal. "So, I suggest omitting the issue and not mentioning anything." A majority agreed with Rida's view. As a compromise, they voted to state only that the official religion of the king (not the state) was Islam.[35]

Rida then joined a group of deputies, including Darwazeh and Atassi, the Congress president, in composing a letter to Faisal based on the deputies' comments. The letter would form the basis of the declaration text. They presented the letter to Congress and won majority approval. The few pro-French opponents—most conspicuously the vice president, Abd al-Rahman al-Yusuf—remained silent.[36]

Atassi, Darwazeh, and Rida then led a delegation to the royal residence in the northern neighborhood of Muhajirin. Guards stood outside in booths painted black, red, white, and green, the colors of the flag. Faisal opened the door of the modest two-story villa and invited the men to sit down in the salon. The walls were white, and the draperies were colored pistachio and raspberry. Faisal sat at his desk, inlaid with mother-of-pearl, and opened the three-page letter.[37]

Congress's letter thanked Faisal for leading the Arabs to victory and praised him for embracing "the lofty principles of President Wilson." It then recommended that Syria implement the Damascus Program of the previous summer, but in terms much more expansive and specific than what Faisal had proposed:

> The temporary occupation [of Syria], imposed by wartime
> conditions, must come to an end. It is time to fulfill
> the nation's aspirations. [Congress therefore] decides by
> consensus on the full, absolute independence of our Syrian
> country—in its natural borders including Palestine—based
> on civil representation, the protection of minority rights, and
> the rejection of Zionist claims to make Palestine a Jewish
> homeland or a destination for migration.
>
> By consensus, we have chosen you as the constitutional
> monarch for the Syrian country, due to your outstanding
> wisdom and sound judgment, as well as for your honorable
> character and your everlasting accomplishments in the fields of
> battle and politics in the interest of the nation.

Faisal made no comment. He simply thanked the deputies and asked God's blessing to ensure the nation's independence and well-being. As he bade the delegation good night, however, his mind likely churned with worry. Demanding independence beyond the limits of the territory that the Arabs now occupied, including Syria's Western and Southern zones, would be likely to trigger a diplomatic crisis. Also alarming was that Congress intended to remain in session after the declaration of independence as a constituent assembly. The government would be responsible to Congress, not to the king. While Faisal had invoked Wilson's principles to justify the call to national sovereignty, Congress had deployed those same principles to establish popular sovereignty.

"The Day of Resurrection"

Monday, March 8, 1920, was the day Syrian nationalists had anticipated since the Ottoman evacuation seventeen months earlier. "The Day of Resurrection," *al-yawm al-mashhud*, as Rashid Rida called it, was the day Arabs truly arose as a nation from centuries of Turkish enslavement. It was the day that the lands of Syria became free. It was the day that Faisal ibn Hussein took the oath as king.

Overnight, the mayor's office had plastered the walls of Damascus with a schedule of events. Under a picture of the new Syrian flag, the posters invited citizens from all classes and quarters to gather at Marjeh Square at two o'clock in the afternoon. Parades through the city would follow, ending with nighttime festivities in its major marketplaces. The Flower Theater Café, located across from city hall, was reserved for female spectators. Nazik al-Abid, the feminist who had so impressed the King-Crane Commission, was among them.[38]

That morning, Congress met at the Arab Club to choose Faisal's escort, which included Hashim al-Atassi, Rashid Rida, and Ahmad Qadri. Upon arrival at the royal residence, they found Izzat Darwazeh. Rida took the occasion to make a few final, grammatical edits to the declaration, which Abd al-Hadi had written out by hand.[39] Faisal, dressed in his military uniform, took his place in the royal horse-drawn carriage. He would ride behind members of Congress. Back in October 1918, Faisal had entered Damascus leading troops on horseback. Now, the civilian government required a new political order. Arab soldiers cheered, "Long live the King!" and women showered the carriages with flowers as they rode toward Marjeh Square.[40]

At three o'clock in the afternoon, Darwazeh took his position as Congress secretary on the balcony of city hall. Beside him stood political, religious, and tribal leaders, as well as foreign consuls from Spain, Persia, and Italy. George Young, the American consul, took a place alongside Faisal's French liaisons, Colonel Toulat and Colonel Cousse. The British liaison was absent. Below the balcony stood hundreds of people, their faces turned upward in anticipation. In a loud voice, Darwazeh declared the resolution adopted the previous day by the Syrian General Congress in the name of the Syrian Arab people of the interior, coastal, and southern zones. He began as follows:

> The Arab people, with their ancient glory and flowering
> civilization, mobilized their associations and political parties
> in the time of the Turks. They waged political struggles
> and spilled the blood of their martyrs, not only to liberate
> themselves from Turkish rule, but also to demand full
> independence and a free life as a nation.[41]

As the crowd cheered, Darwazeh praised "the honorable men who fought alongside the Allies to conquer Turkey" and the many Syrians who had sacrificed their sons in military battle. He acknowledged that ordinary Syrians, too, had suffered persecution, torture, and death for their resistance to the Turks.

The declaration was a call to law, not a call to revolt like the American declaration of 1776. The document affirmed Syrians' right to an independent state under international law, listing the seven wartime statements made by British, French, and American officials that recognized the Syrian right to independence. After the war, it continued, the peace conference drafted Article 22 of the peace treaty, which reaffirmed the "promise to give the people their right of self-determination." Syrians had also claimed that right in the Damascus Program submitted to the American Commission in July.

The declaration invoked the political necessity of implementing that law. It noted that the eighteen months of military occupation had done great harm to Syria, economically and politically, and had caused the people great anxiety, which had led to insurrection. That burden must now be lifted and the three zones of Syria must now be reunited, Darwazeh declared:

> We therefore unanimously proclaim the independence of our country, Syria, in its natural boundaries, including Palestine, based on a civil, representative form of government that protects the rights of minorities and rejects the claim of Zionists in Palestine to a national homeland.

> We have informed Prince Faisal, son of His Majesty King Hussein, that in light of his struggle to liberate the country, the nation recognizes him as its constitutional monarch with the title His Royal Highness King Faisal I.

The declaration then affirmed Congress as the guardian of Syrian independence. It also affirmed the decentralized authority of provincial governments, including autonomy for Lebanon, and the independence of a separate state of Iraq. With a nod toward the foreign diplomats present, Darwazeh added: "We have complete faith that the noble Allies and all other civilized countries will welcome this document, which is based on the natural and legal right to life." Only then, Darwazeh emphasized, could the Syrian Arab nation reach its utmost goal, to become an active member of the civilized world.

The crowd burst into enthusiastic applause and loud rejoicing.

Faisal gave a brief speech expressing his devotion to the nation, and a 101-gun salute cracked through the sky. The crowd cheered again as the new Syrian flag was raised. The dignitaries watched a military parade pass beneath the balcony and then slipped inside city hall for the formal oath of allegiance.

Faisal stood on a platform with a draped canopy; there was as yet no throne or actual crown. Over his uniform he donned a fine white headscarf and black robes. To his right stood his little son, Ghazi; and to his left, Prince Zaid. Military officers, ministers, religious patriarchs, and deputies from all three Syrian zones gathered around.

Following precedent set by the Ottoman sultan in the 1908 constitutional revolution, Faisal responded to the deputies' oaths of loyalty
with his own oath to serve the people, including all Syrians in all three
zones. He vowed to obey God, respect all religions, and uphold the
equality of all citizens under the law. He also promised to maintain
order, choose officials on the basis of merit, seek consultation from
the people, and promote the spread of knowledge.[42]

Leaders of the major religious communities then pronounced
Faisal king of Syria. Even Faisal's opponents cherished the moment.
"I was fortunate to be among those who entered to congratulate
him," recalled Dr. Shahbandar. "I will never forget him standing on
the platform, shaking hands with those who pledged allegiance to
him, one by one."[43]

King Faisal reappeared on the balcony to accept the good wishes
of ministers, Congress members, and religious leaders. That evening,
the new government held a banquet at the Arab Club.[44] For three
nights the markets opened and torches lit the streets for festivities.

The celebrations attracted thousands and remained calm, in contrast to the angry crowds of November, Colonel Cousse reported.
That evening, Faisal reassured Cousse that he would endeavor to
mitigate any semblance of rebellion against the Paris Peace Conference. He had, as advised, avoided any anti-French rhetoric during
the ceremony, and would now send diplomatic announcements to
reassure Syria's allies of its continued loyalty. If Faisal managed
the diplomacy well, Cousse believed, Syrian independence might
well succeed.[45]

Conclusion: The Question of Sovereignty

Two months later, the Syrian Congress published a commemorative
volume dedicated to King Faisal and to Syria's future.[46] *Souvenir of
Syrian Independence* documented the historic day of March 8, 1920,
with a reproduction of Faisal's speech to Congress, the declaration
text, and a fifty-page gallery of photographs honoring government
officials and religious leaders. The preface hailed the revival of Arab
glory that had faded in the millennium since the Umayyad, Abbasid,

and Andalusian caliphates. The Great War may have brought Arabs down low, under the knife of Jemal the Butcher, but Syrian youth "rose up against the Turks and with promises that they would obtain their full independence, they joined the Allies in liberating the Arab lands."

The volume concluded, however, with a commemoration of the Congress itself. It featured photographs of the Arab Club, where independence was decided; and of city hall, where it was declared. The last page featured a composite poster of eighty-five Congress deputies, members of the cabinet, and, at the center, the king. Each photograph had been taken on the day of the declaration.[47]

The volume was, in effect, an assertion of sovereignty in the face of continued controversy. Within inland Syria, the reaction to Congress's declaration had been overwhelmingly positive. Several cities had staged simultaneous independence celebrations on March 8. In Aleppo, the governor distributed handbills proclaiming independence and the brotherhood of Muslims, Christians, and Jews. Arab Club speakers honored the day as a collective redemption for Syrians' long suffering during the war. In nearby Hama, hundreds of men, women, and even children gathered at city hall to celebrate independence. In Jerusalem, a crowd gathered at the Damascus Gate to hail Syrian independence and the rejection of Zionist claims in Palestine.[48]

Response in the coastal zone, however, was mixed. Tripoli's Muslim ruling elite embraced inclusion in the new Syrian Arab Kingdom. Flyers placarded on Beirut's public walls hailed "the dawn of a new era." But protests broke out on Mount Lebanon, where the Maronite patriarch rejected the declaration and any affiliation with the Syrian Arab Kingdom.

The response in Arabia was ambivalent. Hashim al-Atassi, as Congress president, had formally notified Sharif Hussein of the declaration on March 9. The king of Arabia reportedly opposed it. That is perhaps why Faisal postponed informing his father personally until March 20, when he finally picked up a pen. Faisal knew Sharif Hussein would not welcome news that Syria had severed itself from his dominion. He was currently battling Abdulaziz ibn Saud of Riyadh, who threatened his Hijaz kingdom at Mecca. The son chose to soften the blow with a bit of diplomatic hyperbole and a white lie. He reminded his father of the glory he had already won since launching the great Arab Revolt. The Declaration, he wrote, was a step toward completing Arabs' ultimate liberation and unity. Iraqis had declared their independence on the same day, Faisal reported: "With the help of God, we have started the work by declaring Syria and Iraq independent under the overall kingship of your majesty."

Sharif Hussein reportedly opposed the Declaration, but he did not publish an open condemnation of his son, as he had done in February. Residents of Jeddah, meanwhile, staged a parade in celebration at the end of March.[49]

By then, Faisal had dissolved the military government and appointed a new civilian government, once again under Prime Minister Rikabi. Known for his diplomatic flair, Rikabi inaugurated a correspondence with Syria's former allies on the Supreme Council to defend the legality of the Declaration of Independence. He reassured the British and French that Syria's independence would not threaten their friendly relationship. Rikabi explained that the long delay in fulfilling the Allies' many promises of independence had become an intolerable strain. The Declaration of Independence was a political necessity: the Syrian people, impatient to gain their rights, were on the brink of revolt. "The enlightened section of the citizenry felt it their duty to correct the situation before it became much worse," he wrote.

Rikabi also asserted Syrians' legal right to claim sovereignty. Syria was ready to take its place among the family of civilized nations, he argued. Independent Syria would cooperate in ensuring peace in the Middle East and would rule according to the principles of the peace conference, with equal justice, regardless of religion or race.

At first, Faisal had reason to believe that France might be persuaded. Cousse and Toulat, the French liaisons, had attended the declaration ceremony. And on March 10, General Gouraud had surprised Faisal by cabling personal congratulations to him, "as a general who had the honor of giving him the Legion of Honor medal at Strasbourg." But as high commissioner, he withheld further comment.

Unbeknownst to the Syrians, however, Gouraud sent a letter the same day to Premier Millerand expressing alarm that a Syrian leaflet proclaimed autonomy for Lebanon within a united Syria, on condition that all foreign influence be excluded. "On the one hand, the Prince announced to me that relations between our two countries can remain friendly. On the other hand, he pretends to impose upon us . . . the creation of a kingdom that promises the exclusion of our influence in Lebanon and the immediate disappearance of the Western Zone."[50]

On March 15, Faisal received word from Paris and London, transmitted through Gouraud. "The French government, in full agreement with the British government, cannot accord the Congress of Damascus the right to determine the future of Syria as well as Palestine, Mesopotamia, and Mosul. These regions were conquered from the Turks by the Allied armies and their future, under examination by the peace conference at this very moment, can only be determined by the Allied Powers acting together," the March 15 cable declared. "The Republic is therefore obliged to declare that it considers the acts of this Congress as null and void."[51]

Four days later, on March 19, the United States Senate voted a second time to reject the Treaty of Versailles and membership in the League of Nations. The "Great Power" that Rida had hailed in 1918 as God's instrument for world peace, and that had inspired establishment of the Syrian Congress in 1919, now abandoned Syrian leaders to fight alone.

Chapter 11

Wilsonism Colonized
at San Remo

The international press reported the Syrian Declaration of Independence through a web of entangling sectarian tensions and imperial ambitions. Gone was the simple joy of liberation that had inspired reporting a year earlier, when journalists still believed that democracy and peace might emerge from the Paris Peace Conference. Now, few photographs of Faisal appeared. Scant notice was paid to the Syrian Congress or the constitution that it was drafting. Despite these disappointments, Syrian leaders maintained faith in the power of the press. The peace conference had proclaimed an era of public diplomacy and open covenants. Diplomats were still forced to take notice of world opinion. But behind closed doors, as Rustum Haidar bitterly discovered, France and Britain continued their old-style imperial dealmaking.

Public Debate on Syria and the Turkish Treaty

On March 16, 1920, *The Times* of London published an article on Faisal's coronation that highlighted the presence of Christian clergymen at the ceremony. The paper portrayed the ceremony as an act of emancipation, noting how Faisal vowed that Arabs "would not consent to be enslaved."[1] However, readers of *The Times* that day also would have noticed reports on protests against the occupation of Constantinople that cast the conflict between the peace conference and Ottoman peoples in sectarian terms. One article quoted Indian Muslims who called the occupation an act of war by Christianity against Islam. They demanded respect for Muslim unity under the Ottoman caliph's spiritual leadership. Letters to The Times demanded Muslims' inclusion in the new world order as a reward for war service and as a fulfillment of Wilson's Twelfth Point, promising a "secure sovereignty" to Turkey.[2]

The eminent British historian Arnold J. Toynbee disputed these Muslims' views in his own letter to The Times: "The bolstering up of Turkey will not alter the real balance of power between Christendom and Islam, and therefore will not allay the fundamental resentment of Moslems," he wrote.[3]

The New York Times supported Faisal's coronation with a front-page headline: "Syria Proclaims Freedom and King." Other headlines declared, "Christians in Syria Back Independence" and "Still a Friend, Faisal Says."[4] "Faisal's position rests on grounds both solid and valid," wrote Frederick Jones Bliss in another front-page article. A retired archaeologist of the Holy Land, Bliss was born in Lebanon and was the brother of Howard Bliss, the Syrian Protestant College president who had testified in support of Syrian self-determination in February 1919. In his article, Bliss maintained that Faisal could be trusted to build a modern, tolerant state. Noting that Christians were among the king's closest advisors, Bliss described Faisal as "democratic, liberal minded, strong, patriotic, not personally ambitious."[5]

In the French press, however, only the socialist L'Humanité expressed such support for Syrian independence. In a March 14 article, the paper called on France to satisfy the Syrian Congress's demands and warned against military aggression. "The times are too troubled to think of raising Arabs against us in Syria; conditions in Cilicia are serious enough, and the clashes at Marash, where we have suffered cruel losses, must serve as a lesson."[6]

Most French papers followed the views of the colonial lobby and de Caix. They rejected the Syrian Congress's authority either to declare independence or to crown Faisal. However, not all of them supported de Caix's proposal to punish Syria, like Turkey, with military occupation. "The so-called Syrian Congress has no mandate," Le Journal des Débats declared, scolding officials for letting events reach such a crisis. In an article titled "The Syrian Hornet's Nest," *L'Homme libre* advised, "Let's be vigilant in safeguarding our protégés in Syria; but let's be more vigilant not to strike an Arab movement that will draw us into expeditions that we must avoid." *Le Temps* also warned, "Any hostile attitude by the Powers will only make it [Congress] more popular among the Muslim masses."[7]

In the French parliament, socialists took up Syria's cause as another battle in their long war against the colonial lobby. Their leader was Marcel Cachin, the son of peasants from Brittany; before the war, he had published reports on France's mistreatment of Arabs in Algeria.[8] In December 1918, Cachin had condemned foreign minister Stephen Pichon's speech asserting France's treaty claims to Syria. He agreed that France must oppose British colonial claims, but not through occupation. Rather, France must reaffirm its friendship with Arabs based on shared republican values of liberty and fraternity, Cachin argued: "Syrians demand to be free: That is France's essential contract."

Now, a year later, Cachin criticized Gouraud's mission as a military threat to Syrians' right to self-government. Clemenceau had rejected any plan for permanent occupation, he argued.[9] (The former premier was still traveling in Egypt and learned of the Syrian declaration through letters received at his hotel in Luxor. Clemenceau made no public comment, but referred to it as "Faisal's Revolution" in a March 19 letter to his son.)[10]

On March 26, 1920, Cachin stood up in the Chamber of Deputies to defend the Syrian Congress. He admitted that voting rights had not yet been extended freely into the Syrian countryside. "But it will come," he insisted. "How can this republican Chamber protest against the general exercise of universal suffrage?" The opposition loudly objected. "All right, I have been misunderstood. Currently in Syria [universal suffrage exists] in the great cities of Syria. These cities are very advanced, you know, very intelligent," Cachin continued. "In Damascus, remarkably, there are a dozen daily papers, which indicates an advanced moral and intellectual level.

"A few days ago, there was a meeting of notables, elected as properly as is possible in that country," Cachin continued. "They made decisions that you must consider quite sacred. They declared they want complete independence in Syria and they chose a regular government. They even chose a king." Protests rose from the Right in the Chamber.

Cachin persisted. "It would be very dangerous to go against the will of these men who fully respect . . . the freedom of every people to govern themselves." Applause from the Left side of the Chamber. "When this assembly met, our High Commissioner in Syria, General Gouraud, sent one of his officers to congratulate Prince Faisal. This officer was praised."

To drive home to French deputies their sacred duty to uphold democracy, Cachin then read out the entire Syrian Declaration of Independence. "Do not believe that Western democracies have made resounding propaganda for five years without bearing fruit," Cachin concluded, referring to propaganda that cast the Great War as a battle for democracy. "The peoples who heard it are astonished today to see that, when they claim their freedom and full independence, we respond by sending cannons and bayonets." The age of imperialism, Cachin declared, was over.[11]

Rustum Haidar's gloom lifted. He sent a triumphant telegram to Faisal that described how Cachin had read the Declaration to the Chamber. Sympathetic journalists sought him out for interviews. But Haidar's enthusiasm was dimmed by the reaction of Lebanese Maronites, who called Faisal a "devil." Their influence was evident when a French diplomat gave a public lecture on Syria that focused only on the need to protect Christians.

In his diary, Haidar complained about the double standard regarding democracy in Syria versus Germany: "Ebert's government represents an assembly elected by the people," he wrote. "But it seems the [Peace] Conference won't recognize the Syrian Congress, which also truly represents Syrians." He lamented that Syrians needed much more money, men, and time to convince Europeans that they were fit for independence. When Haidar visited the Quai d'Orsay to plead Syria's case on March 30, the French still refused to recognize Faisal as king.[12]

By this time, de Caix had already mobilized his networks to silence French supporters of Syrian independence. In the Chamber, the colonial lobby discredited socialists' liberalism by linking it to the Bolshevik threat. From Beirut, de Caix amplified the lobby's warning by suggesting that Faisal himself was a Bolshevik agent. In a March 23 letter to a French delegate to the peace conference, he wrote: "[Faisal plays] on Wilsonism to make M. Cachin cry with tenderness. . . . He will also raise the specter of Bolshevism, poised in Asia, if Europe does not give in to the Arab nation."

De Caix's letter declared openly what he had previously only hinted: the Syrian Arab Kingdom must be destroyed. "We cannot tolerate such a regime for long," he wrote. "[Faisal] will never resign himself to being king of Damascus and Aleppo under French tutelage."[13] De Caix dismissed the Syrian government as "mostly a bluff," and its Congress as "camouflaged Wilsonism" used to mask an extremist attack on France. He accused Syrian deputies of building popular support not through elections, but by attacking Christians in order "to show that we are unable to protect our clients."[14]

Robert de Caix was not alone in seeing the Syrian declaration crisis as an opportunity.

Curzon Comes Out of the Closet

In February, President Woodrow Wilson had defended his principles in sharply worded notes to the London Conference on Turkey. But after the Senate's March 19 vote rejecting the Versailles treaty and the League, Wilson could no longer pretend that the United States had a role in drafting the Turkish peace treaty.

With the American exit from the negotiations, the imperial gloves came off. Even as Britain and France paid lip service to the Supreme Council as an impartial godfather of the League of Nations, they hitched it to their own state interests. Tellingly, Lord Curzon had characterized the League as a confederation of sovereign states—not as a supreme body with authority over the states—in his speech at the League Council's inaugural session in January. His remarks had acute relevance for Syria. As Secretary of State Robert Lansing had warned Wilson a year earlier, the mandate system's fundamental flaw was that it did not establish where sovereignty lay. That left the coop open to the foxes.[15] The issue of sovereignty would remain in question for another year, until the League of Nations established the Permanent Mandates Commission to address it.

And so in April 1920, Britain and France were free to exploit the ambiguity of the mandate system for their own profit. Without restraint from President Wilson, they doubled down on their Middle East designs, as set in their secret December 1, 1918, meeting. What followed was a messy bit of dealmaking that historian Leonard Smith has called "imperial contracting."[16]

The consequences were profound not just for Syria, but also for the future of the League and international law across the Middle East. Britain and France converted the instruments Wilson had intended for the protection of small nations' rights into legal tools of imperialist domination. They used mandates to vacate the rights of the governed in favor of imperial powers, all under the aegis of the League of Nations.

This time around, the prime ministers left the details to be handled by their subordinates, Curzon and de Caix. Curzon believed that the British Empire was an instrument of God's will on Earth. His assistant was none other than Hubert Young, who had accompanied the Arabian army into Damascus in October 1918. While Lloyd George had effectively washed his hands of Syria after withdrawing British troops, Curzon still cast a covetous eye upon it. He did so, cynically, by claiming to uphold Wilson's ideals. "For the safety of our Eastern Empire, I would sooner come to a satisfactory arrangement with the Arabs than I would with the French," Curzon wrote. "Ought we not to play the policy of self-determination for all it is worth?"[17]

De Caix colluded in hijacking the Wilsonian apparatus: he convinced French statesmen to jettison Clemenceau's minimalist interpretation of the mandate in order to impose France's full and exclusive sovereignty. Once awarded, de Caix argued, the mandate would eliminate Britain's interference in Syria and enable the destruction of Faisal's state. De Caix enlisted the support of Paul Cambon, the elderly French ambassador in London and a former governor of Tunisia. The two men ultimately outwitted Curzon, the former viceroy of India. Curzon, more experienced as an administrator than as a politician, walked straight into the trap that de Caix prepared.[18]

For Curzon, the moment of truth came the day he learned of Syria's Declaration of Independence. He loathed the choice before him: to cede Syria to the French or to recognize Syrian sovereignty. To the empire-hungry Curzon, both options regrettably excluded Britain. In February, discussions at the London Conference had virtually awarded the Syrian mandate to France. His hand was forced by Syria's March 8 Declaration. It broadcast to the world that a majority of Syrians favored national independence, a fact that the British had tried to cover up by suppressing the King-Crane report.

Curzon's aide, Hubert Young, favored a compromise: Britain could insist on the Supreme Council's sovereignty over the future of Syria and at the same time signal respect for consent of the governed by promising Faisal's rule under mandate. A thirty-five-year-old former soldier, Young had witnessed Faisal's entry into Damascus in October 1918 and remained one of his strongest supporters at the Foreign Office.[19]

Young later published an account of the crisis that Curzon faced in his negotiations with the French:

> When the news reached London the French Ambassador immediately asked for an interview with Lord Curzon. There was a meeting of the Conference of Ambassadors in Lord Curzon's room that afternoon, and he said he would see the French Ambassador immediately after it. I was in attendance at the meeting, and when tea was brought in after the discussion I reminded Lord Curzon of his promise.
>
> "But I don't know what to say to him," Curzon replied. "Come out with me and let us discuss it quietly." He led me into the tiny cloak-room next door to his room and we started an animated discussion among the hats and coats of the assembled diplomats. I wanted repudiation of the Damascus proceedings to be coupled with some kind of encouraging message, but Lord Curzon did not agree, and we were still arguing when one of the secretaries put his head in and tried to say something. . . .

After a few minutes the secretary again put in his head and was nearly blown through the roof. "Cannot I be left undisturbed for one moment?' cried the Secretary of State. "I am discussing a most important question." "I am sorry, sir," said the secretary, "but the French Ambassador is still waiting in your room and wants to know if he is to stay or go away." Lord Curzon turned to me impatiently and said, "You are the man who is preventing me from seeing the Ambassador. Why do you not let me say what I want to say?" "Because I think you are wrong, sir," I said. "And I think you are wrong," he replied. "Well, I must go and see him, and say something," and he sailed away.[20]

Curzon and Cambon subsequently agreed to send the joint message to Faisal refusing to recognize his status as king or the legality of the Syrian Congress. The March 15 note, conveyed by Gouraud (see Chapter 10), invited Faisal to Europe to settle Syria's future status, an act that would force him to recognize the Supreme Council's sovereignty over Syria. In effect, the two men agreed to uphold the edifice of nineteenth-century empire by ignoring the Wilsonian support of Congress as an elected representative of the Syrian people with a voice in the adjudication of colonial questions. Cambon and Curzon accomplished this not by openly disputing Wilson's principle, but by dismissing Congress as a "self-constituted body without representative character or authority." Their scheme disquieted even Lloyd George, who sent a private note to Curzon that very day, saying he was "very perturbed about the decision of the Foreign Office . . . to refuse to recognize the Damascus decision."[21]

Ultimately, Curzon won support for his policy because of Syrians' inclusion of Palestine in their declaration, and the simultaneous declaration by Iraqis in Damascus of independence in Mesopotamia. Zionists saw peril in ceding authority to the Damascus government, and hard-liners in the India Office opposed any form of Arab self-rule in Mesopotamia. All feared a slippery slope—if one occupied people were granted sovereignty, then others would demand the same. As Young later disclosed to the British parliament, the Foreign Office was forced to accept a *"parallélisme exacte"*: if Britain wanted a free hand in Mesopotamia, it had to accord France such license in Syria.[22]

The Syrians might have stood a chance of winning British and French support had they chosen to declare only partial independence, of the East Zone in the Syrian hinterland. British imperialists were angered that the March 8 declaration not only included southern Syria—British-occupied Palestine—but also was accompanied by a separate Iraqi declaration of independence. And French liberals could never have prevailed against the colonial lobby to cede Lebanon. A partial call was never a political option, however. Only half of the deputies who convened on March 8 were from the East Zone. The other half came from Lebanon and Palestine.[23] Because the Syrian Declaration was an assertion of right and principle, it would have been difficult to exclude some Syrians in favor of others.

On April 1, Faisal wrote a desperate letter to President Woodrow Wilson, begging him to come to Syria's aid. "[U]se your power and influence to defend our cause according to your just principles," Faisal pleaded. His appeal went unanswered.[24] It had been almost exactly a year since Faisal shared a rare glass of champagne with T. E. Lawrence to celebrate the Supreme Council's vote to send the commission of inquiry to Syria. It had been six months since the King-Crane report was shelved after Wilson's stroke. And it had been barely two weeks since the US Senate had foreclosed any American role in the League of Nations.

For the first two weeks of April, Rustum Haidar tried to gain an audience with Lord Curzon. Millerand's staff at the Quai d'Orsay insisted they could not recognize Faisal unless the British did. So Haidar had traveled to London with Faisal's second envoy, Nuri al-Said. They found Philippe Berthelot at his Hyde Park hotel. Haidar knew Berthelot well, from the intense period of negotiations that had led to the January 6 accord with Clemenceau. Berthelot had lost his senior post at the French foreign ministry when Clemenceau resigned, but had later been assigned as a delegate to the London Conference on Turkey. Berthelot regretted that he could not help. He warned the Syrians that Millerand did not share Clemenceau's sympathetic views regarding Faisal. "Personally, I endorse his being named king of Syria. Please pay my respects to him and his wife," Berthelot said in parting.[25]

The Syrian envoys decided to seek Curzon's leverage against Millerand, and to ask for a renewal of Britain's subsidy to the Hijaz delegates. Their salaries had not been paid for some time. Finally, on April 15, Curzon agreed to a meeting. They would have to come to his residence, because he was ill.

Rustum Haidar and Nuri al-Said arrived at Curzon's home at six fifteen in the evening and did not leave until nearly eight o'clock. Every moment was full of anguish. Curzon claimed he could not recognize the Syrian government, because it was in occupied enemy territory under a temporary military regime. The Syrians rejected his logic: the peace conference had recognized Armenia's independence, so why not Syria's? Both had been part of the Ottoman Empire—and both had rebelled against it. Curzon deflected their argument by claiming —contrary to the views he himself had previously expressed—that only the peace conference had the authority to decide Syria's fate. The conference was scheduled to reconvene in San Remo, Italy, in two days.

Curzon feigned regret that Faisal had not accepted his invitation to attend the conference. Haidar reminded Curzon that if the Allies would recognize his title as king, Faisal would attend. Hubert Young, Curzon's aide, intervened to strike a compromise. They composed a new telegram for Faisal:

> We have no objection to the independence of Syria but this
> can only be recognized by the Peace Conference. You may
> assure the people that it is in order to enable us to recognize
> it officially that your presence is essential. We fully realize
> that conditions have changed and that you are now no longer
> merely an allied commander but it is only the Peace Conference
> that can recognize you in any other capacity.[26]

In reality, Curzon still intended to collude with de Caix to void the January 6 accord that had recognized Syria's provisional independence.

The Wilsonian Moment was passing quickly into history. Anti-imperialist liberals in Europe voiced only muted opposition in the press. American voices had gone silent.

To the Syrians' dismay, Howard Bliss, the president of the Syrian Protestant College, fell ill with tuberculosis and soon died. Syrians were devastated. Members of the royal court, the Congress, and the cabinet, including war minister Yusuf al-Azmeh, sent passionate condolences to his family. "To Mrs. Bliss," wrote Faisal's chamberlain, Ihsan al-Jabri, "Your affliction is the affliction of the whole country." Rashid Rida wrote, "The Syrian Congress extends its sympathies" upon the loss of a "beloved President." The Arab Club, labeled extremist by the French and British alike, organized a public memorial in Damascus "to reveal the high esteem the American Nation and her noble Principle[s] have in the hearts of the Syrians."27

Syria's fate would now be determined by veterans of the great imperial game, statesmen who met in heavily draped Victorian hotels and offices. Curzon and Cambon took no notice that the Syrians demonstrated an ability to practice modern government. French intelligence reports on the impressive and productive hearings conducted by the Syrian Congress were disregarded.28

Notably absent in these crucial weeks was the man who had first publicized the Syrian cause, T. E. Lawrence. "I failed badly in attempting a piece of work which a little more resolution would have pushed through or [which I should have] left untouched," Lawrence confessed in February to Stewart Newcombe, a former fellow officer.29

His letter betrayed the feelings of a depressed man. Since September, when he suggested to Curzon that independent Syria should be recognized just as Poland and Slovakia had been, Lawrence had suffered political isolation. Hubert Young personally condemned Lawrence for airing diplomatic secrets in The Times. And in the end, publicity had not helped the Syrian cause. Britain had washed its hands of Faisal, forcing him to go to Paris.

Lawrence suffered acutely from the effects of steady press coverage, which made him famous for his exploits in Arabia just as he faced total defeat in London. Most galling was that Lloyd George continued to praise him to reporters as a hero.30 In response, Lawrence decided to change his name. He wished he could change his face as well, so that he would be "more beloved." He slipped into hiding, disclosing his new address to only a few people. "I have abandoned Oxford and wander about town in Pimlico [London]," he confided to Newcombe, his old comrade. "It's nicer than looking at Lord Curzon."

In his room at Pimlico, Lawrence struggled to finish the manuscript that would be published, too late, as *Seven Pillars of Wisdom*. He condemned the "disgraceful bargain" the British made with France in order to gain Mesopotamia. As atonement for his failure, Lawrence channeled his moral disgust into his book. The introduction to its first edition called out the stubborn racism of the international system:

> If I have restored to the East some self-respect, a goal, ideals:
> if I have made the standard of rule of white over red more
> exigent, I have fitted those peoples in a degree for the new
> commonwealth in which the dominant races will forget their
> brute achievements, and white and red and yellow and brown
> and black will stand up together without side-glances in the
> service of the world.[31]

Wilson Dressed for the Imperial Ball at San Remo

Events rushed forward. By the time Haidar met him, Curzon had already shared confidential reports on the Syrian Congress with Cambon. In secret meetings, the two men ironed out a common understanding on the mandates. Contrary to the telegram composed by Young, Curzon proposed that the peace conference confirm Faisal as king only after he had been confirmed in a valid election. But Cambon refused this proposal, insisting that the conference could not recognize the decisions of the illegal Congress. Elections could be held only after France assumed the mandate. The two men finally agreed to omit details on governance in the mandates that the Supreme Council would confer at San Remo.[32]

De Caix still feared that Berthelot might "let Syria go to the devil." Berthelot was ignoring de Caix's alarmist telegrams from Beirut. In desperation, de Caix unleashed his panic on the junior delegate to the conference, Albert Kammerer. De Caix warned the delegate that "Wilsonian nitwits" were ignoring the Syrian Congress's aim to boot France out of Lebanon as well as Syria. "When men like M. Cachin support Sharifianism as the expression of a conscious national will, they are usually motivated by a mania to oppose all expansionist policies of our country, rather than a desire to assure peace and progress in the Orient," he wrote. De Caix also advised Kammerer to beware of the opinions of the Damascus liaisons Toulat and Cousse, who worshipped "St. Faisal." He recommended that they be transferred out of Syria.[33]

Meanwhile, Gouraud warned Millerand that France should prepare for a violent Syrian reaction to the mandate. "The Damascus opposition is ready to rise against us at the least pretext," he wrote. "I am waiting for the date of arrival for six battalions."[34]

On April 17, Curzon crossed the Channel, paused in Paris, and then traveled south to San Remo in the company of the French delegates. Lloyd George traveled separately by sea, docking at Marseille. The Italians played host as the delegates converged upon the Villa Devachan, an ornate hotel in the lush hills that overlooked the Italian Riviera. This was to be a relatively small session of the Peace Conference, with only two representatives from each of the four principal Allied powers. Wilson, upset about French aggression in the Rhineland, had only begrudgingly authorized the American ambassador to Italy to attend as an observer.[35] Opening receptions at the seaside resort took on the atmosphere of a holiday.

Faisal did not attend. To protest the Allies' refusal to recognize his son as king of Syria, Sharif Hussein broke off all ties to the peace conference.[36] That left Rustum Haidar and Nuri al-Said to confront a dilemma. As employees of Sharif Hussein, they no longer had standing to attend at San Remo. How could Arabs be absent from this momentous decision on their fate? With no official funding, they scraped together the price of two train tickets.

At the conference, Syria was almost an afterthought. Discussion focused on the Turkish threat and the Armenians' plight. The mood sobered as the powers realized that none of them had the will or the means to save Armenia. Lloyd George later confessed that European commitments limited their ability to handle the Armenian crisis. "[The Allies] had incurred heavy obligations involving the employment of considerable forces for some time—on the Rhine, in Syria, Palestine and Mesopotamia and also in Constantinople and the Straits," he wrote in his memoir. So Lloyd George and Millerand fatefully decided to postpone a decision by asking the United States to take the Armenian mandate.[37] That decision virtually ensured that no Armenian state would ever be erected in Anatolia.

Oil was the second hot topic at San Remo. With tensions still high in the German Rhineland, France and Britain worried about the need for petroleum in future wars. On the morning of April 24, they finalized the deal that had been broached back in December 1918: France would receive a 25 percent share of Mosul's oil; Britain would route the pipeline to suit French preferences. Millerand and Lloyd George congratulated one another on their near total agreement on the Turkish peace treaty.[38] The Americans, by contrast, were "stunned" to learn of their exclusion from a share of Iraqi oil, condemning the April 24 deal as a violation of the mandate principle of open markets.[39]

That afternoon, the Council took up the question of mandates, beginning with Palestine. Berthelot surprised the British with a last-minute objection to including the Balfour Declaration in the mandate charter. His intent was less to protect Arabs in Palestine than to force Britain to respect France's claim to hands-off control of Syria. Curzon stubbornly defended the Balfour promise of a Jewish home, assuring Berthelot that Britain would honor the political rights of non-Jewish peoples. The French and Italians also pressured the British to grant them the right to protect their religious institutions in the Holy Land. This satisfied Catholic lobbyists.[40]

Nuri al-Said and Rustum Haidar arrived on April 24. By then, the hotels in San Remo were swarming with lobbyists and journalists. "We drove to the Grand Hôtel des Anglais," Haidar wrote. "We found the place only with great difficulty because the city was full of people. The Italian delegation was at the hotel. They told us the British were at the Royal Hotel and the French in the Savoy."

Curzon could not contain his annoyance at their arrival. "Syrians, Zionists, Armenians," he wrote to his wife. "They take rooms at the same hotel as we are in and they dog our footsteps wherever we go." Nuri al-Said complained, too. Out of all the peoples who faced future rule under a mandate, only the Armenians had been invited to speak to the Supreme Council at San Remo.[41]

At eleven o'clock in the morning on April 25, delegates finally met at the Villa Devachan to discuss the mandates for Syria, Palestine, and Mesopotamia. Berthelot proposed that the Turkish treaty explicitly assign the mandates and set their political boundaries. Curzon objected. He still intended to use Wilsonism as an instrument to preserve British prerogatives. "If we want to obtain peace in this part of the world, it is necessary that we seek to live in harmony with Prince Faisal," he said. Curzon insisted that Faisal be present at any discussions regarding his authority and Syria's relationship to Palestine. "If Prince Faisal arrives after the Conference has already assigned Palestine, established its boundaries, and settled the Zionism question, there may be serious protests in the new state, which he will use to his advantage. It is better not to offer him this opportunity," Curzon argued.

Berthelot demanded that the mandates be assigned immediately. "We must come to agreement so that neither France nor England can reopen discussions by relying on Prince Faisal or on any events that might occur in the region." He made it clear that France intended to assert total control over Syria once the mandate had been assigned.

This time, Lloyd George backed Berthelot against Curzon. "The difficulties that had existed on the subject of Syria have disappeared," he said. Over Curzon's head, he agreed to insert into the treaty the text that Millerand proposed: "The mandatories chosen by the Principal Allied Powers are France for Syria, Great Britain for Mesopotamia and Palestine." Mandate charters, which would set the terms of mandatory rule, would be drawn up later and submitted to the League of Nations.[42]

When discussion turned to the Hijaz, in Arabia, Lloyd George spoke in favor of holding off. "I think Prince Faisal should be present for this discussion," he said. Berthelot admitted that Faisal's envoy, Nuri al-Said, had just arrived and demanded to be heard. "But I had to tell him that the Conference will be concluded after our meeting this afternoon." Curzon then opened the discussion, wherein the Council agreed to award the Hijaz independence from Turkish rule. The Syrian Arabs were never heard at San Remo.

Haidar learned of the mandate assignments later in the evening on April 25. He had awkwardly accepted an invitation from the British to attend dinner at the Royal Hotel, only to find guests celebrating the partition of Syria. His diary entry described a pleasant dinner conversation with Zionists, who talked of future economic cooperation. Lloyd George came to their table and inquired about their thoughts on Prince Faisal. An Arab guest corrected the prime minister, saying, "King Faisal." Lloyd George made a joke and laughed it off. Britain's future high commissioner of Palestine, Herbert Samuel, told Haidar that he personally accepted Faisal as king of Syria. But Samuel wondered whether France would recognize Faisal's reign. Neither Haidar nor Nuri al-Said slept well that night.[43]

At the train station the next day, April 26, Millerand proclaimed France's victory to the press, then hurried back to Paris to report to the Chamber. Curzon departed San Remo unaware that he had fallen into Robert de Caix's trap. T. E. Lawrence, by contrast, immediately understood what the French had won. Forecasting armed revolt, he joined a prominent group of critics in sending a petition to Lloyd George that urged him to take the Middle East out of the hands of Curzon's Foreign Office.[44]

Zionists celebrated the San Remo decision as the final achievement of their dream for a Jewish homeland in Palestine. Rabbi Samuel Wise, who had introduced Faisal to Wilson in January 1919, personally thanked the American president and praised him at a Zionist celebration of the mandate in New York City.[45]

The Arabs, by contrast, responded to San Remo with bitter disenchantment about the promise of a new world order. The facade of transparency simply shrouded old-style imperial diplomacy. The Supreme Council had simply dressed the secret deal of December 1, 1918, between France and Britain in the deceptive clothing of a mandate. Only Italy had abstained from the deceptive charade, and then out of its own grievances more than adherence to principle.

Michel Lutfallah lodged the first Syrian protest. "The decision of the San Remo conference concerning the dismemberment of Syria annihilates its political, geographic, and ethnic integrity," Lutfallah wrote in an April 26 telegram sent on behalf of the Syrian Union Party. "This arbitrary decision contradicts all Allied declarations and breaks the heart of the Syrian Arab Nation."

Haidar and Said did not yet comprehend that France regarded the mandate as a writ to unseat Faisal's government. Only on April 28, after returning to Paris, did Haidar learn the truth, from newspaper reports on Millerand's speech to the French Congress.

Two days later, Haidar lodged a forceful protest against the San Remo decision, which he also sent to a Damascus newspaper. Haidar focused on the violation of Article 22 of the League covenant, which required that popular opinion be a principal consideration in assigning the mandate.

> The Hijaz delegation wishes to inform the Supreme Council of its surprise at learning, through public sources, of the decision taken at the San Remo conference on the Arab countries detached from Turkey. We cannot help noting a certain contradiction between the principles it [the decision] embodies and the promises of liberty and self-determination that have been solemnly proclaimed.

Not only had the Council not consulted the people; it had willfully rejected the will of the population as publicly expressed to the King-Crane Commission and in the Declaration of Independence. In short, the Entente powers had betrayed their loyal allies, the Arabs, who had fought beside them and hoped to take their rightful place in the family of civilized nation-states, Haidar concluded. "The San Remo decision destroys this hope."[46]

PART IV

The Constitution:
A Civil Weapon
Against Colonization

Chapter 12

The Sheikh versus the King:
A Parliamentary Revolution

In the seven weeks between the March 8 Declaration of Independence and the April 25 San Remo accord, the Syrian Congress continued to meet. Even though Faisal had agreed to Congress's oversight on all issues regarding Syrian independence, he did not routinely share diplomatic correspondence with the deputies.

In ignorance of developments in London, Paris, and San Remo, Congress drafted articles of the constitution. Like Faisal, deputies loyal to Fatat and the Syrian Union Party regarded the establishment of a modern constitutional regime as a "civil weapon of the nation" against colonialism.[1] They also regarded the constitution as their legal assertion of power against Faisal's prerogative. Leaders of Congress aimed to go beyond constitutionalism to establish a truly democratic regime.

Asserting Parliamentary Sovereignty

On March 27, 1920, the Syrian Congress summoned Prime Minister Rida al-Rikabi to its chamber, now located in the Abid office building facing Marjeh Square. Seats had been installed in a large hall on the second floor in front of a platform for speakers. Offices for the Congress president and staff were furnished nearby. Izzat Darwazeh, as Congress secretary, had overseen the move from the Arab Club just three days before.[2]

The physical move prepared the ground for the political revolution that occurred inside the chamber that day. Congress president Hashim al-Atassi welcomed his old friend Rikabi and asked him to take a seat on the speakers' platform. The two men knew one another from Ottoman times. Rikabi, a fair-headed man with a reddish beard who came from a prestigious Damascene family, had outranked Atassi as a military general with the title "pasha," and had served as governor of Basra and Medina, deputy governor of Jerusalem, and military commander of Baghdad. Atassi, despite his gaunt face and grizzled goatee, was twelve years Rikabi's junior, at age forty-four. He came from the leading family of a provincial town (Homs) and had served before the war as a mid-level Ottoman administrator in nearly every district of Greater Syria, including Homs, Hama, Baniyas, Baalbek, Tyre, Salt, and Jaffa.[3]

In the old days, a prime minister would have clearly outranked a leader of parliament. That was certainly the case in the Ottoman Empire, under which the grand vizier was all-powerful, responsible only to the sultan. In the summer of 1919, when the Syrian Congress was first convened, Rikabi had enjoyed tremendous authority as the civilianized military governor of Syria. But his power had diminished in November, when the popular uprising and Congress had forced Prince Zaid to remove him from office. However, upon returning in January, Faisal reappointed him, preferring a mature and pragmatic statesman who recognized the need for diplomacy in dealing with the Europeans.

That morning in March, though, the tables had turned. Atassi had summoned Rikabi to submit his cabinet's political program for congressional approval. Rikabi had at first refused to appear, sparking the Syrian Arab Kingdom's first crisis in a battle of legislative against executive power.

Shortly after Independence Day, congressional deputies voted for a resolution requiring that cabinet ministers be responsible to them as the people's representatives, not to the king. While Atassi did not have the demeanor of a revolutionary, he cultivated influence as an honest broker among deputies from the many regions in Syria where he had previously worked. Since March 8, he had quietly worked behind the scenes—as president of both the Congress and the constitutional committee—to set the democratic terms of independence.

Faisal and Rikabi had immediately denounced the vote and ignored the summons. But Fatat leaders in Congress dug in their heels. They had been fighting against monarchical tyranny since the 1908 revolution. To assure democracy, they believed, sovereignty must lie with the Syrian people and the legislature, not in the executive branch.

The Sheikh to the King:
Islam Demands Democracy

Three days passed in a tense stalemate. Finally, Rashid Rida stepped in to mediate. During one of his usual morning visits to the royal residence, the king asked about the sheikh's view of the crisis. Rida replied that he was surprised by the congressional vote, which was nearly unanimous. He personally had abstained from voting because he thought the complex issue needed more discussion. Faisal, encouraged by the possibility that he had found an ally, invited Rida to elaborate.

Rida paused in his reply to the king. Back in Beirut, he had warned Faisal that he would not become a yes-man. So now he decided to speak bluntly. Their debate that day would become a legendary moment in Syrian history. [4]

"My opinion is that the policy must be implemented once it has been approved," Rida advised.

Faisal was disappointed. "Congress doesn't have that power, because it is not a parliament," the king insisted.

"Yes, it does! It has more power than a parliament because it is a constituent assembly," replied Rida.

"I am the one who founded it and I don't give it the right to obstruct the government," Faisal declared.

"No, it is the Congress that appointed *you*! You were just an Allied general under Allenby's leadership. The Congress made you king of Syria," Rida retorted. "It has the superior power, since it represents the nation. That is according to the law of your religion, Islam; and according to all modern laws."

The king fell silent. He had not expected Rida to justify Congress's power with religious law. Since he was the victorious commander of the Arab Revolt, Faisal thought, Islamic law must surely be on his side. Ottoman sultans had justified their rule through Islam for centuries.

Rida, however, belonged to a new breed of religious reformers. They believed that Islam did not support unbridled kingship but rather required its leaders to consult the people. Rida's mentor, Muhammad Abduh, had supported a constitutional revolution in Egypt in 1881. At the turn of the century, Rida had published Abd al-Rahman al-Kawakibi's book against tyranny in his own magazine, *The Lighthouse*. Along with many leading Ottoman clerics, he had supported the 1908 revolution against the despotic Sultan Abdulhamid. And in 1915, Rida had drafted an "organic law" for the future Syrian Arab state that envisioned "a sort of republic" that would separate religion from state, base sovereignty in the people, and privilege parliamentary power over the executive. It became the basis for the Syrian Union Party's constitutional proposal presented to the King-Crane Commission in 1919.[5]

To Islamic modernists like Rida, popular sovereignty was necessary not only to counterbalance the despotic tendencies of kings, but also to guarantee Muslims' independence against European imperialism. Only with full sovereignty could their societies exercise the fair and just rule of law. Rida believed that legislatures exercising the authority of popular sovereignty could block corruptible monarchs from selling out their countries to Europeans, as the Iranian shah and the Egyptian khedive had done in the late nineteenth century. Rida also believed that liberal constitutionalism was an authentic expression of Islamic values, not a Western corruption. As he explained to readers of *The Lighthouse*, leaders of Islam's first generation taught that authority should lie with knowledgeable representatives chosen by the people. Rida believed so strongly in Islam's essential democracy that he had earned an arrest warrant during the 1908 revolution for demanding an elected parliament that would govern through leaders of merit, against the corrupt cronyism of the Ottoman sultan.[6]

Faisal also embraced the principle of constitutional monarchy. In January, his government's official newspaper, *The Capital*, had even affirmed its commitment to democracy in a front-page editorial. The two main principles of democracy, the paper declared, were that laws must be based on equality and justice, and that "power lies in the hands of the people, as exercised by representatives elected to draft those laws."[7]

But the king felt he had already given up enough power. In discussions before Independence Day, he had demanded the right to dissolve the Congress after the declaration. Rida and Fatat leaders, however, had insisted that Congress remain in session as a constituent assembly and as a temporary legislature. Once the constitution was ratified, they argued, elections could be held for a true parliament. The two sides then struck a compromise: Congress would remain in session on the condition that it wield power over the cabinet only in matters concerning Syrian independence.

That compromise was now a problem for Faisal. He felt that he could not trust inexperienced deputies in a time of crisis. Britain had already occupied Constantinople and arrested 150 Turkish nationalists. France would be likely to exploit that precedent to justify the use of force against Arabs, he feared.

But Rida did not back down. He suspected that Faisal had agreed to become king only to gain the freedom to negotiate unilaterally with France. "Congress placed a condition on the formation of your government—that it must answer to it on all matters regarding independence. The political program of this government is directly related to maintaining that independence," Rida explained.

Faisal still did not budge. Rida warned Faisal that if he did not mend the rift with Congress, there would be dire consequences. "It will make us look very bad and give foreigners an excuse to claim we are not fit for independence. This, my Majesty, you will not accept."

The king and the sheikh brought their argument to a meeting that afternoon with Prime Minister Rikabi and Prince Zaid. We have no records of what they said, but in the end, Faisal relented and agreed to obey the summons.

That is how Rikabi came to appear before the Congress on March 27, 1920, a day that marked the fulfillment of the revolution Fatat had fought for since 1908. The Syrian prime minister was not the personal assistant of the monarch; he was the servant of the legislature. Rikabi

consequently outlined his plans to develop the economy, expand education, establish a proper administration, and defend the country. The
deputies debated the merits of these proposals and then gave Rikabi
their vote of confidence.[8]

The revolution at Damascus was distinctively democratic compared with the Turkish national movement that was emerging simultaneously north of Syria, in Anatolia. Like the Syrians, the Turks
had organized a congress in late 1919 to defy the dictates of the Paris
Peace Conference. On March 19, their leader, Mustafa Kemal, called
for elections to an independent parliament at Ankara, the Grand
Nationalist Assembly. The Ankara government opposed the Ottoman
sultan's regime in Constantinople, which had capitulated to European occupation. Like the Syrians, the Turks declared independence
by invoking Wilson's principles. And like the Syrian Congress, the
Grand National Assembly began drafting a constitution in 1920.
But the Turkish movement differed in critical ways. First, Mustafa
Kemal commanded formidable military power, built on the remnant
of the Ottoman army that had been posted on the Russian border.
While Kemal could back nationalists' demands with force, Faisal
had only the "civil weapon" of the law. Consequently, the Turkish
movement was built on the supreme military power of Mustafa
Kemal; the Grand National Assembly remained weak. Second, in
contrast to the Syrians' revival of the liberal and inclusive principles
of 1908, the Turkish movement explicitly defended Turkish and
Muslim claims to Anatolia against those of Christian Greeks and
Armenians. The Turkish constitution would include neither the
protections of civil rights nor the guarantees of equality among
citizens that the Syrians' did.[9]

From comments like Rida's to Faisal, we can surmise another reason
why the Syrian Congress was more motivated than its Turkish counterpart to establish democracy: it needed to prove itself to the Great
Powers at Paris, where capacity for self-rule was ostensibly measured
in liberal terms. The Turks were not threatened with a mandate and
were in complete revolt against the Supreme Council. Syrian leaders
were snared in the Paris peace process. Like nationalists in Egypt's
1919 revolution, they understood that including non-Muslims was

essential to attaining independence. France and Britain used claims of protecting non-Muslims from Muslim tyranny to justify their rule: Lebanon was to be a haven for Christians, and Palestine a homeland for Jews. They maintained the pretense of extending similar protection over an Armenian homeland. The Syrians aimed to block Europeans' sectarian project by rejecting sectarianism and promoting a democracy that would include citizens of all religions.

By contrast, the Turkish movement responded to the European threat by building an explicitly and exclusionary Turkish Muslim state. It was built upon the morbid foundation of war crimes that had aimed to cleanse Anatolia of Armenian and Greek Christians. Turkish liberals who opposed this exclusionary nationalism were weakened by association with European occupiers, especially after the Supreme Council declared all Turkish people responsible for the mass murder of Armenians.[10]

The Syrian leaders' preference for democracy was not merely an opportunistic tactic, however. They acted from long-held political conviction. Many of them had joined the Decentralization Party before the war to fight for the equality of Arabs, Christians, and other minorities in the Ottoman parliament. Given the circumstances in 1919–1920, their designation of Syria as an Arab nation must be understood in an inclusive spirit, bridging the religious differences to unite Arabic-speakers. At the time, Armenian-speakers were expected to return to their homeland in Anatolia. The Kurdish population in what is today northeastern Syria resided in a distant frontier zone far from Faisal's consciousness and unvisited by the King-Crane Commission. Turkish-speaking former Ottoman officials were the one group singled out for exclusion from the Syrian nation.

"The Arabs have always been the most democratic of peoples and were the first to teach the world equality," Sheikh Kamil al-Qassab proclaimed in a speech attended by Faisal and published in a Damascus newspaper on April 12. Qassab praised the king for permitting Congress to complete the independence that he had fought for and for his effort to explain the truth about Syria to the Great Powers. "We desire every nation in the civilized world to see that we are a self-subsisting people," he continued, according to a rough English translation of the speech submitted to the Foreign Office two weeks before San Remo.[11]

For Congress president Atassi, this was a personally significant moment, to realize the democratic dreams of nearly a half century, since his father had joined the first Ottoman parliament of 1876. That parliament had initially accorded a disproportionate number of seats to non-Muslims as a strategy to hold the empire together. But Sultan Abdulhamid suspended parliament during a war with Russia and promoted an Islamic ideology instead. As mayor of their hometown, Homs, during that time, Atassi's father had permitted Christians to ring their church bells. When conservative Muslims complained to Istanbul, he was ousted from his post. In Atassi's view, sectarian division more than anything else had caused the empire's downfall. He now intended to ensure equality of all Syrians under the rule of law.[12]

Under Izzat Darwazeh's efficient management, Congress immediately put these ideas into action. Darwazeh's secretariat strictly enforced rules of procedure to guard against cronyism. It issued new identity cards and set a monthly salary schedule for all deputies. It organized congressional votes to approve a democratic set of procedures. Speakers could join debate only by placing their names on a list. No decision could be taken without a quorum—a majority of Congress members present in the room. Resolutions were to be adopted with a simple majority of votes among delegates present. Newspapers published weekly reports on Congress's activities and its statements on public issues. Congress also established standing committees to develop policy on taxes, the drafting of the constitution, and foreign affairs. By April, it had become a truly independent branch of government.

However, even as the deputies grappled with constitutional issues, they continued to worry about Syria's military weakness. Turkish nationalists had captured control of an Ottoman army stationed far east of Constantinople. But the Syrian government had relatively few forces and even less matériel. The Ottomans had either taken armaments with them or destroyed these in their retreat. Syrians could not equip their new army, because they were hemmed in on all sides by Allied powers that limited the import of weapons. And their dynamic military commander, Yasin al-Hashimi, had been kidnapped and transported to Palestine by the British.

Rida had supported the Declaration of Independence as a way of staking a political claim to Syrian territory in advance of military claims. "But I thought that without a defensive force that the country can rely on, these facts on the ground would have no value," he recalled. During the month of April, Rida pressured both Faisal and Rikabi to build a national defense force out of Bedouin tribes. He was deeply frustrated by Rikabi's inaction. At heart, the prime minister sympathized with Faisal on prioritizing a diplomatic compromise and remained unconvinced that Syria could ever build a force to resist France.[13]

A Constitution to Secure the People's Sovereignty

This political background explains why Syrian politicians gave priority to writing a constitution even as the threat of a French invasion loomed. Deputies took to heart Faisal's directive to make the constitution both a "civil weapon" to block colonial rule and a "basis for democratic life."[14]

Some Syrians even compared themselves to the Americans who had gathered in Philadelphia in 1787. As the official newspaper, *The Capital*, put it, "The difference between the American government and the Arab government will be this: the first is a constitutional republic, the latter will be a constitutional monarchy."[15] Like the Americans, Syrians labored under pressure to unite their people—and extract tax revenues from them—in a common defense against foreign threats.[16]

Unlike the Americans, the Syrian constituent assembly did not work in secret. From their rooms overlooking Marjeh Square, the members could hear the sound of popular rallies. Newspapers reported on their debates. Women, minorities, and progressives lobbied against traditional interests for a more inclusive polity. Religious conservatives rallied to protect religious tradition and clerical authority from elitist reforms that appeared too secular or too European.

Drafting the constitution was, in the best democratic tradition, a passionate exercise in crafting a social contract. Congress leaders understood that public engagement—such as the American constitution had earned through state ratification—ensured the staying power of constitutions.[17] Unlike constitutions imposed from above that were then quickly suspended—as in Tunisia in 1861 and the Ottoman Empire in 1876—the Syrian Constitution promised to be a living document forged at the popular level.

In addition to Atassi and Darwazeh, the constitutional committee included four lawyers, two Muslim clerics, and two civilians, one of whom was Christian.[18] For months they had quietly met at the Arab Club to study Ottoman and European constitutions. Just as Wilson had advised in his text *The State,* they sought to design a government suited to the particular conditions of their country. Their starting point was the Damascus Program presented to the King-Crane Commission: Syria must be sovereign; it must unite all three zones; and it must treat all its peoples equally, regardless of sect. Zionism, as a threat to these goals, was to be rejected.

The first three articles the committee presented to Congress were: (1) The Syrian Arab Kingdom's government is a civil, parliamentary monarchy. Its capital is Damascus, and the religion of the king is Islam. (2) The Syrian Kingdom's provinces form a political unit that may not be partitioned. (3) The constitution guarantees Syria's provinces administrative autonomy and grants Congress the power to determine their boundaries (this third article was later omitted).[19]

Concerning the king's powers, the committee proposed to require the king to swear to "respect the divine laws, remain loyal to the nation, and uphold the constitution" (Article 6). The king would be commander in chief; however, any declaration of war and any peace treaty would be subject to Congress's approval. No member of the royal family could serve in the cabinet. Other articles reviewed in April addressed less controversial matters, such as the administration of the courts, the disposition of Ottoman imperial lands, commercial and naval laws, and the public treasury.

These initial articles codified understandings recently reached between Faisal and the Independence Party. They also revealed the

Syrian Constitution as the rebellious child of its Ottoman predecessor. In the 1909 constitution, Article 1 stipulated that the Ottoman provinces formed an indivisible whole (as similarly stated in the Syrians' second article), and Article 2 established Constantinople as the imperial capital (as in Syria's first article). But Article 3 of the Ottoman constitution had set terms of rule that Syrian Arabs rejected in their constitution:

> The imperial Ottoman sovereignty, which carries with it the Supreme Caliphate of Islam, falls to the eldest prince of the House of Osman. . . . On his accession the Sultan shall swear before parliament . . . to respect provisions of the Sheri [Islamic law] and the Constitution and to be loyal to the country and the nation.[20]

The Syrian articles omitted reference to the caliphate, and in place of "Islamic law" they substituted "respect for divine laws." The vaguer language reflected the committee's effort to reach compromise among factions. In a similar spirit, the Syrian Constitution notably omitted anything like the Ottoman articles 4 through 6, concerning the sultan's sacred person and his role as protector of the Muslim faith, and the legal immunity of his family.

The virtual disestablishment of Islam was revolutionary. Aside from the requirement that the king be Muslim, Faisal was to be a constitutional monarch with no sacred status. None of the articles on individual rights, the legislature's promulgation of law, or the law courts even mentioned Islamic law.

Articles proposed later in April departed even further from the Ottoman model to lay the basis for a truly democratic regime. Articles 9 to 26 proposed to empower citizens with a full range of civil and social rights, affirming freedom of belief, association, and speech; protecting citizens from torture, arbitrary arrest, or exile; banning forced labor; protecting private property and the home from unwarranted state confiscation and searches; and guaranteeing public education for all children. All Syrians, without distinction, would be equal before the law.

Other articles granted power to the legislature that the Ottoman parliament had never enjoyed and ensured the separation of powers against old, corrupt habits. The constitutional committee proposed a bicameral legislature, outlining its powers and electoral procedures in articles 47 to 95. It also proposed to grant suffrage to every Syrian in good legal standing of age twenty or more (gender was unspecified but presumed male). A Chamber of Deputies would be elected by the people in a two-stage process. Most members of the Senate would be elected by provincial assemblies; the remainder would be appointed by the king. The cabinet would be responsible to the Chamber of Deputies, which could vote no-confidence. Ministers would also be required to answer the summons of either the Senate or the Chamber. The king would have a limited power to dissolve the Chamber of Deputies, only in cases of a sustained dispute between the Chamber and the cabinet, and only if the Senate decided against the Chamber.

By the end of April, the Syrian Congress had debated no fewer than eighty-six articles. A typical session would begin when a member of the constitutional committee, usually Darwazeh, read aloud the proposed text of an article. Deputies would discuss it and decide whether revisions were needed. If so, they sent the text back to the committee. Congress deleted some articles altogether.

Debates were often lively and hotly contested, forcing drafts back to the committee for revision. Like the American constituent assembly at Philadelphia, the Congress at Damascus split into factional fights over the extent of state power and the balance of power between the central government and the provinces. The Progressive faction, which was aligned with the Independence Party and Fatat, favored a strong central government uniting all three zones. Its leaders included Darwazeh, from Palestine; Atassi, from the Syrian interior; and Riad al-Solh, from Lebanon.

In the middle ground was the small Democratic faction. They were populists who militantly fought the French threat and who accepted religious reform under the inspiration of Kamil al-Qassab. While the Democrats held few seats in Congress, they wielded the power of street politics through the HNC.[21]

Qassab offered Rida the presidency of the Democratic faction, on the strength of their former partnership in the Syrian Union Party.

But Rida chose to stay with other SUP members in the Fatat-backed Progressive faction, which elected him its president.[22]

Conservatives gathered in the Moderate-Liberal faction, linked to the short-lived Syrian National Party founded by Faisal in January. They were led by Abd al-Rahman al-Yusuf, one of the most influential politicians in Damascus. At nearly fifty years old, Yusuf was also said to be the city's wealthiest man. Born the son of an Ottoman official of Kurdish descent, Yusuf became director of the annual pilgrimage to Mecca at a relatively young age. At his baroque-style home, he often convened political meetings to settle city disputes. By 1914, he had become an Ottoman senator. Given his close Ottoman ties, he had opposed the Arab Revolt during the war. He and other wealthy conservatives saw Faisal's government as a threat to their prestige. They referred to Faisal and to deputies who came from the Lebanese coast and Palestine as foreigners.[23]

Another leader of the conservative faction was Rida's archenemy, Abd al-Qadir al-Khatib. Although he came from a more modest background than Yusuf, Khatib's family had long been prominent among preachers at the great Umayyad Mosque. At age forty, Khatib was fifteen years younger than Rida. But he held beliefs that were far more traditional. In 1909, when Rida gave a reformist sermon at the Umayyad Mosque, Khatib had roused a crowd against him. The British had dubbed Khatib a "fanatical humbug" for his activism within the Higher National Committee.[24]

At a session in late April, Khatib took advantage of a visit by a cabinet minister, Yusuf al-Hakim, to attack what he viewed as the heretical Progressive project to establish a secular state. He stood up and waved a report signed by thirty-three members of the Moderate-Liberal faction. "The ministry of education, which educates our young, does not respect the sanctity of religion," Khatib declared. He complained about its secular, nationalist curriculum and the mixing of boys and girls in schools. He had personally seen girls enter public buildings without veils on their heads.

Ahmad Qadri, Faisal's physician, who also served as a deputy, tried to interrupt him. But Khatib continued to complain. Hakim, a Greek Orthodox former Ottoman bureaucrat from the Latakia region, advised Khatib to take his concerns directly to the education minister. Khatib claimed he had already done so, with no result.

"Representative government is a series of links in a chain. If issues are not resolved after going to those in charge, then the public has the right to protest," Hakim conceded. To applause, he added, "I assure you that our government respects all religions and all opinions. We should not mix private and public matters, but I admit that I share the gentleman's opinion."[25]

Khatib had launched only the first salvo in the debate on religion and government. It exploded the next day, when another deputy proposed to grant women the right to vote. Rida once again stepped in to mediate, to bridge a chasm between secularists and religious conservatives that threatened the future of Congress and democracy itself.

Chapter 13

Women's Suffrage and the Limits of Islamic Law

On Sunday, April 25, 1920, Ibrahim al-Khatib, a deputy from Mount Lebanon, stood up during a debate on Article 78, concerning Syria's electoral law. Khatib (no relation to Abd al-Qadir al-Khatib, the conservative cleric) cleared his throat and proposed that educated women be granted the right to vote.[1]

The chamber erupted into chaos. Sheikh Sa`id Murad, a deputy from Gaza and a professor at Damascus's new law school, calmed the room. Murad then spoke in support of Khatib. Islamic law granted women rights equal to men's, and therefore demanded women's suffrage, he argued.

The room exploded again. Unable to restore order, Congress president Hashim al-Atassi postponed the debate until the next day.

The Women's Movement

Khatib spoke in the name of the new Syrian women's movement. During the war, women from Syria's most prominent families had opened hospitals, schools, and orphanages for children; organized famine relief; and provided destitute women with wage-earning work. After the armistice, women mobilized to demand independence for their nation and rights for themselves. They had, after all, proved their patriotism.[2] They had read in foreign magazines that educated British women had just won the right to vote and that the United States was about to ratify the Nineteenth Amendment, granting women suffrage. German, Polish, and Russian women had recently earned the right to vote, too. Closer to home, Muslim women in Albania and Azerbaijan had also obtained suffrage, and a prominent Turkish woman who had spent time in Beirut during the war, Halide Edib, had even run for parliament in Constantinople.

The Muslim women who led the suffrage campaign in April 1920 were well known to deputies in Congress—and to the king. From Beirut, Anbara Salam had invited Rida to speak at her women's club the previous December. After his speech in support of women's civic engagement and their gradual emancipation, Salam had praised Rida as the supreme guide to Muslims in the modern world. She called on him to enlighten Muslims on women's rights, so that women might contribute even more to rebuilding their nation.[3] In January, Salam brought a women's delegation to meet Prince Faisal upon his return from Paris. She had been introduced to Faisal by her father, a former Beirut mayor and member of the Ottoman parliament. Faisal lent a sympathetic ear. Even though his own wife lived secluded in their royal residence, he admired the industry and education of women in Europe.[4]

A few days later, in Damascus, Nazik al-Abid, leader of the women's delegation to the King-Crane Commission, organized a welcome celebration for Faisal. Women and their children joined men in waving flags and "pouring love from their hearts to revive the nation with equality, justice, and fraternity."[5] Faisal granted subsidies to Abid's girls' school for orphans of war martyrs, and to her magazine, *Light of Damascus*. Abid was such a prominent personality in the city that she inspired a novel by a visiting British writer.[6]

Abid publicly called for women's rights on the front page of her magazine's inaugural issue in February 1920. Like Anbara Salam, she framed her appeal in terms of social need. Her magazine was to be a forum for men and women to "understand each other and arrive at truths worth expressing, and so lift this wretched nation from the ruin of misery."[7]

When Congress slated its discussion of Article 78 on the electoral law, Salam joined Abid's suffrage appeal. She and a Lebanese delegation boarded a train to Damascus. So as not to excite unnecessary opposition, they remained veiled and sat in the harem section.[8] Abid greeted them upon their arrival at the Hijaz Station.

Women were not, however, permitted to enter the Congress chamber. They therefore turned to Ibrahim al-Khatib to present their case. He had contributed an article to Abid's magazine on the history of Arab women's rights, claiming they had once enjoyed "rights that American and Western women didn't even have."[9] Khatib eagerly accepted the mission of making their case to Congress.

Religious Backlash

The women had no illusions about the religious opposition they faced in Congress. Muslim women across the Middle East and South Asia based their demand for equal rights on the egalitarian spirit of Islam. But their opponents quickly labeled them apostates, enemies of Islam, and even stooges of European rule. These opponents denounced the men who supported women's rights as Freemasons, or worse.[10]

In Syria, conservative Muslim clerics had already shown their determination to protect religious tradition in public affairs. As soon as Congress opened in June 1919, for example, they had proposed that each session open with the customary recitation of a Qur'anic phrase used in the Ottoman government: "In the name of God the merciful and compassionate." Opponents, mostly lawyers, argued that in the new era, politics must reflect the values of the entire nation, not those of a particular religion. Yusuf al-Hakim, the Greek Orthodox deputy from Latakia, had brokered a compromise. Pluralism did not contradict the belief in God, he argued, noting that even the British expressed religious sentiments in their secular government. He persuaded the deputies to open their sessions with a one-word invocation, "Bismallah," which simply meant "In the name of God."[11]

Ten months later, the same conservatives regarded any proposal to expand women's rights as an existential threat. Women's status had traditionally been defined under Islamic laws on marriage, divorce, and inheritance that were adjudicated by judges in autonomous religious courts. During the war, however, the Young Turk regime had transferred legal authority on personal status issues to the centralized state under the Family Law of 1917. A year later, Muslim clerics had greeted the Ottoman defeat as an opportunity to recoup their own lost power. But now it appeared that the new Syrian government intended to roll back their authority even more. On March 29, Prime Minister Rikabi had announced a new directorate of clerical affairs that would have the power to review and appoint muftis, preachers, and teachers in a new system of religious schools funded in part by donations.[12]

And so, in late April, conservatives in Congress were bristling to wage battle not only against secularists, but also against liberal religious reformers like Rida. Reformers aimed to sweep away archaic traditions by shifting emphasis from the letter of outdated, medieval laws to the basic principles found in sacred texts. These included principles of moderation and balance in religion, and also of the equality of all believers before God, women included.

The suffrage debate conjured these critical political conflicts into a perfect storm. It would finally force Rida to confront his hostile enemies among the conservative deputies. The terms on which he helped Congress to resolve the issue set a historic precedent for reconciling divine law with democratic government.

Resumption of Debate on Women's Suffrage

On Monday morning, April 26, Congress secretary Izzat Darwazeh reopened the debate with a motion to approve women's suffrage. "Mr. Said Murad shouldered the burden of explaining—with compelling arguments and conclusive proof—that Islamic law grants women rights no less than men," he remarked. Because the law permitted women to be judges and religion scholars, it could not deny them participation in public affairs.

Darwazeh framed the debate around procedures, not goals. What was the most effective way to introduce women's suffrage into Syria's conservative society? he asked. If the state were to order sudden changes to old customs, there was likely to be backlash. Darwazeh proposed that gradual change would be more productive. "Does

Ibrahim Khatib propose a sudden break with custom, or a gradual one?" he asked.

"I see it as gradual," replied Khatib.

Darwazeh's colleague on the constitutional committee, Saadallah al-Jabiri of Aleppo, seconded Khatib's motion to grant educated women suffrage. That drew an immediate response from one of the clerical members of the constitutional committee, a deputy from Hama, Sheikh Abd al-Qadir al-Kilani. He strode to the podium in his long robe and turban, a contrast to the tight collared suits and neat mustaches worn by Jabiri and Khatib.

Kilani angrily opposed the motion. He conceded that Sheikh Murad might be right to say that Islamic law granted women equality. "But we must set aside this perspective, and look at the moral and administrative sides of the issue," he argued. "Show me a European state that grants females this right."

Voices from the benches shouted, "England, Sweden, Turkey!"

Kilani spoke again. "Gentlemen, ninety-nine percent of our women are not educated," he said. "If you want the educated women as you call for, then open schools for them and teach them to be teachers to their children. Then look to the next generation. Every building not built on a solid base collapses."

Kilani then raised another issue—the mixing of the sexes. "If we give the right to vote to women who deserve it, then there would be a female deputy. Do you want her among you?" he asked.

Jabiri pointed out that such mixing already occurred to a certain degree. "We see her going to the market to shop," he said.

Kilani was not satisfied. "That is a different issue," he argued. "In my view, the presence of women as voters or elected officials, or deputies—with their ignorance and with society's corrupt morals—is harmful and not useful."

Da`as Jirjis, a Christian member of Kilani's own Moderate-Liberal party, spoke up in favor of women's suffrage. He agreed that the uneducated majority of women should not vote. But he insisted on following principle, which required granting educated women the right.

"The Turkish government is at the forefront of Islamic governments that adhere to the rule of the holy law. Even so, it gave the right to vote to women," Jirjis argued. "You have witnessed during the war, Muslim women's service in the army is proof that the help of the gentle sex was of great importance."

Ahmad Qudmani of Damascus interjected, "God gave her [woman] half a brain and half an inheritance."

Jirjis dismissed such prejudice to invoke political need: "Establishing such a law is very important, especially in our current political circumstances. I therefore demand that this proposal be accepted and referred to the committee."

Applause broke out from the right side of the hall.

Adil Zu'aytir, a conservative notable from Darwazeh's hometown, Nablus, stood up. "I see it as harmful, because it does not conform to the spirit of the nation," he said. "You know, gentlemen, that some European nations granted this right only after six hundred years of development. Do we wish, at the beginning of our social development, to give them rights and so become a joke among sociologists?

"Each nation has its customs and habits and if the laws don't align with them, then it causes revolts and unrest in the country." Applause rose from the center. "We came to this place to express the views of the nation. If we gave an opinion or passed a law that the nation does not accept, have we then kept the nation's trust?"

Voices called out, "No!"

Subhi al-Tawil of Latakia stood to rebut Zu'aytir. "The educated woman is better than a thousand ignorant men," he argued. "Why do we give them the right to vote and deprive educated women of it?"

Qudmani called from his bench: "How many are like you in Latakia?"

"If you have something to say, honor the podium and do not speak from below," Tawil responded. "We can take the idea of representation from Europeans. There is no harm in following them, if we do so gradually."

Qudmani: "We in Damascus don't want that. You can do it in Latakia!"

Tawil: "With all my might, I support the proposal of brother Ibrahim al-Khatib. I request a vote by name."

At this point, Sheikh Sa'id Murad of Gaza, the champion of women's rights, stood up to applause. Seeing that some delegates remained silent, the young deputy Riad al-Solh intervened: "It is our duty to respect knowledge. For that reason, he deserves our applause." Louder clapping filled the room.

Citing the Qur'an, Murad acknowledged that differences of opinion among men were natural. "It is the order of the universe," he said. But argument should focus on essential issues. Deputies must set aside frivolous religious debate and worries about veils to focus on what is really at stake with women's suffrage: Syria's sovereignty.

"My main motive in speaking on this subject is from what I've read in Westerners' reports and newspapers. They say: 'The East needs the protection of the West because it consigned half of itself to ignorance. Meaning, women.'"

The hall exploded again in an uproar, but Murad continued. "I speak in formal Arabic so that all may understand: Westerners say that the East that consigns half of itself to ignorance, indefinitely, requires that we [Europeans] protect it."

Another uproar. Qudmani stormed out of the chamber with five other deputies: Sheikh Abd al-Qadir al-Khatib and Sheikh Muhammad al-Mujtahid of Damascus, like Qudmani; Ibrahim al-Sheikh Hussein of Deir ez-Zor; Sheikh Ahmad al-Ayashi of Idlib; and Khalil al-Talhuni of Maan.

President Atassi called out, "We have lost a quorum!"

But Darwazeh counted heads in the room and confirmed: "We still have a quorum."

Rashid Rida's Intervention

Murad had touched another raw nerve in Syrian politics. Since before the war, political debate had polarized into two positions on the issue of imitating the West. Conservative Muslims felt that imitation of the West would lead to the loss of society's soul. For that reason, Kamil al-Qassab and the Democratic Party adamantly rejected any reform in women's rights. HNC members had begun harassing women on the street, seeing it as an act of pious patriotism.[13] They resented Europeans' contention that women's veils were a symbol of Islam's backwardness.[14] Abd al-Qadir al-Khatib and his faction heard echoes of such a colonial view in Sheikh Murad's argument at the April 26 session.

The debate had struck directly at the mission of the Congress. Syrians had convened it to prove to Europe that they could govern Syria as a modern nation, without the assistance of a foreign mandate. But was the democratic procedure enough proof? Must the Congress adopt European-style laws, as well? Answering these questions was critical to the survival of the Congress. The fragile consensus of March was now in peril. If the six deputies did not return, would the Congress survive?

This kind of binary logic—that to accept European-style reforms was to betray Arab culture—also struck at the heart of Islamic reformism. Scholars like Rida had defied accusations that they were simply tailoring Islam to fit Western culture. They argued that Islam shared basic values with all civilizations, and that their reforms were rooted deep in Islamic principles. Regardless of what European Orientalists wrote about the backwardness of Islam, Muslims could forge a modernity true to themselves.[15]

In this spirit, Rafiq al-Tamimi, a deputy from Palestine, tried to rescue the moment. He argued that granting women's suffrage would not require the renunciation of Islam. "We can, gentlemen, compromise between old and new schools," he said. He suggested that women and men vote at separate locations, to avoid the mixing of the sexes. Or perhaps women could be required to vote with the counsel of their male guardians. Tamimi also pointed out that some women might choose not to vote at all.

"I commend Congress for standing up adamantly for women, for raising their status when the riffraff and fools in the capital attack the gentle sex," Tamimi argued, in a direct reference to the HNC harassers. "If Congress, which speaks for the nation, does not rein in those fools who attack respectable women in the streets, then you can say good-bye to freedom!"

Ibrahim al-Khatib jumped up. "Had I realized [deputies'] ideas were ready to support my proposal so much, I would have proposed we grant women more rights!"

Uproar exploded in the hall, echoing the noise of the "riffraff" outside in Marjeh Square. In anger, Khatib threatened to resign from the Moderate-Liberal Party, with its "ignorant" members. He backed down but demanded an immediate vote. "We have had enough discussion!"

Rashid Rida thought otherwise. After remaining silent for the entire day, the president of the Progressive Party stood up to long applause. He felt a bit weak, for he had suffered a bout of malaria over the previous week.

Rida began by apologizing for not having been able to review the Islamic law on women's rights, but he assured the assembly that this was not a problem. Rida explained that after following debates on women's rights in Egypt, he had decided it was essentially a political issue, not a religious one.

"We must maintain our status with the nation, especially since it delegated us for a certain task, and not for general issues. The public interest requires that," Rida advised. "The suffrage issue has no public benefit now. It might even have a negative effect," he warned. "In these difficult circumstances, one single outcry is enough to provoke the public."

At a superficial level, Rida was arguing that the women's issue was not important enough to warrant such conflict. The Congress was convened to ensure Syria's independence. Suffrage was a side issue. At a deeper level, however, Rida spoke from years of thinking and writing about the role of Islamic law in the modern world. The key term in his comment was "public benefit," or *maslaha* in Arabic. The purpose of government was to serve the public in a wide variety of matters that extended well beyond the jurisdiction of Islamic law. In his view, Islamic law should govern only a restricted arena of public affairs relating to clearly defined matters of religion, regulating ritual, and family life. Beyond that arena, politicians must formulate new laws to address current needs.[16]

Rida's belief in limits to the jurisdiction of Islamic law did not mean he did not believe in Islamic government. He believed in the ethical and spiritual need for a Muslim caliph. And he believed government must rest on Islamic principles of justice, harmony, consultation, and compromise. In short, Islam should guide how politicians rule, but not necessarily define the laws they pass.

Pertinent to the debate at hand, and revolutionary to both sides, was that Rida did not believe women's suffrage was governed by Islamic law at all. It did not matter, as Sheikh Murad argued, that Islam demanded equality. Nor did it matter, as Kilani and Qudmani argued, that Islam placed women under men's guardianship in the family or granted them only half the inheritance of men. What mattered on April 26, 1920, was that Congress must lead the nation at a time of existential crisis. Rida feared that if Congress imposed laws against the popular will, it would risk its future. Rida returned to the pragmatism that animated Islamic reform.

"If you want to adopt a practical law, then you must consider the nation's sentiments," Rida declared. "Religious issues are determined according to religious texts. But secular issues are determined according to public interests, which change with time and place." If leaders decided that women's suffrage served the nation's interest, Rida noted, "then we can find support for it in Islamic law."

But, Rida explained, this held no public benefit today. "I ask that the proposal for women's right to vote be rejected and ask that it not be included in the constitution." He made clear, however, that his negative view was no capitulation to rigid tradition on women's seclusion. Rida called for a constitutional requirement for girls' education. "I say that we must fight those hard-liners who want to keep women ignorant."

A deputy from Latakia rushed to alert Rida to his self-contradiction. "I read in the interpretation of the Qur'an published by *The Lighthouse* the following verse: 'And due to the wives is similar to what is expected of them.' He [God] gave women rights as he gave men rights."

Rida dismissed the idea that Islamic law unambiguously demanded that women be granted suffrage. "We said that we have no public interest in this issue."

Apparently upset, Rida then recalled the violent backlash he had suffered for proposing reform in a sermon at the Umayyad Mosque. "My brothers, ten years ago when I began to teach a lesson on matters of faith, the whole world rose against me," he complained. "Now you force me to say that this issue will provoke a great deal of uproar, speeches in mosques against the Congress. There is no practical benefit in that."

In 1909, Rida was able to visit Syria from his exile in Egypt, owing to the restoration of civil liberties after the constitutional revolution. Religious reformers invited him to lecture at the Umayyad Mosque. Abd al-Qadir al-Khatib, an opponent of reform and the revolution, organized an attack on Rida. During his lecture on the need to study science and to ban praying to Sufi saints, an audience member interrupted Rida, accusing him of being a Wahhabi (like the Saudis). Khatib stood up to endorse the accusation. Thousands of people rioted in Damascus that night, and Rida fled the city. Rida later learned that Khatib and the provocateur had planned to exploit his lecture to rally support for their antirevolutionary party in the coming parliamentary election.[17] Now, old tensions threatened to sabotage the new era of independence.

Dr. Said Tali`, the Tripoli deputy who published the Independence Day memorial volume, came to Rida's defense. The time was not right for such a dramatic reform, he argued. "Poor is the woman whom you discuss in the assembly, while she is being insulted in the streets." Tali` reminded the deputies that the Japanese wrote their constitution in a pragmatic way as well. They prioritized what was appropriate for their country, and left aside the theoretical arguments of legal specialists.

"If I were in Europe, I would join those who defend giving women that right," Tali` argued. "But because I am Syrian living in Syria, I am not able to do that. . . . Any law that is does not accord with the spirit of the nation will not be useful. Syria cannot withstand such a law."

But Riad al-Solh, delegate from Sidon, insisted on principle, not politics. He dismissed the departure of the six delegates as a case of rigid people who were unable to confront a compelling argument. "When I stand on this podium, I don't ask whether the cafés and houses are against me or not. I accept granting this right to women in principle. So if the cafés of Damascus don't support it, other districts will be glad to accept it."

After making his point, however, Solh extended an olive branch of compromise. "To satisfy the intellectuals, we should set this issue aside for now," he said. "I propose that Congress inform the government that it absolutely condemns attacks on women in the capital. It is a shame to accept that."

George Harfoush of Beirut made a last pitch to support Sheikh Murad. "With this debate, the Congress has proved that it is joining the free, modern world. Tomorrow, when Europe reads in its newspapers that the members of the Syrian Congress proposed to give women the right to vote, we will certainly have an impact greater than sending twenty delegations. So I agree with those who would grant women their rights."

President Atassi then asked, "Do you think we have had enough discussion?"

Voices responded, "Enough!"

Uthman Sultan, another deputy from Tripoli and a member of the constitution committee, made a motion to postpone the vote on women's suffrage: "We will keep a record of the proposal, but leave the article as it is." Fifteen deputies supported the motion.

Attasi followed. "Whoever agrees, raise your hands, please."

A majority raised their hands.

Atassi then asked for a vote on the proposal to crack down on men who attacked women in the street. A majority raised their hands in approval, and the session concluded.

A Setback for Liberal Ideals

It was not Islam but rather the public pressure of the HNC's demonstrators that undermined women's suffrage, Darwazeh believed.[18] Nearly all the deputies had agreed that the Qur'an granted women political equality. A majority actually recorded their approval of suffrage in the Congress minutes. When Darwazeh and the constitutional committee met, they decided to leave open future interpretations of the electoral law. Rather than stipulate that only men could vote, they used the generic word "Syrian," which could be read as encompassing both male and female.[19]

Rida, however, only briefly noted the discussion on women's suffrage in his personal diary that night of April 26. His entry concerned another meeting that same evening, convened to address the latest threat to Syrian sovereignty from San Remo.[20]

In other circumstances, Rida might have joined Progressives in support of women's suffrage. But the grave news about the Supreme Council's award of a French mandate in Syria cast dark clouds over the debate. The nation's highest priority that day was Syria's independence, which could be defended only through political unity. The Congress could not afford to split apart.[21]

Nazik al-Abid agreed on the higher priority. "Leave your hiding place [in your home] because your homeland needs you," she urged her readers in the May 1920 issue of her magazine. "Inspire and motivate others with your activity, . . . raise your voice and remind everyone of their national duty."[22]

Chapter 14

A Democratic Constitution for Christians and Muslims

Two days before the suffrage debate opened a schism in Congress, deputies had stumbled upon the even greater, diplomatic threat kept hidden by the government. On April 24, Congress interrogated Yusuf al-Hakim, the minister for commerce, agriculture, and public works on troubling incidents in the French-controlled coastal zone. Deputies had received alarming reports that France was circulating a petition against the Congress, that it had lowered the Syrian flag at the Arab delegation office in Beirut, and that it had arrested a Muslim preacher for mentioning King Faisal's name during Friday prayers.

The interrogation revealed the connection between events in Lebanon and the San Remo Conference. Both weaponized sectarianism to threaten the pluralist democracy being founded in Damascus. Congress responded by forcing a change in government and—under its new leadership of two Muslim clerics—writing into the constitution legal protections for minority rights and equality. In May and June, as threats multiplied and as the government instituted a military draft for Syria's defense, the Congress finished writing the constitution. The full text, establishing a democratic, parliamentary monarchy, was unveiled to the public on July 5, 1920.

San Remo and the Second Fall of Rikabi

Yusuf al-Hakim, a deputy from Latakia before he joined Rikabi's cabinet, drew cheers from his former colleagues as he strode to the

The Ottoman governor of Syria executed twenty-one prominent Arab leaders as traitors in Beirut and Damascus on May 6, 1916. The executions sparked the Arab Revolt, launched one month later.

A wartime famine caused by the Allied blockade and Ottoman military needs killed up to 500,000 people in Greater Syria, turning the population against Turkish rule.

Sharif Hussein of Mecca, father of Prince Faisal, who launched the Arab Revolt with British promises of Arab independence.

François Georges-Picot, French negotiator of the 1916 Sykes-Picot agreement and French high commissioner in Syria and Cilicia.

Troops of the Arab Northern Army enter Damascus, passing British soldiers in a car, October 1, 1918.

Damascus citizens near the Darwish Pasha Mosque on October 2, 1919, the day after Arab and Allied troops entered the city.

Lt. Col. T. E. Lawrence, British liaison to Prince Faisal during the Arab Revolt.

The Deraa Rail Station, south of Damascus, from which Prince Faisal staged the conquest of the Syrian capital. A protest in Deraa launched the Syrian democratic uprising in 2011.

Faisal ibn al-Hussein, Arab Revolt leader and later king of the Syrian Arab Kingdom.

General Edmund Allenby, Commander of Britain's Egyptian Expeditionary Forces.

Prince Faisal leaves the Victoria Hotel, October 3, 1918. He had just been informed by Gen. Allenby that the Arabs must wait for independence to be granted by the Paris Peace Conference.

The Northern Arab Army enters Aleppo in late October 1918. Their banner reads, "His Greatness Prince Faisal to Restore Arab Independence." Faisal arrived a few days later, when he proclaimed a constitutional regime with equal rights for all Arabs, Muslim and non-Muslim, rich and poor.

Gen. Rida Pasha al-Rikabi, appointed the first military governor of Syria and later prime minister.

The Umayyad Mosque in Damascus, built in the seventh century on the site of a church and Roman temple, and housing the tomb of Saladin, who defeated European Crusaders in the twelfth century. Mass meetings were held in the mosque in support of Arab independence. Syrians still repeat the legend that French Gen. Goybet, who conquered the city in July 1920, visited Saladin's tomb, and proclaimed "We're back."

Rustum Haidar, Faisal's advisor and head of the Hijaz Delegation in Paris, whom Europeans later shut out of the critical San Remo conference.

Awni Abd al-Hadi, advisor to Prince Faisal at the Paris Peace Conference and later his secretary in Damascus.

The "Big Four" on May 27, 1919. Negotiations at the Paris Peace Conference were controlled by representatives of the "Big Four" Entente powers. Shown here, from left to right: David Lloyd George, prime minister of Great Britain; Vittorio Orlando, premier of Italy; Georges Clemenceau, premier of France; and Woodrow Wilson, president of the United States.

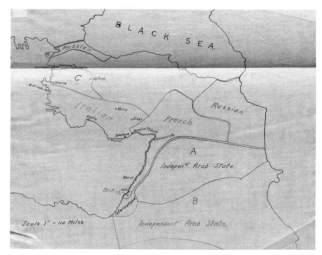

This hand-drawn map from the archive of the American delegation to the 1919 Paris Peace Conference shows its understanding of how the Entente powers intended to divide Ottoman land. Americans assumed that Syria, comprising much of regions A and B, would be an "Independent Arab State."

Pres. Woodrow Wilson addressing the Paris Peace Conference at its opening session, January 18, 1919. "This is the supreme conference of mankind," Wilson proclaimed, urging delegates to embrace a truly universal program of peace.

Cover of the December 1918 issue of *The Lighthouse*, where Rashid Rida hailed American President Wilson as an instrument of God's will in assuring the rights of Arabs and all small nations.

Rustum Haidar and Prince Faisal attended the opening session of the Paris Peace Conference on January 18, 1919. The French at first blocked their entry, but the British persuaded them to permit Haidar and Faisal to attend as delegates of the independent regime of Sharif Hussein of the Hijaz—not as representatives of Syria.

Howard Bliss, president of the Syrian Protestant College in Beirut who spoke in favor of Syrian self-determination and against a French mandate at the Paris Peace Conference.

Robert de Caix, journalist, leader of the French colonial lobby, and advisor to Gen. Henri Gouraud.

Prince Faisal welcomed by a crowd in Damascus, upon his return from the Paris Peace Conference, May 3, 1919.

"His Mandatory Wives—oh, Sam!," published in the *New York Herald* on February 23, 1919, shortly after Pres. Wilson had unveiled the League of Nations Covenant. The cartoon shows Uncle Sam leaving the "International Matrimonial Bureau, League of Nations" with multiple wives, including a veiled Arab woman, representing non-white societies.

Charles R. Crane, leader of the American King-Crane Commission of inquiry to Syria.

Prince Faisal with the King-Crane Commission of inquiry, Damascus, 1919. Seated in the front row, from left to right, are: Henry Churchill King, Prince Faisal, Gen. Edmund Allenby, Charles R. Crane, Albert Lybyer, commission member. Two commission members stand in the middle row: Capt. William Yale, second from the end and George Montgomery is at the far right end. The military governor of Syria, Rida Pasha al-Rikabi, is standing behind them, at the far right in the back row.

Sheikh Rashid Rida, publisher of *The Lighthouse* and later president of the Syrian Arab Congress.

Nationalist demonstrations like this one drew thousands of city residents into the streets in the fall of 1919, protesting against plans to withdraw British troops in favor of the French. Popular pressure from the Higher National Committee forced the Syrian Arab Congress to demand independence in November 1919.

Damascus covered in snow, February 1920. During the storm, the Syrian Arab Congress and Faisal negotiated the terms of the Declaration of Independence.

Hashim al-Atassi, president of the Syrian Arab Congress that declared independence, became prime minister in May 1920.

The coronation of King Faisal I of Syria on March 8, 1920. He was chosen on authority of the Syrian Arab Congress and surrounded by Muslim, Christian, and Jewish clerics.

Lt. Col. Edouard Cousse, the French liaison to King Faisal, who attended the Declaration of Independence ceremony and opposed the overthrow of the regime.

A souvenir postcard of an independence parade on March 8, 1920, in Aleppo commemorates Faisal's coronation.

Syria's Declaration of Independence was printed in this commemorative volume in May 1920. The cover, shown here, features a map of Syria extending from the boundaries of Arabia and Gaza northward along the Mediterranean coast, to the Taurus mountains in Anatolia (now in Turkey) and eastward toward Deir ez-Zor.

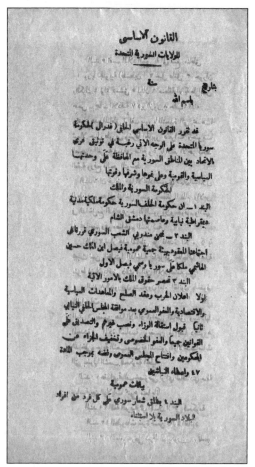

Abd al-Rahman al-Yusuf, conservative leader in the Syrian Arab Congress.

A July 1919 draft of the Syrian constitution submitted to the King-Crane Commission. Titled "The Constitution of the United States of Syria," it called for an independent government uniting all territories of Greater Syria under a constitutional monarchy. The draft was likely drawn up by the Syrian Union Party in Cairo and carried to Damascus by Abd Al-Rahman Shahbandar.

Nazik al-Abid, the Damascus feminist whose appeal for women's suffrage launched a critical debate on the Syrian constitution.

Marjeh Square, the government center of Damascus, in the 1920s. The multistory Abed Building, behind the pillar, housed the Syrian Arab Congress on its second floor between March and July 1920. It was there that the Syrian Constitution was debated and drafted.

 Shakib Arslan, Lebanese Druze prince and advocate of a united Syria and Arab independence.

 Monsignor Elias Hoyek, patriarch of the Maronite Church and advocate of Lebanese independence from Syria.

Sheikh Kamil al-Qassab, popular preacher and leader of the Higher National Committee in Damascus.

Izzat Darwazeh, secretary of the Syrian Arab Congress who read the Declaration of Independence to the public on March 8, 1920.

Triumphant meeting of the Fatat organization at Dummar, on March 20, 1920. This photo was reproduced in the memoir of Izzat Darwazeh, who stands at the right end of the back row, with his arms crossed. Standing to Darwazeh's right, third from the left end of the back row, is Riad al-Solh, future prime minister of independent Lebanon. Third from the left in the middle row is Shukri al-Quwwatli, future president of independent Syria. Seated in the middle of the front row, Faisal's personal physician, Dr. Ahmad Qadri, hugs Awni Abd al-Hadi, Faisal's secretary. Lying down at the end of the row, in white, is Dr. Sa`id Tali`, who published the independence memorial volume.

The San Remo conference of April 1920 was held in a luxury hotel. Seated at the table, on the far left are Philippe Berthelot and Alexandre Millerand of France; next to them sit Vittorio Scialoja and Premier Saverio Nitti of Italy. To Nitti's left, bending down and blurred, is David Lloyd George. Lord Curzon sits next to him. At the far right is Matsui Keishiro of Japan. The Americans attended as observers only, since the US Senate had voted to reject membership in the League. The Arab Hijaz delegation to the peace conference was not invited.

Alexandre Millerand, French premier who ordered the invasion of Syria and overthrow of Faisal's government in July 1920.

Marcel Cachin, defender of Syrian independence in the French Chamber of Deputies.

George Nathaniel Curzon, commonly known as Lord Curzon, led British efforts to expand British rule over Arab lands, at the price of conceding Syria and Lebanon to France.

Gen. Yusuf al-Azmeh,
commander of the Syrian
army who lost the battle
and his life at Maysalun on
July 24, 1920.

Gen. Henri Gouraud, French
high commissioner of Syria and
Lebanon, conqueror of Syria.

French troops, recruited mostly from West Africa and North Africa, enter Damascus under
the command of Gen. Mariano Goybet on July 25, 1920. The day before, the French had
defeated the Syrian army at the town of Maysalun, west of the city. Faisal and the Syrian
government fled to Deraa, the town from which they had launched their conquest of
Damascus nearly two years earlier.

The Syro-Palestinian Congress in Geneva, 1921. The Congress appealed to the League of Nations to reject the San Remo conference's assignment of mandates. Sheikh Rashid Rida, left end of the front row, traveled to Europe in search of liberals who would uphold Wilson's principles. He is talking with Prince Michel Lutfallah of Lebanon, who financed the delegation. On the right in the front stands Shakib Arslan, who would remain the Congress's chief representative in Geneva. He was joined there by Riad al-Solh, standing in the top row on the right end.

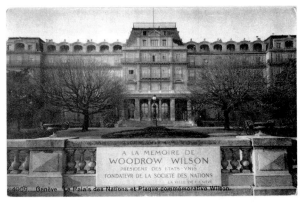

William Rappard, chief administrator for the League of Nations Permanent Mandates Commission in Geneva, who met with the Syro-Palestinian Congress.

A plaque, commemorating Pres. Woodrow Wilson as the founder of the League of Nations, installed at the League's headquarters in Geneva in 1924. By then, the League had all but abandoned Wilson's principle of self-determination in favor of the colonial powers that controlled the Permanent Mandates Commission.

Damascus in flames after French artillery shelling during the Syrian Revolt of 1925. Urban Syrian nationalists, led by Abd al-Rahman Shahbandar, joined Druze tribes in a general insurrection against French mandatory rule. By the spring of 1926, several quarters of Damascus had been destroyed and the leaders of the Revolt were living in exile.

"One against Ten: The Heroism of our Troops in Syria." The French magazine portrayed colonial troops brutally suppressing the Syrian Revolt in 1925. The Revolt caused much alarm at the League of Nations, which, under French pressure, ignored Syrian appeals.

Dr. Abd al-Rahman Shahbandar, foreign minister in the Syrian Arab Kingdom and a leader of the 1925 Syrian revolt, addressing a crowd after his return to Syria from exile in 1937. He regained popularity by opposing the National Bloc's collaboration with the French and by recalling the 1920 Declaration of Independence. Shahbandar was assassinated in his medical office in June 1940.

King Faisal I of Iraq announces independent Iraq's membership in the League of Nations, October 6, 1932. Faisal, formerly king of Syria, raised the hope of Arabs in other mandates that they may soon achieve independence in a reunited Arab state, thereby rolling back the betrayal of San Remo in 1920.

By 1930, Sheikh Rashid Rida had lost faith in European liberalism and promoted a new style of Wilsonian peace in his book *The Muhammadan Revelation*. He inspired the Egyptian teacher, Hasan al-Banna [pictured], to establish a populist, anti-Western Islamic movement—the Muslim Brotherhood.

Protest at Deraa, the town where Faisal staged the conquest of Syria in 1920. Here, on August 19, 2011, demonstrators demanded political rights, civil liberties, and the ouster of the regime of Pres. Bashar al-Assad. Leaders of the Syrian uprising invoked the constitutional past of Syria to justify their demands.

podium to reassure Congress that the government had taken action against the coastal threats to Syria's sovereignty. The government had already lodged a complaint about the petition, demanded the release of the preacher, and restored the kingdom's colors. "Our flag is fluttering in the wind and it will remain there, as our nation wishes," Hakim declared, trying to soothe worries that the Rikabi government was failing in diplomacy.[1]

But Dr. Ahmad Qadri, Faisal's personal physician and deputy from Hebron, was not at all comforted. The preacher's arrest was cause for war, he declared. "It is an intervention into religious affairs." To much applause, Qadri urged preemptive action against the French while their troops were deployed north in Cilicia.

Next, a deputy from Aleppo demanded that Hakim disclose details of the meeting of the Supreme Council at San Remo. Newspapers had reported that two Syrian envoys were there. Who were they? What was the government's policy at San Remo? Hakim insisted that the cabinet could not reveal those details.

A deputy from Tripoli, a town in the coastal zone, stood up to protest. "It is for the people to decide their future. It must not be decided in Paris or London or San Remo. It must be decided in the Syrian Kingdom!" he declared.

Hakim bristled at the implication that the government might sell out the country, "No one should portray it that way," he insisted. Hakim's hometown was also in the coastal zone. As a child, he had attended the American mission school in Latakia. As one of two Christian ministers in the cabinet, he might have felt vulnerable to suspicions about his loyalties.

Another deputy from the coast, Riad al-Solh of Sidon, stood up to defend him. Restating Congress's demand for vigilance on national defense, he led a round of applause for Hakim.

However, the damage had been done. It became clear that Rikabi's cabinet had kept Congress in the dark at a critical moment, when the Supreme Council's refusal to recognize Faisal as king had prompted King Hussein's withdrawal from the peace conference. With no further official word, the Supreme Council voted the next day, April 25, to assign France the Syrian mandate.

Because Rikabi broke his agreement to permit Congress oversight on issues touching on Syrian independence, Congress exercised its right to remove him.

San Remo and Rida's Rise as Congress President

On April 26, following the suffrage debate, Rashid Rida spent what he called a "useful and unforgettable evening" with King Faisal; Izzat Darwazeh; Sati` al-Husri, the education minister; and several deputies at the home of Faisal's chamberlain Ihsan al-Jabiri. The men discussed the decision at San Remo and Rikabi's lack of preparation for it. "It became clear that the King has lost trust in the Rikabi cabinet," Rida wrote that night in his diary.[2]

A crisis atmosphere took hold in Damascus. Anti-French demonstrations had already broken out to protest the arrest of the preacher and the lowering of the flag. Now protesters flooded the streets to condemn the San Remo decision.

The next night, the group confronted Rikabi. This time the king was absent, but opposition leaders like Abd al-Rahman Yusuf attended. Rikabi rejected their accusations of poor planning and resisted pressure to build up Syria's army. Military defense was futile, he argued, insisting that Faisal and the cabinet agreed it was better to sign a treaty with France. Rida marveled that an experienced politician like Rikabi could believe France would respect Syrian independence under mandate, as called for in the discredited Clemenceau accord.[3]

Contrary to his prime minister's claims, Faisal was persuaded that Syrians must make a show of force to pressure Europe into respecting their independence. The king agreed that Rikabi had to go.[4]

On May 2, Congress exercised its new legislative powers to vote no-confidence against the Rikabi government. The old soldier resigned for a second time in six months. Several deputies pushed hard for a strong "defense cabinet." Rida proposed Yusuf al-Azmeh, head of the army, to replace Rikabi. He was a young, passionate, and militant patriot. But Faisal preferred the calm, well-mannered Congress president, Hashim al-Atassi. The king hoped Atassi might restore confidence between the palace and the Congress.

The next day, Faisal announced the new Atassi government, which retained most of Rikabi's cabinet but installed Yusuf al-Azmeh as the new war minister and Abd al-Rahman Shahbandar as the new foreign minister. Rida was pleased that Faisal had accepted his recommendation of Shahbandar, a fellow SUP member.[5]

On May 5, the Congress held an election to replace Atassi as president. The Progressive Party nominated Rida as president, and Sheikh Abd al-Qadir al-Kilani as vice president. The Moderate-Liberals nominated Rida al-Solh (Rashid Rida's old friend) for president and Sheikh Abd al-Qadir al-Khatib (Rida's antagonist from the 1909 Umayyad Mosque incident) as vice president. Rida came out on top in the final round of voting. But Khatib was elected as his vice president.[6] Izzat Darwazeh remained Congress secretary.

Rida accepted his own post reluctantly. "I told [Riad al-Solh] that I would be the first to vote for your father," Rida wrote in his diary that night. "And I told the Progressive Party to vote for [Rida al-Solh] but they would not accept him because they are the majority party." Rida conceded that he was better equipped than Rida al-Solh to handle the primary task of the president, to adjudicate the drafting of the constitution. The senior Solh was a better administrator than politician.[7]

There was a clear political benefit of choosing Rida and Khatib: to mend differences in Congress after the stormy suffrage debate. Khatib had walked out of the chamber with other conservative clerics, and Rida had successfully played the role of mediator. In light of the news from San Remo, the need for unity was paramount.[8] In the same unifying spirit, Rida immediately resigned as president of the Progressive Party in order to ease lingering suspicions of his partisanship. "I had to be equally fair to both parties," he wrote. "Most of those who were not very pleased with me—when I insisted on maintaining order or stopped them from talking—were from my own party."

Rida's first act as president was to summon Foreign Minister Abd al-Rahman Shahbandar to present the Atassi government's program. On May 8, Shahbandar, presented three policy goals: (1) to support full independence with full rights of foreign diplomatic representation; (2) to insist on the unity of Greater Syria against claims of Zionists in the south; and (3) to reject all foreign intervention that undermined national sovereignty.

Congress gave its vote of confidence, and the Atassi government immediately announced a universal military draft and a national loan to cover military costs. After heated debate, Congress approved the loan, which would be guaranteed by state lands. Shahbandar then sent a letter to the British repeating Syria's request for recognition of Faisal as king, so that he might accept the peace conference's invitation to Europe. The British again declined.[9]

In the face of looming conflict, Congress accepted Rida's proposal to complete a draft of the constitution as soon as possible.[10] It spent the next two months (with a short break at the start of Ramadan) debating, revising, and approving articles on minority rights, provincial government, and the judiciary system.[11]

At first, conflict flared under the new clerical leadership. Young secular nationalists who had, before March 8, voiced support for a secular republic bristled at Rida's efforts to reintegrate the disaffected conservative faction. "The disruptions are tarnishing Congress's good image," Rida complained one day to his vice president, Abd al-Qadir al-Khatib. "We need more cooperation."

Just then, Izzat Darwazeh walked in. Khatib accused Darwazeh of disrupting Congress sessions. When Atassi was president, Darwazeh had helped to keep order in the chamber, he remarked. But now, under Rida, Darwazeh no longer even sat next to the president. Darwazeh apologized to Rida, explaining that he had left his seat on the platform only to consult some deputies on drafting a law.

Rida was surprised and gratified that Khatib, his archenemy, had stood up for him. "It upset him that the 'Effendis' [men in suits] found it difficult that the president was a religious scholar wearing a turban."[12]

Tarbush and turban eventually learned to cooperate. Darwazeh, who had considered Atassi a personal mentor and friend, at first regarded Rida with awe, as an eminent scholar and elder. Unlike the even-tempered Atassi, Darwazeh noted, Rida would often lose his temper in the chamber. In private, however, Rida was neither terrifying nor condescending. He thought of Darwazeh as "a pillar of the party." The two men soon developed a respectful and even affectionate working relationship.

Committed to maintaining a united front against foreign threats, Rida also tried to foster a spirit of pragmatism and negotiation among other deputies as well. "I used to advise not to rebel against the government, saying it was better to work with the government than undermine it," he recalled.[13]

Maintaining unity was not only a matter of bridging the secular–religious divide, however. It also required maintaining the good faith of non-Muslim Syrians, whose loyalties were severely tested by the sectarian rhetoric of the French, the Lebanese Christian nationalists, and the Muslim nationalists. Even as the Syrian Congress prepared to address the controversial issue of equal rights for non-Muslims, mutual trust was shaken by conflict outside its chamber.

Guerrilla warfare in the Bekaa Valley took on a sectarian hue. Syrian militias often attacked Christian villages on suspicion of their pro-French sentiments. Combat between Turkish nationalists, the French, and Armenians sent new waves of refugees over Syria's northern border. Efforts made since Independence Day to foster cross-sectarian brotherhood were threatened. "Aleppo is a hotbed of Arab, Turkish, Kurdish and Circassian propaganda," wrote the American consul. He relayed rumors that Faisal's Arab officers in the city were socializing with Turkish nationalists, who were once again "endeavoring to exterminate the Armenians."[14]

Lebanese Declaration of Independence

Faisal and the Fatat organization had long prioritized the need for Muslim-Christian unity against France's divisive claim that Christians needed its protection. No Fatat leader worried more about a potential Muslim-Christian schism than Rustum Haidar. His hometown, Baalbek, lay in the Bekaa Valley, where fighting between the French and Syrians since December had upset relations between Muslims and

Christians. Events since Faisal's return to Syria had only deepened his anxiety about the conflict.

Syria's alliance with the Turks was backfiring, he thought: Europe saw it as a renewal of Islamic jihad, and in response Europeans were playing the religion card. "Let's support rapprochement with the Turks in foreign affairs, but internally, we must kill these sentiments [of Islamic unity] and foreign germs," he wrote. "The homeland is for both Muslim and Christian together."

Haidar worried, too, that talk of establishing a separate Armenian Christian state would lead to splitting Lebanon from Syria on sectarian lines. He knew that Christians of the Bekaa, especially in its capital city, Zahle, still mourned the thousands massacred in the 1860 civil war. But in the sixty years since then, relations had improved under the rule of the cross-sectarian Lebanese Administrative Council.[15]

But wartime atrocity and foreign occupation had upset the old Ottoman order.[16] Since October 1918, politicians and intellectuals of the French-occupied West Zone had advanced rival visions of a post-Ottoman polity. While some proposed unity with Damascus based on a common Syrian identity, others emphasized the distinct history of Mount Lebanon and the coast in arguments for a separate state. Still others fully embraced the Arabism of Fatat.[17] Political fluidity had encouraged the Damascus government to open an office in Beirut and to engage in the competition for hearts and minds.

Towering over the various factions, in size and influence, was the movement led by the patriarch of the Maronite Church. Monsignor Elias Hoyek had lived through the wartime famine that had killed 200,000 people on Mount Lebanon and the coast, most of them Christian. At the start of the famine, thousands of Armenian survivors had arrived in Lebanon. The decimated villages of Mount Lebanon were proof to him and his flock that the Ottoman military governor, Jamal Pasha, aimed to annihilate Christians of all sects within the empire. At war's end, Hoyek ignored the fact that the famine had been caused not only by Ottoman mismanagement, but also by the Allied blockade and the hoarding of grain by Maronite elites, most notoriously by the Sursock family.[18] He gratefully accepted French protection, reestablishing a relationship that was centuries old. Premier Clemenceau formally renewed that commitment in November 1919 at a personal meeting with Hoyek in Paris. He even issued a note assuring Hoyek of an independent Lebanese state.

As the primary provider of food to the starving people of Mount Lebanon, the Maronite Church had emerged from the war with more power than the cross-sectarian Lebanese Administrative Council. In his appeal to the French, Hoyek tied the massacres of the 1860 war to the recent famine in order to demand an independent state of Greater Lebanon, expanded beyond Mount Lebanon, as reparation for past injustice.[19] The church's campaign, supported almost exclusively by Christians and opposed by most Muslims and Druze, exerted a sectarian influence on politics in Beirut, pitting Christian "Lebanists" against Muslim "Unionists," who favored unity with Syria. Beirut newspapers routinely cast Syrian politics in sectarian terms, claiming that the goal of Damascus was to "kill Christians," Haidar angrily confided to his diary.

"Christians used to respect their Muslim brothers, but since the arrival of the French, they have taken a different view," Haidar remarked. He scorned accusations by leaders of the Maronite Church that Faisal must be a dangerous sectarian leader simply because he was a descendant of the Prophet. "And what should Muslims say about a leader who comes to the Orient and declares he is a descendant of Crusaders?" Haidar asked, referring to Gouraud. "Will the day come when Christians recognize Muslims honestly, and extend their hands to them sincerely, as the Copts in Egypt have done?"[20]

Shortly after Haidar penned those lines, he met the members of the third Maronite-led delegation to Paris sent by Monsignor Hoyek. The delegation, led by Bishop Abdullah Khoury, was composed of three Maronites and one Druze prince.[21] They received a warm welcome from the colonial lobby, which arranged for meetings between the Lebanese and French legislators. On February 20, the French Senate's foreign relations committee adopted a resolution supporting an independent Greater Lebanon, which was to include Rustum Haidar's hometown in the disputed Bekaa Valley.[22]

In a note to Premier Millerand, Bishop Khoury's delegation dismissed the "parody" of a Congress meeting to declare independence in Damascus. Gouraud assured the premier that he would forbid Lebanese deputies to attend Faisal's coronation, which was likely to "boost Muslim nationalism." In mid-March, fearing "embarrassing demonstrations" in French territory, Gouraud decided to tour the French-occupied West Zone to declare publicly that the Syrian declaration was null and void. He claimed four thousand Christians had fled Sharifian terrorists for French protection on the coast.[23]

On March 22, with the blessings of both Gouraud and Monsignor Hoyek, a Lebanese group issued a rival declaration of independence. Hundreds of notables, village leaders, and city officials from across Mount Lebanon gathered at Baabda, seat of the Lebanese Administrative Council. As they unfurled a new flag based on the French tricolor, the delegates rejected the authority of the Damascus Congress and proclaimed the independent state of Greater Lebanon under French mandate. They also condemned the Lebanese deputies who had defied Gouraud's ban to attend the Syrian Congress, two of whom were in fact Maronite Christians: George Harfoush and Arif al-Naamani from Beirut.[24]

Although the Maronite Church commanded the largest bloc of Lebanese Christians, there were other, more flexible political factions in Lebanon. Some Christians, especially Greek Orthodox, supported the March 8 declaration's proposal to incorporate an autonomous Mount Lebanon within independent Syria. Politicians in Damascus had reason to believe that they might cultivate even more support on the coast. To that end, Faisal staged his own tour of Lebanon later in March. Gouraud complained that Syrian flags were flying everywhere in the Bekaa Valley.[25]

Under the pressure of the rival Lebanese declaration and sectarian violence in the borderlands between the West and East zones, Congress took up debate on minority rights in the Syrian Constitution.

Establishing Minority Rights in Syria

We have no official count of Christian deputies in Congress, but biographical data suggest there were at least a dozen. Darwazeh claimed there were as many as twenty. Rough population estimates suggest this number was proportional to the population of Greater Syria. In the absence of an accurate census, the King-Crane Commission had estimated in 1919 that 18 percent of the population in all of Greater Syria was Christian. The dozen Christian deputies fell just short of that proportion, equaling 14 percent of the total of eighty-five deputies portrayed in the official commemorative portrait of the 1920 Congress.[26]

However, the Christian population varied by zone: in the East Zone (inland Syria and Jordan), Christians represented 8.3 percent; in the South Zone (Palestine), 10 percent; in the West Zone (Lebanese coast), 37 percent. While Christians' representation exceeded their proportion of the population in the East and South zones, Christians in the West Zone correctly argued that the Congress underrepresented them. It was disingenuous, though, to blame Congress for the underrepresentation of Lebanese Christians. Not only had the French blocked open elections in 1919, but also the Maronite Church and Lebanese Administrative Council had refused to send any delegates.

Jews were also underrepresented in Congress: while King-Crane estimated that 110,000 Jews lived in Greater Syria (more than half of those in Palestine), the only recorded Jewish deputy was Yusuf Linado from Damascus. Zionists in Palestine had declined to send deputies. Out of either conviction or fear, Linado raised no public protest against the Congress's condemnation of Zionism. Other groups were also ignored, most saliently Kurds. Thousands lived in their own quarter of Damascus, led most prominently by Abd al-Rahman Yusuf as well as the family of Nazik Abid, the feminist. Thousands more lived in Aleppo and in the northeastern deserts of Syria. Most urban Kurds spoke Arabic and were socially distant from desert and rural communities. No organized Kurdish nationalist movement yet existed in Syria.[27] We have no record of petitions by Kurds who may have objected to the designation of Syria as an Arab Kingdom. Nor is there evidence of a discussion of their rights in Congress.

Events in Lebanon and pressure from the Supreme Council, in the end, focused Congress's debate about minority rights on Christians more than any other group. The promise of legal equality had long been accepted by political leaders, but the concept of minority rights was new. In the Ottoman era, Arab officials had never shared the anti-Christian hostility of the Turkish ruling elite. In 1908, Muslim clerics in Beirut and Damascus had publicly embraced the promise of Christians' legal equality.[28]

Because Rashid Rida was president of the Congress, his views on Muslim-Christian relations would be consequential. Rida had grown up in a Muslim household that had cordial relations with Christian neighbors in Tripoli (Lebanon). After his move to Cairo, however, he had grown critical of the evangelical aggressiveness of Christian missionaries. He engaged in polemics to defend Islam against European Orientalists, and to exhort fellow Muslims to strengthen their learning and faith in the modern world. However, Rida maintained close friendships with Arab Christians, especially Syrian emigrants in Cairo. And he carried on a dialogue between the faiths in his magazine.[29]

Rida was personally impressed by the relatively egalitarian and tolerant atmosphere in Damascus. "Muslims were not favored in the government of Damascus over Christians or Jews," he wrote. "Muslims didn't expect any better treatment from Muslim ministers. They expected the same from both Muslim and non-Muslim ministers."[30] In April, Rida gave a lecture in Congress on Islam and legislative government. Once non-Muslims understood Islamic teaching on the subject, he argued, they should find it satisfactory. To his satisfaction, several Christian deputies told him they were pleased with his lecture.[31]

But Rida warned readers of The Lighthouse that Muslims, including himself, were often insensitive. At war's end, Ottoman-trained Muslim officials had rushed to take posts vacated by the Turks, without thinking to include Christians. And in late 1919, when Rida helped to raise money for an Islamic college in Beirut, he himself had been unconcerned about the sectarian appearance of his campaign. When Christians complained about favoritism, Rida responded by advocating public schools for both Christians and Muslims.[32]

Since January, Faisal had promoted Christian participation in government. Three Christians served in his cabinets: Faris al-Khoury, Yusuf al-Hakim, and Iskander Ammoun. Faisal named the Maronite priest Habib Istifan to a prominent post in the culture ministry, a post he used to tour Syria to rally Christians to the regime. While he continued to subsidize the Greek Orthodox patriarchate, Faisal also began to support the prominent literary salon of Mary Ajamy, which attracted a mix of Christian and Muslim notables. Ajamy also published a women's magazine that promoted Arabism among Christians as well as Muslims.[33]

The political concept of Christians as a minority group was introduced only at the end of the Great War, in the Paris peace process. It was a by-product of the process of carving out states based on the nationality of a supposed majority population in the various districts of the Hapsburg and Ottoman empires. Peacemakers were acutely aware that groups deemed external to the majority ruling nation might suffer discrimination.

It was in response to such concerns at Paris that Prince Faisal first proclaimed there to be no minorities in Syria: citizens of all religions were all Arabs with equal rights. He essentially sought to abolish the Ottoman system that organized non-Muslims into separate and inferior communities called millets. However, upon his return to Damascus in May 1919, Faisal began to publicly use the terms "minority" and "rights" in addressing the status of non-Muslims. After accepting a blessing of gratitude from the archbishop of refugee Armenians, Faisal proclaimed, "The claims of the minority groups will definitely be given preference over the views and wishes of the majority" in order to reverse the sectarian hatreds sown by the wartime Ottoman government. "We must prove to [the Allies] that we are a people who want to be independent. Let us protect the great and small among us, our neighbors, and those who seek refuge with us." Faisal repeated the message in Aleppo, warning that ignorant Europeans might use discrimination against minorities to undermine the cause of Syrian independence. "The government to be established," he vowed, "will undoubtedly do whatever is necessary to support the rights of the minority and will make written pledges for the record."[34]

Likewise, Rida and the Syrian Union Party had long stressed that constitutional guarantees of full rights were crucial to winning popular support in Syria and European support at the peace conference. "We must always mention the rights of minorities to reassure the Christians," a member stressed at a January 1919 party meeting. "We

must work to erase the fear in Christians' hearts." Rida and Shahbandar served on the SUP's minorities committee. That spring the SUP
adopted its own "Fourteen Principles," the seventh of which called
for protection of minorities.[35]

At first, in October 1918, Christian leaders of Damascus were
split in their views toward Faisal's regime. But at Faisal's coronation
on March 8, 1920, all of the city's Christian patriarchs confirmed
their public support for a constitutional Syrian Arab Kingdom. They
exchanged vows of loyalty with the new king, on the condition that
he continue to uphold his promises of equality. Afterward, they convened a high-profile meeting at the Damascus residence of the Greek
Catholic patriarch, Dimitri Qadhi. Like many Syrian Catholics, Qadhi
had at first rejected Faisal's rule, but he became so dismayed by the
inefficient and divisive tactics of High Commissioner Georges-Picot
that he turned against the French in late 1919. A British official, who
met Qadhi at that time during a visit to Syria, estimated that 40 to
45 percent of Christians opposed the French.[36]

The Muslim and Christian spiritual leaders who convened at Qadhi's
home on March 11 agreed to establish a permanent committee to
promote "unity and agreement among all sects that had recently
rejected the international mandate in any form." They further vowed
to work hand in hand with one another and the government against
"enslavement" (meaning discrimination and subordination) and to
"preserve freedom for themselves and their children."[37]

Debate on minority representation in the national and provincial assemblies lasted two weeks in the first half of June. Heated
argument exploded on June 7 over the question of minority quotas. A bloc of deputies proposed that half the seats in the national
assembly be reserved for all minorities, meaning non-Sunni Arab
Muslims, the various Christian sects, Jews, Druze, and Kurds. The
group was led by Teodor Antaki, a Christian deputy from Aleppo
who was also a member of the constitution drafting committee.
However, on June 7, a majority of deputies voted to reject that
proposal in favor of strict proportional representation. Antaki and
several defeated deputies stormed out of the chamber and headed
to the Greek Orthodox patriarchate for a strategic meeting hosted

by Monsignor Gregorios. This was just the sort of split that Faisal and the SUP had long feared.

A compromise was hammered out after more argument the next week. On June 14, Congress finally approved an amended Article 129, setting minority quotas in provincial elections. The article granted minorities a slightly higher rate of representation (one representative per fifteen thousand inhabitants compared with one for every twenty thousand Muslims). A similar compromise was struck for the national assembly, where one minority deputy would be elected for every thirty thousand inhabitants, compared with one per forty thousand inhabitants for Muslim deputies. Supporters argued that this arrangement would guarantee minorities one-third of the seats in the national and provincial assemblies.[38]

The compromise represented an improvement over the 1909 Ottoman constitution, which made no special provisions for minority representation. But it did not fully satisfy advocates for fuller minority representation. Several deputies boycotted the June 14 vote for reasons that, owing to the loss of congressional records, remain unclear. Tension may have risen because non-Muslims distrusted the clerical leadership of Rida and Khatib. Dissent and fear are also understandable reactions to a political context where non-Muslims and non-Arabs confronted violence along the Lebanese and Anatolian borders; their leaders proposed sectarian segregation as a safer alternative to the Congress's liberalism. On the very day that the six deputies stormed out of the chamber, June 7, Congress issued a summons to the foreign minister to discuss a new round of French threats.[39]

After taking the June 14 vote, Congress approved a ten-day recess for the end of Ramadan. Upon their return from the holidays, the deputies completed a full review of the constitution on June 29. Every one of the 148 articles had been discussed in Congress sessions.[40]

Despite the controversy, the electoral provisions for minorities—combined with the constitution's guarantee of equal rights regardless of religion or ethnicity and its disestablishment of Islamic law—represented significant steps beyond its Ottoman predecessor toward establishing an inclusive, democratic political system. These steps were taken through democratic procedures involving debate and compromise. While Arabic was designated the official language, the constitution did not require citizens to speak it. And while the state threatened to deport former Turkish officials, it permitted those born in Syria or married into native Syrian families to gain citizenship. Even the official name of the country, the Syrian Arab Kingdom, represented a compromise between those who sought to found the state on the particular mix of populations in Syrian territory and those who sought a broader federation of Arabs. The denial of suffrage to women fell short of democratic ideals, but it was a shortfall shared by France and other democratic countries of the time.[41]

"The Muslim majority in the Eastern Zone of Syria treated minorities as brothers in terms of rights and duties. The government did not discriminate between Muslims and Christians in distributing posts," recalled Yusuf al-Hakim, the Greek Orthodox minister. Hakim had run for Congress president in March and won forty-three votes, landing in third place. His experience with the "clerical" Congress after May 5 was not entirely negative. In his memoir, Hakim remembered Abd al-Qadir al-Khatib as a man of exemplary and modest opinions, not as a fanatic.[42]

For Rida, the ratification of a constitution that included Christians as full citizens with equal rights was the achievement of an aspiration born in 1908, when he celebrated the revolution at an Armenian church in Cairo. Muslims in the crowd had carried him on their shoulders to the altar to embrace the Armenian bishop in brotherhood. To readers of The Lighthouse, Rida wrote with pride about how the Syrian Arab Kingdom had established a true democracy:

> Freedom in all its aspects ruled—including freedom of association, speech, and publishing—which were envied in other parts of Syria and Egypt. The exaggerated salutations and aggrandizement of officials and notables (that Damascus was famous for) disappeared. People sensed their own honor and dignity.

The kingdom ruled with greater justice than the French and British, Rida argued: non-Muslims were equal to Muslims in every way. In Lebanon and Palestine, by contrast, Muslims suffered discrimination.[43]

Presentation of the Constitution

On July 5, 1920, Congress held a public reading of the entire draft constitution. More than eighty deputies gathered in the Abid building on Marjeh Square. They represented districts of Greater Syria that today lie in five separate states: about half were from Syria, a third from Lebanon and Palestine/Israel, and the remainder from Jordan and Turkey.[44]

Uthman Sultan, a deputy from Rashid Rida's district of Tripoli, spoke on behalf of the constitution committee. A young professor from Damascus Law School, Sultan was humbled by the honor. He handed a copy of the constitution to Congress president Rashid Rida. The document was 148 articles long and bore the signatures of the twenty-four deputies who served on the constitutional committee and in Congress leadership.[45]

Sultan stepped to the podium. From beneath a tight tarbush that accentuated his plump cheeks, he looked across the chamber and addressed his fellow deputies:

> Today, our Syrian nation prepares for a new era of
> independence. His Royal Highness Prince Faisal charged
> the Syrian General Congress, enjoying the trust of all the
> nation whom it represents, to draft a constitution for the new
> Syrian Kingdom, to organize it under a new structure, and
> to safeguard especially the rights of minorities. His Highness
> expressed the urgent need to set down the constitution now, as
> a civil weapon to protect the nation from the shock of colonial
> politics, whose propagandists use a variety of pretexts to take
> control of our country under misleading terms like tutelage,
> protectorate, and mandate.

Sultan presented the constitution as "shining proof to the civilized world" that Syrians were sophisticated enough to run a modern state.

Syria had matured in the eighteen months since the Supreme Council voted to establish the mandate system, he declared. Syrians now had a system of government that met the criteria for full independence.[46]

Sultan's speech presented the constitution as a living document, tailored to the specific needs of Syrian society. It was not a foreign model of government plucked from textbooks, imposed on Syrians in order to please Europeans at the peace conference, Sultan explained. "The committee studied carefully the roots and bases of democratic life, while minding the conditions of the country and the people, with their differing sects and hopes," he explained. Members finally settled upon a civil, parliamentary form of government because it would balance freedom and rule of law. The proposed regime would mobilize public opinion, but also guard against "exclusionary and religious elements in politics and government."

This was the logic behind Article 1, which Sultan read aloud: "The government of the Syrian Arab Kingdom is a civil, representative monarchy. Its capital is Damascus, Syria, and the religion of its king is Islam." The article ensured the people's right to rule, and did not leave politics to the control of "religious factors," Sultan explained. But freedom of religion and safeguards against discrimination among sects were also guaranteed in the constitution.

Sultan acknowledged that some Syrians would have preferred to go one step farther, to establish the greater freedom of a republic "after the hardships they suffered under cruel, authoritarian rule." But the committee believed Syrians were not ready yet for a republic. Without a transition period of social education, a republic would result in anarchy.

The committee chose Faisal as king, Sultan explained, also to suit Syria's special needs. Faisal's heroic record of leadership on the battlefield would inspire the people and help them "forget the abyss into which they fell under past governments." But some Syrians asked, "How can a son of the Hijaz step up to the Syrian throne?" The committee addressed their concern by making Faisal king not by claim to dynasty or geographic origin, but rather "because he is chosen by election of Syrian citizens." Faisal would not, and could not, become a despot like the Ottoman sultan, he continued, because the government would be responsible to Congress, not to the king. "Article 9 addresses this issue: The King is respected, but not responsible."

Because Syrians had opposed the centralized rule of the Young Turks, the constitution established a decentralized, federal-style government, Sultan continued. Provincial assemblies would hold all local authority, while the General Congress would issue national laws on health, education, labor, and defense. Unity would be fostered through the common official language and through a national school curriculum.

Sultan also emphasized the "bill of rights" embedded in the constitution's third chapter. It guaranteed citizenship to all residents of Syria, with equal rights under the law. It also protected freedom of belief and religion, as well as freedom from censorship in the press. Forced labor or exile, torture, and unauthorized entry into private residences were completely banned. A free elementary education was obligatory for all citizens. Religious schools, including Christian schools, were permitted.

The young professor spoke at length of constitutional guarantees to protect minorities, to protect their schools and religious rites. Electoral laws would ensure that no ruling clique dominated government, by allowing all (male) citizens to vote and by setting quotas for minority representation.

Sultan concluded by proposing that Congress send a request to Prime Minister Atassi to begin organizing the polls, so that as soon as the constitution was ratified parliamentary elections could be held.

With an elated spirit of achievement, the deputies voted to accept the entire constitution in principle, pending a second round of review, article by article. They also agreed to launch the process of organizing elections.[47] Within a week, Congress formally ratified the first six articles with minor revisions. These articles established in Syria a civil, representative monarchy and established the powers of the king, who had to obey the constitution and the laws of God (not Islamic law, as in the Ottoman constitution).

Exactly a year after the Congress first unveiled the constitutional project to the King-Crane Commission, Syrians were ready to implement the constitutional democracy they had promised.

Conclusion: Maronite Support at the Eleventh Hour

While Catholic newspapers generally ignored events in Damascus, other papers in Beirut followed Syrian politics closely. In the spring of 1920, *Lissan al-Hal,* published by a Protestant Christian family, ran a regular column on Syria that followed constitutional debates, especially on minority rights. The paper simultaneously ran critical articles on General Gouraud's project to draft a separate constitution for Lebanon. The general insisted upon appointing the members of the constitutional committee himself and made it clear that a Frenchman, not a Lebanese, would serve as governor. In the week between June 30 and July 7, *Lissan al-Hal* published enthusiastic articles about the Syrian Constitution's emphasis on minority rights and its presentation to Congress, along with an editorial insisting that the people had the right to appoint their own ruler.[48]

Doubts about French intentions in Lebanon had first resurfaced in early May. Leading nationalists worried that Lebanon had not even been mentioned at the San Remo Conference. Its fate had been folded into the decision to award France a mandate over all of Syria. Christians, including Maronites, who had insisted on Lebanese independence now suspected there would be no quick passage from French mandate to full independence. Some of them took a second look at the March 8 Declaration of Independence, which had promised Lebanon full autonomy on condition that all foreign powers (France) be excluded from the territory.

Amid public debate, Lebanese deputies to the Syrian Congress had begun to engage erstwhile opponents of union with Syria in secret talks. The talks that Riad al-Solh, deputy from the coastal city of Sidon, held with the Lebanese Administrative Council produced surprising and dramatic results.

Solh believed that the future of Syria rested on Lebanese opinion. He aimed to puncture France's pretense as protector of Christians by winning Maronite loyalty to the Syrian state. Shortly after July 5, he carried an advance copy of the Syrian Constitution to a meeting of the Lebanese Administrative Council. Many of the councilors were satisfied that non-Muslims would indeed enjoy equal rights of citizenship in Syria. Solh also brought with him a promise from Faisal that the federal state of Syria would rule the coast as an autonomous state of Lebanon stretching from Sidon in the south to Tripoli in the north. Council members were also swayed by false news reports that Faisal and Gouraud were close to sealing an agreement that might leave Lebanon under French control.

On July 10, a majority on the Lebanese Administrative Council—seven of twelve members—voted to defect to the Damascus government. Led by the Maronite patriarch's brother, Saadallah Hoyek, the seven councilors set out secretly for Damascus that very night to pledge their oath of loyalty to Faisal. They would then travel to Paris to proclaim their support for the Syrian Arab Kingdom to the Supreme Council. But as their train paused at a mountain checkpoint, a Senegalese soldier arrested them on charges of treason. Gouraud immediately abolished the Lebanese Administrative Council.[49]

The defection of the Maronite patriarch's own brother was a welcome endorsement of Syria's democratic constitution as a "civil weapon of the nation" against colonial designs. It was "the most wonderful event that pleased our hearts," Yusuf al-Hakim recalled. The Lebanese, who had lived in freedom in the Ottoman era, within the district of Ottoman Mount Lebanon, could not bear to submit to direct French rule under the mandate.[50]

Hakim's optimism was short-lived. Events unfolded quickly in the next two weeks, overwhelming Syrians' plans to finally establish their democracy by holding elections. The Congress woke to the diplomatic maneuvers that were about seal Syria's fate.

In Palestine, the Declaration of Independence had provoked popular celebrations. But the British had firmly blocked any actual move toward incorporating the region into Greater Syria. In mid-June, Izzat Darwazeh and other Palestinian deputies had raised futile protests in Congress against Britain's appointment of the first civilian high commissioner to Palestine.

And on the Lebanese coast, the French high commission was working secretly to preempt any flood of support for joining a united

Greater Syria. Following the precedent of San Remo, French Premier Millerand intended to use force to quash popular opinion on the choice of mandatory power. Throughout the month of June, even as the Congress debated the last articles of the constitution, he and General Gouraud had been planning the absolute destruction of their state.

PART V

Syria's Expulsion from the Civilized World

Chapter 15

Battle Plans for Syria

"Our policy in Syria is worse than at any moment since the General arrived," de Caix wrote to Berthelot on May 4. Far from rejoicing over the mandate award, de Caix agonized over the uncertainty about France's sovereignty. To him, the Damascus government was an "abscess" that would infect all of Syria, unless removed. "We must finish with the Faisal question, either by reducing the Damascus government to proper proportions, or by eliminating it," he advised. "The English continue to favor Faisal as a way to oust us."[1]

By agreeing to omit details at San Remo, British foreign secretary Curzon had left the field open for the French to define the terms of the mandate. De Caix stepped in to convince French officials that the mandate granted them exclusive sovereignty over the Syrian interior. They must now shut Britain out and ensure Faisal's downfall. By month's end, de Caix had convinced Millerand and Gouraud to draw up plans to invade the Arab East Zone. This radical shift in French policy, fully abandoning the January 6 Clemenceau accord, was enabled by the waning of threats from both north and south of Syria. While de Caix negotiated a cease-fire with Turkish nationalists, Faisal's father, Sharif Hussein, suffered defeats by Ibn Saud. Few Turks or Arabs would likely come to Faisal's aid.[2]

Striking, in retrospect, is how long it took Faisal's government to discover France's new plan. On May 1, Gouraud forwarded to Faisal a note on the San Remo decision. With the mandate, it said, France confirmed "its recognition of the right of Arabic-speaking peoples of all confessions residing in the Syrian territory to govern themselves as an independent nation." He assured Faisal that France would protect Syrian independence from foreign aggression "within borders fixed by the Peace Conference, while taking into account necessary autonomies."[3]

Unbeknownst to Faisal, three days later Millerand gave Gouraud instructions "to settle the Syria question with the Prince." Only France, not the Syrian Congress, had the right to name Faisal king or to constitute a government, Millerand reiterated. Gouraud should therefore draw up plans to impose French authority: "I give you full freedom of action," he said. In anticipation of protests, Millerand ordered the war ministry to transfer troops to Syria. He also sent de Caix to Ankara, to negotiate a cease-fire with Mustafa Kemal so that additional French troops could be transferred from Cilicia to Syria.[4]

The May 1 French note surprised the Syrians. Based on communications from the British, they had understood that San Remo recognized their provisional independence. On April 27, General Allenby had sent a telegram reflecting the compromise that Hubert Young had composed in Curzon's home earlier in the month. Allenby's cable had reassured Faisal that the Allies provisionally recognized Syria and Mesopotamia as independent states and that he would be recognized as king of Syria: "While His Majesty's Government are prepared to recognize Your Highness provisionally as head of an independent Syrian State, they hold strongly that your claim to Kingship can only be formally established by Peace Conference."[5]

Faisal wanted to believe Allenby's promises. "I am pleased to note that the San Remo conference recognizes Syria and Mesopotamia as two independent states," he responded on May 15. "And with joy I note the readiness of our great ally Great Britain to recognize me as King of the Syrian state."[6] By then, however, Faisal had learned of France's very different reading of San Remo. On May 14, Faisal had written to Millerand to dispute the premier's suggestion that Syria was not a united nation deserving of sovereign rights, but rather a collection of various "Arabic-speaking peoples." Millerand's note, the king wrote, "has caused among my people a painful effect and a great uproar. First of all, in recognizing the right of Syrian peoples to independence, the French government has not given Syria a new right: this right is granted by nature. Second, Syrians do not belong to different nations distinct from one another, but to the same, single nation that has inhabited the same territory for more than a thousand years." Syria would accept France's aid only under the January 6 accord, Faisal declared: "It is impossible to accept it under the form of 'mandate.'"[7]

In a similar defiant spirit, Syria's new foreign minister, Abd al-Rahman Shahbandar, had vowed to the Congress on May 8 to defend Syria's sovereignty and to fight the San Remo decision: "The power and courage of peoples are the best guarantee for the defense of rights."[8]

Syrians' defiance, and especially their continued references to Britain, enraged Millerand. He ordered the French ambassador in London, Paul Cambon, to set matters straight with Curzon: the mandate awarded France full sovereignty over Syria and prohibited Britain from interfering in the matter—just as France would not interfere with the British mandates of Palestine and Mesopotamia.

Curzon denied that Britain had encouraged Faisal to resist the mandate. But as a dyed-in-the-wool imperialist, he was still reluctant to cede unilateral power to France. So Curzon recommended that the two powers send a joint ultimatum to Faisal. They could lure him to the Peace Conference with threats to cut his subsidies and strip him of his title as Hijaz representative.

Millerand accepted Curzon's proposal on two conditions: that the joint ultimatum be sent only through Gouraud, and that Britain suspend all contact with Faisal and renounce recognition of him as head of state.[9] Millerand also demanded that the ultimatum deny any future role in Syrian affairs to Sharif Hussein and the Hijaz delegation. In Millerand's view, Faisal was no longer acting as an Allied officer; therefore, the basis of the January 6 accord no longer held.[10] But Curzon was uneasy with those terms. A copy of the joint ultimatum sat on his desk for the remainder of the month of May, unsigned.[11] Millerand decided to act unilaterally.

On May 27, the French premier sent an ultimatum to Faisal. The document stated that as a mere "military commander" of residual occupying forces left over from the Great War, Faisal was now required to submit to the internationally recognized sovereign, France. Continued Syrian protests against the mandate were unjustified, Millerand declared, because the sovereign authority of the Supreme Council of the peace conference could not be contested. The Council represented "the union of Powers who, at the price of immense sacrifice, liberated the oppressed peoples, and especially the Arabs." Now only the Supreme Council—not the Syrian Congress—had the right to define the laws and borders of new states under mandate.[12]

That very same day, Millerand ordered Gouraud to draw up a battle plan to invade the Syrian interior and occupy Damascus against the "insolent and threatening Sharifian government." He noted that conditions were ripe, with the Turkish cease-fire and the award of the mandate.[13]

Gouraud readily accepted the call to battle. In language as militant as Millerand's, the general blamed the Syrians for the shame of his defeat in Cilicia and for his weak position in Lebanon. Faisal had shown "bad faith," and made "perfidious insinuations" to challenge France in Lebanon, he claimed. In his view, Syria's refusal to grant access to the railway needed to send troops to Cilicia was a "stab in the back" by an erstwhile ally.

The copious use of the term "Sharifian" by various French diplomats was a sign of de Caix's growing influence. The term cast the Syrian Arab Kingdom as an alien, Hijazi presence and demonstrated a denial of the Syrian Congress's position as representative of the population. In fact, Faisal had long ago cut ties with his hostile father. He protested the French ultimatum, arguing that there were no "Sharifians" in his army and that most officers in the Damascus government were from Greater Syria. Elected Syrian deputies had elected him their king.

Awni Abd al-Hadi, Faisal's longtime secretary, recognized the term "Sharifian" as an attack on the Arabs' claim to equal membership in the family of nations. By contrast, he remarked, Clemenceau had treated the Syrian Arabs as fellow liberals. Clemenceau had sympathized when Faisal had warned him that stationing French troops in Syria would weaken the hand of liberals to the benefit of those who joined Mustafa Kemal's armed movement in Anatolia. To Abd al-Hadi, the January 6 accord and the Declaration of Independence were bulwarks of liberal values—against both the French colonial lobby and the "hidden hands" of despair who were organizing futile militias to wage Islamic jihad. In letter after letter, Abd al-Hadi and the king had reiterated their desire for Muslims, Christians, and Jews to live together, with equal rights.[14] But Curzon and the British had turned a deaf ear to their appeal to uphold the Great War's promise of a new democratic world order.

In June 1920, the French succeeded in isolating Syria diplomatically. They convinced the Allied powers that the mandate superseded not only Clemenceau's January 6 accord but also the King-Crane report of August 1919, and even the Sykes-Picot accord, which had designated the Syrian hinterland as a zone of French influence, not French rule. France now claimed full dominion over the entire territory. In effect, the French did not recognize a Syrian nation at all. While they referred to Mustafa Kemal and Turkish rebels as "nationalists," they called their Syrian opponents "rebels" and "bandits," who mounted "disorders."

By early July, Syria was so isolated that communication with the outside world had to be funneled through the office of General Gouraud, through a single telegraph line linking Damascus to Beirut. Faisal was also denied the right to travel to Europe. In desperation, Syrians hastily arranged an alternative telegraph line to the Hijaz. The Italian consul in Damascus occasionally allowed Syrian politicians to contact the outside world using the consulate's diplomatic links.[15]

Faisal and Gouraud never met face-to-face. They communicated solely through telegrams and couriers. Gouraud rejected every offer of cooperation that Faisal sent him.[16] Gouraud also dismissed the advice of his couriers, colonels Edouard Cousse and Antoine Toulat, who had served as liaisons in Damascus for more than a year. They urged Gouraud to compromise, arguing that the Syrian Declaration of Independence was not incompatible with the mandate.[17] But as T. E. Lawrence knew well, prime ministers preferred grand imperial strategy and routinely dismissed the wisdom of local officials.

The Plan to Destroy the Syrian Arab Kingdom

Once Damascus had been cornered, the French moved in for the kill. As of May 27, Millerand had not yet planned to occupy more than the Syrian interior. But his goals radicalized rapidly over the following two weeks, in response to growing friction with Britain.

On June 11, Millerand flew into a rage upon learning that Allenby was continuing to meddle in Syrian affairs. "The French government, having decided against intervention in the organization of the mandates of Palestine and Mesopotamia," he wrote to Cambon, his ambassador in London, "expects the same respect of the English government." Allenby had dared to propose that Prince Zaid attend the peace conference in Faisal's place. "[Allenby] still thinks he is head of the military occupation in Syria," Millerand wrote in a second letter.[18]

Between the two letters to Cambon, Millerand issued Gouraud a new directive: void the January 6 accord and destroy the Syrian Arab Kingdom. He saw no point in negotiating with the "hostile Sharifians." Millerand blamed Faisal for his own demise. "So far, the latter's policy has been to fight us and to spread an artificial, xenophobic nationalism throughout Syria; his attitude has consistently undermined the conciliatory spirit expressed in the provisional January 6 accord," he wrote. Millerand instructed Gouraud to plan to replace Faisal and the Congress with a new government of docile, "indigenous" authorities.[19]

Millerand's directive echoed an earlier conversation he had with de Caix, on June 5. De Caix had warned Millerand not to work with Faisal. "Syrians are both too intelligent to negotiate with and too disorganized to control," he said.[20] De Caix followed up that meeting with a memo that concluded, "It seems therefore absolutely necessary to completely domesticate or better, to eliminate the Sharifian government before discussing [the form of] the mandate."[21]

De Caix's central role in the decision to destroy the Syrian Arab Kingdom is also revealed in recently discovered secret correspondence between him and Gouraud. Their handwritten notes were not codified at telegraph offices and were usually sent to home addresses. Like Iago with Othello, de Caix sowed insecurity and doubt in Gouraud and then promised him redemption if he followed his subordinate's advice. "They [Millerand, Paléologue, and others] criticize you for working too much on a day-to-day basis, reacting to events without making your own policy," de Caix warned Gouraud in a June 8 letter. "There is only the impression that things are going badly in Syria." De Caix also warned Gouraud to keep this advice secret, "not to signal that you know what I write to you when you write to Paris to justify the High Commission's policy. It will make you out as a complainer." Instead, he advised, "what I recommend is that you act according to what I find."

De Caix conjured a reality that did not yet exist in either Paris or Beirut. In the same letter, he told Gouraud that Millerand would be pleased to "erase the occupation of Cilicia," and he advised the general to undertake an "energetic act" in Syria (implying military intervention). De Caix claimed that the sentiment in Paris favored regime change following France's occupation of Syria. The January 6 accord was dead and resurrecting it was a dead end. De Caix closed his June 8 letter with a final warning to the general: an invasion that left France without a solid base and that did not justify its cost would prompt Paris to disband the entire Army of the Levant.[22]

Your letter "shocked me," Gouraud replied, in a letter addressing de Caix as "my dear friend." Gouraud maintained that the delay and drift of policy in Syria were not his fault, but had resulted from decisions made by Picot and Clemenceau. "I understand quite well that M. Millerand is upset," Gouraud wrote, "but he unloads the consequences of their errors onto my back." Gouraud placed his trust in de Caix. "Luckily, as in March, you are there to defend us with the truth."[23]

Faisal recognized de Caix's hand in France's changed attitude. "I returned from Paris last January full of hope," he wrote to Millerand on June 10. Now, ever since the cease-fire with Turkey, he was being treated with hostility by French officials. "I intend to neglect the actions of your officials, especially those who work ceaselessly to dismember Syria and to annihilate my personal influence, the goal [that was] clearly indicated by the proposals that M. de Caix has submitted to you and that intend to establish in Syria several, separate governments," Faisal wrote.[24]

Faisal's appeals to Berthelot to defend the January 6 accord against de Caix's plots went unanswered.[25] The cordial lunches they enjoyed at each other's homes the previous winter were a distant memory.

In his advice to Gouraud and Millerand, de Caix targeted not only the Arab king, but also Syria's democratic government. He incorrectly portrayed the Syrian Congress as an instrument deliberately created by the British to delegitimize France. The British never permitted a political body to represent popular opinion in Mesopotamia, he observed to Millerand. "The clamors of the Syrian Congress will permit hypocritical members of the League of Nations who wish to serve England (no doubt Italy and Japan) to declare that the situation in Syria is different from Mesopotamia," he warned Millerand.

Significantly, de Caix anticipated that the politically sophisticated Syrians might succeed in convincing the League that Article 22 requiring a mandate did not apply to them. "It is quite possible British policy will maneuver to draw us into a discussion of the mandate with Faisal before the Council of the League of Nations," de Caix wrote. France must therefore block Faisal from attending the peace conference.[26]

De Caix understood that the liberal threat posed by the Syrian Congress was as lethal as Wilsonism. Rashid Rida, Hashim al-Atassi, and other members of Congress had rejected rebels' calls to mount an armed revolt with the Turks. They had instead placed their bets for Syria's future on a new world order based on rights, law, and equality. That was why, even after San Remo, Rida urged Congress to continue debating and drafting the constitution.

The French were so nervous about the potential influence of the Syrian Congress that they deployed spies to file regular reports on its debates. Gouraud took particular notice of a report on the June 7 debate over the rights of non-Muslim minorities: "None of their proposals was accepted. The non-Muslim delegates stormed out of the meeting room," read the report. Gouraud perceived political advantage in the dispute. "I will not fail to take advantage of this news to open the eyes of Christians to the dangers they risk by indiscriminately engaging in Faisal's government."[27] Gouraud's intelligence staff cultivated the loyalties of Christian, Druze, Shiite, and Allawi minorities by offering protection, distributing weapons, and promising autonomy once France established rule of the hinterland.

Sectarian thinking pervaded French discourse. Using populist language ripped from the tabloids, Millerand based his May 27 call to battle on the need to defeat Faisal's support for "brigands who massacre Christians." He advised Gouraud to make a public declaration upon the invasion to promise a "light and liberal" mandate. "Occupying the four cities will reassure the Christians who have begun to doubt us," Millerand reasoned.[28]

Faisal, in response, scolded Gouraud for stirring sectarian fears. If he had worked instead to uphold the French Republic's own ideals of equality and tolerance in Syria, peace would have prevailed. "[Y]ou would have seen by now no need of drawing your sword to submit the people to the yoke of a minority, nor to make menacing speeches as you have recently done," Faisal wrote.[29]

Meanwhile, Maronite leaders continued to lobby French officials for a separate, independent state of Greater Lebanon. The delegation met with de Caix at the Quai d'Orsay to discuss Lebanon's future borders. De Caix assured the Lebanese that France would protect Christians under a new system of autonomous, sectarian states.[30]

The Chamber of Deputies Debate

The French Chamber of Deputies, much like the Syrian Congress, demanded a say in foreign policy. Wilsonism's last echo was the continued expectation that the public had a say in matters of war and peace. On the first anniversary of the signing of the Versailles treaty, the French Chamber convened hearings on whether to finance an invasion of Syria. The deputies reopened the painful debate on the wages of the Great War, pitting pleas for peace against desires to avenge blood spilled. In retrospect, the debate also reveals how uncannily prescient some French citizens were of the long-lasting effects that an invasion would have on relations with the Muslim world. "France is not alone in facing the perils of the Eastern problem," wrote Senator Paul d'Estournelles de Constant, former diplomat and Nobel Peace

Prize winner, in a June 17 newspaper column. "It is the whole world that is threatened. Rather than turn our Oriental friends into rebels, France should promote peace under international law," he argued.[31]

The public had no interest in Syria, the socialist paper *L'Humanité* agreed. The budget must instead go toward postwar reconstruction in France.[32]

Advocates of peace in Syria converged at the offices of the Hijaz delegation in Paris. They included representatives of the Human Rights Association, members of the foreign affairs committees in the Assembly, and journalists. With guarded optimism, Rustum Haidar remarked that support for peace in Syria was growing. "And it appears that the Senegalese will refuse to go to Syria, complaining that their service has ended," he said.[33]

In the French press, however, pacifist voices were drowned out by loud demands for an invasion. "This is the moment to take responsibility," wrote a prominent journalist and member of the colonial lobby, Auguste Gauvain, on June 23. His front-page editorial in *Journal des Débats* argued that France must recover all the Ottoman territory it had sacrificed to win in the war. If France pulled out, he warned, the nation "would be covered in shame throughout the Orient."[34]

Gauvain's article launched three days of debate in the Chamber of Deputies. The socialists took the lead, as they had done during the March debate. Because Marcel Cachin was absent (he had departed for the second Comintern congress in Russia), Ernest Lafont spoke for the party. A deputy from the Loire valley, Lafont warned against imperial overreach driven by the simplistic notion that France must "not let England, by herself, indulge her own appetite."

Lafont turned to Millerand and demanded to know what France had received in return for the millions it had spent in Cilicia, Syria, and beyond. The answer was Mosul's petroleum the "Asian Devil" luring France into sin. "Will we stay in Syria? To conquer by force the consent that the inhabitants will not freely give us?" Lafont asked. Loud applause rose from leftists in the Chamber.[35]

Édouard Daladier, a socialist veteran recently elected to the Chamber, reopened debate the next morning. "You have not taken account of the profound emotion that reigns, especially since the Great War, in the Muslim world," he declared. "It is completely mistaken to characterize Faisal as a kind of desert Bolshevik or a Wilsonian in a turban," he said. "Faisal is, to the contrary, a moderate who risks being overwhelmed by extremists and who uses every means in his power to divert this dangerous current.

"[Syrians] have proved, through continuous evolution, that they want to promote liberty and independence, to organize a real state," Daladier warned. "In reality, you are offering them a mandate at the point of our bayonets. If you persist in this foolish policy you risk a catastrophic end."

The debate then turned into a referendum on the rival policies of Millerand and Clemenceau.[36] Aristide Briand, Clemenceau's old nemesis, stood up to teach a few lessons to his younger peers. The Sykes-Picot accord was not an imperialist treaty, he lectured them. It was negotiated at a bleak moment, during the battle of Verdun. "It was our duty not to neglect any aspect of defense and to honor the rights and interests of France," he scolded. "To say that our country has imperialist views is a truly baseless accusation."

Briand insisted that France pursued an altruistic civilizing mission, in contrast to Britain, which worked tirelessly to maximize only its own interests. That was why the British had disregarded the 1916 accords and placed Faisal in the French zone of Syria.

Louis Lenail, a leader of the colonial lobby, called the Chamber's attention to the vast expanse of Ottoman territory that the British had occupied. "England has taken 3 million square kilometers and we, 220,000," Lenail noted. He balked at the proposal to give France's small portion—Syria—"to the Sharif of Mecca."

Lenail, a veteran wounded during the Great War, was a newly elected deputy from the Lyon region, home to Catholic and industrial groups that favored the mandate. Reflecting his frequent meetings with the Maronite-led Lebanese delegation, he painted a dark image of Faisal, unrecognizable to those whom the king (then prince) had charmed at Paris salons in the winter of 1919.

Faisal would not fulfill Wilson's principle of self-government, Lenail argued. The king and his father came from Mecca, "the dirtiest, unhealthiest city in the world." Oriental Christians, Armenians, and Lebanese were begging France to rescue them from the Muslims' backward regime, he claimed. "We will not let you be massacred," Lenail cried, to a loud round of applause.

The next speaker was also a newly elected veteran. Georges Noblemaire represented the finance committee, which de Caix had already lobbied.[37] Noblemaire argued that if the French did not invade Syria, France would become a second-rate power. "[A]nd that is not why 1.5 million French have died," he said. The right side of the Chamber exploded into applause.[38]

On the third day, Saturday, June 26, debate turned to French failures in Cilicia. A deputy recalled the massacre of a French garrison there. "I belong to a region where many men who died at Urfa came from," he declared. "I demand that you concentrate your forces, and abandon what we cannot hold."

Millerand jumped in. "The plan you just proposed is the one that the War Minister and I recommended to General Gouraud, who is ready to implement it!"

Another deputy advocated a preemptive strike against jihad: "Behind Turkey, Islam stands against Europe," he warned, to vigorous applause.

Léon Blum, the future socialist prime minister, dismissed fear of jihad as a phantom of nationalist propaganda. He also disputed colonialists' depiction of Syria as a Christian country that loved France. "In this region, we do not confront the unanimous enthusiasm of the people that M. Lenail mentioned yesterday. Occupying the entire territory that we have been granted by international mandate actually resembles, whether you like it or not, a conquest," Blum said. "Let go of this alluring mirage of grand memories and legends and inspire yourselves with the immediate interests and needs pressing upon France."

Millerand cut leftists' applause short to insist that the so-called legends were a present danger. "There are military operations under way that are nothing but a necessary response—as limited as possible —to attacks directed by you know whom," he warned, apparently referring to Faisal. France must honor its obligation to uphold the sacred trust of the mandate.

"You ask the government what it plans to do," Millerand continued, addressing Blum directly. "It answers you that France, a great Mediterranean power, that France, allied to Syria by so many memories and traditions, does not have the right . . . to abandon Syria." Loud applause broke out across the Chamber. "We are in Syria. We refuse to leave it."[39]

Minutes later, the Chamber approved the budget for the Syrian invasion, 478 votes to 83.[40] It was a towering victory for de Caix and a confirmation of the colonial lobby's pervasive influence. The Chamber's decision to invade Syria also reflected events that had transformed the Syria question since Clemenceau's January 6 accord: the election of a conservative French government, the rise of Turkish nationalists in Cilicia, and Curzon's choice to cede Syria in order to protect Britain's imperial gains.

Beneath the Chamber debates flowed a current of lingering regret for the tremendous sacrifices made during the Great War. In June 1920, France had only recently begun building cemeteries for those who had been killed during the war. Both sides of the Chamber framed the Syria question in terms of redemption. While *Le Temps* hailed the vote as a victory for imperial rivalry against England, *L'Humanité* cast the invasion as a defeat for weary veterans. In an article bearing the headline "It Is Done," Blum lamented that the Syria campaign would prolong mandatory military service.[41]

In fact, so few Frenchmen wanted to serve the empire at this point that Gouraud was forced to amass an army composed almost entirely of colonial troops from Africa.

Syrians' Final Appeal

In response to the Chamber vote, Syrian Union Party president Michel Lutfallah sent his brother to the French Senate on June 29. Habib Lutfallah, the SUP's representative in Paris, arrived at the Luxembourg Palace for an afternoon meeting with the Senate's finance and diplomatic committee in the inauspiciously named Berthelot Room.

Philippe Berthelot, Clemenceau's erstwhile diplomatic advisor, came from a family whose political prominence extended back to the eighteenth century. His father was Marcellin Berthelot, a famous chemist and politician buried in the Pantheon along with France's national heroes. Marcellin had also been friends with France's most famous Orientalist, Ernest Renan, who had argued that Islam was a backward religion. That same afternoon, Philippe Berthelot was working in his Quai d'Orsay office to prepare a boundary map of Syria for Gouraud's invasion.

The Lutfallahs were a prominent family as well. The father of Michel and Habib was a Greek Orthodox entrepreneur from the Syrian coast who had made a fortune in the Egyptian cotton industry. He later became the banker of Sharif Hussein, who granted male members of the Lutfallah family the title "prince."[42] Unlike the Berthelots, the Lutfallahs could not achieve their political goals within their hometown, Cairo, where they owned one of the most opulent palaces along the Nile River. They were well accustomed to the practices of colonial politics.

Habib Lutfallah was a square-jawed man who wore a homburg hat, in contrast to his brother Michel's tarbush. Impeccably dressed in a European suit, he made an appeal to the French senators that displayed his deep understanding of European politics. He set aside Wilsonian ideals and instead employed realpolitik to battle de Caix's plan to weaken Syria.

Rather than invade, Lutfallah proposed, France should make Syria the Poland of the Middle East. Just like Poland, a strong Syria could block the spread of Bolshevism and uphold civilization against barbarism. "Public opinion in France is poorly informed on Syria," he warned the committee. "It neglects that our history is tied to that of humanity, that we are an evolved Nation that possesses a cultivated elite, youth familiar with the French 'grandes écoles,' a significant press corps spread across Asia, Egypt, and the two Americas."

Syria would be more useful to France as a strong, free nation than as a weak colony, Lutfallah continued. "In Balkanizing Asia Minor, in multiplying small principalities, dust particles of states, [France] leaves the road open to the anarchy that will create an endemic state of war. There is one way to prevent the invasion of this anarchy," Lutfallah advised. "Create a solid barrier by letting an Arab state rise in Asia Minor. Strong, united, it will be able to resist the Red Grip and avert danger. World peace is at stake."[43]

The Senate committee likely listened with interest. Earlier in June, several of its members had expressed skepticism when Berthelot proposed to invade Syria. They questioned the wisdom of unseating a king and the legality of occupying the Eastern Zone of Syria, which wartime agreements had promised would be an independent Arab state.[44]

While Lutfallah met with the committee, Rustum Haidar lobbied the Senate's leading anticolonialist, Victor Bérard. Bérard had joined forces with Paul d'Estournelles de Constant, author of the article opposing intervention in Syria that had sparked public debate in mid-June. The two anticolonialists had convinced a significant minority in the Senate to vote against the invasion.[45]

But after winning the Chamber's budget approval, Millerand was in no mood to heed dissidents. In response to the premier's triumphant speech to the Chamber on June 30, Haidar rushed to the office of Maurice Paléologue, the officer in charge of Syria at the Quai d'Orsay. Little did Haidar know that Paléologue had already been forbidden by Millerand to even suggest a return to diplomacy based on the January 6 accord. After Haidar expressed his concern about the Chamber vote, Paléologue curtly replied that he could not discuss military plans. He would only confirm that France intended to impose the mandate. Haidar was alarmed. That evening he sent Faisal a telegram: France intended war.[46]

Chapter 16

The French Ultimatum and Faisal's Dissolution of Congress

Faisal waited a nervous week for Rustum Haidar's cable. He had asked Haidar on June 24 for an update from the French foreign ministry. Five days earlier, he had learned that the French signed an armistice with the Turkish nationalist leader, Mustafa Kemal. Faisal worried (correctly) that the truce might free France to redeploy its troops from Cilicia to Syria. Haidar's cable, reporting French plans for war, confirmed his worst fears.[1]

The king hid these dark developments from Congress and even from his own cabinet. As late as June 20, Foreign Minister Shahbandar reassured Rashid Rida that the San Remo accord recognized Syria's independence, just as General Allenby had told the Syrians back in May. Shahbandar still believed it was possible to negotiate virtual independence under the French mandate, along the lines of the January 6 accord. Although he did not share Shahbandar's faith in the peace process, Rida conceded that it would be wise to send a delegation to Paris to negotiate terms.[2]

Rida's diary suggests he had no inkling of France's battle plans until early July. However, his summary thoughts at the end of June were uncannily perceptive. The government was weak, he confided to his private pages. Hashim al-Atassi's so-called defense cabinet showed no backbone. In the six months since his return from Paris, Faisal had failed to impose discipline among his palace staff or his ministers. His government had no consistent vision or policy and had achieved few reforms. In the old Turkish way, his subordinates just aimed to please him even as they helped themselves to the benefits of office. When problems arose, Faisal angrily put off his critics and tried to impose his unilateral will. He had been better as a diplomat in Paris than he was proving to be as a ruler.

Drift at the palace made Kamil al-Qassab's populist politics in the street all the more dangerous. Rida's opinion of his old friend had changed. "He is patriotic, but he is bold to the point of recklessness," Rida lamented.[3]

Syrians knew they stood little chance of defeating the French army on a battlefield. Their best hope lay in shaping terms of submission to the mandate. But the conflict between king and Congress—ignited with the tinder of Qassab's powerful street politics—made for an explosive and chaotic response to news of France's battle plans.

July 1–8: First Signs of the French Threat

By the time Uthman Sultan presented the constitution to Congress on July 5, rumors of invasion had already begun to circulate. But when Sultan and others urged a quick ratification, Rida insisted that the draft be reviewed properly in a second, article-by-article reading.[4] Uthman was convinced by those who argued that Faisal would use completion of the constitution as a pretext to dismiss the Congress. Leaders in Congress instead demanded a full hearing from the cabinet on the crisis.

In retrospect, signs of trouble had been evident since late June, with reports that conservative politicians were meeting with the French. Abd al-Rahman al-Yusuf, leader of the elitist Syrian National Party, was seen paying a visit to the French mission.[5] Christian patriarchs, including the Greek Orthodox patriarch Monsignor Gregorios, had also begun frequenting the French mission. In the last week of June, an SNP rally had attracted three hundred supporters. In response, Faisal invited twenty-three city notables to his residence.[6]

On July 4, the city's mood suddenly changed. People panicked at the news of Haidar's warning of war. Rumors of imminent invasion grew in response to war minister Yusuf al-Azmeh's order that day to requisition food for 25,000 soldiers and commandeer all automobiles and carriages for military use.[7]

"You could feel clearly that a storm was rising," Cousse reported. As demonstrations broke out, he reported that a number of Christians complained that they feared a massacre. While there had been no actual attacks, Christians had clearly lost confidence in the government.[8]

Kamil al-Qassab began attracting large crowds among the city's middle and lower classes. His sermons called on citizens to defend their land, and his pamphlets demanded "independence or death." Hundreds of Damascenes, including some women, rushed to enlist in popular militias. Through the Higher National Committee network, Qassab commanded a thousand-man militia in the city and built links to branch militias in other cities and in rural areas.[9]

By July 8, populist attacks on French garrisons were undermining Faisal's efforts to build trust with General Gouraud.[10] In response to reports about French troop movements toward the Syrian border, Faisal had asked Haidar to make another visit to the Quai d'Orsay. Haidar cabled back that Paléologue was quite hostile. Accusing the Syrians of plotting with the Turks against France, he had warned, "I will not hide from you the gravity of the situation right now."[11]

That same day, July 8, Faisal hosted a meeting to raise funds for the Syrian army. The level of contributions was disappointing. Rumors circulated that the elite families of Damascus welcomed French rule as a way to regain the political power they had lost to Congress and to the so-called Arab foreigners from Arabia, Iraq, and Palestine.

A secret nationalist group called the Spying Eye sent threatening letters to the members of the Syrian National Party, accusing them of selling out to the French. The tracts specifically named the party's leaders—Congress deputies Abd al-Rahman al-Yusuf and Sheikh Abd al-Qadir al-Khatib—as traitors. Turnout at SNP meetings dwindled.

July 8–12: Showdowns in Damascus and Spa

On July 7, Rida and Congress moved to challenge the Atassi government. Since May, they complained, Atassi had based his misguided policy on a simplistic and literal reading of the San Remo accord, which mentioned merely provisional recognition of Syrian independence. Continued negotiations with the French were dangerous.[12]

In Atassi's defense, Faisal threatened to dissolve Congress on the pretext that it had completed its task of drafting the constitution. He invoked a provision in the draft constitution that permitted the king to declare martial law if a threat to public security emerged while Congress was not in session.

As in their confrontation in March, Rida stood up for the legislative branch. He had deputies sign an oath vowing to remain in session until a new parliament was elected. Faisal called a group of deputies to his residence to argue that they had no place in negotiating Syria's future with the French. Only he understood the necessary subtleties of diplomacy.[13]

On the morning of July 13, Congress summoned the cabinet to its chamber in Marjeh Square to submit a public report on the crisis. Prime Minister Hashim Atassi, Foreign Minister Abd al-Rahman Shahbandar, and War Minister Yusuf al-Azmeh filed into the hall just as deputies were discussing Article 7 of the constitution, on the king's powers.

The handsome Azmeh, with his thick wavy hair and a mustache curled upward, spoke for the cabinet. He reported that the French had occupied two points in Syria's Eastern Zone, along the Aleppo–Rayak railway. Deputies peppered Azmeh with questions about war preparations. But the war minister responded only vaguely.[14]

"We have asked that this issue be referred to an international committee," Azmeh assured them. The prime minister would send a delegation to Paris "to prove to the world and all the nations that we are not enemies to anyone and not opposed to the Peace Conference's decisions as long as they respect our independence and honor."[15]

Meanwhile, the king ordered his personal secretary, Awni Abd al-Hadi, to draft protests to international bodies. "Faisal based his appeal on the agreement with Clemenceau," Abd al-Hadi recalled later. He still hoped to bring France back to moderation, to the League of Nations. To avoid French censors, he cabled the protests through the Italian consulate.[16]

Then, Faisal decreed martial law.

In shock and anger, Rashid Rida gathered thirty dissident Congress members that night, July 13, at Dr. Ahmad Qadri's house. (While Qadri remained Faisal's physician, with access to the palace, he was also a Congress deputy active in the "rejectionist" camp.) They agreed that Atassi's cabinet had to go. Syria needed a vigorous defense. They preferred Yasin al-Hashimi, the former war minister, as prime minister.[17] As Rida and the dissident deputies returned home to sleep, they did not yet know that Faisal had already made an offer to Hashimi, but that the dynamic soldier, having been arrested by the British in November and only recently freed from jail in Palestine in May, had refused to serve.[18]

Meanwhile, from Paris, Robert de Caix urged General Gouraud to speed the invasion. Faisal had asked to travel to the Supreme Council meeting being held that week at Spa, Belgium. The French were still nervous, fearing that Britain might intervene on his behalf. "Our eviction," de Caix wrote, "is still the desire of the entire British political machine." And the international community might yet support Britain, he warned. "[T]he British might bring a 'Faisalian' delegation before the League of Nations to dispute our mandate."[19]

Gouraud took the bait. On July 10, he refused Faisal's request to travel to Belgium, using the pretext that there was no ship available. He then wrote to Millerand, promising to issue an ultimatum to the Syrians by July 20.[20]

De Caix had also warned Gouraud that, given enough time, the Syrians might turn Christians against the mandate. That same night of July 10, de Caix's prediction seemed to come true, as members of the Lebanese Administrative Council tried to escape to Damascus. Gouraud was relieved at their arrest. To protect French prestige, he censored press coverage of the affair, and he forced Maronite leaders to send pledges of loyalty to Paris.[21]

In another office at the Quai d'Orsay, Haidar met Paléologue to learn why Faisal's travel request had been denied. Because the king was still colluding with Britain against France, Paléologue explained. "He must understand that the English are not behind him."[22]

Haidar had a sense of doom. "Paléologue thinks that the Oriental can be subdued only by threats and fear," he wrote that night in his diary. "And he might be right. The Oriental must wipe the shame of fear from his brow and go to war again, condemning the world to a continuing funeral."[23]

That same day, in Spa, Premier Millerand staged a showdown with Lord Curzon. During a meeting break on July 12, Curzon casually mentioned that Britain had offered Faisal a boat to Europe from the port of Haifa. Millerand exploded. Faisal had forfeited his right to attend the peace conference after violating France's rights in Lebanon, the French premier declared, referring to the king's sponsorship of guerrilla bands in the Bekaa Valley. "The response to Faisal must be that France has the mandate for Syria and that it is to her that he must address his concerns."[24]

Curzon listened in silence. Later that day, he quietly advised Allenby to inform Faisal that there would be no place for him at the Council meeting.[25] The door to Syria's international recognition, opened by Britain in January 1919, slammed shut.

July 14: General Gouraud's Ultimatum

On July 14, 1920, the French Assembly paused to dedicate the French national holiday to Joan of Arc. Since the time of Napoleon, Joan had been honored as a national heroine for her fifteenth-century victory at Orleans over the English. On May 16, 1920, Pope Benedict XV had canonized her.[26] Linking the secular holiday, invented by the Third Republic to commemorate the storming of the Bastille in the French Revolution, with that of Saint Joan represented the radical shift in postwar French politics: the Sacred Union of 1914–1918 became the sacred mission of imperial rivalry against Britain.

Georges Clemenceau, a founding father of the Third Republic, spent that July 14 in the resort town of Vichy. Not only was the old Tiger an atheist, he was also a believer in the need for a close alliance with Britain. He vowed to well-wishers that day that he would never return to politics. In fact, he was already planning another foreign excursion, this time to indulge his lifetime passion for Buddhist art and philosophy in India and Southeast Asia.[27]

In Paris, Rustum Haidar, stayed home to avoid celebrations held across the city. "Things here are in a very bad moral state," he wrote in his diary. Former President Poincaré had published an article disputing the existence of an Arab nation in Syria. Arabs were only one among many nations in a territory also occupied by Chaldeans, Syriacs, Phoenicians, and Assyrians, Poincaré had declared. "He is ignorant in Eastern affairs and his ignorance comes from nothing but blind racial fanaticism," Haidar wrote.[28]

The pro-Syrian French paper L'Asie arabe condemned plans for war in Syria as "a Crusade cleverly devised by Jesuits and clerics, with the aid of prominent fanatics and lobbyists, who have skewed French policy by portraying Syria as a Christian country that merely seeks liberation from the Muslim yoke, personified by Faisal."[29]

Following the new religio-nationalist mood, Gouraud orchestrated the celebration of July 14 in Lebanon with full pomp and color. He paraded through Beirut in his white dress uniform, riding on horseback alongside General Mariano Goybet, commander of the Army of the Levant's Third Division. The men strutted through city streets lined with soldiers, as residents waved from balconies above. Afterward, Christian leaders and politicians came to the Serail to pay their respects to France.[30]

General Goybet had arrived in Beirut in April to help plan the invasion. His friend Father Claudius Chanteur, at St. Joseph University, had informed him that Lebanese Christians were terrified of Muslims and massacre. "Occupy Damascus and send Faisal back to the Arabian desert!" he advised.[31]

In Damascus, King Faisal also declined to join the July 14 festivities. A year earlier, he had festooned the city with French flags. Syrian musicians had played the "Marseillaise," the French national anthem, as Faisal paid an official visit to the French mission. Faisal had even hosted a banquet for 250 citizens in honor of Colonel Edouard Cousse, the high commissioner's liaison who had fought in the Arab Revolt.

This year, precisely at noon, Colonel Cousse paid a visit to the king's residence. Cousse handed Faisal an envelope containing General

Gouraud's ultimatum: submit to the French mandate or face France's conquering army.[32]

The ten-page document set out the case for invasion. Because Faisal had failed to fulfill the conditions of the January 6 accord, Gouraud declared, France was forced to assert its rights as granted by the peace conference. Gouraud listed each of the Syrians' violations of the accord, including guerrilla attacks on the French zone boundary, an illegal Syrian entry into the Bekaa, and massacres of Christians. Gouraud condemned the provocative, defensive posture of the Atassi government as "an insult both to France, whose aid it rejects, and to the Supreme Council, which gave to France the mandate for Syria." Gouraud accused Atassi of treating France's supporters as criminals and its enemies as heroes, and of bribing members of the Lebanese Administrative Council to sell out their country.

The ultimatum went further, to dismiss Arabs' claims related to their role as war allies. Syrians had never truly defeated the Ottoman Turks, Gouraud asserted. Therefore, Syria's civil government, including the Congress, was illegal. Faisal was merely a commander of an occupying army; consequently, his coronation was simply an act of rebellion against the peace conference. Missing entirely from the document was the spirit of the "A mandate" as a temporary period of advice and assistance envisioned by Woodrow Wilson in January 1919.

The use of force to impose a mandate explicitly violated the spirit of Article 22 of the League covenant, which required that mandates be assigned according to the wishes of the people. Gouraud acted instead according to the lesson he learned from the great colonial ruler of Morocco, Gen. Hubert Lyautey: France's duty was to bring order, not to uphold the Rights of Man.[33] He had not hesitated to cancel Lebanese rights to representative government when he dissolved the elected Lebanese Administrative Council on July 10. He now intended to replace it with a commission strictly controlled by the French governor. Likewise, Gouraud did not recognize the Syrian Congress and made no plans to hold elections to replace it.

"It is no longer possible to trust a government that has so clearly demonstrated its hostility to France, and that has done such serious wrong to its own country," Gouraud concluded the ultimatum. The

Syrian people, he claimed, had suffered from chaos in government, agitation by militias, and exorbitant taxes; and a general lack of economic investment had caused the population to suffer. "France is therefore obliged to take measures to guarantee the safety of her troops and of the people of the country."

The general threatened invasion unless Faisal accepted five conditions, in writing, by July 18:

1. Grant France control of the Rayak-Aleppo railroad and its stations.
2. Abolish military conscription and reduce the army to its size as of December 1, 1919.
3. Accept the French mandate, which will not involve annexation or direct administration.
4. Accept Syrian currency issued by the French-controlled Bank of Syria.
5. Punish those guilty of hostile acts toward France.

If Faisal did not fulfill these conditions by July 31, he would face violent consequences.[34]

July 14–20: Syrians' Response to the Ultimatum

The ultimatum arrived in Damascus like a bomb, engulfing the isolated Syrian capital in a frenzy of fear. "The severe tone of the ultimatum shook our nerves and our minds," Izzat Darwazeh recalled. "For the next ten days, Damascus and Syria boiled over with agitation, tension, and confusion."[35] Darwazeh rushed to a meeting of the Higher National Committee called by Kamil al-Qassab at the Arab Club. A majority voted to reject the ultimatum and prepare for war. The crowd of three hundred supporters sang patriotic songs and swore oaths to defend their country. They then paraded to a rally with the Democratic Party, rival to the notables' Syrian National Party.

"O brothers! Our forefathers were not cowards," Qassab declared. "They waged war against their powerful enemies with hearts full of faith and conviction. Let us emulate our forefathers and mix our blood with tears in the earth which we inherited from them." At the end of his speech, 1,500 new party members signed up.[36]

That night Darwazeh attended a second meeting, organized by Rida. It was larger than Qassab's, attended by Fatat members who had supported Faisal since the Arab Revolt. Their vote on the ultimatum was split. Rida al-Rikabi's loyalists, most of whom had joined Fatat only after the war, voted to accept it. Older members, like Darwazeh, remained true to principle and rejected it.

"We argued that France would enter Syria the way it did Algeria and Morocco. It would come under the pretext of offering aid, then implant a colonial regime . . . with force and terror," Darwazeh explained. "If we accepted the ultimatum, we would accept our doom."

Like Darwazeh, Rida believed that Syria would forfeit its rights if it did not fight to defend them. Those who surrendered passively deserved their oppression, he had warned in *The Lighthouse*. Rida still held a sliver of Wilsonian hope that small nations could and should claim equal rights with strong ones. "We still have hope that they [the British] will recognize the new social revolution caused by the war," Rida wrote. "If those men are able to overcome their imperial ambitions and if they manage to make their states adopt a new policy that agrees with the interests of Egypt, India, the Arabs, Persia, and other nations, then they will establish the everlasting, greater glory of their Saxon nation."[37]

The best strategy was to recruit enough volunteer militias to slow the French advance, Darwazeh proposed, admitting that ultimate defeat in battle was certain. "Then we would draw the attention of Europe and force it to intervene and find a more dignified solution based on European ideas."[38]

Qadri, who also attended the meeting, agreed. "The point of fighting to the end was to influence the conscience of the civilized world that emerged from the massacre of the Great War, and the conscience of the governments that called for righteousness to prevail."[39]

Syrians saw the French ultimatum as a test of both their own faith in international law, and the League of Nations' commitment to the rights of small nations. But no consuls and no international bodies responded to their appeals. The American consul told Syrians that his country had washed its hands of European politics. Earlier in the month, President Wilson had lost the nomination for reelection in a Democratic Party that had turned its back on his international vision.[40] The new secretary-general of the League of Nations, Eric Drummond, advised Faisal's envoy against making any public appeal. That would only make it harder for France to make concessions, he contended.[41]

On July 15, the Congress convened an extraordinary session. Riad al-Solh, the deputy who had recruited the Lebanese Administrative Council to join Faisal, now proposed that Congress adopt the constitution wholesale, based on the draft distributed after the July 5 session. He wanted the constitution ratified in order to establish Syria's legal existence. But Uthman Sultan pointed out that after ratification, King Faisal would have grounds to dissolve the Congress. His proposal to postpone ratification won a majority vote.

Qadri followed up with a resolution to keep Congress in session throughout the crisis. The deputies unanimously adopted the resolution, promising they would uphold three principles: unity and full independence; the constitutional basis of the monarchy; and congressional oversight in foreign affairs. "The Congress will not recognize any treaty, agreement or protocol concerning the country's future unless the Congress has approved it."[42]

That night, Rida led a congressional delegation to the royal residence to urge Faisal to reject the ultimatum. They argued as fiercely as they had in March. Faisal again threatened to dissolve the Congress. "This arrogant and crazy man," Rida wrote in his diary that night. "I intend not to visit him again."[43]

On Friday, July 16, Faisal took the ultimatum issue to the people. Hundreds had gathered in the seventh-century Umayyad Mosque for weekly prayers, including Bedouin horsemen who had galloped through city streets. Faisal informed the crowd of Gouraud's conditions. "Reflect and make your decisions; whatever you do, I am with you. If you want peace, we will make peace. If you want war, we will make war." But he did not get the answer he wanted.

The crowd cried, "War! War! War! Fire, not dishonor. Death, not slavery!" They marched from the Umayyad Mosque to the Hamidiye military barracks, waving flags and yelling, "Defense until death!"

Speakers called on young men to enlist in the army. Organizers claimed that four thousand had signed up by evening. Critics claimed the number was closer to four hundred.[44]

That very night, King Faisal discovered an awful truth. He gathered a panel of military leaders to discuss preparations for war. They reported that the army had so few bullets and trained personnel that a battle against the French would last only a few hours. Some officers feared that it might last only five minutes.[45] Qadri rushed to the Italian consulate, seeking information about the strength of French troops. The consul estimated that the French had at least 75,000 fully equipped troops in Syria and Cilicia. After his meeting with the Italians, Qadri headed to the Syrian War Ministry to meet with the highest-ranking officer on duty. "I found that he was ignorant of the great capacity of forces that France had amassed to attack us. He was astounded by what I said," Qadri wrote.

Qadri reported his findings to Faisal that same night. "Among the things he [Faisal] told me, in great pain, was that the better wisdom now was to seek peace with France."[46]

Atassi's cabinet agreed. "Rejection of the ultimatum would lead to a war in which our army would be swiftly crushed and lose everything, including honor, and come under the direct administration of the French," Sati` al-Husri, the education minister, explained.[47]

Atassi sent a note the next morning to Rida, inviting Congress to the royal residence on Saturday evening, July 17. Rida, still fuming over his argument with Faisal, reluctantly accepted. He held only the slimmest hope that the king might yet be convinced. The crowd was so large the guests were forced to gather in the garden outside.

Faisal exposed the military's weakness and listed his reasons for accepting Gouraud's conditions. Darwazeh protested loudly: it was unfitting for Faisal, as leader of the nationalist struggle since 1916, to hand Syria to the French; the cabinet should resign in protest. Faisal resorted to a tactic he had tried the previous February, when Fatat leaders had rejected the Clemenceau accord. To prevent peer pressure, he asked everyone present to cast a secret vote on a paper ballot. He would act on the majority opinion. Rida refused, sensing the king's intent to divide them.[48]

After the meeting, Qadri and Rida confronted the war minister, Yusuf al-Azmeh. "How did we get into this predicament?" Qadri asked. Azmeh admitted that he had been bluffing, in order to scare the French. He had known all along that the army was ill-prepared. "He said he never thought they would attack an ally while the Peace Conference was still in session," Qadri recalled.[49]

Rida was appalled at this deception. He had nominated Azmeh for war minister because he had trusted Azmeh's promise to lead the Syrians to rebel as Mustafa Kemal's Turks had done. Now Azmeh confessed that his bravado had rested on the tenuous belief that Bedouin tribes would rally to Faisal. Rida rebuked Azmeh harshly. "I am guilty, and I bear responsibility for what I've done," Azmeh replied. "Yesterday, I was about to commit suicide out of grief."[50]

The next day, Sunday, July 18, Faisal called Colonel Cousse to his office and asked him to transmit his oral acceptance of General Gouraud's conditions to Beirut. It was a gamble, the king explained to the liaison. By consenting to the ultimatum, he was putting Syria into Gouraud's hands. Cousse, uninformed of France's battle plans, reassured Faisal that the French government would respect Syrian independence.[51]

On Monday morning, July 19, Congress convened a special session to issue its own ultimatum to Faisal. Rida opened the chamber to the public. City notables and party leaders crowded in to watch a majority of deputies vote to outlaw the acceptance of a mandate. The March 8 declaration of independence, which Atassi had endorsed in May, declared the mandate a violation of Syrian unity. If the prime minister betrayed his vow, Congress would declare his government unconstitutional. Congress distributed copies of the resolution throughout the capital.[52]

Rida led another delegation to Faisal's residence that evening. A week earlier, the doors had been open to a stream of visitors eager to share their views with the king. Now, guards stood at the gate. Inside, the king was agitated. The two men argued again.

"Who are you people? It is I who created the state of Syria," Faisal cried.

"It is you who created Syria?" Rida replied. "Syria was there before you were born!"[53]

After Rida left, Faisal cabled written acceptance of Gouraud's ultimatum. Gouraud had extended the ultimatum deadline another twenty-four hours, to give the government time to implement his conditions. The chastened Azmeh ordered the Syrian army to demobilize. Troops even evacuated the garrison of Majdal Anjar, which guarded the mountain pass between Lebanon and Damascus.

The next morning, July 20, Hashim al-Atassi and Yusuf al-Azmeh appeared at the Congress chamber. Azmeh read a royal decree suspending the Congress for two months. Members jumped from their seats to speak, but Azmeh ordered them to sit down. "The law requires you to adjourn," he said sternly. Military police evacuated the hall. With pale faces, the ministers exited in silence.[54]

Rida was not completely unhappy that Congress had been shut down. It would not suffer the blame for the catastrophe ahead. In Rida's view, Faisal bore sole responsibility. He had ignored Rida's pleas to organize Syrian Bedouin as a defense force, supplemented by tribes from the Arabian Peninsula. Instead, Faisal's authorization of guerrilla attacks on Lebanese villages now provoked the French invasion.[55]

July 20: A Popular Revolt

French planes appeared over Damascus on July 19 and 20. They dropped thousands of leaflets that denied France was acting out of colonial aims. "France seeks to advance its interest in the country's [Syria's] prosperity, under the guarantee of the Syrian people's independence, which has already been formally recognized," Gouraud proclaimed. Congress was run not by founding fathers of a democracy but by renegade fanatics, the general continued: "Syrians, you are not ignorant of the fact that in the past six months the government of Damascus, pressured by an extremist minority, has exceeded all limits in pursuing the most aggressive policy against the French." In language long deployed by Jean Gout and Robert de Caix, the leaflet closed with a threat against Muslims:

> Out of humanitarianism common to all French people, I have
> no intention to use planes against unarmed populations, but
> on condition that no Frenchman and no Christian is massacred.
> Massacres, if they occur, will be followed by terrible reprisals
> from the air.[56]

Down below, on the streets of Damascus, an armed revolt erupted.
It began on July 19, when Sheikh Kamil al-Qassab led thousands in
a demonstration against accepting the ultimatum. Habib Istifan, the
ex-priest, joined him and others in speeches. Crowds surged in size,
shouting, "Down with Faisal! Down with the traitor!" Some chanted
praises of Congress, which was meeting nearby.

Yasin al-Hashimi, governor of Damascus, sent police into the streets
to fire on the demonstrators. Overnight, dozens were arrested, including Qassab himself. Istifan fled for exile in Egypt.[57]

The next day, July 20, shops closed and soldiers mutinied in protest
against Qassab's arrest. As night fell, the soldiers streamed from their
barracks "brandishing their weapons and shouting [that] the government has surrendered to the French," reported Taha al-Hashimi,
Yasin's brother. The soldiers joined members of Fatat, who fired guns
in the air to whip up crowds of protesters.

In a Syrian version of the 1789 storming of the Bastille, protesters
stormed the medieval Citadel, located at the entrance to the old city.
They freed Qassab and others who had been imprisoned there. They
also looted weapons from the prison storehouse and called upon citizens to defend their nation, since the king would not. Gunfire could
be heard across the city, causing panic among the people. "Damascus
was the scene of horror, panic, and extreme rage," Izzat Darwazeh
recalled.[58]

Qadri, who had long condemned Qassab's street politics, also witnessed the scene. "Voices echoed into the night, 'Down with the government!'" Qadri recalled. "During this revolt, some demonstrators
yelled at the top of their voices that Faisal shared blame with his
government in this shameful deed." One "malevolent" group broke
off from the main demonstration to march north toward the royal
residence. Rumors spread that they intended to kill the king.[59]

Police and military units battled the rebels all night. Eyewitnesses claimed they saw Prince Zaid himself shooting protesters with a machine gun. Central Damascus was strewn with corpses. Rida heard that 50 or 70 had been killed, and 150 wounded. Darwazeh likewise claimed 200 were killed or wounded.[60]

That same night, Faisal handed Colonel Cousse his final written acceptance of Gouraud's conditions. It had to reach the general by the midnight deadline. Cousse, who sympathized with Faisal, took it immediately to the telegraph office.

The king stayed up late into the night, angered by the violence and appalled by threats to his person. "I will not be intimidated!" he yelled. His bodyguards turned the rioters away. In the wee hours, the royal household finally settled down.

But the people of Damascus were not at peace with their king. "Muslim families are seized with panic," French intelligence reported. "[They are holding] meeting after meeting in the homes of top political leaders like Abd al-Rahman Pasha al-Yusuf, Sheikh Kamil Qassab, Rida Rikabi, and Prince Zaid."

Gouraud was no doubt pleased to learn of the disorder in Damascus. He was certainly pleased to learn that a pliable elite might facilitate France's takeover. Yusuf's Syrian National Party was "not hostile" to French administrative control. The party thought French leadership would be good for business and trade, the intelligence report continued. The party's elite had forced Faisal to accept France by donating "not one centime" to his national loan appeal and by refusing to donate their horses to the army.[61]

On July 20, days before the French army arrived, the political community in Damascus had shattered. Christian patriarchs who had blessed Faisal's coronation in March now openly supported the mandate. Nationalists who had fought alongside Faisal in the Arab Revolt now turned against him. Ordinary citizens who had once mobilized to participate in a democratic process now fueled Qassab's violent street politics. In response, the conservative elite that had once engaged in constructive debate in Congress now supported its dissolution.

The rebels' attack on the Citadel prison was a desperate attempt to defend Syrian democracy against a tyrant king who had closed the Congress. Even the Young Turks, who had hanged the best and brightest of the Syrians during the war, had not machine-gunned ordinary citizens on the streets of Damascus. But unlike the French mob that stormed the Bastille prison, this mob faced a foreign army that stood ready to sweep away the entire regime.

Chapter 17

Maysalun: The Arab State's Last Stand

On the morning of Wednesday, July 1, Faisal awoke to reports that French troops had marched into Majdal Anjar, heading toward the capital. Because the Syrian army had demobilized, they met no resistance.[1]

Faisal summoned Colonel Cousse, who appeared, utterly bewildered. The colonel swore he'd sent the telegram accepting General Gouraud's ultimatum shortly after six o'clock the previous evening.

Cousse and several of Faisal's officers jumped into a car and drove out to the Beirut road. They encountered General Goybet marching toward Damascus. His soldiers, mostly Africans, were dying of thirst under a sun already grown hot. Pale with emotion, Cousse asked, "What are you doing, my General? You have invaded Sharifian territory even though Prince [sic] Faisal has accepted all of the High Commissioner's demands!" Goybet pointed behind him and answered, "I am executing a clear military order. Search back there for diplomatic questions." Cousse's car sped toward Gouraud's mountain headquarters at Aley.[2]

Cousse reappeared at Faisal's residence in the afternoon. "The telegram accepting the conditions of the ultimatum was late in reaching Gouraud because the wires were cut in the region of Sarghaya," the colonel reported. "The General ordered the advance before he got the telegram."³ Later investigation revealed that the telegram had arrived shortly after French troops had left their camp. Critics argued that Gouraud had a duty to verify whether communication had been attempted before ordering the march.⁴

Syrians regarded the preemptive advance as another step in their humiliation and exclusion from the rights enjoyed by full—meaning white and European—members of the family of nations. Frustration unleashed Syrians' lower instincts. Rebels raised a racist battle cry against the largely African Army of the Levant: "We can crush a few negroes!"⁵

For two days, Faisal tried to retrieve some dignity. While Azmeh remobilized the army, the king cabled Gouraud to halt his forces. "This is, my General, a violation of the given word and an act against the rights of man and international morality," Faisal wrote.⁶ He dispatched Sati` al-Husri to consult with Gouraud face-to-face. Excruciating hours passed, for Husri's travel was slowed by French military movements.

Husri returned late on the night of July 22. Gouraud admitted he knew that the telegram had been sent when he ordered the army to advance, he reported. The general agreed to another twenty-four-hour extension, but with a new condition: that a permanent French mission be established at Damascus. Faisal, with a look of exhaustion, listened without comment.

The next morning, Friday, July 23, the Atassi cabinet convened for the last time to discuss Gouraud's newest condition. The ministers were upset by the demand for a permanent French headquarters in Damascus, a violation of the provisional independence promised by the League.

Cousse interrupted the meeting to deliver another telegram from Gouraud, with yet another condition: permit the thirsty French army to advance to the Syrian base at Khan Maysalun, the site of plentiful water springs. "General Gouraud's obvious purpose was to bring his troops to within twenty-five kilometers of Damascus, wait for another opportunity to make a new demand, and then march them right into the heart of the capital," Husri recalled.⁷

All talk of accepting terms ended there. Husri rushed to urge foreign consuls to raise the alarm. It was a last appeal to liberal world opinion. Only the Italians agreed to spread word of France's illegal invasion. The French press was silent. In Britain, T. E. Lawrence and a few journalists published protests, but the War Office and Lloyd George held their tongues.[8]

The call to war went out across Damascus.[9] Faisal again attended Friday prayers at the Umayyad Mosque. This time, he urged citizens to fight for their religion and their nation. Rashid Rida, by contrast, declined invitations to give sermons urging jihad. "I won't deceive anyone," he wrote in his diary. It was too late to mount a credible defense. He could not in good conscience urge citizens to fight a war that would bring only destruction upon them.[10]

Meanwhile, thousands scrambled to obtain weapons and find transport to the front. National defense became increasingly sectarian, further splintering the inclusive, liberal polity that Faisal and Congress had long promoted. Christians and Jews who had received death threats from the Spying Eye now cowered in their homes. And while some Muslim groups guarded Christian and Jewish neighborhoods, Muslim clerics rallied their faithful to war.

Sheikh Kamil al-Qassab led a cheering crowd to the royal residence. Faisal now greeted his opponent with open arms. "We support what you have always preached, to respond with force. Show us your work!" Qassab extended his hand to the king and vowed, "As long as you have decided to resist, I promise you that I will recruit 10,000 armed men by evening."[11]

Women also mobilized. Faisal had granted Nazik Abid, the feminist leader, an honorary rank within the war ministry's health department to organize a nurses' battalion called the Red Star. For her service in battle, Abid would later be dubbed Syria's "Joan of Arc."[12]

Cousse returned to Faisal's residence at sunset to learn the response to Gouraud's new conditions. There was none. The cabinet only confirmed that it would fulfill the original ultimatum of July 14. This time, communication with Gouraud was easy. Toulat simply telephoned the general and told him the answer was "no." For good measure, Gouraud added a second justification for invasion: France had been provoked by a surprise attack by two hundred Sharifians at Tel Kalakh near Homs.[13]

After dinner, Azmeh came to the royal residence to bid farewell to the king. As he departed, Azmeh took Husri aside to ask him to look after his wife and daughter. Husri had the morbid sense that the war minister would not return.

July 24: The Day of Maysalun

Before dawn, General Goybet surveyed his forces, all nine thousand of them: Algerian riflemen in the lead; to the north, several Senegalese battalions, a company of tanks, a regiment of Moroccan cavalry. At first light, reconnaissance planes took to the air. Three squadrons of bombers followed. "All eyes turned East where, under the rising sun, on its opulent oasis, awoke Holy Damascus, Mysterious Damascus, which we had dreamed of for so many days," Goybet later wrote in a memoir circulated by the French war ministry.

Goybet had no doubt about the righteousness of his mission. In an account published by the French defense ministry in 1922, Goybet related his battle story like a fairy tale set in a landscape of translucent hues, like a delicate watercolor. Soldiers scrambled across rocks and gorges, down the foothills of the Anti-Lebanon mountains. They heard a sudden "tac-tac-tac" of machine guns, coming from a ruined house where the Syrians hid.[14]

Behind Goybet, stationed along the Syrian border, stood the Army of the Levant. Once consisting of only thirty-two battalions, it now comprised fifty-two battalions of infantry, three tank companies, twenty-nine batteries of artillery, and ninety airplanes. The number of troops stationed in Cilicia and Syria combined exceeded eighty thousand.[15]

The forces of Goybet's Third Division rolled out toward Khan Maysalun, a village located twenty miles outside Damascus. By nine o'clock, their forces had breached defensive trenches and fully engaged Syrian troops.

The Syrians had mustered barely half the troop strength of the French, at most four thousand Syrian troops. Qassab's ten thousand volunteers were nowhere in sight. The Syrians also lacked aircraft and tanks.[16] When the French reached the first crest, the Syrians' front line quickly evacuated. The second defensive line soon followed.

At noon, the battle was over. Yusuf al-Azmeh lay dead at his command post. Syrian volunteers abandoned their cannons and machine guns as they tried to outrun the planes that gunned them down. The field was strewn with bodies. In the early afternoon, remnants of the Syrian army regrouped ten miles south of Damascus. The French had lost forty-two men; the Syrians had lost more than twelve hundred. By then, French troops had already occupied Aleppo. Homs and Hama surrendered without resistance on July 28. Gouraud sent his congratulations to Goybet and his troops, promising that their names would be "inscribed on a glorious page of the history of France and Syria."[17]

Faisal had begun to watch the battle from the second defensive line. However, he was forced to seek shelter from the onslaught of French planes. Azmeh's driver appeared to inform him that the war minister had been martyred. Tempted to head toward the battlefield, Faisal decided they should retreat. He stopped at Prince Zaid's house, west of the city, and sent Qadri into town alone to inform the ministers and mayor of the defeat.[18]

The army of the Arab Revolt was valiant no more. France and Britain had forced its dismantlement in 1919 and, through their control of ports and roads, deprived it of weapons shipments. Subsidies had been cut. Under constant foreign pressure, the government never reached the level of stability required to assess taxes and formulate battle plans.[19]

"It was not long before the expected news of crushing defeat spread," Darwazeh recalled. He had spent the previous two days assisting the war ministry. "Survivors returned to Damascus in a woeful state. Havoc and confusion ensued."[20] Fatat leaders distributed travel money to party members. Darwazeh took forty pounds and left half of it at his home. "I took the train with the others, carrying a bag of clothes, to Deraa."[21]

The Hijaz Railway Station was filled with panicked nationalists fleeing French retribution. Husri met Prime Minister Atassi there. They planned to establish a temporary government at Kisweh, twelve miles south of the city. Other activists, like Darwazeh, went farther south to Deraa, where they could organize military resistance. Rashid Rida chose not to join them. He still hoped to stir the conscience of the civilized world, he told Qadri, by standing his ground as the French overran the country's rights.[22]

Colonel Cousse accompanied General Nuri al-Said to Maysalun. At four-thirty in the afternoon, they met General Goybet to talk terms. The general demanded food immediately for his troops. He would wait until tomorrow to lead them into the city.

At sunset, Faisal drove to Kisweh, the town from which he had launched his triumphant entry into Damascus twenty-one months earlier. Waiting for word from Nuri al-Said, the defeated king refused any discussion. "I saw him sitting next to his train, surrounded by his sad and gloomy entourage," Darwazeh recalled.[23]

France Occupies Damascus

The next morning, Faisal appointed the pro-French minister of the interior, Alaa al-Din al-Durubi, as his new prime minister. Durubi's cabinet included the Syrian National Party leader, Abd al-Rahman al-Yusuf; and two Christians who had served under Atassi: Faris al-Khoury and Yusuf al-Hakim. Faisal hoped that the presence of Christians in this new government would encourage the French to keep him as head of state.[24]

Late in the afternoon on July 25, the French army marched into Damascus, with Moroccan cavalry leading the procession. Children ran into the street to marvel at the tanks. Some Europeans saluted from the balcony of the Victoria Hotel, where Rida had first stayed almost a year earlier. Now, the French staff took rooms there.

General Goybet paraded through Marjeh Square and turned north, marching past hospitals and consulates toward Faisal's residence and Mount Qassioun, the point from which the German emperor William II had viewed the city twenty-two years before. Goybet paused to admire the view. "It was impossible to believe there had been a bloody battle the day before," he recalled.

At dinner, Goybet received a request from Faisal to reenter the city. Faisal had Awni Abd al-Hadi write the note in French, reminding the general that he had tried to prevent war. It was better to cooperate than to abandon Syria completely to the French, Faisal thought. Nuri al-Said and Cousse had given him the impression that the French might yet let him rule.[25]

"I saw no problem letting him spend a last night in Damascus," Goybet wrote. It would be better to have Faisal close, in case Gouraud ordered him taken as a prisoner to Beirut.[26] Goybet finished his meal and headed to Prince Zaid's house to sleep.

When Faisal returned to his residence later that night, he discovered that Goybet planned to dethrone him in the morning.

In a quiet ceremony at the French mission early on Monday, July 26, Goybet pronounced the end of the "Sharifian" regime. "Prince Faisal brought his country to near destruction. His responsibility for all the bloody troubles that Syria has witnessed these past months is too great and too obvious for him to continue to govern." Goybet imposed an indemnity of 200,000 dinars (10 million francs) on the population for attacks on the Western Zone. The funds would go to families who were harmed or killed, he promised. Goybet also promised that hostile agents would be punished and that the Syrian army would be downgraded into a gendarmerie.[27]

Minutes later, General Gouraud ordered Faisal expelled from Syria.[28]

Faisal spent his last evening in Damascus, July 27, receiving visitors. Notables and young activists came to say farewell. He asked each of them to sign a petition to the Allied powers demanding that he remain as Syria's leader, freely chosen by the nation. He continued to defend his decision to negotiate with the French. He had sought only to save the country—unlike the notorious Egyptian monarch, Khedive Tawfiq, who sold out his citizens to the British occupation in 1882. "When I saw the danger with my own eyes, I pointed out the need for a wise and moderate policy," Faisal explained. "But no one listened. My opinion went with the wind."[29] Faisal apparently did not yet understand that the French had been planning his expulsion for months.

Despite their frosty relations, Rida also decided to say good-bye to the king. He arrived after ten at night to find policemen stationed throughout the palace, supposedly guarding the furniture from looters. They were more likely guarding Faisal.

The Congress president and the king spoke for nearly an hour. Faisal was remarkably calm, smiling for the first time in two weeks, Rida noted. He reminded Faisal that the tremendous losses suffered by Syria were due to his government's poor planning. Faisal flinched, but vowed that he would continue the struggle until victory, or death. Rida could not hold his tongue. Faisal's foolish negotiations had squandered the one chance Syria had for independence. "You have nothing," he told Faisal before taking his leave.[30]

The king and sheikh would never meet again.

Faisal's Exile

Just before midnight, Colonel Toulat escorted Faisal and Abd al-Hadi by car to the Hijaz Railway Station. There they met Husri, Dr. Qadri, Faisal's bodyguard Tahsin Qadri, and others in the royal entourage. Cousse came to bid them farewell, along with only a half dozen others.[31]

As they boarded the train, Abd al-Hadi handed Toulat two letters from Faisal. The first declared all of Gouraud's commands "null and illegal before the League of Nations." The second likewise declared Faisal's expulsion illegal under international law. France was throwing the world back to the age of barbarism, Faisal warned:

> If today's nations lived in the Middle Ages—where force alone made the law and where the sword alone settled conflicts— your conduct would conform to the established law. But if the Great War that we waged alongside the Allies to obtain our freedom and independence has actually reached its goals of consecrating rights by law and abolishing militarism . . . then the French force occupying the Eastern Zone, which I rule, must be considered an instrument of oppression and must be treated as such.

Toulat delivered the notes to Gouraud with a sarcastic remark: "Obviously composed by Mr. Abd al-Hadi. No comment needed."[32] Once again, Faisal's words fluttered away on the wind.

As the train pulled away from the station, "the skies were bright red because of a fire raging in the city," Husri recalled. At Deraa, they joined the nationalists at their makeshift government headquarters. "The King descended from the train with his habitual smile, but it concealed great pain. We joined him at the station cafeteria for breakfast, which we ate in silence. There was none of his friendly banter," recalled Asad Daghir, a Christian nationalist from the Lebanese coast.[33] "The King and his entourage slept and ate in their own train car," Darwazeh recalled. They held numerous strategy meetings in that car.

Deraa was a crossroads. Faisal could travel south toward Amman to organize an armed revolt, or he could take the train east to the port of Haifa in British Palestine, to wage a diplomatic battle in Europe. He was hamstrung by lack of money, having brought none from Damascus.[34] Faisal summoned local leaders, just as he had done at Deraa during the September 1918 advance north to Damascus. This time, however, he sensed that local tribal chiefs and rural leaders would not join the fight. "I was then determined to demand our rights in front of the international conclaves," he explained to his father.[35]

On Faisal's third day at the camp in Deraa, French planes appeared in the sky. They dropped copies of Durubi's order for Faisal and his entourage to evacuate Syria. If they refused, the planes would bomb nearby villages. Faisal decided it was time to take the train to Haifa.[36]

On August 1, 1920, the men who built the Syrian Arab Kingdom said their good-byes in the small town where they had launched their conquest of Syria. From Deraa, they dispersed across the Middle East, to carry on their political struggle in the mandatory states of Iraq, Jordan, and Palestine; in the Hijaz and in Egypt; and, eventually, back in Syria and Lebanon.

Erasure of the Syrian Arab Kingdom

On July 29, Millerand ordered a complete takeover of Damascus. "All traces of Faisal's illegal, improvised government must disappear," he commanded. De Caix had warned him and Gouraud that the Syrians might challenge France at the League of Nations.[37] General Goybet seized and secured all government buildings, including the Congress's chambers. Gouraud also ordered the confiscation of all property belonging to Faisal and his brother Zaid. On learning that Faisal had been permitted back into his residence, Gouraud angrily scolded Toulat.[38]

That same day, much to de Caix's delight, Gouraud arranged to fire both Toulat and Cousse. By month's end, the French mission at Damascus was in the hands of Georges Catroux, a veteran colonial administrator with little sympathy either for the "Sharifians" or for Article 22's recognition of provisional independence. His first task would be to arrest eighty of Faisal's top military officers and suppress the revolt brewing near Deraa.[39]

Rashid Rida's name did not appear on the French blacklist, perhaps because he had kept a low public profile during the July crisis. On the evening of July 31, he even had dinner with the new prime minister, Durubi. They discussed the need to insist on Syrians' right to maintain their army. But Rida soon realized that there was nothing he could do for Syrian independence. He moved quietly to a house out of town to wait for an exit visa.[40] Likewise, the quietly prudent Hashim al-Atassi avoided arrest. He slipped back to his family estate in Homs.

Gouraud began implementing de Caix's plans to partition Syria into cantons. He explicitly defined the states on a sectarian basis, "one Christian-majority state and two Muslim states."[41] Millerand insisted that no large Syrian state remain. Gouraud accordingly detached the Bekaa Valley from Syria, and joined it to Lebanon, along with the coastal city of Tripoli. Northern Syria was divided between a state of Aleppo and an Alawite territory on the coast, north of Lebanon. Catroux governed a shrunken entity called the State of Damascus and began negotiations for a separate Druze state south of it.

On August 5, the League of Nations rejected Sharif Hussein's demand to protect the rights of legally elected Syrian officials, which the League was created to do. The League's first secretary-general was Sir Eric Drummond, a former advisor to Balfour who shared his boss's anti-Wilsonian views. The League had no right to intervene,

Drummond responded, because Syria was still part of the Ottoman Empire. It was therefore technically still a war zone, so the League covenant did not apply. "The League was created to maintain peace after it has been established by the Treaties, and one cannot ask it to intervene in countries where this condition has not yet been realized."[42]

Drummond's August 5 letter effectively erased the Syrian Arab Kingdom's existence. In the League's eyes, only a temporary Allied military regime had existed in Syria since October 1918. Drummond's claim was highly contentious. In no commonly understood sense did Syria still belong to the Ottoman Empire. Article 22 of the League covenant, which entered international law in January 1920, had designated Syria as provisionally independent under the mandate system. On that basis, San Remo had assigned Syria to France as a mandate under the trust of the League. And on the basis of that trust, Premier Millerand had asserted the right to occupy the hinterland. Only in the narrowest legal sense could Drummond claim that the League would have no jurisdiction until after the formal peace settlement, the Treaty of Sèvres, which would be signed the following week.[43]

"Syria is still a mess," Lloyd George admitted to Woodrow Wilson that same day. "But the establishment of French authority ought to clear the air."[44] Lloyd George colluded in the erasure of Syrians' claim to their provisional independence. Wilson, too, effectively endorsed the destruction of the Syrian Arab Kingdom by failing to make even a symbolic gesture toward upholding the original spirit of the mandate system. The outgoing American president was a broken man with broken dreams.

"You have nothing to fear from the international order," de Caix wrote to Gouraud a few days later. "Lloyd George joyfully led the funeral of Sharifianism when he told Millerand the last time he saw him, 'Faisal is not a serious boy [garçon].'"[45]

On Saturday, August 7, Gouraud made his formal entry into Damascus at the Hijaz Railway Station, the terminus of the rail line that the Northern Arab Army had captured two years earlier. It was now festooned with French flags, and a military band played the "Marseillaise." The audience, mostly Christian, was respectful but subdued. Gouraud mounted his horse, tall and erect in his saddle, to ride through the Muslim neighborhoods of the city. Few homes or shops displayed a French flag. No crowds cheered.

Gouraud arrived at Faisal's former residence to join the heroes of Maysalun for lunch. The villa became Gouraud's Damascus headquarters and remains today the French ambassador's residence. From there, Gouraud established a mandatory government, working through the cabinet that Faisal had appointed before his exile. French rule took on the aspect of a reversal in time, to the days of Ottoman tyranny before the 1908 constitutional revolution. Prime Minister Alaa al-Din al-Durubi had been Sultan Abdulhamid's private physician; the governor of Aleppo was a retired Ottoman colonel who had once directed Abdulhamid's secret service in the city.[46]

That evening Gouraud hosted a banquet at city hall, in the very room where Faisal had been crowned five months earlier. Guests eagerly displayed their knowledge of French. Next to Gouraud sat Prime Minister Alaa al-Din al-Durubi and his chief advisor, Abd al-Rahman al-Yusuf. Yusuf was one of several conservative former deputies in the Syrian Congress who embraced French rule. Both men proudly told Gouraud they had sons studying in France. The high commissioner then stood to offer a speech, in which he drily recited Faisal's sins to a silent audience. "France was patient for a long time," he said. "We do not come as masters, as colonizers, or as enemies of Islam," he declared. "My ambition is to work for the prosperity of all Syria and especially this pearl of Islam embedded in the emerald of Damascus."[47]

Gouraud's promises echoed General Frederick Maude's speech upon conquering Baghdad in 1917: Maude also announced that Britain had come as a liberator, not a conqueror. This was the old language of European colonialism: Napoleon had claimed to liberate Egyptians upon his invasion of Egypt in 1798, only to impose heavy taxes and a brutal rule of force.

The next day, Sunday, Gouraud joined officials at the Latin Church for Mass. Monsignor Giannini, the papal delegate, hailed France's arrival as "one of the most beautiful triumphs for true civilization."[48] Afterward, Gouraud took a car to the Umayyad Mosque and the tomb of Saladin. Sheikh Abd al-Qadir al-Khatib, Rashid Rida's long-time antagonist, welcomed the general on behalf of the city's Muslim clergy.[49] Decades later, rumors still circulated in Damascus that Gouraud stood at the tomb of Saladin, who had defeated the Crusaders in the twelfth century, and said, "We have returned."[50]

On August 9, the day Gouraud departed Damascus, the French military court handed down dozens of death sentences to Syrian nationalists. Among those condemned in absentia were Kamil al-Qassab, Ahmad Qadri, Awni Abd al-Hadi, Izzat Darwazeh, and two future prime ministers of Lebanon and Syria: Riad al-Solh and Shukri al-Quwwatli.[51]

The following day, August 10, Millerand hosted the formal signing of the Treaty of Sèvres in a Paris suburb. The treaty partitioned the Ottoman Empire among the Allies and implemented the San Remo decision to assign Syria to France. Not only did it divide Arab lands into multiple mandates, but it also divided Anatolia among the French, British, Greeks, Armenians, and Turks. With additional provisions for reparations and war crimes trials, the Ottoman state was made to pay a far harsher price than even the Germans. The treaty stripped it of three-fourths of its territory, leaving a rump state on the northern Black Sea coast.

Arab and Turkish nationalists condemned the treaty outright. Unlike the Syrians, however, the Turks were able to support their protest by launching a war against the Allies. By August, Iraq had already broken out into a mass armed revolt that would take Britain months to crush.

In Syria, renegade nationalists managed only a symbolic revolt at Deraa. On August 20, top Syrian officials took a train south to calm unrest in the region. Some two hundred rebels ambushed their train as it pulled into the station one stop north of Deraa. They pulled the officials from the train, killing twelve. Among the dead were Gouraud's August 7 dinner partners: Prime Minister Durubi and Syria's wealthiest landowner, Abd al-Rahman Yusuf.[52]

Rashid Rida had worked closely with both Durubi and Yusuf. The day after their murders, he obtained permission to leave Syria. He had suffered the previous three weeks with a fever, alone in a hotel room. He had closed his house and sold all his furniture before falling ill. It was time to leave. A merchant advised him not to go home by way of Deraa and Palestine. The uprising in the south made travel too dangerous. Trainloads of French soldiers were heading there.

On August 23, 1920, just short of a year after his arrival, Rida departed Damascus on a train heading to Beirut. Through friends, he obtained a visa for Egypt. Fortunately for Rida, the police chief in Damascus had neglected to mention in his travel documents that he was publisher of The Lighthouse and had been president of the Syrian Congress. Rida boarded the first ship he could find on August 30. It was an uncomfortable British merchant vessel. He refused to wait for the passenger ship due to depart two days later, because the French were to proclaim Greater Lebanon on September 1. He could not bear to witness it.

By then, French officials had begun using a new term for nationalist rebels: *apaches*.[53] It was a racialized term reserved for barbarians without rights. Like North American Indians, members of the Syrian resistance deserved only conquest and even death. General Gouraud imposed an indemnity on Syrians for the cost of defeating their revolt, much as the Entente intended their archenemy Germany to pay the cost of World War I.

And so the patriotic remnants of the Arab Revolt, who had fought as allies in the Great War for democracy, were finally expelled from international society. The Treaty of Sèvres assigned Arabs a subordinate place in the postwar world, as humbled subjects of an enemy power. In the deafening silence of the outside world, the Syrian Arab Kingdom was erased from history. Memory of the betrayal haunted Qadri years later. "It was as though the Arabs were never Allies."[54]

Chapter 18

Wilson's Ghost in Geneva

August 13, 1921, was Eid al-Adha, Feast of the Sacrifice, the biggest holiday of the year. A year after he had left Damascus, Rashid Rida lay on his back, seasick, aboard the *Cleopatra*, an Italian liner bound for Trieste. "I prayed to God to cure my son, bless my family, and bring all of us here (on board) to safety." Traveling with him was a Christian friend, George Youssef Salim, who knew enough Italian to help the imam avoid pork dishes in the dining room—when he felt well enough to eat. The seas had grown rough near Crete.

Michel Lutfallah, president of the Syrian Union Party, was leading the party on a delegation to Geneva. They intended to appeal against the mandates in Syria and Palestine when the League of Nations opened at month's end.

Rida had almost not come. He had returned home to Cairo the previous September, to his joy, in time to see his son Muhammad Shafii attend the first day of kindergarten. At age fifty-five, he had fathered a third child that summer. But the baby did not survive long after birth, and Rida's wife was still suffering through a long recovery. Then in early August, Muhammad Shafii had come down with a serious stomach illness. Rida stayed at his bedside himself. He had put off Lutfallah's entreaties to travel.

But when Lutfallah appeared at his door on August 10, Rida relented. "I realized that service to the nation should come before family. I decided to go, putting my trust in God," Rida wrote. They had set sail from Alexandria two days before the holiday.

The *Cleopatra* finally docked at Trieste on August 17. The group was held up at customs because Lutfallah was carrying so many cigarettes. While waiting, Rida rushed to the telegraph office to send word to his family—and to send articles back for publication in *The Lighthouse*. He depended on income from his publishing business.[1]

Rida was enchanted by Europe. The train trip from Trieste to Geneva took them though the Lombardy plains. The Alpine landscape full of wildflowers reminded him of his birthplace in Lebanon. "The mountain lakes like this [Lake Maggiore] and Lake Lucerne are among the most beautiful things that God created on this earth," Rida wrote. "This scenery has inspired the sublime contemplation of philosophers and fired the imagination of poets." His optimism dimmed a bit as they crossed the Swiss border. Their train pulled into Geneva under a heavy rain.

Rida made the trip to Geneva because, despite the disaster at Damascus, he still had faith in the universal potential of liberalism. "I am a believer who sees despair of God's mercy as a form of infidelity," he wrote to his *Lighthouse* readers in June 1921.[2] The Supreme Council had violated Wilson's principles by endorsing France's forcible occupation. But now, the League of Nations Assembly was finally holding its first session in Geneva. It might yet be persuaded to reverse the violation, for, according to Article 22, the League (not the Supreme Council) had the final authority to assign mandates. To this end, Rida and other exiles in Cairo had continued since July 1920 to campaign for Syria's rights.

For Syrians and other peoples around the world, Geneva was the center of international society and a magnet for opponents of European imperialism. Lobbyists converged on the city to petition the League of Nations. It was after the Syrians' defeat at Maysalun that the League moved into its headquarters on the Lake Geneva waterfront, and only the previous spring that the Permanent Mandates Commission had formed. These international institutions renewed the SUP's hope that the Wilsonian world order might yet prevail.[3] Rida understood the epic importance of the moment: if the League denied Muslims their rights under international law, a century of conflict between East and West would follow.

The League of Nations:
Between Empire and Law

En route from Milan to Geneva, Rida's train passed near Lake Como, where Faisal had stayed for three months in the fall of 1920. Sympathetic Italians had offered the fallen king a refuge and a lawyer. Faisal drew up Syria's legal case, based on documents that he and Sati` al-Husri had carried from Damascus, to file protests with the League of Nations.

Rida, as Syrian Congress president, filed his first protest with the League in September 1920, against France's destruction of villages and "massacres of women and children" following the assassination of Prime Minister Durubi. The League's secretary-general, Eric Drummond, a former assistant to Balfour, was not inclined to interfere with the French occupation. He replied that the matter was "not within the competence of the League of Nations."[4]

Rida had higher expectations of the League of Nations Assembly. While Drummond headed the executive branch of the League, the Assembly was its general deliberative body, consisting of representatives of all member states. A smaller body, the League Council, functioned as a kind of senate, or precursor to the United Nations Security Council, with membership dominated by the Great Powers. The Assembly had first convened on November 15, 1920, gathering delegates from forty-two countries in a meeting hall near the League's headquarters in a magnificent old hotel. Its first action was to adopt a resolution honoring Woodrow Wilson as the League's founding father.[5]

Rida had sent the Assembly a congratulatory telegram, which he signed as president of the Syrian Congress. To his good wishes he added a plea: "On the occasion of your general meeting, members of the Syrian Congress—elected representatives of the Syrian nation who were obliged by French military force to seek exile in Egypt— have the honor to remind you of Syria's independence proclaimed by Article 22 of the League covenant," Rida wrote. "We protest against the overthrow of a national government [in] Damascus [by] foreign militarism."[6]

To Rida's satisfaction, the League of Nations Assembly voted for the immediate organization of the Permanent Mandates Commission (PMC), against the stonewalling of Britain and France. The two Great Powers had wanted more time to establish faits accomplis without League oversight.

However, the League Council stepped in to block the Assembly's move. Imperialist members of the Council insisted that the PMC include representatives of the mandatory powers. It appointed to the PMC a French former governor of Indochina, a British former colonial governor of Nigeria, and a Dutch colonial officer.

Balfour, the British representative on the League Council, then urged the PMC to postpone action on the Arab "A" mandates because Colonial Secretary Winston Churchill was planning a meeting in Cairo to discuss Britain's territories in the Middle East.[7] By approving Balfour's motion, the PMC permitted Britain to tighten its colonial hold on Arab lands.

When Rida sent a telegram in November 1920 protesting France's overthrow of the Syrian Arab Kingdom, it never reached the Assembly for review. Paul Mantoux, Clemenceau's former secretary and now a League official, diverted the telegram to the French delegation. "I think we should not distribute this document, because there is no reason for the Secretariat to handle propaganda from every group of exiles or malcontents from every country," he told the French delegates. Much as Millerand had done six months earlier, Mantoux denied the legal existence of the Syrian Congress, and erased it from international memory.

Mantoux blocked the transfer of subsequent telegrams to the Assembly, including protests by Syrian Union Party president Michel Lutfallah against the dismemberment of Syria, and by Kamil al-Qassab, Riad al-Solh, and Awni Abd al-Hadi against their death sentences. All of these petitions went unanswered. A protest from Rustum Haidar of the Hijaz delegation received a more careful review because he represented a state that the Treaty of Sèvres recognized as sovereign.[8]

The decision to send a delegation to Geneva emerged when the SUP held a ceremony in Cairo's Continental Hotel to observe the first anniversary of the March 8 declaration of independence. Delegates sent a telegram demanding their national rights. In April, Rida and Lutfallah followed up by sending out invitations to reconvene in Geneva.[9]

Faisal had also marked the March 8 anniversary in a separate telegram demanding that the Treaty of Sèvres be revised to free and reunite Arab lands. The imprisonment of army officers who had fought for the Allies, he protested, was a violation of the League's trust.[10]

Faisal by then had chosen a different path in the struggle for Arab independence. He continued working within the Great Powers system rather than rebel against it. After weeks of lobbying, T. E. Lawrence had convinced Lord Curzon to invite Faisal to London for consultation. Faisal accepted the invitation because he had heard rumors that he might be named king of Iraq. After repressing the Iraqi revolt in late 1920, the British decided they needed an Arab face for their mandatory regime there.[11]

Faisal's hopes were raised in early 1921 during talks in London. Colonial Secretary Churchill then convened the conference on Middle Eastern affairs in March 1921. Faisal was informed then that Britain would be proud to nominate him for the Iraqi crown. But he would have to demonstrate first that Iraqis would welcome him. Just after his thirty-eighth birthday, Faisal made his way to Baghdad, accompanied by Rustum Haidar and Sati` l-Husri. They spent the summer attending banquets with religious and tribal leaders. In July, Faisal won the British-engineered plebiscite. He intended to rule with greater discipline in Iraq than he did in Syria. This time around, he would insist on the power to control policy and chart a more gradual path toward independence.[12] Faisal's coronation ceremony was set for August 23, 1921, just after Rida arrived in Geneva.

Earlier that summer, Rida had published a scathing criticism of Faisal's Iraq strategy in *The Lighthouse*. He wrote that Sharif Hussein and his sons thought of displeasing England as "like apostasy, losing God's mercy." Faisal and his brother Abdullah, who had been installed as king in Transjordan, colluded in Britain's violent repression of Arabs. "They [the British] gave him all the military power and planes needed to subdue any Arabs of this country who resist their plans."

"I would like Arab nations to know that mandates are not inevitable and that the League of Nations will not be a puppet in the hands of colonialists," Rida wrote in the same article. "There is great hope for establishing a connection between East and West on the basis of justice and mutual exchange." The future of Arab democracy, he advised, must unfold without the Hashemite monarchy.

At Geneva, Rida planned to teach Britain and France that they would not succeed in oppressing Arabs. "I still hope to convince the two countries not to divide our lands and deny our rights," he wrote. "It is unfortunate that my previous quest was with their extremist colonialists. I hope to reach an agreement with the Liberals among them. There are many of them, thank God for that."[13]

Rida at the Permanent Mandates Commission

On August 24, 1921, the day after Faisal accepted his crown in Baghdad, Rida and other SUP members went to the League headquarters to meet with William Rappard, the administrative director of the Permanent Mandates Commission. Rappard was a Swiss scholar born in the United States and a fan of Woodrow Wilson. He regretted that Wilson's vision of mandates, as a limited form of neutral guidance, had been subverted by Britain and France. They had, in fact, imposed their mandates by force against popular opposition. But Rappard, like Rida, was still an optimist. He believed the PMC could "hold those powers accountable to a democratizing world," according to historian Susan Pedersen.[14]

Rappard was a "decent fellow," Rida remarked. "Our conversation began with Wilson's theory on the project of the League of Nations. We spoke of the plot by two imperialist countries to deceive Wilson into introducing the idea of the mandate into the League's covenant." Mandates, Rida argued, contradicted the League's primary purpose, to ensure peace by guaranteeing nations their freedom. He said that Britain and France regarded mandates as a means "to make their enslavement of nations legal, with the support of the whole civilized world."

"If the occupying army withdraws, and leaves the country to you, could you maintain security and order?" Rappard asked.

"Yes," Rida responded, explaining that Syrians had done so in 1918. "That is because the actual government, during the Turkish era, had been in the hands of the people."

"We knew nothing about this," Rappard answered. They ended the meeting on a friendly note.[15]

Manifesto of the Syro-Palestinian Congress

A second goal of the Geneva trip was to reunite the Syrian Congress in exile. Lutfallah rented a meeting room at another hotel. In addition to Lutfallah, the Lebanese delegates present included Riad al-Solh; Suleiman Bey Kanaan, one of Lebanese Administrative Council members who had been arrested before the battle of Maysalun; and Prince Shakib Arslan, a Lebanese Druze who lived in exile in Germany. Delegates from the Syrian interior included George Youssef Salim, Rida's travel companion; and Ihsan al-Jabiri, Faisal's former chamberlain. Four delegates from Palestine joined the meeting as well, along with delegates who had just arrived from the United States, Argentina, and Chile.

Conflict flared when the Palestinian delegates proposed changing the group's name to the Syro-Palestinian Congress (SPC), to reflect the fact that Syria and Palestine were now ruled by two different powers. Lutfallah opposed the name change because it compromised the Syrian Congress's claim to unity. Rida offered a compromise: they would change the name, but prioritize unity in their charter. After a long debate, the delegates accepted Rida's proposal.

The Congress's Muslim majority then elected Lutfallah as president because his Christian faith would emphasize their commitment to cross-sectarian national unity. They elected Rida and a Palestinian delegate, Tawfiq Hammad, as vice presidents; and Shakib Arslan as secretary. Arslan was an Islamic reformer like Rida, but the two had split during the Great War, when Arslan insisted on supporting the Ottoman caliphate and Rida opted to rebel against Ottoman tyranny.

Reconciled at Geneva, they would become active partners and close friends over the next decade.

After this initial conflict, the Congress achieved consensus in drafting a formal petition to the League of Nations Assembly, demanding that it rescind the mandate. The delegates submitted the resulting twenty-two-page manifesto on September 21.[16]

In language that anticipated the anticolonial movements following World War II, the Syro-Palestinian Congress called for a world made equal and free of colonial oppression:

> We approach your Assembly with trust in the founding
> principles of the League of Nations. It revived the hope of
> all nations that they would gain respect for their people, for
> their right to self-determination, and for justice and honor in
> international relations, that the policies of colonialism would
> be denounced, and that treaties regulating relations among
> member states would be observed faithfully.

The manifesto reasserted Arabs' status as wartime Allies who had supported the rule of law against militant aggression. "The long war that has ended and that gave birth to the League of Nations was a struggle between two ideologies, that of force and occupation against that of right and freedom," it observed. "Leaders of the Allied nations announced . . . that the war will not lead to new conquests or annexation of new countries; rather, it must result in the victory of civilization and the independence of nations."

The manifesto then stated the case for Syrian self-rule, based on Article 22. The people had proved their maturity by "establishing a Syrian state based on order, freedom, and peace." Their elected Congress, as a constituent assembly, had declared independence in accordance with public opinion.

The French had violated the spirit of Article 22 in Syria, the manifesto continued. "The mandate they impose upon us has annihilated our independence and plunged us in the abyss of colonization," it read, chastising General Gouraud for behaving like a conqueror. He had imposed a war indemnity, arrested the elected members of the Lebanese Administrative Council, and expelled Syria's elected king. Now, he was preventing Syrians still in Damascus from coming to Geneva.

The manifesto warned that this was a moment of reckoning for the League. "We present these incidents to the League of Nations because they have been committed in its name. There is no doubt that you—respected representatives—reject the enslavement of an entire people in the name of your sublime aims." The manifesto concluded that the League would have to redeem itself by ordering France and Britain to withdraw their armies and to permit Syria, Lebanon, and Palestine to unite under a "responsible civilian government before a parliamentary assembly elected by the people."[17]

Rida's Last Hope in European Liberals

Rida regarded the SPC as an instrument to save the soul of the League. He lobbied Assembly members to join the SPC's campaign against the colonial corruption of the mandates. Iran and China were most sympathetic to his call for solidarity.

Rida told the Iranian Assembly member that Britain was the worst enemy of the Muslims. British imperial expansion would provoke a violent backlash from its subjects, he warned. "We have already begun to see signs of regression, with bloody revolutions in Ireland, Egypt, and Iraq. Palestine has started a political revolution and India, a social revolution," he said.

Rida told the Iranian that it was the sacred duty of independent states to support the resistance. "We have seen signs of God in harnessing the Russian nation to help two Islamic states—the Ottoman and the Iranian," Rida said, and the Iranian agreed: "Had it not been for Mustafa Kemal Pasha, every Muslim in this world now would have been humiliated," he remarked.

Rida issued his boldest ultimatum to the president of the Assembly, Paul Hymans. He warned Hymans that Britain and France had turned the purpose of the League against itself.

> It does not befit the honor of this League, which President
> Wilson proposed to include all civilized nations for the
> good of all human beings, nor the honor of its nations and
> governments, nor the honor of its principles and its intended
> goals, for it to be used as a tool by the two colonial states.
> These states seek to use this Assembly to guarantee, in the
> name of a mandate, the subjugation of peoples.

World peace and the future of law were at stake, Rida continued. "If
the Balkans are the spark of war in the West, then Syria, Palestine,
and other Arab countries will ignite the fires of war in both the West
and the East."[18]

Rida drew inspiration from conversations with journalists who
flooded Geneva for the League meeting. "I met liberals in Geneva
and elsewhere," he wrote to readers of The Lighthouse. "I discovered
that they believe this war did nothing but increase greed and intrigue
among the leaders of the Great Powers, who spread strife, evil, and
bloodlust." They didn't believe their leaders' slander against Muslims,
or those leaders' false claims "to protect Eastern Christians from their
fanaticism." He especially enjoyed a conversation with the editor of
the Geneva Tribune at a dinner at Lutfallah's hotel. The editor did
not share Rida's faith in liberals. "Without compelling force, these
politicians will not turn away from the ambitions and intrigues they
are accustomed to," the editor said. "Unite yourselves, preserve your
religion, your ethics and your virtues, and prepare to take advantage
of the upcoming war," the editor advised.[19]

Rida departed Geneva in late September, after submitting the SPC's
appeal. The members of the SPC had voted to establish permanent
offices in Geneva and Cairo to follow through on their campaign. To
their deep disappointment, however, the League Council and Assembly both voted to retain the mandate system. And while Rappard
filed their appeal with the PMC, its members agreed that they could
not challenge the vote to retain the mandate system. The PMC also
decided it had no authority to question the terms of the mandates
set by Britain and France. It would limit its oversight to a review of
annual reports and of methods of rule. In the coming months, the

SPC would send additional petitions as the League Council prepared its formal vote to ratify the assignment of mandates. Rappard never forwarded them.[20] The voices of the Syrian exiles were silenced once again, filed away in the drawers of the PMC.

Equally disappointing was the silence in France. Although socialists published the SPC's manifesto, *Le Temps* dismissed it as the word of the "so-called Syrian delegation," full of ambitious men with no link to the Syrian people. At the foreign ministry, Berthelot dismissed the "noises" made by "some kind of pan-Islamist congress in Geneva."[21]

Charles Crane and Shahbandar's Protest in Damascus

As the League Council's final vote on ratification of the French mandate drew near, tensions rose in Damascus. SUP member Abd al-Rahman Shahbandar, the Syrian Arab Kingdom's last foreign minister, had planned to come to Geneva but, just beforehand, he was granted amnesty to return home to Damascus. As soon as Shahbandar reopened his clinic, he founded a secret nationalist organization. He saw an opportunity to go public in April 1922, with the visit of Charles Crane.

Crane, friend of Woodrow Wilson and former head of the King-Crane Commission, was one of the liberals whom Rida and the SUP had approached in the months after Maysalun. They urged him to publish the King-Crane report. "It was useless to say that these people were not fit for self-government," Crane later wrote. "These people were certainly much better equipped for self-government than the Bulgars, Serbs or Greeks were when they got independence."

In early 1922, Crane decided to visit Syrian exiles in Cairo. "Mr. Crane, all we Moslems feel that Mr. Wilson is the most important man to come into the world since the time of Mohamed," one Syrian told him. "We believe his doctrines are just as good Moslem doctrine as they are Christian doctrine." The exiles asked Crane to choose several of Wilson's speeches to be published in proper Arabic translations. "Mr. Wilson was very much touched by that request," recalled Crane, who would personally deliver the chosen texts a year later.[22]

But before returning to the United States, Crane decided to make a stop in Damascus. He was curious to see how the city had changed in three years. When word spread of his arrival on April 1, Syrian nationalists thought it was an April Fools' prank. They had lived in utter isolation from the outside world, under the repressive eye of the French regime.

A letter of introduction from the president of the American University of Beirut, Shahbandar's alma mater, prompted the former foreign minister to meet Crane at the Hijaz Railway Station. Crane's face was more wrinkled and his back a bit bent, but with prompting he remembered Shahbandar as his translator in 1919.[23]

That evening, Crane invited Shahbandar to his room at the Damascus Palace Hotel, near Marjeh Square. Crane explained that he had come to Damascus to prepare the belated publication of the King-Crane report. "I want you to bring me to meet the people of this country, especially the scholars among them, to see if their minds have changed, and to see if the information we collected in our report was right," he said.

Shahbandar seized the opportunity to organize a nationalist meeting with Crane. Members of his secret group, the Iron Hand, agreed to make three demands: full independence, the unity of Greater Syria, and maintenance of the Ottoman caliphate, which would provide solidarity among the smaller Arab and Muslim countries. To avoid French spies, they decided to hold the meeting in an orchid garden outside the city.

"In the gardens of that city members of the uleima [Muslim clergy] wanted to hear Wilson stories," Crane recalled. "I told them many stories to indicate that in all essential points of view Mr. Wilson was a good Moslem. The essential doctrine of the Moslem world is to be at peace with the Lord and to be at peace with one's neighbors." In response, a religious scholar chanted the verses of the Qur'an about Jesus Christ, whom Muslims consider a prophet. French secret police stationed on the garden's perimeter listened too. They tracked Crane's every step. Their reports landed on the desk of Robert de Caix in Beirut.[24]

Crane tried to avoid political controversy, but the Syrians who had gathered in the garden kept raising pointed questions. They wanted to know why the King-Crane report had not been published and why the Americans had lost interest in their cause. They complained of French taxes and brutality, and they still scorned the British for permitting Faisal's expulsion. They begged Crane to take up their cause. "We cannot get any word out, so you must carry it!" Shahbandar stirred political excitement by embellishing his translation of Crane's mild speech.

"Damascus blew up while I was there and some people said that it was because I had been making political speeches," Crane recalled. "I had just been telling them stories."[25] Crane's assistant, Donald Brodie, worried that Muslim-Christian relations in Syria had suffered under French rule. "In 1918 there was an excellent opportunity for a much closer and more sympathetic reproachment [sic] between the Moslem and Christian worlds," he wrote. "There is much evidence in Syria today that this unprecedented opportunity has been lost by European blunders and that the religious chasm has widened, not narrowed."

In the early morning on April 6, the day Crane planned to leave Damascus, dozens of Syrians arrived at the lobby of the Damascus Palace Hotel. As Brodie told the story, Crane was surprised to see them when he came downstairs from his room. He graciously thanked his visitors and wished them well. As he opened the door to his car, the Syrians began to chant, demanding independence and unity for Syria. At their head was a prominent Syrian woman, who approached the car, threw back her veil, and appealed to Crane in Arabic. The crowd cheered her as the car pulled away. It could only inch along the narrow street, now filled with protesters. Some jumped on the running board and forced the driver to steer toward the city's central square. Local police ran after them, but the crowd drowned out their orders to hault.

After about twenty minutes, Crane stopped the car at Marjeh Square, said his final farewells, and headed to Beirut. His visit had touched off the most vigorous cycle of protests since the day of Maysalun. That night in Beirut, Crane heard that police had arrested five prominent citizens, including Shahbandar.[26]

The next day, after Friday prayers at the Umayyad Mosque, a procession of eight thousand citizens protested the arrests. Muslims and Christians marched together through the city markets. They arrived at the Citadel, where Shahbandar sat in a cell not far from where Kamil al-Qassab had been jailed two years earlier. The French were not going to let the crowd storm the prison as had happened in July 1920. They brought in tanks, armored cars, and cavalry to clear the streets. Another forty-six Damascenes were arrested.

On April 8, Shahbandar's wife led forty other women in another huge demonstration. Among the protesters was Nazik al-Abid, the suffragist who had nursed Yusuf al-Azmeh at Maysalun. The crowd chanted, "We will buy our independence with our blood!" The French struck with deadly force, killing three demonstrators. Dozens more were thrown into the Citadel. In response, protests broke out in Homs, Hama, and Aleppo.

Faris al-Khoury, formerly Faisal's finance minister and now the city's leading lawyer, defended Shahbandar at the trial. But they lost the case. Shahbandar was sentenced to twenty years in prison for organizing the protests and taking money from Crane for an armed revolt in Syria. Nazik Abid was caught with a similar amount, $1,000. Crane insisted the funds were donations for scholarships to study in the United States. Rumors flew that Crane himself had also been condemned in absentia.[27]

Just before he was jailed, Shahbandar penned a letter in English addressed to "H. Ex. Dr. W. Wilson, Ex-President of the U.S.A." He reminded Wilson that he had sent a letter to him during the war. "Your well-known pledges at Mount Vernon were in those days, as they are now, an inspiration to all people in the East.

"But alas! What we tried to avoid most fell as a crushing stone on the head of our people," Shahbandar wrote. "Your most reliable friend, Mr. Crane, the God-sent messenger to suffering Syria, will tell you after his short visit lately to our country in what miserable condition our people are." Shahbandar informed Wilson that he and his friends had been arrested for simply speaking to Crane. "It is a crime in this country to ask for independence or the application of the principles of the American nation as expressed in the words of

Dr. Wilson." He signed the letter, "A. Shahbandar, ex-minister for foreign affairs in the Syrian national government."[28]

Just as the Syrian dissidents hoped, the world press played the Crane affair as a scandal.[29] In interviews, Crane claimed Syrian opposition was so strong that the French would need to spend a half billion francs to maintain an occupying army of 100,000 troops.

The *New York Times* published an article quoting Michel Lutfallah, who predicted that there would be another war if the League Council approved the French mandate. "It is now evident that imperialists are making a parody of your noble principles in Syria, making mandated people enslaved colonies," he told the paper. "The Syrian people . . . have placed all hopes and confidence in the American people."[30]

Crane used the public outcry to win President Wilson's permission to publish the King-Crane Commission report. This would not appear in print, however, before the League of Nations took its fateful decision to inscribe the mandates over Arab countries into international law.[31] Little did Crane know that President Harding's State Department was then negotiating the formal recognition of the British and French mandates in Palestine, Syria, and Lebanon in separate treaties. The United States made no stipulations regarding the sovereignty or consent of the local populations; negotiations focused on Americans' desires to protect their missionary and educational institutions and for fair terms for commercial and industrial investment. The terms of these side agreements were kept quiet.[32]

The Empire Strikes Back

Whether intentionally or not, it was symbolic that the League Council chose to meet in London to decide on ratification of the mandates. The proceedings conformed more to the norms of an imperial capital than to the ideals of Geneva. In response to the mass demonstrations in April, the French mobilized their propaganda machine to ensure approval of the Syria mandate.

"The winds of independence blow in the Orient," Gouraud wrote to his sister after Crane's visit. He noted that in February, the Egyptians had successfully negotiated a treaty that ended the British protectorate.

Gouraud's office sponsored the publication of books and articles on how the French had stabilized Syria after it suffered "Sharifian anarchy." French experts blamed Syria's problems on Muslim fanaticism and British influence.[33]

De Caix supplied the League Council with an annual report on France's first year of rule. He blamed continued problems on the incompetence of Syrians. All experienced bureaucrats, de Caix argued, had fled back to Anatolia after the Great War ended. Given this vacuum, France had been compelled to insert its own cadres. The report virtually erased the twenty-two-month period of self-rule under the Syrian Arab Kingdom, making reference in passing to discontent with "the excesses of the centralizing regime instituted by Faisal."[34]

Michel Lutfallah led a delegation to London to submit a final appeal. Although newspapers publicized their cause, the League Council refused to meet the Syrians. The 613 petitions that the League had received from Syria and Lebanon were quietly ignored.[35]

On July 24, the League Council announced its approval of the mandates at a public session held in St. James's Palace. The French Council member hailed the mandates as a generous undertaking, noting that France and Britain could have simply annexed Palestine and Syria at the moment of victory. Balfour, the British Council member, merely assured the audience that Britain would protect the holy sites of Palestine and treat Palestine's Arabs justly. The Italian member made no comment and simply wished Balfour a happy birthday.[36] To no avail, the Turkish nationalist government at Ankara protested against the presumptuous allocation of mandates, which severed Ottoman territory before the signing of a formal peace treaty.[37]

France's mandate charter, setting the terms of its rule in Syria and Lebanon, was published in August. French would be an official language alongside Arabic. The advice of "native authorities" was not required in government until three years later, when the adoption of a constitution was required. The French were not required to respect the civil rights that had been guaranteed in the 1920 Syrian Constitution; rather, they were obliged only to guarantee the freedom of religious belief and the rule of religious law. Most cuttingly, the charter obliged the Syrians to pay for their own colonization. The local population was liable to pay the cost of maintaining France's occupying troops. Once the constitution was adopted and even after the mandate was terminated, Syrians were also obliged to reimburse France for all administrative costs, including the pensions of the French staff.[38]

Back in Geneva, Lutfallah warned the Assembly not to endorse the Council's decision. The nations of the world still trusted the League to ensure peace, he advised. "But if the general assembly limits itself to approving the Council's decision and justifying this injustice, this trust will vanish which will make the nations believe no more in the League of Nations. Once again, force will prevail over truth."[39]

In Syria, a tract circulated condemning the "despotism" of the French and British who denied the people's right to choose their rulers. "Our Allies have changed into enemies," it complained. "[They have] done things that they have not even done in the most savage and least civilized countries, like Senegal."[40]

The defeat hit Rashid Rida hard. In November 1922, he published a bitter, apocalyptic letter to European liberals in *The Lighthouse*. Rida warned that history would judge them harshly unless they pried the League away from the control of the Great Powers. "We hope that scholars, writers, workers, and farmers will cooperate in overturning the politics of greed whose rifles and cannons lead to war after war. Their wars will not end until they ruin the earth and destroy all living things," Rida wrote.

> The war taught the East that Europeans are liars who call things by their opposites. . . . Why? Because they had made so many promises about liberation and independence, publicly and privately. . . . Then the land of Arab Palestine was sold to the Jews. The Arabs were humiliated and enslaved at the hands of those who claimed to liberate and rescue them! These were the mandatory powers, sent in the name of the League of Nations.

Like Lutfallah, Rida conjured a bleak vision of the future: "If European Liberals deny this appeal, or if they are unable to establish peace between East and West, then Eastern national leaders will understand that the League of Nations has agreed to serve as the most evil instrument that has ever existed on earth," he wrote. "The result would be the destruction of Europe."[41]

At that very same moment, in November 1922, General Gouraud quit his post as high commissioner. As soon as the mandate charter was officially published in August, he had submitted a nineteen-page letter of resignation in protest against budget cuts. Opponents of the Syrian invasion, including a veteran decorated for valor at the battle of Verdun, argued for the drastic reduction in the size of France's occupying force. The Army of the Levant was twice the size of the British occupying armies in either Iraq or Egypt, the veteran remarked, and yet, it could not prevent a simple demonstration during Charles Crane's visit from blowing up into an international scandal.

Gouraud underlined the transcript where the deputy called for a lighter mandate that permitted Syrians freedom and autonomy. He understood what the Chamber in Paris did not: Syrians would not accept the mandate without strong military repression. "For a last time I beg your Excellency to demand from Parliament and obtain from it 13 million [francs] that are needed," he wrote to the prime minister. But Paris did not come through with the funds, and on November 20, 1922, Gouraud set sail from Beirut, leaving de Caix behind as interim high commissioner.[42]

A mere sixteen months after occupying Damascus, the most ardent public advocate of France's mission in Syria had abandoned it. Parliaments in both London and Paris also turned their backs on the mandates. As the postwar economic crisis continued in Europe, deputies who had voted to uphold national honor in 1919 now slashed budgets. But they would not go so far as to liberate the Arabs.

Instead, they chose to run the mandates on a shoestring in a less humane, more brutish manner, using racial prejudice to justify their actions. In Iraq, Churchill fashioned a deadly solution to Britain's lack of financial capacity for rule. In place of gendarmes on the ground, the Royal Air Force would patrol the countryside from the air, bombing tribes and villages that refused to pay taxes.[43] In Syria, the French had already introduced air terror during the battle of Maysalun; the burning of villages became a routine tool of repression. Every department of government in the regimes they built in Syria and Iraq, even public health, became a branch of the intelligence service.[44] Their mandatory states were templates for future Baathist dictatorships in both countries.

Rida retained a sliver of hope that a new Turkish peace treaty might abolish the mandates. In late 1922, Mustafa Kemal finally defeated the Greek army, and negotiations began in Lausanne, Switzerland. But the Turks did not push for the liberation of their former Arab subjects. In the Treaty of Lausanne, signed on July 24, 1923, they finally relinquished all claim to sovereignty over the Arab territories of the former Ottoman Empire in exchange for their own independence.

Hope died forever on September 29, 1923, when the mandates officially entered international law. By then, Robert de Caix had taken up his new position as France's representative on the Permanent Mandates Commission in Geneva. The imperialists now ruled their mandates with no Wilsonian restraint. For the next fifteen years, de Caix personally wrote whitewashed annual reports and ensured that no dissident Syrian petition would ever be considered by the PMC. He protected the regime of minority cantons he had installed against nationalists' struggle to build a common community. The effect of de Caix's sustained power at the League was disastrous and permanent.[45] He claimed to fight Arab nationalism; in fact, he undermined any basis for Arab liberal democracy to flourish again.

"The collapse of the Faisal era was a great shock in history [with] multiple strong effects on the rest of the Arab-Ottoman countries," wrote Izzat Darwazeh years later. He blamed the collapse primarily on the "Allies' treachery," but also on weak leadership. The Syrian Arabs had no time to gain the experience needed to combat the wily methods of Europe's imperial diplomats.[46]

Woodrow Wilson's Ghost

Four months after the mandates became law, Woodrow Wilson died. Charles Crane joined the pallbearers at a small funeral service held in Wilson's home in Washington, DC, on the chilly afternoon of February 6, 1924.[47]

Syrians sent their condolences to Edith Wilson. A year later, a booklet entitled *The Democratic President Wilson* appeared in Cairo. It was published by the Eastern Bond society, of which Rashid Rida was vice president. The booklet presented an Arabic translation of a memorial address for Wilson, given to a joint session of Congress in December 1924 by Edwin Anderson Alderman, president of the University of Virginia and Wilson's childhood friend. Alderman recalled Wilson as a Christlike martyr for his ideals, a man motivated by religious principle to serve the public interest. "I am of those who believe he gained more than he sacrificed at Versailles, and I know that he alone among mortal men could have salvaged out of that sea of passion the League of Nations," he said.

But the last four years of Wilson's life had turned bleak, Alderman acknowledged. "A vast disillusionment, a chaos miscalled peace, a kind of shamefacedness and cynicism in the recollection of its dreams, and faith in the triumph of moral ideals, seem to hold the Nation and the world in its grasp."[48]

Alderman could have been describing the state of Rashid Rida's soul and the grim prospects that Shahbandar confronted after his release from prison. The era of liberal mass politics seemed to have died. A new era of populist militarism—and even fascism—had emerged. Memories of Wilson's popularity faded. Even former supporters dismissed Wilsonism as false idealism, an idea that was doomed to fail.[49]

In Geneva, the League of Nations memorialized its founding father by renaming its lakefront headquarters the Palais Wilson. Like a gravestone, a massive plaque read, "IN MEMORY OF WOODROW WILSON." The hulking old Victorian hotel, soon to be abandoned for a new League building, became a virtual mausoleum for Wilson's ideals.[50]

Epilogue

Parting of Ways:
The Liberal, the Sheikh,
and the King

Dr. Abd al-Rahman Shahbandar returned to Damascus in the summer of 1924, two years after his arrest. He had spent seventeen months in prison and then several more months in exile. During that time, he traveled to the United States to visit Charles Crane and to raise funds for the Syro-Palestinian Congress. The election of a new left-wing government in Paris opened the door for Shahbandar to resume his political activism. Not only did Paris grant him amnesty, it also lifted political restrictions. The former foreign minister resumed his medical practice and quietly reconnected his old networks in the Syrian capital. He also maintained his links with Rashid Rida and other members of the Syro-Palestinian Congress in Cairo.

In June 1925, Shahbandar announced his new People's Party at the opera house of Damascus. His rousing speech promised liberation from the "despotic" mandate, reunification of Syria, and restoration of a constitutional government. The People's Party claimed to have one thousand members, including the two Christian ministers from the 1920 government, Faris al-Khoury and Yusuf al-Hakim; and the capital's leading Muslims. "This is, no doubt, a new stage in the political history of Syria," Shahbandar proclaimed.[1]

Shahbandar planned to expand the People's Party to Syria's other major cities. The party was bankrolled by the SPC and local merchants. Rustum Haidar's family in Baalbek financed its newspaper. The

People's Party explicitly revived the liberal spirit of the Progressives in the Syrian Congress. Shahbandar's close partner, Hasan al-Hakim, possessed a rare remaining copy of the 1920 constitution, which he would one day publish.

But those plans were upended by an armed uprising in southern Syria in August 1925, led by Sultan Pasha al-Atrash, leader of the Druze community. The Druze rebelled against an intrusive, modernizing French governor. Shahbandar jettisoned peaceful politics and allied himself with the Druze to organize a national revolt. In its manifesto, the Great Syrian Revolt roused the population to avenge those defeated at Maysalun, reclaim independence, and restore democracy. "Remember that the hand of God is with you and that the will of the people is the will of God," the manifesto declared. It called on Syrians to fight the French in order to uphold "the principles of the French Revolution and the Rights of Man."[2]

This time, in contrast to July 1920, tens of thousands of Syrians volunteered to fight the French. They came not just from Damascus, but also from Druze country in the south to Aleppo in the north. By October 1925, the revolt had swept through the countryside to the orchards surrounding Damascus. The French responded with a massive bombardment of the capital by plane and artillery. An entire section of the city was flattened and hundreds of civilians died. International outrage forced the high commissioner to resign.

From his refuge in Druze territory, Shahbandar proclaimed a provisional government and declared Syrian independence. For a time, he became as famous in the Middle East as Mustafa Kemal of Turkey and Saad Zaghlul in Egypt.[3] Meanwhile, the SPC office in Geneva issued press releases and translations of Shahbandar's tracts. Riad al-Solh, who had joined the SPC while in exile in Lebanon, traveled to France to appeal to public opinion over the heads of the powerful colonial lobby.[4] As winter approached, the revolt spread to northern Syria.

In the spring of 1926, France unleashed a fierce counterrevolutionary campaign, forcing Shahbandar into exile. Across the border in Palestine, he again met his good friend Charles Crane. They took a walk through the Mount of Olives in Jerusalem. "He seemed to be steady and clear about the position, status and aims of the revolutionary movement," Crane recalled. The American was especially impressed by the Syrians' expertise in guerrilla warfare, and by the level of public support for the fighters.[5]

However, by year's end the rebels were beaten down. Any hope that the League of Nations might intervene also died. Once again, the League dug in behind a wall of legal exclusion. Although the Permanent Mandates Commission scheduled a special session in Rome on the Syrian Revolt, it refused to allow Syrians to testify. It was impossible to allow a Syrian native to sit alongside a Frenchman on equal terms, William Rappard explained.[6] At the hearing, Robert de Caix denied that a Syrian nation existed. Defending the need for French military action, he insisted, "It is pure fiction to claim, as certain Syrians and French do, that we found in the Levant an organized nation, ready to rule itself."[7]

De Caix had blocked all petitions to the League originating from within Syria. When the PMC asked why none had been received, he lied and theorized that the Syrians had been so terrorized by Ottoman rule that they still feared to send petitions. Seventeen years after Sultan Abdulhamid announced that the Ottoman peoples were mature enough for constitutional government, de Caix argued that Syrians were not yet mature enough to rule themselves.[8]

This second military defeat, now with the collusion of the League, transformed Syrian-Arab politics. After 1926, no one had any hope left in Geneva, the League, or European liberals. Loss of international faith undermined faith in justice at home, too. Wilsonism had been the glue that had held the democratic coalition together in postwar Damascus. It revived an Ottoman-era belief that a constitutional government would ensure state sovereignty—by limiting the power of monarchs who might be corrupted by foreign states. That formula had failed in the Ottoman case, but Wilsonism gave Syrians faith of a new kind: that a constitutional government would ensure international protection against foreign aggressors. That faith had brought unlikely allies together in the Syrian Congress: the wealthy Damascene Abd al-Rahman Yusuf and the postal clerk from Nablus, Izzat Darwazeh; the conservative Sheikh Abd al-Qadir al-Khatib and a populist like

Sheikh Kamil al-Qassab. Faith in Wilsonism was also the common ground on which King Faisal and Rashid Rida could argue.

Following defeat in the Syrian Revolt, the liberal constitutional community that had existed in 1920 steadily and irrevocably split apart. The deafening silence of the League and international public opinion undermined support for liberal politicians. The prolongation of supposedly temporary mandates also made a return to the 1920 liberal-Islamic constitutional coalition less likely. France's repressive apparatus and patronage of an antidemocratic elite raised new structural barriers to democratic politics. Propaganda on both sides conspired to erase 1920 as a moment of brief democratic success, substituting instead politicized memories of moral failure, weak leadership, and national betrayal.[9]

Amid this confusion and heartbreak, the seeds of dictatorship and antiliberal Islamism sprouted.

Schism in the Syro-Palestinian Congress

The Syro-Palestinian Congress had been founded in 1921 not only to represent Greater Syria to the League, but also to revive the Syrian Congress. Rashid Rida continued to sign petitions as Congress president and act as mediator between religious conservatives and secular liberals. Michel Lutfallah continued to finance the SPC, as well as Shahbandar's People's Party and the early phases of the Syrian Revolt.

When Lutfallah's funds ran low, Rashid Rida turned for support to Abdulaziz Saud, who had just conquered Mecca and ousted Sharif Hussein from the Hijaz. Wheras Faisal's father had been a petty and divisive leader, Ibn Saud unified and stabilized much of the Arabian Peninsula under the sole independent Arab state to survive the Paris Peace Conference. Rida did not, however, fully embrace the Saudis' brand of Islam, Wahhabism. In his usual pragmatic spirit, Rida embraced Ibn Saud because of the political importance of his leadership. In 1923–1924, the Turks had established a republic and abolished the Ottoman caliphate, which could no longer unite Arabs and Muslims.

But Lutfallah, longtime banker to Sharif Hussein, resented Saudi influence. He saw it as a turn away from the tolerant secularism of

1920. Shahbandar agreed. They both resented, as well, the growing influence of Rida's friend Shakib Arslan, a Muslim Lebanese exile who had taken Saudi citizenship. Amid disputes over the spending of Saudi funds on the Syrian Revolt, Shahbandar and Arslan became bitter enemies.[10]

Under these and other political pressures, the SPC finally split into rival camps in 1927. While Shahbandar and Lutfallah chose to negotiate with France and accept the division of Syria and Lebanon, Rida and Arslan denounced them as traitors.[11]

The SPC split mirrored a wider political schism across Greater Syria. Under Hashim al-Atassi, Syrian nationalists drafted a constitution for a Syrian republic. On paper it resembled the 1920 constitution in requiring the president to be Muslim and omitting reference to Islam as a state religion or basis of legislation. In spirit, however, the draft constitution was divisive. Muslim clerics and conservatives whom Rida had cajoled in the 1920 Congress were not part of process. Liberal constitutionalism in Syria became an elite and secular affair. It stoked opposition from conservatives who cooperated with the French. And it provoked protests from Islamic populist groups who did not share the commitment to democracy as Kamil al-Qassab did.[12]

In contrast to Hashim al-Atassi and nationalists in Damascus, veterans of 1920 in Palestine maintained a strict line of noncooperation with the British mandate. Izzat Darwazeh had opened a national school in his hometown, Nablus, that taught Arabic language and culture from textbooks he wrote himself. He also offered lessons in civil disobedience, modeled on the methods of Mahatma Gandhi, and became president of the local Young Men's Muslim Association (YMMA), modeled on the YMCA. It recruited men from popular classes to the nationalist cause. This became the base for reviving the Independence Party, which he established with Awni Abd al-Hadi after a new round of political violence in Palestine, the Wailing Wall riots of 1929.[13]

While secular liberals aligned with colonial powers, the resistance aligned with Islamic populist groups. This political schism broke the coalition that had sustained the Syrian Congress. The mutual trust that Rashid Rida had nurtured revived briefly during the Syrian Revolt, but then collapsed in defeat. The Muslim-Christian solidarity forged in the Syrian Arab Kingdom also collapsed, under the weight of the sectarian policies of the French and British, and the Islamic rhetoric of the resistance.[14]

Jerusalem 1931: A Last Chance of Return?

A last attempt to reunite veterans of the Syrian Arab Kingdom came in 1931, as a sideshow to a religious gathering in Jerusalem.

In 1929 the holy city in Palestine had suffered deadly riots, sparked by a dispute over access to Jewish and Muslim holy sites. In response, the mufti of Jerusalem convened a General Islamic Congress with substantial support from Indian Muslims. The congress that convened in December 1931 was the largest Muslim gathering since the fall of the caliphate in 1924. Rashid Rida and Izzat Darwazeh helped with preparations. Nearly 150 clerics and political leaders arrived from the farthest reaches of the Islamic world, from Morocco to Russia and Southeast Asia. They shared a Muslim concern for the religious monuments in Jerusalem, considered Islam's third-holiest city. The Ottoman caliphate had protected and maintained these monuments for centuries. Now, at a time of conflict over the site, there was no responsible authority.

The General Islamic Congress opened at the eighth-century Al-Aqsa Mosque, located above the wall of the Jewish temple where the 1929 riots had begun. "It was majestically prepared," Darwazeh recalled, "which made that night one of the historic nights in the history of Palestine."[15]

Rida gave a lecture on the Prophet's night journey to heaven, said to have been launched from that spot. Thousands of Palestinians gathered outside to welcome the delegates, a testament to the growth of religious organizing by the mufti and the YMMA.[16] Among workshops held in the next days, Rida chaired a session on Islamic reform and education, during which he proposed to unite Muslims around a common curriculum. He regarded this congress as an important step toward building the international brotherhood of Muslims he had advocated for thirty-five years.[17]

Awni Abd al-Hadi, never known for his piety, decided to take advantage of the gathering to reunite veterans of the Syrian Arab Kingdom.

Many had not seen one another for ten years. "It was a nice opportunity," Darwazeh recalled, "to renew the era of the Arab movement since these Arab men had been so busy with local politics." Among those who gathered at Abd al-Hadi's home on December 13 were Rida, Kamil al-Qassab, and Riad al-Solh. Faisal was absent, because the British had discouraged his attendance.

That night they signed an Arab National Pact, which called on politicians to resist colonial methods of divide-and-rule and to focus their struggle on the common goal of Arab unity and independence. The pact condemned all cooperation with mandatory powers. It also appointed an executive committee (including Abd al-Hadi, Darwazeh, and Asad Daghir, a Lebanese Maronite) to plan a larger conference at a future date, perhaps in Baghdad. The first signature at the bottom of the document belonged to Rashid Rida.

The 1931 Arab National Pact aimed to renew the spirit of unity lost in 1920, but with a critical difference. Whereas the Syrian Congress and the drafting of a constitution were integral to the struggle for democratic independence in 1920, the 1931 pact made no reference to democracy, legislative authority, or civil rights. The goals of unity and independence remained the same, but the methods for achieving those goals were left open. Nationalism was detached from liberalism.

Faisal's Antidemocratic Path to Iraqi Independence

Although unable to attend the Jerusalem reunion, King Faisal of Iraq was enthusiastic about the idea of holding a follow-up meeting in Baghdad. He sent Rustum Haidar to talk with nationalists in Syria and Palestine. They agreed to hold the Baghdad Arab congress in the fall of 1933. But once again, the British intervened to force Faisal to abandon the plan.[18] Faisal was unable to resist the British demands, because he was in the final stages of negotiations to end the mandate. On October 3, 1932, Iraq was formally admitted as an independent country into the League of Nations.[19]

Iraqi independence had come at great personal cost to Faisal. He had left Damascus a young man. In 1931 he was not yet fifty years old, but he looked like a wizened man of sixty. He chain-smoked, from habit and stress. He had suffered bouts of serious illness that prompted him to spend summers in Europe, where he still impressed English ladies with his talent at playing bridge, and often attended the horse races. In 1925, after the fall of Mecca to Ibn Saud, Faisal's wife and children moved to Baghdad. Faisal worried that his neglected eldest son, Ghazi, was mentally unstable and unfit to succeed him as king.[20]

Independence had come at a great political cost, as well. In the early 1920s, Faisal had accepted Britain's proposals for a constitution like Egypt's, whereby he would exercise a preponderance of power in government. He still blamed the Congress for the collapse of the Syrian Arab Kingdom, and he was determined never to suffer another Maysalun. The Iraqi constitution denied the popular sovereignty that Rida had defended in Syria, stating that "the authority of the people is a trust given to the king." As a legal advisor at the time admitted, "it cannot be said to have been a truly democratic constitution."[21]

By 1929, Faisal looked for inspiration to the regimes of Mustafa Kemal, Reza Shah Pahlavi of Iran, and even Benito Mussolini, who sent a sculptor to Baghdad to carve an equestrian statue of Iraq's first king. Faisal also appointed to his cabinet military veterans of the Syrian Kingdom, Jaafar al-Askeri, Nuri al-Said, and Yasin al-Hashimi. They wielded influence by doling out imperial lands and government offices to local leaders. Iraqi peasants were reduced to penniless sharecroppers. While the British consul worried about the emergence of a "palace autocracy," the Foreign Office was so impressed by the apparent stability of Iraq that it decided to grant independence—at a price. Faisal had to rig the elections of 1930 to ensure that parliament would sign the unpopular independence treaty, which extended Britain's military presence on Iraqi soil for twenty-five years.[22]

Outside Iraq, Faisal won such admiration for achieving independence that he renewed his effort to hold an Arab congress in Baghdad. In the summer of 1933, he visited Jerusalem, where huge crowds welcomed him, chanting, "Faisal, king of the Arabs!" In Syria, Hashim al-Atassi and other leaders of the new National Bloc also agreed to attend the Baghdad summit, after much prompting from Rida. They had spurned earlier initiatives by Faisal to unite Syria and Iraq under his monarchy, because they were committed to the popular sovereignty of a republic. But unity in a federation with several other Arab states was attractive.[23]

Then the moment slipped away. In June 1933, with Nuri al-Said and Rustum Haidar at his side, Faisal traveled from Jerusalem to London, where King George V recognized him as an independent monarch. Faisal felt unwell, due to complications of heart disease. He cut his visit short to seek medical treatment in Bern, Switzerland. Before he could recover, a crisis broke out in Iraq, and he returned briefly to Baghdad in August. During Faisal's absence, hard-liners in the Iraqi military had brutally suppressed an Assyrian Christian uprising in northern Iraq. They murdered many Christians and expelled others to Syria. It was Faisal's worst nightmare: no sooner had Arabs won independence than they attacked a Christian minority—just as their European opponents had predicted.

The stress proved too much for the ailing king. Faisal was forced to return to Switzerland. During a stopover in Egypt, he confessed to a Syrian nationalist that the Assyrian crisis was the outcome of his own policies. He recognized the high cost of collaborating with Britain and the need to secure Arabs' true independence through solidarity. "We can never accept the kind of life that our British allies have planned for us," he said. "This situation can continue until the volcano of resentment and anger inside us erupts. Or we unite our positions and close ranks."[24]

Faisal then summoned Dr. Shahbandar, who was still in exile in Egypt. "When we met, I saw his pale face and emaciated body," the doctor recalled. Nuri al-Said told him it was only because the king had slept little on his trip from Baghdad. Faisal told Shahbandar that he worried about the power of the military and that colonial rule had broken apart peoples who had coexisted for centuries. "Then he smiled at me and said, 'If only France had given us an opportunity like the Assyrian revolt to open up the Syrian question. Then the world might have listened to us.'"[25]

Six days later, on September 8, 1933, King Faisal died in his Bern hotel room. He was barely fifty years old. News of his death sounded the end of an era. Mourners filled Baghdad's streets with shrill cries of grief, waking those who slept on rooftops at night. Black flags of mourning were raised in cities across Greater Syria, in Damascus, Beirut, Aleppo, Jerusalem, and Amman. On September 14, according to the *New York Times,* 100,000 mourners greeted the arrival of Faisal's coffin at the port of Haifa.[26]

"It shook the Arab movement," recalled Darwazeh. He and Abd al-Hadi piled into a crowded taxi to drive twenty hours across the desert to Baghdad. They joined the long procession of mourners following the king's horse-drawn hearse. It was the largest funeral in memory in the Arabic-speaking world. But when they raised the possibility of proceeding with the Arab congress, the Iraqis refused.[27] Faisal had left behind an unstable Baghdad caught in the grip of anti-democratic nationalists, a militant officer corps, and a very young heir, King Ghazi. Within three years it would be rocked by a military coup.[28]

The Passing of a Generation and Erasure of the Liberal-Islamic Consensus

Faisal's death prompted a collective reckoning of the past. His was the first loss in the aging 1920 generation. Memory of the Syrian Arab Kingdom—often in partial or distorted form—crystallized in funeral orations, obituaries, and so on. Gradually, memory of the liberal-Islamic consensus at Damascus faded.

The *New York Times* praised Faisal for "shaking off the British mandate" in Iraq, but expressed concern that post-Faisal Iraq might follow the path of other new dictatorships, an indirect reference to the rise of fascism in Europe. "The ugly affair of the Syrian massacres would indicate that Iraq has not escaped the lurch into exacerbated nationalism that many bigger countries than Mesopotamia have experienced."[29] The paper ignored the role of colonial powers in subverting democracy in both Iraq and Syria.

The Times of London also took a skeptical view of Faisal's place in history, replicating the imperialist views that had justified the destruction of the Syrian Arab Kingdom. "He had been proclaimed king of Eastern Syria by the impetuous nationalists who surrounded him," *The Times* wrote. "Within a few months the hotheads had been overthrown by a French army and the dethroned king was in exile. But fortune was forgiving."[30] Faisal was lucky in that Britain gave him a second chance. The paper made no mention of Britain's broken promises or its subversion of the mandate system.

Likewise, the leading French newspaper, *Le Temps*, recast history to efface the 1920 betrayal of trust. It featured Faisal on its front page as a dashing Arab soldier who had come into "conflict" with the French in Syria. Despite "difficulties" with extremist nationalists, he continued to be a British puppet as king of Iraq, the paper acidly remarked.[31]

Colonial views of Syria persisted in France, unchecked. General Gouraud was incensed by Shakib Arslan's praise of Faisal in a Geneva newspaper for his "magnanimous character, intelligence, and heart." In an angry letter to a friend, written thirteen years after Maysalun, he recalled that Faisal's commander in Aleppo had issued orders to "throw the French into the sea."[32] Gouraud's bile overflowed again upon his learning that Syrians had erected a monument at Maysalun for General Yusuf al-Azmeh. "He claimed to have fired the cannon that injured me at the Dardanelles," Gouraud complained.[33] Gouraud and de Caix were no doubt bitter that many in France had blamed their policies for the 1925 Syrian Revolt. Their rival, Philippe Berthelot, had even apologized and reconciled with Faisal. Through colonial circles, the two architects of Faisal's defeat at Maysalun worked to undermine efforts to negotiate an independence treaty for Syria.[34]

Memory of 1920 played differently in the Arab world. "The Arab countries were shaken by [Faisal's] death and the Islamic world shuddered, as from a powerful earthquake," Rida wrote in *The Lighthouse*. He died of "a heart attack that struck a heart full of love for his people and his homeland." The popular outpouring of praise for Faisal was "something unprecedented in previous years, except when he entered Syria as a conqueror.[35]

In October 1933, Rida launched a ten-part series called "The Lessons of King Faisal's Life," in order to teach a new generation what the Syrian Arab Kingdom was and why it fell. He began by praising Faisal for overcoming the poor education given him by Sharif Hussein. Unlike his father and brothers, Faisal was intelligent, patient, and principled. However, he was not prepared for the crisis of 1920. His ignorance of three basic truths had led to disaster.

The first truth, Rida argued, was that unity among Arabs must be built through inclusive political systems—not imposed by a dictator from above. Faisal had been reluctant to engage the Syrian masses and he had resented the Congress. Faisal should have stood by the Declaration of Independence and the "facts on the ground," rather than seek compromises with the French. During the July 1920 crisis, Rida reminded his readers, the people had cheered the Congress and turned against Faisal.

The second truth was that Arab unity was the key to resisting Europe. Faisal had never heeded Rida's warning on the need for political solidarity in the weakest link of the Arab world, the Arabian Peninsula.[36] Citing passages from his own diary, Rida showed that he had urged Faisal to secure a truce between Sharif Hussein and Ibn Saud. That way Syria could have called up troops from the peninsula, and united the Bedouin to resist France. Instead, Faisal had squandered his efforts by supporting the raids on Lebanon that had provoked General Gouraud's ultimatum.

The third truth, Rida argued, was that Arabs must never compromise on their sovereignty. Faisal should have dismissed Hashim al-Atassi's weak cabinet, which had focused on negotiating with France rather than building a defense.

The "Lessons" series was a final word between two men who had forged an intense, productive, and stormy relationship in 1920. Rida revealed his role as a close advisor to Faisal, which had not before been widely known. Theirs had been a rich meeting of minds, establishing an Islamic democratic vernacular that had briefly united secular liberals with religious populists. Faisal and Rida never worked together after July 24, 1920. France's ultimatum had broken a unique partnership. By the 1930s, Rida's pivotal role in the Syrian Congress had been largely forgotten.

Rida's Ambiguous Legacy

Just as Faisal broke with the democratic model forged at Damascus, so Rida also departed from the liberal bargains he struck in 1920. Bitterly disappointed by the League of Nations, he turned his attention in the later 1920s to religious matters, publishing books on the modern caliphate, Wahhabism, and women's rights in Islam. He also became vice president of the Eastern Bond Society, which sponsored lectures, conferences, and publications to promote Arab Muslim ties to Asia.

Rida, who had shunned sectarianism in 1920, edged toward a worldview pitting East against West, Islam against Christianity. He had warned Lloyd George in a 1919 letter that if Sykes-Picot were implemented, it would stoke Muslim hatred for Britain. The division of Syria by Britain and France would be proof that in the Europe-made postwar world, "right, justice and freedom were intended only for Christians."[37]

Not only did Lloyd George never respond to Rida's letter, but he put the Muslim-hater Lord Curzon in charge of Middle East policy, Rida reminded readers in his 1923 book, *The Caliphate*.[38] European colonization of Arab lands undercut universal values and the impartiality of international law. Rida also turned against secular liberalism. Soon after his break with Shahbandar, he quit the Eastern Bond Society when secular liberals took over its journal.[39] Rida never publicly rejected the 1920 Islamic-liberal consensus. Even in *The Caliphate* he continued to believe in popular sovereignty. But he no longer believed in the full compatibility of Islamic and European civilizations.

The shift in Rida's views is evident in his last major book, *The Muhammadan Revelation*, published in 1934. It is mainly a passionate defense of the Prophet Muhammad's message, against the criticisms of European Orientalist scholars and Christian missionaries. The book is not hateful in tone. Rida argues that the revelations made to the Prophet in the seventh century were a divine miracle. They did not oppose or contradict the beliefs of Jews or Christians; rather, they articulated the core message in pure form. Rida urged believers to remain moderate and respectful of others. He condemned fanatics who sought to coerce others to adopt Islam. "There is no compulsion in religion," he said, quoting the Qur'an.[40]

The book also had a political message. Rida proposed Islam as a universal doctrine that might substitute for Wilsonism as an instrument of world peace. Islam stirred human beings to choose the path of peace, he argued. Islam also offered a program to fight injustice.

"Thus, the solution to the world's problems is faith in the Book which prohibits tyranny and all other forms of corruption," he wrote. Islam permitted just war, waged only to defend truth against falsehood. Most of all, Rida argued, Islam prohibited aggression for purely material ends, which started World War I:

> In our own times, the peoples of the world have been
> subjected to the worst sort of conflict, even to the point where
> civilization itself was at stake. With the kinds of weapons that
> have come into use—poison gas, machine guns, and bombs
> dropped from airplanes on populated cities—entire populations
> of men, women, and children can be exterminated in minutes.[41]

Like Wilson, Rida insisted that the foundation of peace must be the rights and dignity of individuals. Despite his turn toward conservative moralism, Rida still believed that politics must be based on popular sovereignty.

Islam, Rida further proposed, would foster a truly universal system of world justice, because it called for the common humanity and equality of all peoples. It rejected the racist hierarchy that caused war in Europe and corrupted the League of Nations. Europeans' "insistence on the superiority of their white skin, and their contempt for the rights of black-, brown-, red-, and yellow-skinned people, have led them to all manner of excesses and tyranny, and to disgrace their own civilization."[42]

Charles Crane welcomed *The Muhammadan Revelation* enthusiastically. After meeting Rida on a visit to Cairo in the spring of 1934, he arranged to distribute the book to religion scholars in the United States. He also funded a second Arabic edition for use in institutes of learning across Asia.[43]

Rida considered Crane one of the Arabs' few true friends in the West. Crane had maintained ties to many in the Damascus generation. He kept up a correspondence with Shahbandar, visited Faisal in Baghdad, and met the mufti in Jerusalem about sustaining the General Islamic Congress on a permanent basis. He had also struck up a friendship with Ibn Saud in Arabia, where he ventured on behalf of American oil interests. At the time of his visit with Rida, he was also funding research for the first Arab-authored history of the Arab Revolt in English, *The Arab Awakening*. It appeared in the United States just weeks before Crane died, at age eighty, in 1939. "East and West will alike mourn the passing of this lover of mankind," the *New York Times* wrote.[44]

By the time Rida completed his "Lessons from the Life of King Faisal" series in 1935, he was nearly seventy years old and overweight, suffering from rheumatoid arthritis and hypertension. While Faisal dealt with stress by smoking, Rida did so by eating. He enjoyed his wife's Syrian cuisine and socialized at frequent political banquets in Cairo. However, he still lived on the edge of debt. He had moved his family to a comfortable home near the fashionable Garden City district, but income earned from the Saudis barely covered the costs for his publishing business, located in the same building. Rida still traveled around the city in the second-class section of the tram, which he now found quite tiring.

On August 22, 1935, despite his poor health, Rida offered to drive Prince Saud ibn Abdulaziz to the city of Suez, where he would board a boat for home. Rida saw the trip as an opportunity to offer more advice. It was also a polite gesture to the benefactors of his press. On the return trip, Rida felt extremely tired. He tried to read his Qur'an in the car, but the road was too bumpy. Feeling dizzy and nauseous, he lay down on the back seat and closed his eyes. By the time the car reached Cairo late that afternoon, "his soul went up to his creator."[45]

Dr. Shahbandar met the car as it arrived at the house. Since it was a warm evening, he advised the family to surround Rida's body with ice. "He had always loved ice, even in winter," Rida's nephew remarked. The garden outside filled with mourners. At 7:30 p.m., the radio broadcast news of Rida's death. Because Islamic law required a quick burial, a service was arranged at a nearby school. Rashid Rida was laid to rest next to the grave of his teacher, the former mufti of Egypt, Muhammad Abduh.[46]

While Rida's death drew less press attention than Faisal's death, Charles Crane ensured that Rida was memorialized in the *New York Times*. The paper's obituary featured a photograph and praised him as a leading thinker and activist in the Muslim world. "He called upon the civilized world to bear witness to the suffering endured by Syria," the paper noted, "appealing to the American conscience for the upholding of justice and the avoidance of bloodshed."[47]

A public memorial for Rashid Rida was held on April 2, 1936, at the headquarters of a new Islamic group, Muhammad's Youth. The rector of the preeminent Islamic university, al-Azhar, presided over a gathering that included government ministers, the mayor of Cairo, and numerous religious and literary scholars. Despite their differences with Rida, both Michel Lutfallah and Abd al-Rahman Shahbandar attended the service.

Following several religious speakers, Shahbandar stood up to offer a testimonial. He began by recalling his own early days as a student of reformist Islamic teachers in Damascus. They found much inspiration by reading *The Lighthouse*. He met Rida on his visit to Damascus after the 1908 constitutional revolution. Shahbandar reminded his audience of Rida's political courage. During his famous lecture at the Umayyad Mosque, opponents had run him off the stage. "A group of people who resented religious reform, freedom and the constitution plotted against him. It almost ended in bloodshed," he recalled.

Arabs must continue Rida's battle against antidemocrats who falsified religion to serve their own purposes, Shahbandar advised. "Once we realize the powerful interdependency between religious and political belief," he said, "we recognize the extent of Sayyid Rashid's contribution to the Arab national revival."[48]

The next speaker invoked the spirit of 1920 more directly. Habib Jamati was a Christian journalist from Lebanon who had fought in the Arab Revolt. Tall like Faisal, he spoke in a mellifluous voice as he drew a personal portrait of Rida. "I will never forget that day last August when I traveled to Suez with him and his Highness Prince Saud. Al-Sayyid Rashid was joyful that day, full of life, talk, and laughter. We did not know that—may God have mercy on him—he was bidding farewell to us."

Jamati then offered a historical corrective to those who would shroud Rida's memory in Islam. The rector of al-Azhar had remarked that Rida faced three main opponents: secularists, non-Muslims, and traditional Muslims. Not true, Jamati informed the audience. Rida not only befriended Christians like himself, but struggled in concert with them for their common nation.

"I have the honor to raise my voice at this notable Islamic gathering, at the same time that Arab Easter bells ring, mingling with the voices of the faithful, calling for brotherhood, solidarity, cooperation for the Arab nation, for the sake of the slaughtered homelands!" Rida was true to his second homeland, but he did not forget his first.

"He returned to Syria right after the Great War, and given his lofty status in the hearts of people, the Syrians elected him president for their national congress," Jamati reminded the younger generation. "Al-Sayyid Muhammad Rashid Rida's views, advice and guidance deserve great credit for the success of that blessed movement. But fate turned against Syria's revival."[49]

Rashid Rida's name was eventually placed alongside those of sub-sequent presidents of the Syrian parliament on a wall in the entryway of the new parliamentary building constructed in the French era. His role in drafting the Declaration of Independence was remembered along with that of other founding fathers in the annual anniversary of March 8, which became an official national holiday in 1943, at the end of the French mandate.[50]

The Muslim Brotherhood: Rida's Stepchild

A younger generation also memorialized Rida, but without the memories of the 1908 revolution or the 1920 Congress. Among the students who attended Rida's lectures was a young man from a village in the Nile Delta. Hasan al-Banna had come to Cairo after World War I to study at the teachers college. He was shocked by the lewd behavior of British troops, who patronized music halls and appeared drunk on the streets. More shocking were the policies of elite liberals, who rejected the culture of ordinary Egyptians like him. Banna found comfort in attending lessons with Islamic reformers. With his insistence on action beyond charity work, Rida impressed Banna most.[51]

Indirectly, Rida inspired Banna to found the Muslim Brotherhood, in 1928, in Ismailiya, a company town on the Suez Canal, smaller than Port Said. The situation in Ismailiya magnified the power of the secular European culture that had alienated Banna in Cairo. The street signs were even in French. Arabs lived on their own side of town, where they listened to Banna lecture in coffeehouses. They built a mosque and developed an education program as a form of resistance to European domination. By the time of Rida's death, Banna had moved back to Cairo to build a national headquarters for the Muslim Brotherhood, which now had thirty branches across northern Egypt.[52]

Banna did not attend Rida's memorial, but he decided to take Rida's message directly to Egypt's young new king, Farouk. Later published under the title "Toward the Light," Banna's 1936 letter echoed Rida's views in *The Muhammadan Revelation*. But while Rida portrayed Islam as the perfection of a religion shared by Christians and Jews, Banna emphasized Islam as a social and political system distinct from that of the West.

"Your excellency," Banna wrote, "you will see two ways before you. . . . The first is the way of Islam, its fundamental assumptions, its principles, its culture and its civilization; the second is the way of the West, the external features of its life, its organization and its procedures."[53] Reflecting the economic and political crises in Europe, Banna contended that Western civilization, once brilliant in science, "is now bankrupt and in decline. Its foundations are crumbling and its institutions are falling apart. Its political foundations are being destroyed by dictatorships."

Islam, Banna advised King Farouk, was a remedy for peoples exploited by Europeans. "All of humanity are tormented, wretched, worried, and confused, having been scorched by the fires of greed and materialism. They are in dire need of some sweet portion of the waters of True Islam to wash from them the filth of misery and to lead them to happiness." Unlike European nationalism, he assured the king, Islam did not teach hate. Islam was "not a matter of chauvinism and pride, but of leading the world to its welfare."

Farouk did not respond to Banna's call to unify the Muslim world in opposition to Europe's racist warmongering. Like Faisal's son Ghazi in Iraq, he was a weak leader with no interest in social reform. Within a few years he became an obese playboy in thrall to the luxury and passion that Banna condemned in Europeans.

Banna meanwhile developed the Muslim Brotherhood into a force of mass politics. The terms he used to define Islam's political role could not be farther from Rida's conception in 1920. Banna, unlike Rida, left no room for public legislation outside Islamic law. The Qur'an was to be the blueprint for a social revolution. "O ye Brethren! Tell me, if Islam is something else than politics, society, economy, law and culture, what is it then? Is it only empty acts of prostration, devoid of a pulsating heart?" Banna asked, in a 1938 speech announcing the Brotherhood's entry into politics. "This narrow interpretation of Islam and these closed boundaries to which Islam has been confined is exactly what the adversaries of Islam want in order to keep the Muslims in place and make fun of them."[54]

Banna's totalizing vision contrasted with Rida's insistence that large areas of public interest (like women's suffrage) lay beyond the jurisdiction of Islamic law. There was no room in Banna's program for the Islamic-Liberal compromise that Rida had negotiated in 1920.

Although Banna was not a trained religious scholar, he announced in 1939 that the Muslim Brotherhood would resume publication of Rida's magazine, *The Lighthouse*. "This magazine resumes its jihad and appears in the public square again," Banna wrote in the dedication. He claimed that Rida had praised the Brotherhood before dying. "Glory to Allah, the Muslim Brotherhood is the group that al-Sayyid Rashid (God bless his soul) was hoping for."[55]

The public image of Rida as grandfather of the Brotherhood took hold, even though there is no evidence that Rida directly supported Banna's movement. The recasting of Rida as a fundamentalist leader further obscured from history his principal role in promoting liberal Islam in 1920.

The Dream Ends in Damascus

By 1939, Shahbandar had returned to Damascus. Another leftist government in Paris had granted him amnesty. The political landscape had changed since Shahbandar's departure in 1925. Hashim al-Atassi now headed the National Bloc, which had formed after the Syrian Revolt. Atassi and the Bloc's elite nationalists had drafted a new constitution, establishing the Republic of Syria in 1930. In some respects, it was more democratic than the 1920 constitution. The Senate, which had been partly appointed by the king, was abolished. The president, now replacing the king as executive, was still required to be Muslim.[56] However, the process had marginalized both elite conservatives and Islamic populists, who now opposed the Bloc and the secularist republic. There had been no Rida to bridge the camps.

The Bloc government's dealmaking with the French soon cost it popular support. The Bloc had negotiated an independence treaty with France's Populist Front government in 1936. But while the Syrian parliament ratified the treaty, the French government never did.[57] With the National Bloc government under siege, Shahbandar seized the opportunity to reorient away from accommodation with France and back toward the people.

Huge crowds had welcomed Shahbandar upon his return to Syria in 1937. They remembered him as a hero of the Syrian Revolt, untarnished by the compromises that the National Bloc had made with France. Bloc leaders feared Shahbandar as a rival and so placed twenty-four-hour guards around his home. They denied him a permit to open a party headquarters and forced newspapers to stop referring to him as "the great Syrian leader."

That didn't stop Shahbandar from giving a speech to a large crowd on the nineteenth anniversary of Syria's Declaration of Independence. With firebrand rhetoric, he condemned the 1936 treaty because it permitted the partition of Greater Syria and did not secure immediate entry into the League of Nations, such as Iraq had obtained. He reminded the audience that he and other Fatat members had rejected the Clemenceau accord of January 6, 1919, because it too had compromised Syria's sovereignty. The Allies thought that under the Young

Turks "we, the Arab people, were a nation that was beaten, plundered and killed before it could even open its mouth." But the Syrians had proved them wrong. He then asked the crowd to inscribe the words of the Declaration of Independence in their hearts:

> "We, members of this Congress . . . unanimously proclaim the independence of our Syrian country within its natural borders including Palestine . . . based on civil representation, preservation of minority rights, and the rejection of Zionist claims to make a national home in Palestine."

Shahbandar paused and then demanded that Syrians take historical account of how far they had fallen.

> That was our situation on March 8, 1920. So for God's sake, what have we come to? The foreign administration has established a government in this country that feels no shame in calling a protectorate "independence," and in calling subjugation "freedom." Nor does it feel shame in calling the shackles around people's necks "politics and empowerment."

With the audience calling out, "Right! Right!" Shahbandar continued, "Those who brought this treaty not only encroached on the rights of the nation, but also went to Paris, held secret negotiations and made agreements that are still unknown to even some ministers, . . . conditions that, if accepted, could have turned the country into the depths of Africa."

Shahbandar condemned those who compromised Syrian dignity as traitors to the dream of 1920, and as agents of debasement, humiliation, and dehumanization. "The man who kills the victim and then walks in his funeral is less evil than the one who sells his homeland and then cries for its independence."

Syrians must fight French efforts to fragment the Arab nation, he continued, "not because we have the weapons, planes, and guns, but because we believe that our faith is a heavenly power from God, more powerful than the power of man." Shahbandar concluded with a quote from the Qur'an: "Don't weaken and don't grieve; you will triumph if you are true believers" (Al-Imran 137–39).[58]

The anger and shame that Shahbandar evoked that day echoed the anguish of the handbills that had been distributed in 1919, when Britain had pulled out its troops; and again in 1920, when France lined its colonial army along the border. Two decades later, Syrians remembered the betrayal vividly. The breach of faith and of human dignity perpetrated by Britain and France when they plotted in 1920 to destroy Syria's democracy was not only remembered; it was encoded into Syrian and Arab politics. It opened a wound in Arab politics that inspires pain even today.

Shahbandar became the leading politician in Syria. He held high the torch of 1920, of sovereignty and democracy. He spoke truths that neither elite nationalists nor Islamic populists, much less the French, wanted to hear. He criticized nationalists who wielded influence only through the patronage of a personal clientele rather than through commitment to political principles.

Shahbandar was an outsider with no social base, a middle-class doctor, not a tribal chief or a landowner. His opponents moved in on him. When Shahbandar was seen visiting the British embassy, rumors flew that he was negotiating the reunion of Greater Syria under Faisal's brother, King Abdullah of Jordan.

While Shahbandar understood the risks of antagonizing the National Bloc, he did not foresee the threat from another political movement, the burgeoning network of Islamic populists. At its head was Sheikh Kamil al-Qassab. He too had been amnestied after a long exile in Mecca. He returned with a hardened brand of Islam. Supporters of his Association of Muslim Clerics called for the rule of Islamic law and freely attacked women in public. Qassab's network finally forced the Bloc from power in a fight over Islamic law. The Bloc had cooperated with a French effort to roll back the jurisdiction of Islamic law in favor of a civil code. Reprising his role in 1920, Qassab led crowds into the streets. Unlike in 1920, Qassab was no longer interested in the liberal project. Like Banna, he demanded government based on Islamic law.[59]

On July 6, 1940, Shahbandar was ambushed, shot, and killed in Damascus. Amid public horror and mourning, he was buried as a national hero next to Saladin's tomb. The French brought murder charges against National Bloc leaders, who escaped to Iraq. But the lower-level men convicted of the murder confessed they had killed Shahbandar out of religious motives, believing that he was a friend of Britain and an enemy of Islam. Many Syrians believed that France was actually behind the plot.[60]

Despite the trial and conviction of the assassins, the possibility of a political plot behind Shahbandar's murder remains undetermined. The historical symbolism is nonetheless clear. Shahbandar was loathed by a segment of Syria's population that believed Islam should be the basis of government. They viewed Shahbandar as a westernized secularist. But he saw himself in the terms he had used in 1920, as a pious man who could be both Muslim and liberal. His insistence that Islam should remain outside politics, in the private sphere, had been accepted in the Syrian Congress of 1920.

Twenty years of French mandatory rule had utterly transformed Syria's political landscape, driving a sharp divide between liberals and Islamists. That cleavage has weakened the cause of democracy in Syria ever since. In 1950, after France's departure, Syrians would rewrite their constitution, adding social and economic rights to the list of civil rights first enumerated in 1920. By then, the Islamic movement had united into the Syrian Muslim Brotherhood. It wielded enough political clout to force the insertion of a new clause, against the opposition of liberals, socialists, and religious minorities. Alongside the 1920 requirement that the king/president's religion be Islam, Article 3 now read, "Islam shall be the main source of legislation."[61] Since then, nearly every Arab constitution has incorporated similar language. Shahbandar's fatal defeat sounded the death knell for the liberal Islam that had managed to govern, briefly, in 1920.

Appendix A

Members of Congress
in March 1920

Membership in the Syrian Congress fluctuated between June 1919 and July 1920. We do not have precise records, because the Congress archive disappeared after the French invasion. We do have the reproduction of a poster—the original was made in March 1920—which offers an imperfect snapshot of the Congress deputies who declared Syrian independence. The poster and the names of most of the eighty-four deputies pictured on it are given below (a few names are illegible). Some deputies are not pictured, including Mar'i al-Mallah, vice president of the Congress, and several who engaged in the debate on women's suffrage in late April: an opponent, Ibrahim al-Hajj Hussein of Deir ez-Zor; and three supporters, Subhi al-Tawil and Da`as Jirjis of Latakia and Sheikh Sa`id Murad of Gaza. We can suppose that close to ninety deputies gathered at important sessions of Congress in the spring of 1920.[1]

The poster also illustrates the geographic distribution of Congress deputies in the spring of 1920. Thirty-eight deputies, almost half of those pictured, came from today's Syria. One-quarter—twenty deputies—came from today's Lebanon, and fifteen from Palestine/Israel. Five deputies came from today's Jordan, and two came from towns located in what is now Turkey. Missing from the poster are additional Lebanese and Palestinian deputies whose travel to Damascus on March 8 was blocked by France and Britain.[2]

Finally, the photographs on the poster suggest the differences in social background among the deputies. In the late Ottoman and early postwar eras, the type of headgear a man wore denoted his social position. The tarbush (or fez) was worn by an older generation of Ottoman bureaucrats and professionals. Nearly two-thirds of the deputies on the poster wore a tarbush. A dozen deputies wore turbans that signified they were religious dignitaries like Rashid Rida (pictured third from the right on the top row). Seven wore the kaffiyeh (headscarf) of tribal sheikhs from desert regions. Finally, a dozen deputies wore no headgear at all. They were typically younger men associated with the Fatat nationalist organization, including Riad al-Solh,

Source: Pierre Fournié and Jean-Louis Riccioli, *La France et le Proche-Orient 1916–1946* (Tournai, Belgium: Casterman, 1996), 66–67. Reproduction of an original once archived at the French army archives at Vincennes. It cannot currently be located there.

Dr. Ahmad Qadri, and Dr. Said Tali` (author of the independence memorial volume).

Names of the 1920 Deputies and the Districts They Represented

The current-day states were divided, in 1920, into the three zones of Greater Syria: the West Zone included the Lebanese, Syrian, and Turkish coasts; the East Zone included inland regions of today's Syria and Jordan; and the Southern Zone included territory claimed today by Palestine and Israel. While most deputies actually resided in the districts they represented, there were a few exceptions. The most prominent of these was Dr. Ahmed Qadri, a native of Damascus who represented the city of Khalil, or Hebron, in Palestine.

The names and districts listed below reflect the text on the poster, although in some instances it is illegible or at variance with other sources. Rashid Rida, most notably, is listed here as a delegate from Beirut, although most other sources record that he represented Tripoli. Alternate data is given in brackets.

1. Deputies Circling Faisal in the Center of the Poster

First circle, counterclockwise from left of Faisal

Name	City of Residence	Today's Location
Mourad Ghalmiya	Rashaya	Lebanon
Izzat Darwazeh	Nablus	Palestine
Hashim al-Atassi	Homs	Syria
Dr. Said Tali`	Tripoli [Mount Lebanon]	Lebanon
Salah al-Din al-Hajj Yusuf	Safed	Palestine

Second circle, counterclockwise from left

Riad al-Solh	Sidon	Lebanon
Dr. Ahmad Qadri	Hebron	Syria
Saadullah al-Jabiri	Aleppo	Syria
Wasfi al-Atassi	Homs	Syria

2. Left-Hand Block
(Columns enumerated left to right, read top to bottom)

Column 1

Sheikh Abd al-Qadir al-Khatib	Damascus	Syria
Amin Tamimi	Nablus	Palestine
Khalil Talhuni	Maan	Jordan
Rashid al-Hajj Ibrahim	Haifa	Israel
Muhammed al-Sharif	Latakia	Syria
Izzat al-Shawi	Damascus	Syria
Hikmat al-Hiraki	Aleppo [al-Ma`ara]	Syria

Column 2

Abd al-Qadir al-Kilani	Hama	Syria
Hussein al-Zughbi	Nazareth	Israel
Mahmud Nadim	Manbij	Syria
Da`as al-Jirjis	Latakia	Syria
Georges Harfoush	Beirut	Lebanon
Abd al-Hamid Barudi	Hama	Syria
Sa`id [illegible]	Salt	Jordan

Column 3

Rafiq al-Tamimi	Hebron	Palestine
Ahmad al-Ayashi	Idlib	Syria
Abd al-Rahman Arshidat	`Ajlun	Jordan
Abd al-Mahdi Mahmoud	illegible [Damascus]	Syria
Salim Abd al-Rahman	Tulkarm	Palestine
Abd al-Fattah al-Saadi	Acre	Israel
Adil Zu'aytir	Nablus	Palestine

Column 4

Salim Ali Salam	Beirut	Lebanon
Hikmat al-Nayyal	Aleppo	Syria
Abd al-Fattah al-Sharif	Akkar	Lebanon
Ilyas Ayushaq	Damascus	Syria
Ahmad al-Qudmani	Damascus	Syria
Tawfiq Mufarrij	Mount Lebanon [al-Kura]	Lebanon
Sheikh Tahir al-Tabari	Tiberias	Israel

3. Middle Block, Beneath Faisal's Circle
(Columns enumerated left to right, read top to bottom)

Column 1

Said Haidar	Baalbek	Lebanon
Zaki Yahya	Idlib	Syria
Muhammad Haidar	Baalbek	Lebanon
Yusuf Linyadu	Damascus	Syria

Column 2

Fawzi al-Bakri	Damascus	Syria
Musallam al-Husni	Damascus	Syria
Mustafa Lutfi al-Rifa'i	Antioch	Turkey
Suleiman al-Suri	Jabal Druze [Ajlun]	Jordan

Column 3

Mahmoud al-Fa`ur	Quneitra	Syria
Subhi Barakat	Antioch	Turkey
Rashid al-Mudarris	Aleppo	Syria
Mahmud Abu Rumiyeh	Hawran	Syria

Column 4

Faiz al-Shihabi	Hasbaya	Lebanon
Muhammad al-Mujtahid	Damascus	Syria
Manah Harun	Latakia	Syria

Column 5

Mouin al-Madi	Haifa	Israel
Afif al-Solh	Tyre	Lebanon
Naji Ali al-Adib	Jabla	Syria
Ismail Abu al-Rish	Nabak	Syria

4. Right-Hand Block
(Columns enumerated left to right, read top to bottom)

Column 1

Abd al-Rahman al-Yusuf	Damascus	Syria
Jalal al-Qudsi	al-Izaz	Syria
Tamir Hamadeh	al-Harmil	Lebanon
Uthman Sultan	Tripoli	Lebanon

Ibrahim Hananu	Harim	Syria
Sa`id al-Salibi	Salt	Jordan
Yusuf al-Aqil	Tiberias	Israel

Column 2

Sheikh Rashid Rida	Beirut [Tripoli]	Lebanon
Sharif al-Darwish	al-Bab	Syria
Ibrahim al-Khatib	Mount Lebanon	Lebanon
Arif al-Naamani	Beirut	Lebanon
Nuri al-Jisr	Aleppo	Syria
Ibrahim al-Akka	Acre	Israel
Subhi al-Tawil	Latakia	Syria

Column 3

Teodor Antaki	Aleppo	Syria
Tawfiq al-Bisar	Tripoli	Lebanon
Abd al-Rahman al-Nahwi	Safed	Israel
Jamil Bayhum	Beirut	Lebanon
Rashid Naffa`	Metn	Lebanon
Fuad Abd al-Karim	Idlib	Syria
Nasser Fawaz	Hauran	Syria

Column 4

Fatih al-Mar`ashi	al-Izaz	Syria
Ibrahim Abd al-Hadi	Nablus	Palestine
Issa al-Madana	Karak	Jordan
Yusuf Kikhiya	Aleppo	Syria
Khalid al-Barazi	Hama	Syria
Amin Bayhum	Beirut	Lebanon
Sa`id Ramadan	Zabadani	Syria

The deputies who were not pictured on the poster but who were listed in memoirs as members of the Syrian Congress in 1919–1920 include the following:

Delegates From Today's Syria [Not Pictured]

Damascus: Fawzi al-`Azm (deceased), Fawzi al-Bakri, Sheikh Hussein
   Taj al-Din, Mahmud al-Barudi
Aleppo: Yusuf al-Kayyali, Mara`i Pasha al-Mallah
Homs: Muthir Raslan
Duma: Mahmud al-Shishakli
Zabadani: Hassan [or Sa`id] Ramadan
Hauran: Nasir al-Maflah, Nasib al-Atrash
Deir ez-Zor: Fasil [for Fadil] `Abbud, Mahmud Nuri al-Fatih, Ibra-
   him al-Hajj Husayn
Latakia: Yusuf al-Hakim (who left Congress to enter the cabinet after
   March 8, 1920); Muhammad Khayr
Husn al-Akrad: Da`as al-Hajj Hassan

Delegates From Today's Lebanon [Not Pictured]

Tripoli: `Abd a-Majid al-Maghrabi
Sidon: Riad al-Solh (who left Congress to enter the cabinet after
   March 8, 1920)

Delegates From Today's Palestine/Israel [Not Pictured]

Jerusalem: Raghib Nashashibi, Sa`id al-Husayni, `Arif al-Dajani,
   Ya`qub Faraj
Jaffa: Raghib al-Dajani
Safad: Salah al-Din Fadura
Tulkarim: Sa`id al-Karmi
Gaza: Rushdi al-Shawa, Sa`id Murad

From Today's Jordan

Salt: Sa`id Abu Naji

Appendix B

The Syrian Declaration
of Independence
March 8, 1920

A facsimile of the Declaration of Independence, with signatures, was reproduced in the May 10, 1920, memorial volume composed by Said Tali` and published by Yusuf Suyudi. The English text below is based on a translation by Sidney Glazer.[1]

During its public session of Sunday–Monday Jumada II 16, 1338 (March 7, 1920), the General Syrian Congress which represents all the Syrian Arab people in the three zones—interior, coastal, and southern (Palestine)—passed the following resolution:

During Ottoman times the organizations and political parties of the Arabs, who are the heirs of an ancient glory and brilliant civilization, waged a hard political struggle that culminated in a bloody revolt against the central government, only because they wanted complete independence and a free life as a people possessing an independent existence, unique national spirit, and the right of self-rule like that enjoyed by other peoples who are not superior to us in civilization and progress.

The Arabs joined the Allies in the war on the basis of formal promises made privately and publicly by their parliaments and government leaders, in particular the pledges given to King Hussein regarding the independence of the Arab countries. They relied too on President Wilson's lofty principles espousing the freedom and independence of great and small peoples, equality of rights, the termination of the policy of conquest and imperialism, nullification of secret treaties impairing the rights of nations, and the right of self-determination for liberated peoples. The Allies officially agreed to all this in the following: the statement of Premier Briand on November 3, 1915, before the French Chamber of Deputies; the statement of Lord Grey, British Foreign Secretary, on October 23, 1916, before the Committee on Foreign Affairs; the Allies' answer to the note of the Central Powers, which was submitted by Briand through the American ambassador in Paris; the Allies' answer to President Wilson's note of January 10, 1917; the declaration of the French Chamber of Deputies on the night of June 4–5, 1917; the declaration of the [French] Senate on June 6; and Lloyd George's speech in Glasgow on June 29, 1917.

King Hussein's great deeds on the side of the Allies constituted the major factor in freeing the Arabs from the morass of the Turkish regime, and they will live forever in the annals of the people. The diplomatic and military leaders of the civilized world witnessed how much his sons and the other Arabs suffered when they fought in the regular Allied armies for three years. The sacrifices, persecution, torture, execution, and exile of many of those who joined the Arab movement [in] Syria, the Hijaz, and Iraq—not to mention the accomplishments of the Syrians in their own country—facilitated the victory of the Allies and the Arabs. They contributed to the Turkish defeat and subsequent withdrawal from Syria and thus realized the hopes of the Arabs in general and of the Syrians in particular. Arab flags were unfurled and local governments established in various parts of the country before the Allies arrived.

When military arrangements required the division of Syria into three zones, the Allies officially announced that they had no designs on Syria and that the only reason they were continuing the war in the East was to deliver the peoples from the Turkish yoke once and for all. They said that partition was just a temporary military expedient that would have no effect on the country's future independence or unity. Moreover, in the first paragraph of Article 22 of the Treaty of Peace with Germany they formally recognized our independence in fulfillment of their pledge to grant peoples the right of self-determination. Then they sent the American Commission to ascertain the wishes of the people, who made it clear that they wanted the complete independence and unity of Syria.

The burdensome military occupation and partition have now lasted about a year and a half and done us great harm economically and administratively. The minds of the people are filled with doubts as to their future. The tension prevailing everywhere has led to the outbreak of insurrections with the country's independence and unity and the termination of an alien military rule as their goals.

We the members of this Congress, in our capacity as true representatives of all the Syrians in whose name we speak, hereby proclaim the necessity of putting an end to this intolerable situation. We do so in reliance upon our natural and legal right to freedom; upon the blood shed by our martyrs in a long and holy struggle; upon the aforementioned agreements, pledges, and lofty principles; and upon the ever-growing determination of the nation to demand and achieve by any and all means its rights and unity. We have therefore unanimously proclaimed the full and absolute independence of our country Syria, including Palestine, within her natural boundaries, based on a civil, representative form of government; protection of the rights of minorities; and rejection of the claims of the Zionists to Palestine as a national homeland or place of immigration for the Jews.

Furthermore, we have chosen His Highness Emir Faisal, son of King Hussein, to be the constitutional king of Syria with the title his Majesty King Faisal the First. His tireless efforts to liberate the country caused the people to acclaim him their greatest hero. We have announced the termination of the present military occupation governments in the three zones and their replacement by constitutional monarchy which shall be vested by this assembly with the full authority to deal with any matter that may affect our independence until the representative assembly can be convened. There shall also be decentralized administration of the provinces together with observance of the wishes of the Lebanese for the autonomy of their province within its prewar boundaries, provided that it is free from any foreign influence.

Since the Arab Revolt occurred in order to liberate the Arabs from the Turkish yoke (the reasons justifying the independence of Syria are equally applicable to Iraq) and since the two regions are inextricably linked together by linguistic, economic, natural, and racial ties, we therefore demand the full independence of Iraq and the creation of a political and economic union between the two sister countries.

In the name of the Syrian Arabs who have chosen us to represent them we shall preserve the friendship of the noble Allies and fully respect their interests and those of all the other nations as well. We are certain that the noble Allies and all the other civilized nations will accept this honorable and well-intentioned action of ours, which rests on natural and legal right, and recognize our independence. We know too that the Allies will evacuate their armies from the Western and Southern zones, thus permitting the indigenous regime to assume the task of administration and maintenance of order. Retention of the existing mutual goodwill will enable the Syrian Arabs to reach their lofty goal and become active members of the world community.

It is incumbent upon the Syrian government, which has been formed on this basis, to carry out this resolution.

Appendix C

The Syrian Constitution of July 19, 1920

This is the first published English translation of the Syrian Constitution, as it was drafted on July 19, 1920. The Syrian Congress approved the text in principle, but required full ratification, article by article. Congress completed ratification of only the first seven articles. The text was translated by the author with the help of Basem Elzaawily, an Arabic translator in Washington, DC; and Nael Georges, a Syrian constitutional lawyer affiliated with International IDEA (Institute for Democracy and Electoral Assistance), headquartered in Stockholm, Sweden.

After months of research, I could find no surviving original manuscript. However, I was fortunate to have consulted the late Khairiyah Qasimiyah, author of the first major book in Arabic on the government of the Syrian Arab Kingdom, before her untimely death. Through our colleague Dr. Abdul-Karim Rafeq, also a historian of Syria, Dr. Qasimiyah advised me that she considered the version of the constitution published by Hasan al-Hakim to be definitive. This makes sense to me. Hakim headed the kingdom's ministry of post, telephone, and telegraphs and was a close associate of Dr. Abd al-Rahman Shahbandar, the leading liberal politician of the post-1920 era. It is reasonable to believe that he would have kept a copy of the constitution. His was the 147-article version, reflecting the decision after July 5, 1920, to delete Article 3.[1]

We know that the French obtained a copy of the 148-article constitution presented to the Syrian Congress on July 5, 1920. Philippe

David, an employee of the high commission, included in his doctoral dissertation the text of the Syrian Constitution as translated in Beirut on August 26, 1920, by Louis Mercier, the high commission's top translator.[2] Mercier, who was raised in French Algeria, was known for his excellent Arabic. The serious error made in translating Article 1 is therefore telling. Instead of reading, as the Arabic did, "the religion of the King is Islam," the French version stated, "the religion of the *state* is Islam." The error reflects French diplomats' contention that Faisal intended to establish a theocracy; it effectively erases the existence of an Arab democracy. David made a second error concerning the constitution, reflecting the general lack of citation or precision in his text. He claimed the constitution had been read on July 3—it was actually read on July 5—and that it was approved that day—it was not.[3] Calls for ratification of the entire text, as seen in Chapter 16, were rejected for fear that it would permit Faisal to dissolve the Congress.

In a polemical tone, David dismissed the constitution as inadequate proof of the Syrians' capacity for self-government, as "just an Oriental adaptation of parliamentary regimes in Great Britain or France, an assemblage of formulas from various sources." It was written by a "xenophobic" minority of deputies from the Syrian hinterland, David claimed, despite evidence that more than half of the deputies came from the Western coastal and Southern Palestine zones. The constitution concentrated power in the Chamber of Deputies, he wrote further, and elected officials held power over the king, demonstrating "a shocking lack of equilibrium between executive and legislature."

The political intent of David's analysis also caused him to dismiss the legality of the March 8 Declaration of Independence. He described France's July 24 invasion of Syria as "nothing more than a police action," because Syria was juridically nonexistent in international law.[4] Like his French superiors, David extinguished the legal spirit of Article 22 of the League covenant, which was inserted into all peace settlements and which stated that Syria was provisionally independent. His thesis apparently pleased his employers, for David served more than twenty years under the high commission.

In her book on the Syrian Congress, Syrian historian Mari Almaz Shahrastan disputed David's conclusion. The constitution established Syria's capacity for self-rule, she wrote. "It refutes the flimsy premises and reasons used by the Great Powers to justify their presence, occupation, and mandate."[5]

The accuracy of Hasan al-Hakim's Arabic version is supported by two additional sources. First, slightly different drafts of the Syrian Constitution have been published in Arabic, suggesting that there was more than one manuscript. This is highly likely because we know that on July 5 deputies asked Uthman Sultan of the constitutional committee to have copies printed.[6] We have no record that he ever did so, given the tumultuous events that followed. However, all of the Arabic versions share matching language about the religion of the king, not the state. A second source that supports Hakim's version is the writings of Rashid Rida, which reproduce the debate in which the deputies agreed not to make Islam the state religion. These were presented at length in chapters 10 and 12.

France's attempt to erase the democratic regime in Syria unfortunately had a long-term effect on scholarship in English. First, the eminent historian Majid Khadduri referred to David's French translation in his much-cited article on Syrian constitutional history, replicating the false notion that the 1920 constitution established Islam as the state religion.[7] Likewise, the first English-language translation of the constitution, included in a master's thesis written at the American University of Beirut, also relied on the incorrect French translation.[8]

THE CONSTITUTION OF THE SYRIAN KINGDOM

Chapter 1
General Provisions

1. The Arab Kingdom of Syria is a civil representative monarchy. Its capital is Damascus and the religion of its King is Islam.
2. The Syrian Kingdom is composed of provinces that belong to an indivisible political union.
3. The official language in all of the Syrian Kingdom is Arabic.

Chapter 2
The King and His Prerogatives

4. The throne of the Syrian Kingdom belongs to and shall pass to the eldest in line among the sons of King Faisal I. Following this principle, if a King has no son, the throne shall pass to the eldest of his nearest male blood relatives. If there are no male blood-line descendants of Faisal, then the Congress shall elect, by a two-thirds majority, a King descended from the dynasty of King Hussein I of the Hijaz. The throne shall then pass to heirs of the King on the same principle as for Faisal I.

5. The King assumes the throne at the age of eighteen. Should the throne pass to an heir who has not reached this age, the Congress shall elect, by an absolute majority vote, a Regent who shall rule the kingdom in the name of the King. The Regent must not be from the military. He must swear an oath of respect for divine laws, of loyalty to the nation and the King, and of adherence to the Constitution.

6. When he assumes the throne, the King must swear before the Congress an oath of respect for the divine laws and of loyalty to the nation and adherence to the Constitution.

7. The King is respected and he is not responsible.

8. The King is the commander in chief. He declares war, concludes peace, and signs treaties on condition that he submit them to the Congress for approval. Treaties are not valid unless they have such approval. He also has the power to declare a general amnesty, after obtaining the approval of the Congress. He appoints the prime minister and approves the formation of the Cabinet, and accepts its resignation. He sends ambassadors to foreign nations and accepts their ambassadors. He approves laws and regulations and grants a special pardon or reduces the sentences of the condemned. He opens the Congress and adjourns it according to Article [left blank]. He has the right to call the Congress to an extraordinary session and to prolong the duration of its sessions when necessary. He can dissolve the Representative Assembly according to Article [left blank]. The currency is issued

in his name, and he can award medals, set military ranks, and grant royal offices according to special legislation.

Chapter 3
Individual and Collective Rights

9. The designation "Syrian" is applied to every individual among the people of the Syrian Arab Kingdom. Syrian citizenship can be acquired and forfeited according to conditions set by the law on nationalities.

10. Syrians are equal before the law in rights and duties.

11. Personal freedom is guaranteed against all encroachments. No one shall be arrested except for reasons and in circumstances provided by law.

12. It is forbidden to torture or inflict injury upon anyone for any reason.

13. It is forbidden to infringe upon the freedom of belief or religion or to ban religious ceremonies of any confession, unless they disturb the public order or offend other rites and religions.

14. Oversight of Sharia courts and religious councils that administer personal status laws and the management of public [Waqf] endowments shall be administered under laws issued by the Congress.

15. Inhabitants have the right to submit their private and public complaints, as individuals or collectively, to official authorities and to their representative councils.

16. Associations, meetings, and companies may be organized freely within the limits of laws set by the Congress.

17. All residences are inviolable. They cannot be entered except in cases provided by the law.

18. The property of individuals and legal personalities is protected by the law. The government cannot expropriate the property of an owner except in the public interest and after the payment of an indemnity in accordance with special regulations.

19. Publication is free within the limits of the law and cannot be inspected or verified before publishing.

20. The basis of education in public and private schools in all provinces of Syria must be the same, resting on national principles.

21. Elementary education is obligatory. It is free in public schools.

22. Private schools may be freely established, within the limits of special laws issued by the Congress.

23. It is forbidden to compel anyone to pay any sum of money in the form of tax, fees, aid, or anything else, unless the obligation is based on an article of law.

24. Forced labor and confiscation are prohibited.

25. It is forbidden to try anyone except in courts established by law.

26. Administrative exile is completely forbidden.

Chapter 4
The Syrian National Government
[The Cabinet]

27. The national government for the Syrian provinces shall consist of a Cabinet, which is responsible for its actions before the National Representative Assembly.

28. The Prime Minister shall elect the ministers and submit their names to the King.

29. Upon its formation, every Cabinet must present its plans to the National Representative Assembly.

30. Every minister is responsible for his ministry before the National Representative Assembly.

31. No law or resolution can be issued unless it is signed by the Prime Minister and the minister entrusted with its execution, and approved by the King.

32. Royal decrees must be signed by the Prime Minister and the minister entrusted with their execution.

33. It is forbidden for any member of the royal family to be a member of the Cabinet.

34. The military, navy, foreign affairs, postal and telegraph service, customs, public telephone lines, railways, ports, lighthouses, mines, minting of currency, issue of stamps and banknotes, establishment of the national bank, manufacture of arms, war

matériel, and explosives, and the construction of public roads are all exclusively within the competence of the national government.

35. The national government establishes, funds, and administers higher colleges of arts and sciences. It supervises the unified basis of education throughout the Kingdom.

36. The national government standardizes weights and measures and the units of currency on the basis of the decimal system. It also fixes rates of exchange for foreign currencies in all regions of the Kingdom.

37. The revenues from the farming of state-owned domains and property, public forests, customs, public telephones, the tele-graph, postal service, and state banks are assigned to the national budget, as are all taxes on camels and sheep, monopolies, con-cessions, alcohol, mines, ports, lighthouses, stamps, quarantines, ships, fishing, explosives, and railways. Exempt are tax revenues from the Hijaz Railway and its branches, which are part of the Muslim [Waqf] endowments.

38. The national government may not sell or lease public domains except according to a special law that shall protect the interests first of farmers and then of provinces.

39. If the Kingdom confronts danger or conditions that threaten public security during a period when the Congress is in recess, and if there is insufficient time to convene it to enact the neces-sary laws, then the Cabinet shall take the necessary decisions and enact them by a law approved by the King. These decisions must be submitted to Congress at its next meeting.

40. In the case of revolt in any part of the Kingdom, or if the gov-ernment enters a war or declares a general mobilization, then the national government shall proclaim martial law in accordance with special laws promulgated by the Congress, on condition that martial law apply only in the region under revolt.

41. Every minister has the right to attend, whenever he wishes, the deliberations of the Senate and the Representative Assembly. And he has the right to speak.

42. Every minister must respond to the summons of either the Senate or the Representative Assembly and reply to inquiries

addressed to him either in person or through a delegate chosen from among his department heads. He must provide the Senate or Assembly with all requested information on any matter that pertains to the functioning of his ministry.

43. If a minister is summoned to the Representative Assembly for questioning on an issue, and if he does not receive majority support, then he will lose his post. If the Prime Minister loses his post, the whole Cabinet will fall with him. The minister and the Cabinet may request a postponement of their response.

44. If five or more representatives file a complaint on a matter against the Cabinet or a minister concerning an action within their responsibility, and should two-thirds of the Assembly approve the conduct of an inquiry on the matter, then the Assembly shall entrust it to a commission drawn by lots. This commission will conduct an investigation, summon the minister or ministers involved, collect their explanations on the matter, and then submit its decision to the Assembly. If a two-thirds majority agrees on the need for a trial, the case shall be forwarded to the Supreme Court. A special law shall be issued on the trial procedures to be followed.

45. Should the Representative Assembly decide to put a Cabinet or one of its ministers on trial, the latter loses his portfolio.

46. No distinction shall be made between a minister and another citizen regarding ordinary crimes, private rights, or financial obligations. In such a case, the minister shall stand trial in the ordinary courts.

Chapter 5
The Congress

47. The Congress consists of two chambers, the Senate and the Representative Assembly.

48. The Congress convenes on the first of September each year. Its session lasts four months and, according to need, may be prolonged and convoked outside its official term.

49. The King opens the Congress with a royal speech—including all important political and administrative events that have occurred

during the annual recess and on measures required in the coming year—in the presence of the two chambers and entire Cabinet.

50. The Senate and Representative Assembly must issue special rules on their administrative functions and internal deliberations. Each year they must elect, from among their members, a president and two vice presidents, as well as clerks and an administrative committee, in accordance with the aforementioned rules.

51. The Senate and Assembly must each verify proof of election of its members, accept their resignation, and dismiss those who should be legally removed.

52. All deliberations must be public. A secret session may be convened upon the suggestion of ten members or by demand of the Cabinet, provided that a majority of the Chamber approves.

53. The members of the two chambers are free in the expression of their ideas and remarks in the Chamber. None of them may be held responsible for expressing themselves, on condition that they do not violate the internal rules of the Chamber.

54. Neither Chamber may begin deliberations if more than half of its members are not present. Resolutions shall be taken by majority vote of those attending the session, except in matters requiring the approval of a two-thirds majority.

55. Members vote on resolutions by name or by way of a special signal or by hidden opinion [secret ballot]. The last requires majority approval.

56. If a Senator or Representative is accused of treason, and two-thirds of the members of his Chamber agree to try him, he shall then be referred to the Supreme Court.

57. No Senator or Representative may be arrested or tried for an ordinary crime during the Chamber's session unless two-thirds of the members of his Chamber agree. An exception is made when the member is caught by eyewitnesses in the crime. In this case, the Chamber to which he belongs must be informed immediately.

58. A Senator or Representative may not undertake business for the central government, a local government, or municipalities. Nor shall he enter into any commitments or accept any privileges for himself or in collaboration with others.

59. All Senators, Representatives, and Ministers have the right to propose any bill of laws they want. They can also propose the amendment of existing laws. Laws proposed for approval or amendment must be reviewed first by the Representative Assembly and then by the Senate.

60. The civil, penal, and commercial codes; laws on public health; rights of authors; patent rights; the press; official and private education; meetings; societies; emigration; insurance; nationality; units of weights, measures, dimensions, and currency; and labor laws as well as the laws related to the national government shall be promulgated by the Congress and enforceable in all sectors.

61. If the Representative Assembly adopts a law and submits it to the Senate which amends it and sends it back to the Assembly, but the Assembly persists in its first opinion and the Senate does also the same, in this case the law should be sent back again to the Assembly. If the Assembly rejects the amendments, then a commission composed of equal numbers of both bodies shall be formed in order to settle the difference. In case it cannot, the resolution of the Assembly becomes enforceable, provided that it is approved by its two-thirds majority. However, in the case of the Syrian budget law, the Senate can send it back only once. If the Assembly persists in its original opinion, its decision becomes enforceable.

62. The Constitution cannot be revised unless two-thirds of the members of both chambers agree that it is necessary. In such a case, the chambers shall meet in a joint session to decide on revisions by an absolute majority vote.

63. Laws approved by both the Senate and the Assembly are submitted to the King for his approval and his order to implement them. If this is done within one month, the laws become definitive and enforceable. Otherwise, they are returned to the Assembly with an explanation of revisions requested for a second time. As for laws declared urgent, the time allowed for approval or return is just one week. When laws are returned, the Senate or the Assembly shall review them a second time. After the second review, they shall be approved by the King, who will order their implementation within the designated time.

64. Only members have the right to speak in the two chambers except for Ministers or their deputies.

The Senate

65. Representative assemblies in each province elect Senators: one Senator for every four Representatives in the National Assembly. The King appoints half as many Senators as there are elected ones.

66. If the number of Representatives in the National Assembly cannot be divided evenly by four, then the number is rounded up. This determines the number elected by the provincial representative assembly. Likewise, if the number elected to the Senate from the provinces cannot be divided evenly by two, then the number appointed by the King is determined after rounding up.

67. The number of Senators elected from the minority [groups] shall be one-fourth of the number of Representatives elected from the entire Kingdom to the National Assembly: that is, calculated according to the number assigned for each province. The Congress shall pass a special law setting out the procedures for electing minority Senators, and their number for each province. The same proportion of minority Senators shall be appointed by the King.

68. The term of office for a Senator is nine years. One-third of the Senators shall be renewed every three years. The designation of the first and second third to be renewed during the first six years shall be drawn by lot. The first third to be renewed shall be excluded from the second round of lots. The final third shall consist of Senators who have completed their full term. They may be renewed. A Senator whose term expires, or to whom the lot falls, shall be eligible for reelection.

69. If the lot falls to Senators appointed by the King, then the latter shall nominate their replacements. If it falls to elected Senators, then their provinces shall elect their replacements.

70. Membership in the Senate cannot be combined with another post, except in the Cabinet.

71. The following conditions apply to membership in the Senate:
    a. The Senator must be a Syrian of at least forty years of age who has not been convicted of an offense or been bankrupt, unless he has been rehabilitated. He cannot have been deprived of his civil rights.
    b. He must have previously served in high office—administrative, military, political, or judicial—or have been a Representative who has been reelected, or be known for his knowledge or virtue.
72. If a Senator dies or resigns, or if he loses membership in the Senate for other reasons, then, if he was elected, his provincial assembly shall elect his replacement. If he was appointed, then the King shall appoint his replacement. The term of the replacement shall expire with that of his predecessor.

The Representative Assembly

73. Members of the Representative Assembly shall be elected by secret ballot in two stages.
74. National elections for the Representative Assembly take place once every four years, beginning on June 1 and ending in mid-August.
75. The term of the Representative is four years. He may be reelected when his term expires.
76. The term of a Representative lasts until the next elections are completed.
77. Elections are free and the government cannot intervene in them or obstruct them.
78. Every Syrian who has attained twenty years of age and has not forfeited his civil rights shall have the right to cast a vote as a first-degree voter. Those who hold a high school degree shall have two votes. Every Syrian who has attained twenty-five years of age and has not forfeited his civil rights, or been condemned to prison for one month or more, may vote in the second round, provided he can read and write and is not a civil servant, an officer, or a private servant.

79. Every Syrian who has reached the age of thirty may be elected as a Representative, provided that he has not forfeited his civil rights and is not bankrupt.

80. Soldiers on active duty shall not participate in elections. Those on leave from military duty who have returned to their electoral districts may participate.

81. A civil servant cannot run for office or be elected as Representative of the district where he is employed, unless he has resigned at least two months before the electoral process begins.

82. Leaders of the military, their generals, and officers who are on active duty shall not vote or be elected as Representatives unless they resign from the military ranks before the beginning of the electoral process.

83. A single person may not be both a Representative and a civil servant, except in the Cabinet.

84. The same person may not be both a Representative and a Senator.

85. Each Representative is considered a representative of all Syrians.

86. One Representative shall be elected for every forty thousand Syrian inhabitants. [In districts with a lower population, only those with a minimum of twenty thousand will be taken into consideration.]

87. Every district (mudiriyah) is considered an electoral precinct. Any district with fewer than forty thousand inhabitants but not less than twenty thousand, may elect one representative. Districts with fewer than twenty thousand shall be attached to the nearest other district.

88. For minorities, each province shall be considered a single electoral precinct, on condition that it has no fewer than thirty thousand inhabitants. Below that figure, the lowest fraction to be taken into consideration is fifteen thousand.

89. Every two hundred first-degree voters shall have the right to elect a second-degree voter. Below that figure, the lowest to be taken into consideration shall be one hundred.

90. Districts shall be divided into electoral precincts on condition that the number of voters of the first degree in each precinct be no less than two hundred.

91. A special law shall be promulgated to establish procedures for the conduct of elections, as well as other related issues, regarding minority representatives.

92. If a Representative dies, resigns, or leaves office, then the second-degree voters of his precinct shall elect another. The term of the new Representative shall complete the term of his predecessor.

93. In case of a conflict between the Representative Assembly and the Cabinet, and if the latter did not get approval from the former, then the Cabinet shall fall. If the new Cabinet upholds the policy of its predecessor, then the conflict is transferred to the Senate. If the Senate supports the Assembly, the Cabinet must comply. If the Senate does not support the Assembly, then the King has the right to dissolve the Assembly, provided that elections be held and the new Assembly convene within three months. If the new Assembly upholds the decision of its predecessor, then its decision shall prevail.

94. The term of the new Assembly, reelected in accordance with Article ninety-four [note: 93 after Article 3 was dropped after July 1920], shall be four full years. Not included in the four-year term is the session held after its election in order to complete the annual meeting, during which the preceding Assembly was dissolved.

95. Every Representative shall have the right to demand formation of a committee of Representatives to investigate any incidents that have taken place in a ministry, precinct, or district. If the request is accepted by majority, a committee shall be formed and shall present the results of its investigation to the Assembly. It does not have the right to intervene in executive affairs [of the ministry].

Chapter 6
The Supreme Court

96. The Supreme Court shall convene as necessary by the King's decree and shall be composed of sixteen members, half of them from the Senate and half of them from among judges of the cassation courts. They shall be chosen by lot from their respective institutions.

97. The Supreme Court shall be divided into two parts. The arraignment division shall be composed of seven members, of whom four are Senators and three are judges from the courts of cassation and appeal. They shall be chosen by lot from the sixteen members. The second division shall be a tribunal composed of the remaining nine members.

98. An indictment must be approved by at least five members of the arraignment division. A judgment [qarar al-hukm] must be approved by at least six members of the tribunal division.

99. Verdicts of the Supreme Court are final. They are to be enforced according to existing law.

Chapter 7
Finance

100. Each year, the government is obliged to submit its budget for the coming year to the Representative Assembly, at the beginning of its annual meeting.

101. The general budget shall be a law that explains annual revenues and expenditures in a general manner, divided into articles with subsections on its implementation. The legal articles shall be scrutinized, article by article, by the Representative Assembly. The budget should be verified and approved chapter by chapter.

102. The government must not exceed the approved budget limits except for reasons of emergency requiring extra-budgetary expenditures while the Assembly is on recess. In such cases, the government is permitted to manage and spend the extra-budgetary funds in a manner approved by the King, on condition that this decision be submitted to the Assembly when it reconvenes.

103. Approval of every annual budget is effective only for that year. If the Assembly is dissolved before the budget is approved, then the government may, by the King's decree, follow the previous budget until the Assembly reconvenes.

104. Each year, the government must submit to the Representative Assembly a final accounting for the previous year. This accounting must include revenues and expenditures arranged according to the articles and chapters set out in the budget.

Chapter 8
The Auditing Department

105. The Auditing Department shall consist of a president and four members nominated by the Cabinet and approved by the Representative Assembly. The King shall then ratify their appointments, which are lifetime. They may not be replaced or removed except by approval of two-thirds of members present in the Assembly session, and of the King. If, during the exercise of their duties, they commit an infraction that requires them to be brought to trial, then they shall be tried by the Supreme Court upon the approval of two-thirds of the representatives present in the Assembly session.

106. The Auditing Department shall examine the government's annual budget and the records of the accountants. It shall also oversee implementation of the general budget and submit an annual report at the Assembly's first session. The report shall explain the results of its oversight and inspection that year. It shall also submit a report to the Cabinet every three months on the financial situation, with copies sent to the Representative Assembly.

107. The organization of this department's offices and the qualifications required of its employees, their attributes, and the regulations pertaining to them shall be subject to a special law.

Chapter 9
The Civil Service

108. Employees of the civil service shall be chosen on the basis of Syrian nationality, competence, and merit.

109. National laws shall be promulgated to define the positions of civil servants, their ranks, procedures for their hiring and promotion, and the extent of their responsibilities.

110. In the exercise of his duties, each civil servant shall be responsible for his actions in accordance with the laws and regulations in effect

111. No civil servant may be dismissed or replaced except for reasons specified by laws and regulations.

112. A civil servant must obey the orders of his superior in all matters that do not violate laws or regulations in effect.

Chapter 10
The Courts

113. The courts are independent and protected from all external encroachment.
114. The courts shall be constituted and ranked, and their functions and powers shall be defined, under a special law that covers all provinces.
115. Judges shall be elected and appointed, their ranks and qualifications determined, and procedures for promoting and punishment defined under a special law that covers all provinces.
116. Judges shall not be dismissed or censured except by judgment of a court.
117. Trials shall be public except where the law permits them to be held in secret.
118. Everyone has the right to defend himself in court through legal means.
119. Lawsuits between governmental departments and individuals must be presented in public courts.
120. No courts shall be constituted outside the legal court system; nor shall committees with judicial power be constituted except when stipulated by law.
121. No judge may combine his duties with those of another official position.

Chapter 11
The Provinces

122. The internal administration of the provinces shall be based on the principle of decentralization, except in general issues that fall within the jurisdiction of the national government, as declared in the articles of this Constitution.
123. Each province shall have a Representative Assembly that verifies its budget and passes laws and local regulations according to its needs. This Provincial Representative Assembly shall also

oversee the work of its government. But it has no right to pass laws that violate the text of the Basic Law or the national laws that the Congress has the right to make.

124. Provincial boundaries shall be set on the following basis: A province shall not be less than 25,000 square kilometers in area or hold fewer than 500,000 inhabitants. Its natural and economic links shall be taken into consideration.

125. Elections for Provincial Representative Assemblies shall be conducted in one stage. The qualifications of first electors and Representatives, defined in Articles 78 and 79 of this Law, shall be applied in electing representatives of Provincial Assemblies, except for the provincial Representative's age. His minimum age shall be 25 years.

126. The term for a Representative to a Provincial Assembly shall be two years. He remains a Representative until new elections are held, and he can be reelected.

127. One Representative for every 20,000 inhabitants of the province shall be elected to the Provincial Assembly. The lowest fraction below this standard is 10,000.

128. The number of Representatives for minorities in Provincial Assemblies shall be determined as a proportion of their population in the province: for every 15,000 there will be one Representative. The minimum population shall be 7,500.

129. The provinces shall pass electoral laws for their Representative Assemblies.

130. Elections for Provincial Representative Assemblies begin on July 1 every other year. They convene on September 1 each year for a term of two months. This may be extended if proposed by the Governor or by seven Provincial Representatives and if two-thirds of members present in the session approve.

131. Laws passed by Provincial Representative Assemblies shall be submitted by the Governor to the King for approval and implementation, on condition that the King approves them and returns them to the province within one month.

132. If laws submitted by the provinces are returned without the King's approval on the grounds that they violate the Basic Law

(Constitution) or national laws, then the Provincial Representative Assembly shall review them again. If the Provincial Assembly insists upon the original version, and if it is still not approved [by the King], then the Senate shall issue a final ruling on it, on condition that the second submission for approval be made within two weeks. Regarding the budget law, the first submission must be approved or returned [by the King] within two weeks. The second submission must be ruled on by the Senate. Its ruling shall be final, on condition that it is referred to the Senate within one week.

133. Provincial Representative Assemblies shall issue their internal laws. Each year they shall each elect their president, two vice presidents, clerks, and an administrative staff.

134. Provinces shall be ruled by a Governor appointed by the King, on condition that he is an Arab Syrian who holds the same attributes as those required for Senators.

135. The Governor shall appoint the directors of the main departments of provincial government, excepting those linked to the national government, as set out in Article [left blank] of this Law. He shall confirm civil servants nominated according to specified regulations. He also has the right to supervise departments linked to the national government.

136. The Governor shall be authorized to administer the affairs of the province, to implement its budget, and to enforce its laws.

137. Each year, the Governor shall submit to the Provincial Representative Assembly a general report regarding the actions undertaken by the provincial government during the previous year and actions planned for the following year. He shall also submit a copy of this report to the national government.

138. In the case of conflict between the Governor and the Provincial Representative Assembly, the issue shall be peremptorily ruled upon by the Senate. Its decision shall be final. If it sees fit, the Senate has the power to recommend the Governor's dismissal.

139. If, in the exercise of his duties, the Governor General commits an act that requires putting him on trial, then he must be tried by the Supreme Court.

140. Both the Governor General and provincial Representatives shall have the right to propose draft laws to the Provincial Representative Assembly.

141. Any seven Provincial Representatives may request the formation of a commission of inquiry concerning a significant act that occurred in any government department or in any part of the province. If their request is accepted by the majority, then such a commission shall be formed and shall begin its work. It shall submit the conclusions of its inquiry to the Provincial Assembly, but it shall not have the power to undertake executive measures.

142. If a member of the Provincial Representative Assembly is accused of national treason, and if one-third of the Provincial Assembly's members agree that he must be brought to trial, then he shall be tried by the Supreme Court.

143. Provinces have the right to organize courts of all types and degrees, according to a special law, as set out in Article 120.

144. Provinces are divided administratively into regions [Mutassarifiyahs] and districts [Mudiriyahs]. The National Assembly shall issue a law for each of them, defining their [local] departments and attributes and addressing the organization of villages, the mayors, and their functions.

Chapter 12
General Articles

145. The National Assembly shall issue a law on how to administer the tribes and how to resolve differences that arise among them.

146. Each province shall issue a law to organize its municipalities on an electoral basis and to define their attributes and functions.

147. Current laws remain in force until amended or replaced.

Acknowledgments

This book is the fruit of efforts by Syrians to preserve the memory of events in 1919 and 1920, and of the documents left by journalists and politicians who bore witness to what happened in Damascus at that time. Long before George Orwell warned of Newspeak, they diligently recorded the truth that the powerful sought to erase.

I must therefore thank first and foremost the Syrians who have generously shared with me their research and the documents and photographs they have collected. Because of political sensitivities at the moment, they remain unnamed here. Second, I thank those who believed in the truth of this story so much that they financed my research and the very long time it took me to translate and collate the documents I gathered. The Carnegie Corporation of New York provided a generous start-up grant. The Woodrow Wilson International Center for Scholars granted me a yearlong writing fellowship. My former dean, James Goldgeier, supported a second year of writing when I first joined the School of International Service at American University in Washington, DC. Additional funding for research came from Hani Farsi, donor of the Mohamed S. Farsi Chair of Islamic Peace that I hold, and from Thanassis Cambanis at The Century Foundation, an early supporter of my work.

Next, I thank my colleagues who inspired this project. It began with an essay I wrote in August 2013, just after the army ousted Egypt's elected president, Mohamed Morsi, and massacred his supporters in the Muslim Brotherhood who had gathered peacefully in Rabaa Square in Cairo. My friend Samer Shehata published an editorial about how the "Arab Spring" in Cairo had split between Islamic democrats and elitist liberals. It seemed to describe the split among Syrians after the French occupation.[1] I came to understand that the Syrian Congress was extraordinary for holding the two camps together, and that such a coalition was still today the key to building a democratic revolution against dictatorship. Only the Arab Spring rebels in Tunisia succeeded in building such a coalition. I presented that essay to a Princeton University conference on the mandate era, organized in September 2013 by Cyrus Schayegh and Andrew Arsan. I thank conference participants for encouraging me, especially Dyala Hamzah of the University of Montreal, whose thesis on Rashid Rida opened my eyes to his importance as a political activist.

I was able to ground my study of the Syrian Arab Kingdom in a wider historical context, thanks to my colleagues in the 2014 National Endowment for the Humanities faculty seminar on World War I in the Middle East. I am most grateful to my codirector, Mustafa Aksakal, for his continued encouragement and for educating me about the Ottoman experience in World War I. His comments on several chapters saved me from error. I also thank the NEH seminar's guest scholars, John Milton Cooper and Salim Tamari, for their early counsel on the project. Andrew Patrick and Leonard V. Smith both shared valuable insights and materials on the King-Crane Commission and the 1919 peace conference. I also thank Juan Cole for inviting me to the University of Michigan for a conference on Islamic peace, which helped to shape my thoughts on Rashid Rida's views.

It is impossible to name every scholar who helped me in researching this book. Among my chief guides has been Umar Ryad, an expert on Rashid Rida who so generously shared his expertise and his unique sources with me. Without his help, this book would not have been possible. Sami Moubayed and Amr al-Mallah shared their research and private archives on the Syrian Arab Kingdom, patiently responding to my numerous queries. In long conversations over Skype and in Paris, Mohammad Ali Atassi and Salam Kawakibi enriched my understanding of the deepest roots of democratic activism in Syria. Nael Georges reviewed and corrected my translation of the 1920 constitution. James Gelvin reviewed the manuscript and kindly shared rare documents that he had collected in Damascus thirty years ago. Charlie Kurzman, my intellectual companion in the study of liberal constitutionalism in the Middle East, took the time to read and comment on the entire manuscript. I am deeply grateful to him for suggesting revisions on the chapter concerning Christians.

In France, Henri Laurens, Matthieu Rey, and Julie d'Andurain offered much valuable advice and shared precious documents with me. In my multiple research trips to Beirut, many friends gave freely of their time and expertise, including Abdulrahim Abu-Husayn, Moham-mad Ali Atassi, Tylor Brand, Annia Ciezadlo, Selim Deringil, Nadine Méouchy, Lina Mounzer, Youssef Mouawad, Nadia Sbaiti, and Tariq Tell. In Oxford, Eugene Rogan opened many doors for me and always offered a supportive word. Izzat Darwazeh at the University College of London spent an entire, memorable day with me, discussing his grandfather, the Congress secretary, for whom he is named.

I am grateful as well for the assistance of many archivists and librarians. In Beirut, the staff at the American University of Beirut's Jafet Library helped me to find periodicals and the papers of Howard Bliss. Archivists at the foreign ministry archives at La Courneuve and Nantes opened for me the papers of General Gouraud and helped me to search, endlessly, for a copy of the 1920 constitution in the Beirut collection. Debbie Usher at the Middle East Centre in Oxford opened her archives on a closing day to accommodate my travel schedule. Patrick Kerwin and Ryan Reft at the Library of Congress Manuscript Division helped me to discover the treasures in the collection of the American peace delegation of 1919.

I could not have gathered, collated, and translated all the docu-ments used here without the help of Basem Elzaawily, who has been the best research assistant I could ever hope for. He worked with me patiently for years and now knows as much as I do. Over the past six years, he has become a true friend. Catherine Batruni and July Blalack researched Arabic periodicals for me. Claire Gellner was a delightful help at the French archives in Paris and at the Wilson Center. Samantha Parks was a godsend in navigating online sources in French.

I must also thank those who helped me bring this project to completion. I finished writing this manuscript with the encouragement and support of my new colleagues at the American University School of International Service. I drew strength especially from fellow members of the Historical International Studies research cluster. Most of all, I thank George Lucas of Inkwell and Morgan Entrekin at Grove Atlantic for believing in the project and for bringing it to publication.

This book is an homage to my longtime mentor, Abdul-Karim Rafeq. Thirty years ago, I met Dr. Rafeq at the University of Damascus, where I enrolled in his Ottoman history course. He introduced me to research at the Dar al-Watha'iq Archives. Later, when he took a chair in history at the College of William and Mary, he advised me on my dissertation and first book, *Colonial Citizens*. Dr. Rafeq has generously continued to support and inspire my research since then. His work on the Syrian University and social history of the late Ottoman period remains an inspiration. He read a draft of this book thoroughly and provided extremely useful comments. Dr. Rafeq was also my bridge to the late Khairiyah Qasimiyah, a leading scholar on the Syrian Arab Kingdom.

Finally, I could not have sustained the work of writing over the years without the love and understanding of close friends and family. Anne Bartlett drew me out of my writing den for delightful conversation over dinner every month. Her unwavering conviction that the public needed to know this story helped me to carry on. My intellectual North Star has long been Ariel Salzmann of Queen's University. She is the model of a public intellectual. Her companionship at archives and conferences, and over the phone in between, helped me to find the heart and soul of my work. Most profoundly, I thank my husband, David Waldner, who has inspired and enabled my research and writing for almost thirty years. His insight and analytical precision have enriched nearly every page written here. His patience, love, and support, along with that of our sons, Dylan and Benjamin Waldner, are the reasons that this book has come to successful completion.

For Further Reading

General readers who would like to learn more about various aspects of this story will find suggestions below. This note includes only books in English. Scholars and specialists will find additional sources in the chapter notes.

General Books on Arab, Ottoman, and Syrian History

For a long perspective on Arab history, see Albert Hourani, *A History of the Arab Peoples* (Cambridge, MA: Belknap Press, 2010); and Eugene Rogan, *The Arabs: A History* (New York: Basic Books, 2009).

On liberalism and constitutionalism in the Middle East, see Michelle U. Campos, *Ottoman Brothers: Muslims, Christians, and Jews in Early Twentieth-Century Palestine* (Stanford: Stanford University Press, 2011); Bedross Der Matossian, *Shattered Dreams of Empire: From Liberty to Violence in the Late Ottoman Empire* (Stanford: Stanford University Press, 2014); Charles Kurzman, ed., *Liberal Islam: A Sourcebook* (New York: Oxford University Press, 1998); and Elizabeth F. Thompson, *Justice Interrupted: The Struggle for Constitutional Government in the Middle East* (Cambridge, MA: Harvard University Press, 2013).

On early twentieth-century Syrian and Lebanese history, see James L. Gelvin, *Divided Loyalties: Nationalism and Mass Politics in Syria at the Close of Empire* (Berkeley: University of California Press, 1998); Philip S. Khoury, *Syria and the French Mandate* (Princeton: Princeton University

Press, 1987); Elizabeth Thompson, *Colonial Citizens: Republican Rights, Paternal Privilege and Gender in French Syria and Lebanon* (New York: Columbia University Press, 2000); and Fawaz Traboulsi, *A History of Modern Lebanon* (New York: Pluto Press, 2007).

World War I in the Middle East and the Syrian Arab Kingdom

On the social, military, diplomatic, and political history of World War I in the Middle East, see Mustafa Aksakal, *The Ottoman Road to War in 1914* (New York: Cambridge University Press, 2008); and Eugene Rogan, *The Fall of the Ottomans: The Great War in the Middle East* (New York: Basic Books, 2016). On the Middle East from the view of British diplomats, see David Fromkin, *A Peace to End All Peace: The Fall of the Ottoman Empire and the Creation of the Modern Middle East* (New York: Henry Holt, 1989).

On the particular wartime experiences of peoples living in Greater Syria and in their diaspora, see Conde de Ballobar, *Jerusalem in World War I: The Palestine Diary of a European Diplomat* (New York: I.B. Tauris, 2011); M. Talha Çiçek, *War and State Formation in Syria* (New York: Routledge, 2014); Stacy D. Fahrenthold, *Between the Ottomans and the Entente: The First World War in the Syrian and Lebanese Diaspora, 1908–1925* (New York: Oxford, 2019); Leila Tarazi Fawaz, *A Land of Aching Hearts* (Cambridge, MA: Harvard University Press, 2014); Abigail Jacobson, *From Empire to Empire: Jerusalem between Ottoman and British Rule* (Syracuse: Syracuse University Press, 2011); Hasan Kayali, *Arabs and Young Turks: Ottomanism, Arabism, and Islamism in the Ottoman Empire, 1908–1918* (Berkeley: University of California Press, 1997); Salim Tamari, *The Year of the Locust* (Berkeley: University of California Press, 2015); Melanie S. Tanielian, *The Charity of War: Famine, Humanitarian Aid and World War I* (Stanford: Stanford University Press, 2017); and Keith David Watenpaugh, *Being Modern in the Middle East: Revolution, Nationalism, Colonialism and the Arab Middle Class* (Princeton: Princeton University Press, 2006).

On the Arab Revolt and Arab rule in Damascus after World War I, see Ali A. Allawi, *Faisal I of Iraq* (New Haven: Yale University Press, 2014); Scott Anderson, *Lawrence in Arabia: War, Deceit, Imperial Folly and the Making of the Modern Middle East* (New York: Anchor

Books, 2014); George Antonius, *The Arab Awakening: The Story of the National Arab Movement*, reprint ed. (London: H. Hamilton, 1939); T. E. Lawrence, *Seven Pillars of Wisdom* (Ware: Wordsworth, 1997); Malcolm B. Russell, *The First Modern Arab State: Syria under Faysal, 1918–1920* (Minneapolis: Bibliotheca Islamica, 1985); and Jeremy Wilson, *Lawrence of Arabia: The Authorized Biography of T. E. Lawrence* (New York: Atheneum, 1990). For the viewpoint of Arab soldiers, see Laila Parsons, *The Commander: Fawzi al-Qawuqji and the Fight for Arab Independence 1914–1948* (New York: Farrar, Straus and Giroux, 2016); and Michael Provence, *The Last Ottoman Generation* (New York: Cambridge University Press, 2017).

Woodrow Wilson, the Paris Peace Conference, and the League of Nations

On Woodrow Wilson and the Paris Peace Conference, see John Milton Cooper, Jr., *Breaking the Heart of the World: Woodrow Wilson and the Fight for the League of Nations* (New York: Cambridge University Press, 2001); Thomas J. Knock, *To End All Wars: Woodrow Wilson and the Quest for a New World Order*, new ed. (Princeton: Princeton University Press, 2019); Erez Manela, *The Wilsonian Moment: Self-Determination and the International Origins of Anticolonial Nationalism* (New York: Oxford University Press, 2007); Margaret MacMillan, *Paris 1919: Six Months That Changed the World* (New York: Random House, 2001); and Trygve Throntveit, *Power without Victory: Woodrow Wilson and the American Internationalist Experiment* (Chicago: University of Chicago Press, 2017). On the King-Crane Commission, see Andrew Patrick, *America's Forgotten Middle East Initiative* (New York: I.B. Tauris, 2015).

On racism, colonialism, and empire at the time of the peace conference, see Christopher M. Andrew and A. S. Kanya-Forstner, *The Climax of French Imperial Expansion 1914–1924* (Stanford: Stanford University Press, 1981); Richard S. Fogarty, *Race and War in France: Colonial Subjects in the French Army, 1914–1918* (Baltimore: Johns Hopkins University Press, 2008); Sarah M. A. Gualtieri, *Between Arab and White: Race and Ethnicity in the Early Syrian American Diaspora* (Berkeley: University of California Press, 2009); Marilyn Lake and Henry Reynolds, *Drawing the*

Global Colour Line: White Men's Countries and the International Challenge of Racial Equality (New York: Cambridge University Press, 2008); David Levering Lewis, *W. E. B. Du Bois: A Biography 1868–1963* (New York: Henry Holt, 2009); Cameron McWhirter, *Red Summer: The Summer of 1919 and the Awakening of Black America* (New York: Henry Holt, 2011); and Tyler Stovall, *Paris Noir: African Americans in the City of Light* (Boston: Houghton Mifflin, 1996). On imperialism and the administration of the mandate system, see Susan Pedersen, *The Guardians: The League of Nations and the Crisis of Empire* (New York: Oxford University Press, 2015).

Islamism, Nationalism, and Sectarian Conflict after 1920

On the rise of the Muslim Brotherhood, see Umar F. Abd-Allah, *The Islamic Struggle in Syria* (Berkeley: Mizan Press, 1983); Brynjar Lia, *The Society of the Muslim Brothers in Egypt* (Reading, UK: Ithaca Press, 1998); and Carrie Rosefsky Wickham, *The Muslim Brotherhood: Evolution of an Islamist Movement* (Princeton: Princeton University Press, 2013).

On sectarian and nationalist conflict in Syria and Lebanon, see Adel Beshara, ed., *The Origins of Syrian Nationhood* (New York: Routledge, 2011); Carol Hakim, *The Origins of the Lebanese National Idea 1840–1920* (Berkeley: University of California Press, 2013); Michael Provence, *The Great Syrian Revolt and the Rise of Arab Nationalism* (Austin: University of Texas Press, 2005); Laura Robson, *States of Separation: Transfer, Partition, and the Making of the Modern Middle East* (Berkeley: University of California Press, 2017); Kamal Salibi, *A House of Many Mansions: The History of Lebanon Reconsidered* (Berkeley: University of California Press, 1990); Patrick Seale, *The Struggle for Arab Independence: Riad el-Solh and the Makers of the Modern Middle East* (New York: Cambridge University Press, 2010); Max Weiss, *In the Shadow of Sectarianism: Law, Sh`ism, and the Making of Modern Lebanon* (Cambridge, MA: Harvard University Press, 2010); and Benjamin Thomas White, *The Emergence of Minorities in the Middle East: The Politics of Community in French Mandate Syria* (Edinburgh: Edinburgh University Press, 2011).

Notes

Preface

1. Excerpted from the Declaration of Independence as published in Muhammad Rashid Rida, "Bab al-Tarikh: Istiqlal Suriya wa al-Iraq [A Chapter in History: Independence of Syria and Iraq]," *al-Manar* 21:8 (June 1920): 442.

2. "President Wilson's Fourteen Points," Avalon Project, Yale Law School. Accessed June 13, 2019, at https://avalon.law.yale.edu/20th_century/wilson14.asp.

3. Noura Erakat, *Justice for Some: Law and the Question of Palestine* (Stanford: Stanford University Press, 2019), 6. Mark Mazower argues that the United Nations sustained the League's imperial bias, in his *No Enchanted Palace: The End of Empire and the Ideological Origins of the United Nations* (Princeton: Princeton University Press, 2009) and *Governing the World: The History of an Idea, 1815 to the Present* (New York: Penguin: 2012). See also Antony Anghie, *Imperialism, Sovereignty and the Making of International Law* (Cambridge: Cambridge University Press, 2004).

4. Stacy D. Fahrenthold, *Between the Ottomans and the Entente: The First World War in the Syrian and Lebanese Diaspora, 1908–1925* (New York: Oxford University Press, 2019), 85–111; Rida, "Bab al-Tarikh," 441–44; "Ila al-amam wa la tay`asu," and "Mamlaka Suriyya Jadida" ["Go Forward and Don't Lose Hope" and "The New Syrian Kingdom"], *al-Shams* (Buenos Aires), March 20, 1920, 1 and 5; "Syria Proclaims Freedom

and King," *New York Times*, March 12, 1920; "Feisal's Assumption of Kingship," *The Times*, March 17, 1920; "L'émir Faiçal proclamé roi," *Le Temps*, March 14, 1920.

5. Robert Gerwarth, *The Vanquished: Why the First World War Failed to End* (New York: Farrar, Straus and Giroux, 2016). The roots of inhumane global policy lay in the violence governments visited upon their own people during the war years. See Adam Hochschild, *To End All Wars* (Boston: Houghton Mifflin Harcourt, 2011); Uğur Ümit Üngör, *The Making of Modern Turkey: Nation and State in Eastern Anatolia, 1913–1950* (New York: Oxford University Press, 2011); and Ronald Grigor Suny and Fatma Müge Goçek, eds., *A Question of Genocide: Armenians and Turks at the End of the Ottoman Empire* (New York: Oxford University Press, 2011).

6. David Fromkin, *A Peace to End All Peace: The Fall of the Ottoman Empire and the Creation of the Modern Middle East* (New York: Henry Holt, 1989/2009).

7. T. E. Lawrence, *Seven Pillars of Wisdom: A Triumph* (New York: Doubleday, 1935); George Antonius, *The Arab Awakening* (London: H. Hamilton, 1939); Amin Sa`id, *Asrar al-Thawra al-`Arabiya al-Kubra* [Secrets of the Great Arab Revolt] (Beirut: Dar al-Kitab al-Arabi, 1965); Abu Khaldun Sati` al-Husri, *Yawm Maysalun* (Beirut Dar al-Ittihad, 1965), translated by Sidney Glazer as *The Day of Maysalun* (Washington, DC: Middle East Institute, 1966); Scott Anderson, *Lawrence in Arabia: War, Deceit, Imperial Folly and the Making of the Modern Middle East* (New York: Anchor, 2014).

8. Zeine N. Zeine, *The Struggle for Arab Independence: Western Diplomacy and the Rise and Fall of Faisal's Kingdom in Syria* (Beirut: Khayat's, 1960); Philip S. Khoury, *Urban Notables and Arab Nationalism: The Politics of Damascus 1860–1920* (New York: Cambridge University Press, 1983); Malcolm B. Russell, *The First Modern Arab State: Syria under Faisal 1918–1920* (Minneapolis: Bibliotheca Islamica, 1985); Gérard D. Khoury, *La France et l'Orient arabe: Naissance du Liban moderne, 1914–1920* (Paris: Albin Michel, 2009); Margaret MacMillan, *Paris 1919: Six Months That Changed the World* (New York: Random House, 2001).

9. James L. Gelvin, *Divided Loyalties: Nationalism and Mass Politics in Syria at the Close of Empire* (Berkeley: University of California Press, 1998); Eliezer Tauber, *The Formation of Modern Syria and Iraq* (London: Frank Cass, 1995); Keith David Watenpaugh, *Being Modern in the Middle East: Revolution, Nationalism, Colonialism and the Arab Middle Class* (Princeton:

Princeton University Press, 2006); Ali A. Allawi, *Faisal I of Iraq* (New Haven: Yale University Press, 2014).

10. Ali Sultan, *Tarikh Suriya 1918–1920: Hukm Faysal bin al-Husayn* (Damascus: Tlas, 1987); and Suhayla Rimawi, *al-Hukm al-Hizbi fi Suriya: Ayyam al-Ahd al-Faysali, 1918–1920* [Party Rule in Syria: The Days of the Faisal Era, 1918–20] (Amman: Dar Majdalawi, 1997).

11. Khairiyah Qasimiyah, *al-Hukuma al-Arabiya fi Dimashq bayna 1918–1920* [The Arab Government in Damascus between 1918 and 1920], 2nd ed. (Beirut: al-Mu'assassa al-'Arabiya lil-Dirasat wa al-Nashr, 1982); Muhammad Mufaku Arna'ut, *Dirasat hawla al-Hukuma/al-Dawla al-'Arabiya fi Dimashq, 1918–1920* [Studies on the Arab Government/State in Damascus, 1918–1920] (Amman: Dar al-Shuruq, 2000); Mari Almaz Shahrastan, *al-Mu'tamar al-Suri al-'Amm 1919–1920* [The General Syrian Congress 1919–1920] (Beirut: Dar Amwaj, 2000); Yusuf Mazin al-Sabbagh, *al-Mu'tamar al-Suri: Barlaman al-Istiqlal lil-Bilad al-Sham* [The Syrian Congress: The Independent Parliament of Greater Syria] (Damascus: Dar al-Sharq, 2011).

12. "King Feisal," *The Times*, September 9, 1933, 12.

13. C. L. R. James, *The Black Jacobins: Toussaint L'Ouverture and the San Domingo Revolution*, 2nd ed. (New York: Vintage Books, 1963), 294, 362, 376.

14. Historians who hold to the view that the overworked and old-fashioned leaders who met in Paris could have done no better include MacMillan, *Paris 1919*; Erez Manela, *The Wilsonian Moment* (New York: Oxford University Press, 2007); Fromkin, *A Peace to End All Peace*; Susan Pedersen, *The Guardians: The League of Nations and the Crisis of Empire* (New York: Oxford University Press, 2015); and the editors and authors of the introduction of Markus M. Payk and Roberta Pergher, *Beyond Versailles: Sovereignty, Legitimacy, and the Formation of New Polities after the Great War* (Bloomington: Indiana University Press, 2019). A more critical stance toward Paris dealmaking was taken first by European historians, including Eric D. Weitz, "From the Vienna to the Paris System: International Politics and the Entangled Histories of Human Rights, Forced Deportations, and Civilizing Missions," *American Historical Review* (December 2008): 1313–43.

15. Patrick Roger, "Colonisation: les propos inédits de Macron font polémique,"*Le Monde*, February 16, 2017; "Macron reconnaît à nouveau les 'crimes' de la colonisation," *Le Figaro*, November 28,

2017, accessed April 28, 2019, at https://www.lemonde.fr/election
-presidentielle-2017/article/2017/02/16/pour-macron-la-colonisation-fut
-un-crime-contre-l-humanite_5080621_4854003.html and http://www
.lefigaro.fr/politique/le-scan/2017/11/28/25001-20171128ARTFIG00229
-macron-reconnait-a-nouveau-les-crimes-de-la-colonisation.php.

16. Mohammad Ali Atassi, "My Syria, Awake Again after 40 Years," *New York Times,* June 27, 2011, p. A21.

Chapter 1: Damascus—Enter the Prince

1. Rustum Haidar, *Mudhakkirat Rustum Haidar,* ed. and intro. Najdat Fathi Safwat (Beirut: Dar al-`Arabiya lil-Mawsu`at, 1988), 184.

2. Allawi, *Faisal I,* 52–57.

3. Eugene Rogan, *The Fall of the Ottomans* (New York: Basic Books, 2015), 275–85.

4. Suleiman Mousa, *T. E. Lawrence: An Arab View,* trans. Albert Butros (New York: Oxford University Press, 1966), 185–87; Allawi, *Faisal I,* 132–37; Eugene Rogan, *The Arabs* (New York: Basic Books, 2009), 150–53; Rogan, *Fall of the Ottomans,* 296–309, 333–42, 373–77.

5. St. Antony College, Oxford, Middle East Archive, "Open Letter to the Commander in Chief of the Fourth Army," Private Papers of Feisal, Emir of Hedjaz, box 195, translation of document from Akaba archive no. Akaba I/Q/17.

6. There is some disagreement among historians on the chronology. Mousa argues that T. E. Lawrence entered Deraa with several Arab officers at sunset on September 27, 1918, and raised the Arab flag on the morning of September 28 over the "government house." Nuri arrived on the evening of September 28. Faisal arrived in Deraa on September 29 by car and began planning the attack on Damascus. Lawrence left Deraa by car at dawn on September 30. See Mousa, *T. E. Lawrence,* 200–1. Jeremy Wilson claims Lawrence arrived in Deraa the morning of September 28, in his *Lawrence of Arabia: The Authorized Biography of T. E. Lawrence* (New York: Atheneum, 1990), 558–59.

7. Otto Liman von Sanders, *Five Years in Turkey,* trans. Carl Reichmann (Annapolis: United States Naval Institute, 1927), 301–4.

8. David Garnett, ed., *The Letters of T. E. Lawrence* (New York: Double-day, 1939), 256. Quote is from Lawrence's last contribution to the *Arab*

Bulletin, no. 106, "The Destruction of the Fourth Army." Major Sir Hubert Young, *The Independent Arab* (London: John Murray, 1933), 254.

9. T. E. Lawrence, *Seven Pillars of Wisdom: A Triumph. The Complete 1922 Text* (Blacksburg, VA: Wilder Publications, 2011), 535. [Hereafter Lawrence, *Seven Pillars of Wisdom Complete*.]

10. George Antonius, *The Arab Awakening*, reprint ed. (New York: Routledge, 2010), 235.

11. Sobhi Omari, *Awraq al-Thawra al-'Arabiya*, vol. 1: *al-Ma'ariq al-Ula al-Tariq ila Dimashq* [Papers of the Great Arab Revolt, 1: The First Battle—The Road to Damascus] (London: Riad El-Rayyes, 1991), 289.

12. Lawrence, *Seven Pillars of Wisdom Complete*, 535.

13. Anderson, *Lawrence in Arabia*, 474. Quote from William Yale.

14. Qasimiyah, *al-Hukuma al-'Arabiya*, 47–50; Sami Moubayed, "Two September Weeks That Saved Damascus in 1918," *Arab Studies Quarterly* 37:4 (Fall 2015): 367–85. Reference is on 371.

15. Mousa, *T. E. Lawrence*, 210 (interview with Sa'id al-Jaza'iri); Qasimiyah, *al-Hukuma al-'Arabiya*, 48; Fa'iz El-Ghussein, *Mudhakkirati An al-Thawrah al-Arabiya*, vol. 2 (Damascus, 1939), 590–91; Russell, *First Arab State*, 9–10.

16. Ahmad Qadri, *Mudhakkirat 'an al-Thawra al-'Arabiya al-Kubra* (Damascus: Ibn Zaydun, 1956), 73–74.

17. Allawi, *Faisal I*, 138–42; Moubayed, "Two September Weeks," 382; Russell, *First Arab State*, 8–13; Eliezer Tauber, *The Arab Movements in World War I* (New York: Routledge, 1993), 239–40.

18. Library of Congress, Manuscript Division, Washington, DC [hereafter Library of Congress], William Yale, "The Political Situation in Syria," report no. 112, November 9, 1918, U.S. American Commission to Negotiate Peace, Box 1.

19. Anderson, *Lawrence in Arabia*, 24–26, 46–49, 88–9, 354–57, 386–87, 417–21, 451–53; Andrew Patrick, *America's Forgotten Middle East Initiative: The King-Crane Commission of 1919* (New York: I.B. Tauris, 2015), 56.

20. Library of Congress, Yale Reports nos. 12, 13, 16, 18, 22, 23, and 61, dated January 28, February 4, February 25, March 11, April 8, April 15, and September 12, 1918, Records of the U.S. American Commission to Negotiate Peace, Box 1; Max Reibman, "The Case of William Yale: Cairo's Syrians and the Arab Origins of American Influence in the Post-Ottoman Middle East, 1917–19," *International Journal of Middle East Studies* 46 (2014): 683.

21. Lawrence, *Seven Pillars of Wisdom Complete*, 545; Omari, *Papers of the Great Arab Revolt* 1: 290–91; Qasimiyah, *al-Hukuma al-ʿArabiya*, 50.

22. Special Collections, Bodleian Libraries at the Weston Library, Oxford, UK [hereafter: Bodleian Library], Lawrence to Yale, October 22, 1929, T. E. Lawrence Correspondence, MS.Eng.c.6737, fol. 305–7.

23. Russell, *First Arab State*, 13.

24. Russell, *First Arab State*, 12. Russell rejects Elie Kedourie's argument that Arabs did not liberate Damascus first.

25. El-Ghussein, *Mudhakkirati*, 599.

26. Haidar, *Mudhakkirat*, 186; Omari, *Papers* 1: 296; Allawi, *Faisal I*, 144.

27. Bodleian Library, T. E. Lawrence Correspondence, MS.Photogr.C.123/2, Fol. 203.

28. Young, *Independent Arab*, 255.

29. Russell, *First Arab State*, 14.

30. Bodleian Library, Photo 123/2 fol. 200 of crowd at Town Hall. October 1, 1918, T. E. Lawrence Correspondence, MS Eng.c.6750, Nuri al-Said 1888–1959. Photographs 1914–18.

31. Lawrence, *Seven Pillars of Wisdom Complete*, 547.

32. Young, *Independent Arab*, 257; Qasimiya, *al-Hukuma al-Arabiya*, 52.

33. El-Ghussein, *Mudhakkirati*, 2: 608–9. Excerpt accessed September 2, 2018, at http://www.telstudies.org/discussion/war_service/fayez_al_ghussein.shtml.

34. Allawi, *Faisal I*, 146; Russell, *First Arab State*, 15–17; Anderson, *Lawrence in Arabia*, 480–81.

35. "The Sykes-Picot Agreement: 1916," accessed August 31, 2018, at http://avalon.law.yale.edu/20th_century/sykes.asp.

36. Qadri, *Mudhakkirat*, 46–48.

37. Haidar, *Mudhakkirat*, 187–88.

38. Qadri, *Mudhakkirat*, 75; Stefan Weber, *Damascus: Ottoman Modernity and Urban Transformation (1808–1918)*, vol. II (Damascus: Danish Institute, 2009), 52, 383–85; Allawi, *Faisal I*, 147; Yusuf al-Hakim, *Suriya wa al-ʿAhd al-Faysali* [Syria and the Faisal Era], 2nd printing (Beirut: Dar al-Nahar lil-Nashr, 1980), 23.

39. Bodleian Library, Lawrence to Major Scott, October 14, 1918, MS.Eng.d.3328: Letters from T. E. Lawrence, fol. 148.

40. Wilson, *Lawrence of Arabia*, 568. See also Anderson, *Lawrence in Arabia*, 483–84.

41. Bodleian Library, Lawrence, "Reconstruction of Arabia," 6–7, MS.Eng.d.3348, fol. 56–63.

42. Husri, *Day of Maysalun*, 101–2; Qasimiyah, *Al-Hukuma al-'Arabiya*, 55–56.

43. Qasimiyah, *al-Hukuma al-'Arabiya*, 55.

44. Zeine N. Zeine, *The Emergence of Arab Nationalism*, 3rd ed. (New York: Caravan, 1973), 143. Shaykh Ahmad Tabbara gave slightly lower figures, and excluded Deir El-Zor province in his speech at the 1913 Arab Congress: See al-Lajnah al-Ulya li-Hizb al-Lamarkaziyah, *al-Mu'tamar al-'Arabi al-Awwal* [Higher Council of the Decentralization Party, *The First Arab Congress*] (Cairo: Matba' al-Bosfur, 1913), 86.

45. Coulondre to Pichon, October 5, 1918, two letters reproduced in Antoine Hokayem, ed., *Documents diplomatiques français relatifs à l'histoire du Liban et de la Syrie à l'époque du mandat: 1914–1945*, vol. 1 (Paris: l'Harmattan, 2003), I: 371–73. Quote from 373. [Hokayem vol. I covers 1914–1919; vol. II covers 1920.] See also Tauber, *Arab Movements in WWI*, 240; Meir Zamir, "Faisal and the Lebanese Question, 1918–1920," *Middle Eastern Studies* 27:3 (1991): 404–5.

46. Tauber, *Formation of Modern Syria*, 12–13.

47. Tauber, *Formation of Modern Syria*, 12–16; Tauber, *Arab Movements in WWI*, 2–3, 57–79.

48. Tauber, *Arab Movements in WWI*, 242. There is disagreement. Mousa, *T. E. Lawrence*, 205, says Ayyubi arrived on October 6. Qasimiyah, on 57, also dates his arrival earlier.

49. Tauber, *Arab Movements in WWI*, 242.

50. Colonel de Piépape to War Minister, October 10, 1918; Coulondre to Pichon, October 18 and 20, 1918, in Hokayem, *Documents diplomatiques*, I: 386–87, 391–92.

51. Telegram to Allenby reprinted in Alan de L. Rush, ed., *Records of the Hashemite Dynasties*, vol. 10 (London: Archive Editions, 1995), 131–32. Also in the same volume, Clayton memos to Allenby dated October 12, 1918, 102–7. Russell, *First Arab State*, 16–17.

52. "Sir Edmund Allenby's Assurance to the Amir Faisal," reported to London, October 19, 1918, and reprinted as Annex H in "Report of a Committee to Consider the Correspondence between Sir Henry McMahon and the Sharif of Mecca in 1915 and 1916" (London: His Majesty's Stationery Office, 1939).

53. Russell, *First Arab State*, 18; Allawi, *Faisal I*, 155–58, which draws on Mousa, *T. E. Lawrence*, 220–21; Qasimiyah, *al-Hukuma al-ʿArabiya*, 51–54.
54. Mousa, *T. E. Lawrence*, 206; Tauber, *Formation of Modern Syria*, 242–43.
55. Christopher Bromhead Birdwood (Lord Birdwood), *Nuri al-Said: A Study in Arab Leadership* (London: Cassell, 1959), 90–93; Young, *Independent Arab*, 263.

Chapter 2: Aleppo—A Government and Justice for All

1. "An Introduction," *Lissan al-Arab*, October 2, 1918. Translation from American University of Beirut, Special Collections Library [hereafter AUB Library], Howard Bliss Collection, Box 19 File 4, AA:2.3.2.19.4.
2. Yücel Yanıkdağ, "Ottoman Empire / Middle East," *1914–1918-Online: International Encyclopedia of the First World War*, ed. Ute Daniel, Peter Gatrell, Oliver Janz, Heather Jones, Jennifer Keene, Alan Kramer, and Bill Nasson (Freie Universität Berlin, 2014–12–19) [hereafter *1914–1918 Online*]. Accessed June 5, 2019 at https://encyclopedia.1914–1918 online.net/article/ottoman_empiremiddle_east.
3. L. Schatkowski-Schilcher, "The Famine of 1915–1918 in Greater Syria," in John P. Spagnolo, ed., *The Problems of the Modern Middle East in Historical Perspective* (Reading, UK: Ithaca Press, 1992), 229–30, 238–50; Leila Tarazi Fawaz, *A Land of Aching Hearts: The Middle East in the Great War* (Cambridge: Harvard University Press, 2014); Yiğit Akın, *When the War Came Home: The Ottomans' Great War and the Devastation of an Empire* (Stanford: Stanford University Press, 2018).
4. Manuscript letter to bishops of Homs and Hama, October 11, 1918. I thank Benan Grams of Georgetown University for sharing it with me. The patriarch's name was Gregorius IV Haddad.
5. Russell, *First Arab State*, 20.
6. Diary of Ihsan Turjman, April 3 to May 9, 1915, quoted and translated by Salim Tamari, *Year of the Locust: A Soldier's Diary and the Erasure of Palestine's Ottoman Past* (Berkeley: University of California Press, 2011), 96–113; Melanie S. Tanielian, *The Charity of War: Famine, Humanitarian Aid and World War I in the Middle East* (Stanford: Stanford University Press, 2018), 51–77, 103–6, 235–44; Fawaz, *A Land of Aching Hearts*, 81–120; Ohannès Pacha Kouyoumdjian, *Le Liban à la veille et au début de la guerre: Mémoires d'un gouverneur, 1913–1915* (Paris: Centre d'Histoire Arménienne Contemporaine, 2003).

7. Bedross Der Matossian, *Shattered Dreams of Revolution* (Stanford: Stanford University Press, 2014), 23–31, 113, 119–21; Hasan Kayali, *Arabs and Young Turks* (Berkeley: University of California Press, 1997), 60–72; Watenpaugh, *Being Modern in the Middle East*, 61–75.

8. Gerwarth, *The Vanquished*, 7–8.

9. Young, *Independent Arab*, 262; Russell, *First Arab State*, 20.

10. Khoury, *Urban Notables and Arab Nationalism*, 81–82.

11. Russell, *First Arab State*, 57; Qasimiyah, *al-Hukuma al'Arabiya*, 61–62.

12. Tauber, *Formation of Modern Syria*, 14; Russell, *First Arab State*, 20. Faisal's palace budget was 400,000 Egyptian pounds (LE); the British subsidy in December 1918 was 80,000 LE. The subsidy rose to 150,000 LE in April 1919.

13. Even in well-endowed Beirut, hospital beds at the Syrian Protestant College remained filled to capacity through early December: AUB Library, Letters to Reverend D. Stuart Dodge, November 5 and 27, and December 4, 1918. AA:2.3.2.10.2 File Letters from Howard Bliss to David Stuart Lodge and others, Howard Bliss Collection.

14. Russell, *First Arab State*, 49, 56.

15. Russell, *First Arab State*, 51; Abdul-Karim Rafeq, *Tarikh al-jami'a al-Suriya: al-badaya wa al-namu, 1901–1946* [The History of the Syrian University: The Beginning and Growth, 1901–1946] (Damascus: Maktabat Nubil, 2004), 39–45; Sami Moubayed, *Steel and Silk: Men and Women Who Shaped Syria 1900–2000* (Seattle: Cune Press, 2006), 388.

16. Abdul-Karim Rafeq, "Arabism, Society, and Economy in Syria 1918–1920," in Youssef M. Choueiri, ed., *State and Society in Syria and Lebanon* (Exeter, UK: University of Exeter Press, 1993), 20–25; Russell, *First Arab State*, 48–49.

17. Rafeq, "Arabism, Society, and Economy in Syria," 11–12.

18. Laila Parsons, *The Commander: Fawzi al-Qawuqji and the Fight for Arab Independence, 1914–1948* (New York: Hill and Wang, 2016), 44.

19. Russell, *First Arab State*, 53–54.

20. Margaret McGilvary, *The Dawn of a New Era in Syria* (New York: Fleming H. Revell, 1920), 289, 291.

21. Antony Polonsky, *Politics in Independent Poland 1921–1939* (Oxford: Clarendon Press, 1972), 1–10, 23; Malbone W. Graham, *New Governments of Eastern Europe* (New York: Henry Holt, 1927), 409–39; Josef Gruber, ed., *Czechoslovakia: A Survey of Economic and Social Conditions* (New York: Macmillan, 1924; reprint ed., New York: Arno, 1971), v, 193.

22. Nur Bilge Criss, *Istanbul under Allied Occupation 1918–1923* (Leiden: Brill, 1999), 20–29, 34–35, 41–45.

23. Reproduced in Husri, *Day of Maysalun*, 102.

24. Greek Patriarch to Bishops of Homs and Hama, October 11, 1918, from Benan Grams.

25. Russell, *First Arab State*, 83; `Abd al-Karim Rafeq, "al-Awraq al-Mashiya fi Dimashq min khilal watha'iq al-mahakim al-shara`iya al-`uthmaniya," *Chronos: Revue d'Histoire de l'Université de Balamand* 37 (2018): 76.

26. Allawi, *Faisal I*, 155–56.

27. "Arab Independence," *Lissan al-Hal*, October 2, 1918.

28. Farid Istifan, *Habib Istifan, Ra'id min Lubnan* (Beirut: Dar Lahd Hatir, 1983), 57–59; personal interview in Beirut with Ghassan al-Khazen, descendant of one of the condemned, January 13, 2018. I thank Youssef Mouawad for alerting me to the case of Habib Istifan.

29. Patrick Seale, *The Struggle for Arab Independence: Riad el-Solh and the Makers of the Modern Middle East* (New York: Cambridge University Press, 2010), 120; Qadri, *Mudhakkirat*, 82. Tauber claimed Faisal was a servant of Fatat, in *Formation of Modern Syria*, 39–40.

30. Seale, *Struggle for Arab Independence*, 58–59; Charles Kurzman, *Democracy Denied 1905–1915* (Cambridge, MA: Harvard University Press, 2008), 41.

31. Seale, *Struggle for Arab Independence*, 58–61, 67–70, 84–90, 95–96, 116.

32. Allawi, *Faisal I*, 13–17, 24–30, 36–39; Higher Council, *First Arab Congress*, 113–20, 132–34; Zeine, *Emergence of Arab Nationalism*, 144–45.

33. Qadri, *Mudhakkirat*, 85; Russell, *First Arab State*, 28.

34. Watenpaugh, *Being Modern in the Middle East*, 43, 66–69.

35. `Abd al-Rahman al-Kawakibi, *Taba'i` al-istibdad wa masari` al-isti`bad* (Beirut: Dar al-Kitab al-Lubnani, 2011). The book has not been translated, but Itzchak Weismann gives its title in English as *The Nature of Tyranny and the Struggle against Enslavement*. See Itzchak Weismann, *Abd al-Rahman al-Kawakibi: Islamic Reform and Arab Revival* (London: Oneworld, 2015), 1–2, 22–25, 38–40, 61–63, 101–18; Salam Kawakibi, "Postface," in `Abd al-Rahman al-Kawakibi, *Du despotism et autres textes*, trans. Hala Kodmani (Arles: Actes Sud, 2016), 209–31.

36. Watenpaugh, *Being Modern in the Middle East*, 125.

37. Fa'iz El-Ghussein, *Martyred Armenia* (New York: George H. Doran, 1918); Anderson, *Lawrence in Arabia*, 122.

38. Levon Parian and Ishkhan Jinbashian, eds., *Crows in the Desert: Memoirs of Levon Yotnakhparian* (Tujunga, CA: Parian Photographic Design,

2012), 34, 47, 53, 61–100, quote on 34; El-Ghussein, *Mudhakkirati*, diary entry for July 10, 1918, accessed August 30, 2018, at http://www .telstudies.org/discussion/war_service/fayez_al_ghussein.shtml.

39. Vahe Tachjian, *Daily Life in the Abyss: Genocide Diaries, 1915–1918* (New York: Bergahn Books, 2017); Seda Altug, "1915 Armenian Genocide in Syrian-Arabic Sources," unpublished paper presented at Clark University, Worcester, MA, April 10–11, 2010; British Library, India Office Library and Records, London [hereafter British Library India Office], Mark Sykes to G.H.Q., November 22, 1918, War Office Records, WO95/4372, 279.

40. Qadri, *Mudhakkirat*, 85; Birdwood, *Nuri As-Said*, 94, 101.

41. Husri, *Yawm Maysalun*, 211–12. Translated by the author. An alternative translation of the speech is found in Husri, *Day of Maysalun*, 102–5.

42. British translation reprinted in the *New York Times*, November 8, 1918, accessed on August 30, 2018, at https://wwi.lib.byu.edu/index.php/ Anglo-French_Joint_Statement_of_Aims_in_Syria_and_Mesopotamia.

43. Husri, *Yawm Maysalun*, 214; also Qadri, *Mudhakkirat*, 86–87.

44. Qasimiyah, *al-Hukuma al-`Arabiya*, 63–65.

45. Joshua Teitelbaum, *The Rise and Fall of the Hashemite Kingdom of Arabia* (New York: New York University Press, 2001), 37–43, 104–7, 150, 194–95.

46. Teitelbaum, *Rise and Fall of the Hashemite Kingdom*, 126–29; Tauber, *Arab Movements in WWI*, 186–89; Allawi, *Faisal I*, 162–63.

47. Watenpaugh, *Being Modern in the Middle East*, 95–125.

48. Mehmet Beşikçi, *The Ottoman Mobilization of Manpower in the First World War* (Leiden: Brill, 2012), 98–99, 122–24; Tamari, *Year of the Locust*, 130–35, 155.

49. Qadri, *Mudhakkirat*, 88.

50. Husri, *Day of Maysalun*, 105.

51. Woodrow Wilson, *The State: Elements of Historical and Practical Politics* (Boston: D.C. Heath, 1898).

52. Tauber, *Arab Movements in WWI*, 254.

53. Library of Congress, Yale, "The Political Situation in Syria."

54. Trygve Throntveit, *Power without Victory: Woodrow Wilson and the American Internationalist Experiment* (Chicago: University of Chicago Press, 2017), 249–52.

55. Faisal to Hussein, Damascus, October 29, 1918, and Hussein to Wingate, November 5, 1918, in Sulaiman Musa, ed., *Al-Murasalat al-Tarikhiya 1919: al-Thawra al-`Arabiy al-Kubra*, vol 2 (Amman, 1975), 227–28, 229.

Translation of Faisal's note in Rush, *Records of the Hashemite Dynasties*, 10: 129–30.

56. Faisal to King Hussein, November 12, 1918, and Hussein to Faisal, November 14, 1918, in Musa, *al-Murasalat al-Tarikhiya*, 2: 242. T. E. Lawrence had personally urged Sharif Hussein to delegate Faisal as his representative because the prince's fame might carry influence among Europeans. Lawrence had not, however, consulted Faisal. Lawrence to King Hussein, November 10, 1918, in Musa, *al-Murasalat al-Tarikhiya*, 2: 232; Telegram to Wingate, Cairo, November 8, 1918, in Rush, *Records of the Hashemite Dynasties*, 10: 141.

57. Allawi, *Faisal I*, 171. Allawi dates his arrival to November 19, but local newspapers and the Zeine papers at AUB date his arrival in Beirut as Saturday, November 16. See "His Highness Faisal," *Lissan al-Hal*, November 18, 1918, 1–2.

58. Russell, *First Arab State*, 28; Allawi, *Faisal I*, 171–72.

59. The National Archives of the United Kingdom, London [hereafter TNA-London], Faisal to Commander of Egyptian Expeditionary Force, November 19, 1918, 11, FO 141/438 Papers of the Residency in Cairo.

60. Library of Congress, Yale, "The Political Situation in Syria."

61. "Wilson's Speech," *Lissan al-Hal*, October 15, 1918, 1; "To the Syrian and Iraqi People," *Lissan al-Hal*, November 11, 1918, 2; "Tomorrow," *Lissan al-Hal*, November 14, 1918, 1.

62. Library of Congress, Yale, "The Political Situation in Syria."

63. Manela, *The Wilsonian Moment*.

Chapter 3: Cairo—A Sheikh Prays to an American President

1. Dyala Hamzah, "From '*Ilm* to *Sahafa* or Politics of Public Interest (*Maslaha*): Muhammad Rashid Rida and His Journal *al-Manar* (1898–1935)," in Dyala Hamzah, ed., *The Making of the Arab Intellectual* (New York: Routledge, 2013), 90–127; Dyala Hamzah, "Intérêt général (*maslaha âmma*) ou le triomphe de l'opinion: Fondation délibératoire et esquisses délibératives dans les écrits du publiciste syro-égyptien Muhammad Rashîd Rîdâ (1865–1935)," Thèse/Doktorarbeit, EHESS, Paris, and Freie Universität, Berlin (2008), 140–43, 181–93, 304–9. I thank Dr. Hamzah for sharing a copy of the thesis with me. On Rida's influence in South Asia, see Roy Bar Sadeh, "Islamic Modernism between Colonialism and Orientalism: *Al-Manar*'s Intellectual Circles and

Aligarh's Mohammedan Anglo-Oriental College, 1898–1914," in Susannah Heschel and Umar Ryad, eds., *The Muslim Reception of European Orientalism* (New York: Routledge, 2018), 103–28; Muhammad Qasim Zaman, *Modern Islamic Thought in a Radical Age* (New York: Cambridge University Press, 2012).

2. Tauber, *Arab Movements in WWI*, 165.

3. Ahmad al-Sharabasi, *Rashid Rida, the Owner of al-Manar* (Cairo: Higher Council of Islamic Affairs, 1970), 135, 181, 207–9. Personal interview with Rashid Rida's grandson, Fouad Reda, Minneapolis, July 6, 2017.

4. General Edouard Brémond, *Le Hedjaz dans la Guerre Mondiale* (Paris: Payot, 1931), 53; French Ministry of Foreign Affairs archive at La Courneuve [hereafter: MAE-Courneuve], De France to Pichon, July 3, 1918, Jean Gout Papers, 196PAAP/7. On Rida's politics, see Eyal Zisser, "Rashid Rida: On the Way to Syrian Nationalism in the Shade of Islam and Arabism," in Adel Beshara, ed., *The Origins of Syrian Nationhood: Histories, Pioneers and Identity* (New York: Routledge, 2007), 123–40; Mahmoud Haddad, "Arab Religious Nationalism in the Colonial Era: Rereading Rashid Rida's Ideas on the Caliphate," *Journal of the American Oriental Society* 117:2 (1997): 253–77.

5. Muhammad Rashid Rida, "Change in the Course of the War and the Expected Peace," *al-Manar* 20:1 (October 1918): 444–46.

6. TNA-London, "Comité Central du Parti de l'Union Syrienne au Caire," and "Programme Constitutionel du Parti de l'Union Syrienne," FO 371/4178, 454–57.

7. Rida mentions a bitter argument in February 1918 in his diary, quoted in Umar Ryad, "Like a Mill Donkey: Western Politics in the Aftermath of WWI," paper given at the conference "Human Catastrophe Then and Now," American University of Beirut, June 1, 2016 [hereafter Ryad, "Like a Mill Donkey"].

8. Reibman, "Case of William Yale," 693–95.

9. Rida's diary, December 10, 12, 22, and 25, 1918, as quoted in Ryad, "Like a Mill Donkey."

10. Na`um Bey Shuqair (1863–1922), one of the constitution's authors, had attended the Syrian Protestant College twenty years before Shahbandar. He was a historian and a liaison with the British administration.

11. A version comprising forty-seven articles and dividing Greater Syria into nine states was later presented to an American commission:

"Basic Law of the United States of Syria," in King–Crane Commission Digital Collection, Oberlin College Archive [hereafter KCDC-Oberlin]. Accessed March 13, 2019, at http://dcollections.oberlin.edu/cdm/compoundobject/collection/kingcrane/id/577/rec/4.

12. Rida's diary, December 10 and 31, 1918, as quoted by Ryad, "Like a Mill Donkey"; TNA-London, Walrond to Cornwallis, January 13, 1919, with addendum "Fundamental Statutes by the Party of Syrian Union," in FO 882/24, 85–90.

13. Muhammad Rashid Rida, "Introduction to vol. 21/Fatihat al-Majalid al-hadi wa al-ishrin," *al-Manar* 21:1 (December 1918): 1–8. Rida noted later in the issue that its publication was delayed for two months, until February 1919, owing to a paper shortage.

14. "Address of President Wilson, Opening the Campaign for the Fourth Liberty Loan," New York City, September 27, 1918, accessed September 3, 2018, at https://history.state.gov/historicaldocuments/frus1918Supp01v01/d258.

15. Muhammad Rashid Rida, "Principles of the Great Social Revolution and the Freedom of Nations/Mabadi` al-inqilab al-ijtima`i al-akbar wa hurriyat al-umum," *al-Manar* 21:1 (December 1918): 17–33.

16. Manela, *Wilsonian Moment*, ix–xi, 64–66; Reibman, "Case of William Yale," 681–702.

17. Thomas J. Knock, *To End All Wars: Woodrow Wilson and the Quest for a New World Order* (Princeton: Princeton University Press, 1992), 191.

18. Gerwarth, *The Vanquished*, 98–152.

19. Knock, *To End All Wars*, vii–x, 271–76; Throntveit, *Power without Victory*, 120–21, 252. Wilson's views by 1918 contrasted with earlier attitudes toward American intervention, as in the occupation of the Philippines, articulated in his popular article, "The Ideals of America," *Atlantic Monthly* (December 1902): 721–34. I thank my colleague Robert Adcock for alerting me to this article.

20. Throntveit, *Power without Victory*, 254.

21. "President Wilson's Fourteen Points," Avalon Project, Yale Law School, accessed March 16, 2019, at http://avalon.law.yale.edu/20th_century/wilson14.asp; Charles Seymour, ed., *The Intimate Papers of Colonel House*, vol. 3 (Boston: Houghton Mifflin, 1928), 322–23; Lawrence E. Gelfand, *The Inquiry: American Preparations for Peace, 1917–1919* (New Haven: Yale University Press, 1963), 146.

22. Throntveit, *Power without Victory*, 1–17; Leonard V. Smith, "The Wilsonian Challenge to International Law," *Journal of the History of International Law* 13 (2011): 179–208; Knock, *To End All Wars*, 3–30, 57–147; Manela, *Wilsonian Moment*, 3–26, 35–47.

23. Leonard V. Smith, *Sovereignty at the Paris Peace Conference of 1919* (New York: Oxford University Press, 2018), 1–14; Trygve Throntveit, "The Fable of the Fourteen Points: Woodrow Wilson and Self-Determination," *Diplomatic History* 35:3 (June 2011): 445–81.

24. Knock, *To End All Wars*, 3–14; Throntveit, *Power without Victory*, 18–47, 50–51, 68–78, 100–5.

25. MacMillan, *Paris 1919*, 9–15, 391–94, 405; Fromkin, *A Peace to End All Peace*, 253–62; Manela, *Wilsonian Moment*, 4–5.

26. Robert E. Hannigan, *The Great War and American Foreign Policy, 1914–24* (Philadelphia: University of Pennsylvania Press, 2017), 202–4, quote on 204; Throntveit, *Power without Victory*, 14.

27. Columbia University Rare Book and Manuscript Library [hereafter CURBML], typescript of William Westermann's diary of the peace conference, December 11, 1918, discussion with French ambassador Jusserand; and December 29, 1918, meeting with General Bliss, 4, 14. William Linn Westermann Papers.

28. John Milton Cooper, Jr., *Breaking the Heart of the World: Woodrow Wilson and the Fight for the League of Nations* (New York: Cambridge University Press, 2001), 10–49. Reference to Roosevelt's December 15, 1918, telegram to Balfour on 39.

29. MacMillan, *Paris 1919*, 382.

30. Fromkin: *A Peace to End All Peace*, 305, 312–14, 363–79.

31. "The Prime Minister's Speech," *The Times*, December 21, 1917, 8.

32. Afaf Lutfi al-Sayyid-Marsot, *Egypt's Liberal Experiment: 1922–1936* (Berkeley: University of California Press, 1977), 48–49; Manela, *Wilsonian Moment*, 70.

33. Wilson, *Lawrence of Arabia*, 573–75; Allawi, *Faisal I*, 169–70.

34. Pichon to French ambassadors in Rome and Washington, October 23, 1918; Cambon to Balfour, October 27, 1918, in Hokayem, *Documents diplomatiques*, I: 396–97, 399–400; Jukka Nevakivi, *Britain, France, and the Arab Middle East* (London: Athlone Press, 1969), 69–83.

35. Gout to Pichon, October 12, 1918, in Hokayem, *Documents diplomatiques*, I: 422–23; Gérard D. Khoury, *Une Tutelle coloniale: Le Mandat français en Syrie et au Liban* (Paris: Belin, 2006), 7–8, 16–17; Julie d'Andurain,

Colonialisme ou impérialisme? Le Parti colonial en pensée et en action (Lechelle: Zeillige, 2016), 151–71; Christopher M. Andrew and A. S. Kanya-Forstner, *The Climax of French Imperial Expansion 1914–1924* (Stanford: Stanford University Press, 1981), 151–72.

36. Allawi, *Faisal I*, 174–77.
37. U.S. Army films of Wilson's arrival in Paris, accessed March 13, 2019, at https://www.youtube.com/watch?v=pWRnVıy_JTQ.

Chapter 4: Wooing Woodrow Wilson

1 Haidar, *Mudhakkirat*, 202–5; Allawi, *Faisal I*, 186; Roger Adelson, *London and the Invention of the Middle East* (New Haven: Yale University Press, 1995), 168–69.
2. Allawi, *Faisal I*, 17, 28–29; Columbia University Rare Book and Manuscript Library [hereafter CURBML], Diary of William L. Westermann, January 20, 1919, 23.
3. Haidar, *Mudhakkirat*, 208–9.
4. Robert H. Lieshout, *Britain and the Arab Middle East: World War I and Its Aftermath* (New York: I.B. Tauris, 2016), 322, 329–30, 333–34.
5. "From Prince Faisal to Prince Zaid," London, December 31, 1918. In Musa, *Al-Murasalat al-Tarikhiya*, 259–60.
6. Haidar, *Mudhakkirat*, 205.
7. Awni Abd al-Hadi, *Mudhakkirat Auni Abd al-Hadi*, ed. Khairiyah Qasimi-yah (Beirut: Markaz al-Dirasat al-Wahdah al-`Arabiyah, 2002), 47–48; Qadri, *Mudhakkirat Auni Abd al-Hadi*, 95–96.
8. Abd al-Hadi, *Mudhakkirat*, 50.
9. David Lloyd George, *Memoirs of the Peace Conference*, vol. II (1939, reprint New York: Howard Fertig, 1972), 705; Daniel Yergin, *The Prize: The Epic Quest for Oil, Money, and Power* (New York: Free Press, 1991/2009), 168–89.
10. Allawi, *Faisal I*, 182–83; "Anglo-French Joint Statement of Aims in Syria and Mesopotamia," accessed March 9, 2016, at wwi.lib.byu .edu/index.phop/Anglo-French_Joint_Statement_of_Aims_in_ Syria_and_Mesopotamia.
11. Carl Bouchard, *Cher Monsieur le Président* (Ceyzerieu: Champ Vallon, 2015), 104–5, 213–48.
12. "Guilt of the Kaiser. Germany Must Pay," *The Times*, November 30, 1918, 9.
13. Haidar, *Mudhakkirat*, 219; Allawi, *Faisal I*, 173, 206–7.

14. Throntveit, *Power without Victory*, 254.

15. Abd al-Hadi, *Mudhakkirat*, 61.

16. Bruno Cabanes, *La victoire endeuillée* (Paris: Editions du Seuil, 2004), 36–70, 277–358 ; Leonard V. Smith et al., *France and the Great War 1914–1918* (New York: Cambridge University Press, 2003), 159–65.

17. Gregor Dallas, *At the Heart of a Tiger: Clemenceau and His World 1841–1929* (New York: Carroll and Graf, 1993), 79–189, 501–39, 560–63; Sylvie Brodziak, *Clemenceau* (Saint-Denis: Presses Universitaires de Vincennes, 2015), 66–77.

18. Haidar, *Mudhakkirat*, 214; Khoury, *France et l'Orient arabe*, 173.

19. Haidar, *Mudhakkirat*, 216; T. E. Lawrence, *Diary of the Peace Conference*, fragment from January 1919, accessed October 1, 2015 at http://www.telstudies.org/writings/works/articles_essays/1919_diary_of_the_peace_conference.shtml. On Gout's appearance, see CURBML, William Linn Westermann's diary of the peace conference, 37.

20. James T. Shotwell, *At the Paris Peace Conference* (New York: Macmillan, 1937), 126.

21. Manela, *Wilsonian Moment*, 58.

22. Arthur S. Link, ed., *The Papers of Woodrow Wilson*, vol. 54 (Princeton: Princeton University Press, 1986), 126–32.

23. Aviel Roshwald, *Ethnic Nationalism and the Fall of Empires* (New York: Routledge, 2001), 157–72.

24. Allawi, *Faisal I*, 197.

25. Manela, *Wilsonian Moment*, 72, 145.

26. MacMillan, *Paris 1919*, 21–22.

27. Adam Tooze, *The Deluge: The Great War, America and the Remaking of the Global Order, 1916–1931* (New York: Viking, 2014), 14–30; Knock, *To End All Wars*, 227–45; Khoury, *France et l'Orient arabe*, 176–77, 185–86.

28. Manela, *Wilsonian Moment*, 13.

29. Haidar, *Mudhakkirat*, 120; Wilson, *The State*, 463–67, 555–71.

30. Manela, *Wilsonian Moment*, 40.

31. Shotwell, *At the Paris Peace Conference*, 130–31.

32. Quoted in Patrick, *America's Forgotten Middle East Initiative*, 33.

33. Robert Lansing, *The Big Four and Others of the Peace Conference* (Boston: Houghton Mifflin, 1921), 163.

34. Library of Congress Manuscript Division [hereafter Library of Congress], Curtis to Bliss, January 12, 1919, and Lawrence to Bliss, January 22, 1919, in Tasker H. Bliss Papers, Box 232.

35. Stephen Bonsal, *Suitors and Suppliants: The Little Nations at Versailles* (New York: Prentice-Hall, 1946), 37–38.

36. Melvin I. Urofsky, *A Voice That Spoke for Justice* (Albany: State University of New York Press, 1982), vii, 157–61; Carl Hermann Voss, ed., *Stephen S. Wise, Servant of the People: Selected Letters* (Philadelphia: Jewish Publication Society of America, 1969), 76–77, 84–87; Stephen Wise, *Challenging Years* (New York: G.P. Putnam's Sons, 1949), 161–201.

37. A. James Rudin, *Pillar of Fire: A Biography of Rabbi Stephen S. Wise* (Lubbock: Texas Tech University Press, 2015), 192–98; Bodleian Libraries at Weston Library, Special Collections, Oxford [hereafter Bodleian Library], original of Faisal's addendum, in Lawrence's hand, and text of Faisal-Weizmann agreement in T. E. Lawrence Oddments, MS.Eng. d3348. The memorandum later sparked controversy, as Faisal's addendum insisting on the condition of Arab rule was left off copies. See Allawi, *Faisal I*, 188–89.

38. Link, *Papers of Woodrow Wilson*, 54: 90. Wise's letter was likely prompted by a meeting with Wilson on January 14, when the president expressed concern about Arabs' reactions to Jewish settlement in Palestine. See Urofsky, *Voice That Spoke for Justice*, 156–57.

39. Cooper, *Breaking the Heart of the World*, 24–49.

40. Link, *Papers of Woodrow Wilson*, 54: 224.

41. Haidar, *Mudhakkirat*, 220. Faisal had summarized the conversation at Murat Palace for Haidar. Wilson did not keep a written record of it.

42. Library of Congress Manuscript Division, Woodrow Wilson Papers, Peace Conference Correspondence 1918–1920 [hereafter Library of Congress-Wilson], Wilson to Nubar, January 23, 1919, doc. 7917, and Nubar to Wilson, January 29, doc. 8659; Polk to Wilson on Senate food bill for Syrians and "other Christians," January 24, doc. 7992; Wilson to Cleve Dodge declining invitation to Armenian banquet, January 25, doc. 8124; Wilson's refusal to meet Armenian delegation, January 27, doc. 8303; memo on Hoover foodstuffs appropriations for Europe and Syria, January 25; Hoover to Wilson, January 27, doc. 8348; Wilson to Carter Glass, January 28, doc. 8470. Microfilm Series 5B, reels 391–92.

43. CURBML, Westermann Diary, January 27 and February 12, 1919; Library of Congress Manuscript Division, William Yale, "Great Britain, France and the Near East," Report 174, December 16, 1918, in U.S. American Commission to Negotiate Peace Records, Box 1.

44. Library of Congress-Wilson, James Barton to Wilson, January 31, 1919, docs. 8841–8843.
45. Knock, *To End All Wars*, 213; John Milton Cooper, Jr., *Woodrow Wilson: A Biography* (New York: Alfred A. Knopf, 2009), 454.

Chapter 5: The Covenant and the Colonial Color Line

1. Republic of France, Ministry of Foreign Affairs archive at La Cour-neuve [hereafter MAE-Courneuve], Papiers Jean Gout, 196 PAAP/7, reports of July 3 and 12; November 14, 18, 22, 24, and 27; December 14; and January 2, 10, and 14. Nevakivi, *Britain, France, and the Arab Middle East*, 109–10; William I. Shorrock, *French Imperialism in the Middle East* (Madison: University of Wisconsin Press, 1976), 7, 107; Rita Baddoura, "Chékri Ganem: pionner et vertuose du verbe," *L'Ori-ent Littéraire* 3 (2013), accessed at http://www.lorientlitteraire.com/article_details.php?cid=7&nid=4114.
2. Haidar, *Mudhakkirat*, 225. Haidar records this meeting on January 28, but Allawi and Lawrence date it as January 24. The following account of the conversation is from Haidar, *Mudhakkirat*, 225–28.
3. MAE-Courneuve, "La Question Syrienne et la Révision Eventuelle des Accords de 1916," Gout Papers,196 PAAP/7, 107–27.
4. The National Archives of the United Kingdom, London [hereafter TNA-London], "Oilfields of Persia and Mesopotamia," February 26, 1919, and "Secret: Memorandum on the Oil Fields of Persia and Mes-opotamia," FO 608/97/15, 191–224. Quote is from 197.
5. Fromkin, *A Peace to End All Peace*, 350–51, 394–97; Nevakivi, *Britain, France, and the Arab Middle East*, 68–124. See Lord Milner's March 8, 1919, memo to Lloyd George, in which he proposes acting as the "honest broker" between Faisal and France, but only on the condition that "the French fulfill their promise to us about Mosul and Palestine." Lloyd George, *Memoirs of the Peace Conference*, II: 678–80; MacMillan, *Paris 1919*, 382–83.
6. Andrew and Kanya-Forstner, *Climax of French Imperial Expansion*, 163.
7. David Hunter Miller, *My Diary at the Conference of Paris: Documents*, vol. 4 (New York: Appeal Printing Company, 1924), 297–301.
8. Wilson, *The State*, 366–67; Lloyd George, *Memoirs*, 649–50, 659; Lloyd E. Ambrosius, "Woodrow Wilson and the Birth of a Nation: American

Democracy and International Relations," *Diplomacy and Statecraft* 18 (2007): 693.

9. Sarah M. A. Gualtieri, *Between Arab and White: Race and Ethnicity in the Early Syrian American Diaspora* (Berkeley: University of California Press, 2009); Marwa Elshakry, *Reading Darwin in Arabic. 1860–1950* (Chicago: University of Chicago Press, 2013); Stacy Fahrenthold, "Transnational Modes and Media: The Syrian Press in the Mahjar and Emigrant Activism during World War I," *Mashriq and Mahjar* 1 (2013): 30–54; Khalil A. Bishara, *The Origin of the Modern Syrian* (New York: Al-Hoda Publishing House, 1914), 1, 39–40.

10. The Supreme Council, or Council of Ten, was composed of two delegates from each of the five leading Allies: Britain, France, the United States, Italy, and Japan.

11. Haidar, *Mudhakkirat*, 233–34.

12. Haidar, *Mudhakkirat*, 235.

13. Shotwell, *At the Paris Peace Conference*, 166–67.

14. Link, *Papers of Woodrow Wilson*, 54: 505–8; Miller, *My Diary*, 14: 227–30; MacMillan, *Paris 1919*, 391.

15. Haidar, *Mudhakkirat*, 238.

16. Library of Congress-Wilson, Bliss to Wilson, February 7 and February 11, 1919, docs. 9753–54, 10182, Wilson Papers Series 5B; Ussama Makdisi, *Faith Misplaced: The Broken Promise of U.S.–Arab Relations: 1820–2001* (New York: Public Affairs, 2010), 89–91, 122–24, 136; Betty S. Anderson, *The American University of Beirut: Arab Nationalism and Liberal Education* (Austin: University of Texas Press, 2011), 50–53.

17. Miller, *My Diary*, 14: 391–416, Bliss's quote is on 394; Zeine, *Struggle for Arab Independence*, 255–59, for Bliss's copy of his talk; Anderson, *American University of Beirut*, 18–19; Khoury, *France et l'Orient arabe*, 181–82.

18. Quoted in Cooper, *Breaking the Heart of the World*, 10; Cooper, *Woodrow Wilson*, 474.

19. World Peace Foundation, *A League of Nations*, vol. 2, Special Number, February 1919 (Boston), 413 [emphasis added by author].

20. World Peace Foundation, *League of Nations*, 2: 426.

21. Library of Congress, Minutes of League commission meeting, February 4, 1919, in Wilson Papers Series 5B Reel 392; CURBML, Westermann Diary, January 27, 1919; Knock, *To End All Wars*, 217–19; Throntveit, *Power without Victory*, 275.

22. The draft covenant and discussion are reprinted in United States Department of State, *Papers Relating to the Foreign Relations of the United States: The Paris Peace Conference, 1919* [hereafter *FRUS 1919*], vol. 3 / Minutes of the Plenary Sessions, 208–39.

23. Haidar, *Mudhakkirat*, 250–51; see also World Peace Foundation, *League of Nations*, 2: 432.

24. Haidar, *Mudhakkirat*, 257; TNA-London, Telegram to King Hussein and Sherif Zaid FO 608/92/7, 231.

25. Bonsal, *Suitors and Suppliants*, 45; Shotwell, *At the Paris Peace Conference*, 196–97.

26. "Réception de l'Émir Feisal," *Le Figaro*, January 17, 1919, 1; Faisal's speech of May 5, 1919, upon his return to Damascus, in Husri, *Day of Maysalun*, 107.

27. Jules Chancel, "Les massacres du 28 février 1919 en Syrie," *L'Illustration: Journal Universel*, April 5, 1919, 377; Nevakivi, *Britain, France, and the Arab Middle East*, 128.

28. Lansing, *The Big Four and Others of the Peace Conference*, 163; Lloyd George, *Memoirs*, 673–74.

29. El-Ghussein, *Martyred Armenia*, 48–49.

30. Haidar, *Mudhakkirat*, 261–62, 265–68. The duchesse, originally Élisabeth de Gramont, was known as Lily. Accessed September 7, 2018, at https://fr.wikipedia.org/wiki/Élisabeth_de_Clermont-Tonnerre.

31. Abd al-Hadi, *Mudhakkirat*, 58–61.

32. Haidar, *Mudhakkirat*, 257.

33. Andrew and Kanya-Forstner, *Climax of French Imperial Expansion*, 182–85; Richard S. Fogarty, *Race and War in France: Colonial Subjects in the French Army, 1914–1918* (Baltimore: Johns Hopkins University Press, 2008), 274–86.

34. CURBML, Westermann Diary, January 27, 1919, 28; Knock, *To End All Wars*, 206–7; "Library of Congress Manuscript Division, File 804: Arab State, December 1918–October 1919," Tasker H. Bliss Papers, Box 354; David F. Trask, "General Tasker Howard Bliss and the 'Sessions of the World,' 1919," *Transactions of the American Philosophical Society* 56:8 (1966): 1–11, 17–20, 47, 67.

35. *FRUS 1919*, 3: 766.

36. Knock, *To End All Wars*, 212–13; Library of Congress, Woodrow Wilson Papers, Peace Conference Correspondence, "Resolutions in Reference

to Mandatories," January 30, 1919, Series 5B Reel 391. The debates of January 28 and 30 are found in *FRUS 1919*, 3: 759–71, 785–817.

37. Knock, *To End All Wars*, 31–47; Cooper, *Breaking the Heart of the World*, 16–17; Jean-Michel Guieu, "Pour la paix par la Société des Nations," *Guerres Mondiales et Conflits Contemporains* 222 (April 2006): 89–102.

38. Smith, "The Wilsonian Challenge," quote from 183.

39. Manela, *Wilsonian Moment*, 4, 44, 48–52.

40. Speech at a royal banquet, December 27, 1918, quoted in Smith, "The Wilsonian Challenge," 192.

41. Final text of the covenant accessed September 6, 2018, at http://avalon .law.yale.edu/20th_century/leagcov.asp.

42. Library of Congress Manuscript Division, Woodrow Wilson Papers, Supreme War Council Report on the Occupation of Turkish Territories, February 6, 1919, doc. 9551–56; Wilson to Secretary of War, February 8, 1919, doc. 9908–9; Supreme War Council memo, February 9, 1919, doc. 9993; Secretary of War to Wilson, February 11, 1919, doc. 10175–76; Wilson to Bliss, February 11, 1919, doc. 10183; Wilson to Secretary of Treasury, February 11, 1919, doc. 10198, Series 5B.

43. Knock, *To End All Wars*, 210–19.

44. Cooper, *Woodrow Wilson*, 28, 73, 108, 468.

45. Cooper, *Woodrow Wilson*, 471.

46. Ambrosius, "Woodrow Wilson and the Birth of a Nation," 698–701, 708–9; Michael Dennis, "Race and the Southern Imagination: Woodrow Wilson Reconsidered," *Canadian Review of American Studies* 29:3 (1999): 109–31; Nell Irvin Painter, *Standing at Armageddon* (New York: W.W. Norton, 2008/1987), 344–58.

47. Stephen Skowronek, "The Reassociation of Ideas and Purposes: Racism, Liberalism, and the American Political Tradition," *American Political Science Review* 100:3 (August 2006): 391–94. Skowronek argues that in 1919, Wilson feared the United States might again split in race or class war. However, his solution, gradualism, permitted Jim Crow norms to spread north. See also Robert Vitalis, *White World Order, Black Power Politics* (Ithaca, NY: Cornell University Press, 2015), 39–40.

48. W. E. B. Du Bois, *The Souls of Black Folk* (Chicago: A.C. McClurg, 1903), "The Forethought."

49. Library of Congress Manuscript Division, Woodrow Wilson Papers, General Bliss to Secretary of State, January 29, 1919, doc. 8567, Series 5B; Clarence G. Contee, "Du Bois, the NAACP, and the Pan-African

Congress of 1919," *Journal of Negro History* 57:1 (January 1972): 13–28; Aldon D. Morris, *The Scholar Denied: W. E. B. Du Bois and the Birth of Modern Sociology* (Oakland: University of California Press, 2015), 134.

50. Dallas, *At the Heart of a Tiger*, 69–72; Brodziak, *Clemenceau*, 62–65; Duroselle, *Clemenceau*, 83–86.

51. Marilyn Lake and Henry Reynolds, *Drawing the Global Colour Line: White Men's Countries and the International Challenge of Racial Equality* (New York: Cambridge University Press, 2008), 306–7.

52. Lake and Reynolds, *Drawing the Global Colour Line*, 307; David Levering Lewis, *W. E. B. Du Bois: A Biography* (New York: Henry Holt, 2009), 367–80; Paul Gordon Lauren, "Human Rights in History: Diplomacy and Racial Equality at the Paris Peace Conference," *Diplomatic History*, 2:3 (1978): 257–78; Emily S. Rosenberg, "World War I, Wilsonianism, and Challenges to U.S. Empire," *Diplomatic History* 38:4 (2014): 852.

53. MacMillan, *Paris 1919*, 44 and 99, quoting Headlam-Morley's notes; Jan Christiaan Smuts, "The Mission to Austria-Hungary, Paris, April 9, 1919," in Arthur S. Link, ed., *The Papers of Woodrow Wilson*, vol. 57 (Princeton: Princeton University Press, 1988), 167–75. On 173, Smuts recommended a "Mandatory of the Great Powers for Austria-Hungary" to supervise relations among the new states of Austria, Hungary, Romania, and Czechoslovakia.

54. Gualtieri, *Between Arab and White*, 69–74, discussion of the Fourth Circuit Court of Appeals decision in *Dow v. United States*, September 15, 1915.

55. Andrew Patrick, "Woodrow Wilson, the Ottomans, and World War I," *Diplomatic History* 42:5 (November 2018): 886–910.

56. Library of Congress Prints and Photographs Division, W. A. Rogers, "His mandatory wives— oh, Sam!" *New York Herald*, February 23, 1919, 2. Accessed June 6, 2019, at https://www.loc.gov/item/2010717810/. Rogers was a nationally famous cartoonist hired by the Wilson administration's Committee on Public Information during World War I.

57. Fogarty, *Race and War*, 77–83, 119–29, 282–83; Chris Rominger, "Nursing Transgressions, Exploring Difference: North Africans in French Medical Spaces during World War I," *International Journal of Middle East Studies* 50:4 (October 2018), forthcoming.

58. Miller, *My Diary*, 1: 116; MacMillan, *Paris 1919*, 316–18; Naoko Shimazu, *Japan, Race and Equality: The Racial Equality Proposal of 1919* (New York: Routledge, 1998), 18–19; Library of Congress Manuscripts Division,

Woodrow Wilson Papers, Lansing memo dated January 24, 1919, doc. 8044, Series 5B.

59. Lauren, "Human Rights in History," 271; Throntveit, *Power without Victory*, 281–82.

60. Shimazu, *Japan, Race and Equality*, 30–31; Michael L. Rosin, "The Five-Fifths Rule and the Unconstitutional Presidential Election of 1916," *Historical Methods* 46:2 (April–June 2013): 57–65; Kristofer Allerfeldt, "Wilsonian Pragmatism? Woodrow Wilson, Japanese Immigration, and the Paris Peace Conference," *Diplomacy and Statecraft* 15:3 (2004): 545–72.

61. Siba N'Zatioula Grovogui, *Sovereigns, Quasi Sovereigns, and Africans: Race and Self-Determination in International Law* (Minneapolis: University of Minnesota Press, 1996), 111–42.

62. Library of Congress Manuscripts Division, Woodrow Wilson Papers, Wilson to "Prince Faissal," February 14, 1919, doc. 10668, Series 5B. In addition to Rida's coverage in *The Lighthouse*, *Al-Hilal* ran articles on Wilson and the League of Nations every month between November 1918 and April 1919.

63. Abd al-Hadi, *Mudhakkirat*, 68; Joseph C. Grew, *Turbulent Era: A Diplomatic Record of Forty Years, 1904–1945*, vol. 1 (Freeport, NY: 1952), 372–75, 381–82.

64. Charles E. Neu, *Colonel House: A Biography of Woodrow Wilson's Silent Partner* (New York: Oxford University Press, 2015), 397–403.

65. Knock, *To End All Wars*, 239–44; Cooper, *Breaking the Heart of the World*, 55–71.

66. Crane to Lansing, March 10, 1919, in Crane Papers, Box 4 Incoming Correspondence, Columbia University Library Rare Books and Manuscripts Division.

67. Robert Lansing, *The Peace Negotiations: A Personal Narrative* (Boston: Houghton Mifflin, 1921), 149–61.

68. Isabel V. Hull, *A Scrap of Paper: Breaking and Making International Law during the Great War* (Ithaca, NY: Cornell University Press, 2014), 1–3, 16–41; Note from Paris Bar, February 1, 1919, doc. 9048–50, Wilson Papers Series 5b, Library of Congress.

Chapter 6: A Sip of Champagne, with a Sour Aftertaste

1. Cooper, *Breaking the Heart of the World*, 70–71; Knock, *To End All Wars*, 246–47; Patrick, *America's Forgotten Middle East Initiative*, 29.

2. Shotwell, *At the Paris Peace Conference*, 214.

3. Paul C. Helmreich, *From Paris to Sèvres: The Partition of the Ottoman Empire at the Peace Conference of 1919–1920* (Columbus: Ohio State University Press, 1974), 64–67.

4. Allawi, *Faisal I*, 211–12; Patrick, *America's Forgotten Middle East Initiative*, 43–46; Nevakivi, *Britain, France, and the Arab Middle East*, 129–30; Lloyd George, *Memoirs*, 684–95.

5. Haidar, *Mudhakkirat*, 291; Abd al-Hadi, *Mudhakkirat*, 68; Antonius, *Arab Awakening*, 288; Allawi, *Faisal I*, 211–12.

6. Arthur S. Link, ed., *Papers of Woodrow Wilson*, vol. 56 (Princeton: Princeton University Press, 1987), Faisal to Wilson, March 22, 1919, 243–44.

7. Nevakivi, *Britain, France, and the Arab Middle East*, 145–51.

8. Patrick, *America's Forgotten Middle East Initiative*, 47–48.

9. Haidar, *Mudhakkirat*, 305.

10. Link, *Papers of Woodrow Wilson*, 56: 272–75, 337; Patrick, *America's Forgotten Middle East Initiative*, 46–47; Yale University Library Digital Collections, MSS 466, Edward Mandell House Papers, Series 2, Diaries, vol. 7, 109–23, accessed February 15, 2016, at http://digital.library.yale .edu/cdm/compoundobject/collection/1004_6/id/5270/rec/1.

11. Link, *Papers of Woodrow Wilson*, 56: 584 and 57: 62–71. Wilson's physician, Dr. Grayson, recorded a fever and sore throat, and referred to a "seizure" in his diary; Edward Mandell House, *The Intimate Papers of Colonel House*, ed. Charles Seymour, vol. 4 (Boston: Houghton Mifflin, 1928), 401–4.

12. Haidar, *Mudhakkirat*, 329; Link, *Papers of Woodrow Wilson*, 56: 323, 57: 146; Nevakivi, *Britain, France, and the Arab Middle East*, 136–40.

13. T. S. Eliot, *The Waste Land: A Facsimile and Transcript of the Original Drafts*, ed. Valerie Eliot (New York: Harcourt Brace Jovanovich, 1974), xvii–xxii, 6. Eliot began writing *The Waste Land* later in 1919, while working at a bank that managed German debt. He complained of the tedium of reading through clauses of the peace treaty related to the finances, and finished the poem in 1921, only after a nervous breakdown.

14. Al-Hadi, *Mudhakkirat*, 69; Nevakivi, *Britain, France, and the Arab Middle East*, 141–42; Allawi, *Faisal I*, 219–20; Khoury, *France et l'Orient arabe*, 214–16.

15. Khoury, *France et l'Orient arabe*, 213.

16. Dallas, *At the Heart of a Tiger*, 565–70; Peter Jackson, *Beyond the Balance of Power: France and the Politics of National Security in the Era of the First World War* (New York: Cambridge University Press, 2013), 231–75.

17. Haidar, *Mudhakkirat*, 333–35; Khoury, *France et l'Orient arabe*, 217; Andrew and Kanya-Forstner, *Climax of French Imperial Expansion*, 170–73, 189–96.

18. See, for example, his April 17 note to Clemenceau, where Faisal recapitulated their April 13 conversation as affirmation that "Syria has the right to independence." In Musa, *Al-Murasalat al-Tarikhiya*, 2: 64–65.

19. CURBML, Westermann Diary, April 12, 13, 17, and 23, 1919, 56–67; Patrick, *America's Forgotten Middle East Initiative*, 60–61.

20. Khoury, *France et l'Orient arabe*, 203–9.

21. Haidar, *Mudhakkirat*, 344–59; Allawi, *Faisal I*, 219–24; Khoury, *France et l'Orient arabe*, 223–27; Musa, *Al-Murasalat al-Tarikhiya*, 2: 66–67.

22. Haidar, *Mudhakkirat*, 359–61.

Chapter 7: The Syrian Congress and the American Commision

1. Husri, *Day of Maysalun*, 105–6.

2. "A Word to Citizens," and "Celebration of His Highness Prince Faisal," *Lissan al-Hal*, May 1, 1919, 1–2.

3. Russell, *First Arab State*, 40; "Prince Faisal in the Capital," *al-Asima* [The Capital] 1:23 (May 7, 1919): 3.

4. Husri, *Day of Maysalun*, 106–112; Qadri, *Mudhakkirat*, 115; Russell, *First Arab State*, 41; Shahrastan, *al-Mu'tamar al-Suri*, 27–28; Allawi, *Faisal I*, 232–35.

5. Quoted in Philippe David, *Un Gouvernement arabe à Damas: Le Congrès syrien* (Paris: Marcel Giard, 1923), 48. See also *al-Asima* 1:19 (April 21, 1919), 1:24 (May 9, 1919), 1:25 (May 12, 1919), 1:26 (May 17, 1919), 1:32 (June 5, 1919), 1:35 (June 16, 1919).

6. Shahrastan, *Mu'tamar al-Suri*, 35–41; David, *Un Gouvernement arabe*, 51–63.

7. Patrick, *America's Forgotten Middle East Initiative*, 130–33.

8. Faisal to Commander in Chief, May 28, 1918, in Rush, *Records of the Hashemite Dynasties*, 10: 210–11; telegrams from Faisal to Allenby, May 29, 1919, in Musa, *Al-Murasalat al-Tarikhiya*, 2: 75–76; Patrick, *America's Forgotten Middle East Initiative*, 74.

9. Muhammad Izzat Darwazeh: *Mudhakkirat Muhammad 'Izzat Darwaza, 1887–1984*, vol. I (Beirut: Dar al-Gharb al-Islami, 1993), 350–53, 383–85; Khoury, *Urban Notables and Arab Nationalism*, 86–88.

10. Russell, *First Arab State*, 88.

11. I do not share Shahrastan's doubts about Azm's election as president. He was elected on June 3, when few of the Fatat nationalists had yet

arrived in Damascus. The Ottoman electoral machinery would have favored conservatives over young nationalists. See Shahrastan's discussion, *al-Mu'tamar al-Suri*, 51–58. On Yusuf, see Darwazeh, *97 Years*, 381–83. French officials recognized that the Congress was dominated by conservatives who would resist the democratic plans of Faisal and the nationalists. See David, *Un Gouvernement arabe*, 78–79.

12. Darwazeh, *Mudhakkirat*, I: 363, 366, 377; Muhammad 'Izzat Darwazeh, *Mudhakkirat wa Tasjilat*, vol. 2 (Damascus: al-Jama'iya al-filastiniya lil-tarikh wa al-athar, 1986), 77–78.

13. Rush, *Records of the Hashemite Dynasties*, vol. 10, interview with Michel Lutfallah; Russell, *First Arab State*, 86–88.

14. Republic of France, Ministry of Foreign Affairs archive at Nantes, Fonds Beyrouth [hereafter, MAE-Nantes], "The Central Syrian Union Party in Egypt," in Carton 2368. Program enclosed in a February 12, 1919, memo from Colonel Cousse on the distribution of SUP pamphlets in Damascus.

15. Muhammad Rashid Rida, "Second Syrian Trip (2),"*al-Manar* 21 (August 1920): 428–33. Quote on 428.

16. Muhammad Rashid Rida, "The Syrian Issue and the Parties," *al-Manar* 21 (June 1919): 197–206.

17. Lybyer notes that sixty-nine deputies met on July 2. See untitled memo in King-Crane Digital Collection, Oberlin College [hereafter KCDC]. Accessed February 28, 2017, at http://dcollections.oberlin.edu/cdm/ref/collection/kingcrane/id/2625.

18. KCDC, "Statement of Syrian Conference, Damascus, July 3, 1919." Accessed February 26, 2017, at http://dcollections.oberlin.edu/cdm/ref/collection/kingcrane/id/2525. I have incorporated handwritten corrections and amendments to this translation in my quotation here. Shahrastan discusses the statement in Arabic in *al-Mu'tamar al-Suri*, 61–68.

19. Arnold J. Toynbee, *Acquaintances* (New York: Oxford University Press, 1967), 208.

20. Columbia University Rare Book and Manuscript Library [hereafter CURBML], Charles R. Crane, "Memoirs of Charles R. Crane," Crane Family Papers, 367, and "Personal Diary of William Linn Westermann," April 18, 1919, 64 [hereafter Crane Memoirs and Westermann Diary].

21. CURBML, Lansing to Crane, April 30, 1919. Crane Family Papers, Folder 3, Box 4, Incoming Correspondence (1919–1922); CURBML, Crane Memoirs, 368–69.

22. Henry Churchill King, *A New America in a New World* (Paris: Young Men's Christian Association, 1919), 16.

23. Patrick, *America's Forgotten Middle East Initiative,* 52–62.

24. CURBML, Westermann Diary, April 18, 1919, 66.

25. Harry N. Howard, *The King-Crane Commission* (Beirut: Khayats, 1963), 51, 73; Patrick, *America's Forgotten Middle East Initiative,* 48–49, 66–67.

26. Howard, *King-Crane Commission,* 59–62.

27. MacMillan, *Paris 1919,* 299–301, 427–33; Helmreich, *From Paris to Sèvres,* 94–101.

28. Nevakivi, *Britain, France, and the Arab Middle East,* 154–62; Patrick, *America's Forgotten Middle East Initiative,* 60–72; Ganem to Clemenceau, May 8, 1919, and "Conversation between Wilson, Lloyd George and Clemenceau on Asia Minor and Syria," May 21, 1919, in Hokayem, *Documents diplomatiques,* I: 564–66, 571–77. Quotes on 575, 579.

29. Patrick, *America's Forgotten Middle East Initiative,* 69–73; CURBML, Westermann Diary, May 19, 1919, 78; Howard, *King-Crane Commission,* 77–79.

30. Qadri, *Mudhakkirat,*118.

31. Patrick, *America's Forgotten Middle East Initiative,* 74; Russell, *First Arab State,* 86; Hokayem, *Documents diplomatiques,* I: 582–83, 590, 606–8, 614–18.

32. Allawi, *Faisal I,* 239.

33. CURBML, Crane Memoirs, 371–72.

34. CURBML, Edib to Crane, June 7, 1919, Crane Family Papers. Folder 5, Box 4, Incoming Correspondence (1919–1922).

35. Howard, *King-Crane Commission,* 88–100; Janice Terry, *William Yale* (Limassol, Cyprus: Rimal Books, 2015), 116–17.

36. Faisal to President Wilson, Damascus, June 22, 1919, in Musa, *al-Murasalat al-Tarikhiya,* 83. This is a translation into Arabic from English. Original in E. L. Woodward and R. Butler, eds., *Documents on British Foreign Policy 1919–1939,* Series 1, vol. 4 (London: Her Majesty's Stationery Office, 1952), no. 192. Editor notes there is no record of a response from Wilson.

37. KCDC, "Interview of Commissioners, Advisers Present, with the Kadi, Mufti, and Six Others of the Ulema of Damascus," accessed February 21, 2017, at http://dcollections.oberlin.edu/cdm/ref/collection/kingcrane/id/1839.

38. KCDC, "Menu for Dinner," accessed September 9, 2018, at http://dcollections.oberlin.edu/cdm/singleitem/collection/kingcrane/id/

1380/ rec/17; Terry, *William Yale*, 122; Howard, *King-Crane Commission*, 109–10.

39. Russell called it superb in his *First Arab State*, 90; the date July 1 is penciled on a typewritten copy of the statement in KCDC: "Statement of the Emir Faisal to the Commission (copied verbatim)." The archive website casts the date as July 6, which seems to misread the note and implausibly place the statement two days after the commission left Damascus. Accessed February 27, 2017, at http://dcollections.oberlin .edu/cdm/ref/collection/kingcrane/id/2196. See Rush, *Records of the Hashemite Dynasties*, 10: 223; Howard, *King-Crane Commission*, 120–22.

40. KCDC, "al-Qanun al-Asasi lil-Wilayat al-Suriya al-Mutahidda/The Basic Law of the United States of Syria." Accessed February 27, 2017, at http://dcollections.oberlin.edu/cdm/ref/collection/kingcrane/ id/577. It was found among Henry King's papers.

41. Patrick, *America's Forgotten Middle East Initiative*, 52–62; Howard, *King-Crane Commission*, 116.

42. KCDC, Letter to W. F. Bond, July 23, 1919,. Accessed on February 21, 2017, at http://dcollections.oberlin.edu/cdm/ref/collection/kingcrane/ id/1323. On Lybyer's diary, see Russell, *First Arab State*, 90.

43. CURBML, Crane Family Papers, Box 8 Outgoing Correspondence, Folder 12, January–November, 1919.

44. Howard, *King-Crane Commission*, 134.

45. Jurji Baz, *Nazik Abid* (Beirut: Matba`at al-Salam, 1927); Howard, *King-Crane Commission*, 111, 126–27; `Izzat Aqbiq, "Nazik al-Abid: The Damascus Story of a Woman Activist," *E-Syria al-Mufakkira al-Thiqafiya*, posted November 1, 2011, accessed September 9, 2018, at http:// esyria.sy/sites/code/index.php?site=damascus&p=stories&category =characters&filename=201111012145011; KCDC, "Petition from Ibtihaje Kaddourah," July 5, 1919, and "Petition from Muslim Women of Beirut," July 1919, accessed September 9, 2018, at http://dcollections .oberlin.edu/cdm/compoundobject/collection/kingcrane/id/1459/rec /4 and http://dcollections.oberlin.edu/cdm/singleitem/collection/ kingcrane/id/1863/rec/8.

46. KCDC, Yale to Westermann, July 8, 1919. Accessed March 17, 2019, at http://dcollections.oberlin.edu/cdm/compoundobject/collection/ kingcrane/id/2524/rec/17.

47. Yuval Ben-Basset and Fruma Zachs, "From Şikayat to Political Discourse and 'Public Opinion': Petitioning Practices to the King-Crane

Commission," *New Middle Eastern Studies* 4 (2014): 1–23; Gelvin, *Divided Loyalties*, 150–52; Howard, *King-Crane Commission*, 120, 123, 142–43.

48. Howard, *King-Crane Commission*, 142–45. This section also draws directly on the report as it was published in *Papers Relating to the Foreign Relations of the United States: The Paris Peace Conference 1919*, vol. XII, 751–863 [hereafter *FRUS 1919*], accessed March 19, 2019, at http://digital.library .wisc.edu/1711.dl/FRUS.FRUS1919Parisv12.

49. Howard, *King-Crane Commission*, 221–27; *FRUS 1919*, XII: 859, 861, 863.

50. KCDC, Yale report #65 "Political Situation in the Arab Provinces of the Ottoman Empire," September 16, 1918, 17; Notes to William Yale's lecture, "Arabian and Syrian Situation," by Donald M. Brodie, May 5–6, 1919, at Hôtel de Crillon, 15. Accessed February 21, 2017, at http:// dcollections.oberlin.edu/cdm/ref/collection/kingcrane/id/1198.

51. Patrick, *America's Forgotten Middle East Initiative*, 58, 75, 84, 88–94, 180, 201, 208, 217, 233, 261.

52. Patrick, *America's Forgotten Middle East Initiative*, 72–76.

53. CURBML, Westermann Diary, June 29, 1919, 95. Westermann became a professor of Near and Middle East history at Columbia University, where he remained for twenty-five years, from 1923 to 1948.

54. Howard, *King-Crane Commission*, 218; Nevakivi, *Britain, France, and the Arab Middle East*, 172–85.

55. Trask, "General Tasker Howard Bliss and the 'Sessions of the World,'" 67, quoting August 5 letter to Mrs. Bliss and August 7 letter to Baker.

56. Woodrow Wilson, "Speech at the Stadium in Balboa Park in San Diego, California," American Presidency Project. Accessed March 21, 2017, at http://www.presidency.ucsb.edus/index.php?pid=117390.

57. Woodrow Wilson, Address at the City Hall Auditorium, Pueblo, Colorado, September 25, 1919. Accessed June 6, 2019, at https://www.presidency .ucsb.edu/node/318184.

58. Howard, *King-Crane Commission*, 256–63, 266, 318.

59. CURBML, Crane Memoirs, 273.

Chapter 8: A Democratic Uprising in Damascus

1. Russell, *First Arab State*, quoting *Suriya al-Jadida*, 91–92.

2. Nevakivi, *Britain, France, and the Arab Middle East*, 170, 175–78, 185, 188. T. E. Lawrence published his letter in the *Times* on September 8. Reproduced in Rush, *Records of the Hashemite Dynasties*, 10: 249–51.

3. "Reply by His Highness the Emir Feisal," in Rush, *Records of the Hashemite Dynasties*, 10: 267–71; Nevakivi, *Britain, France, and the Arab Middle East*, 199.

4. Howard, *King-Crane Commission*, 266.

5. Gelvin, *Divided Loyalties*, 234.

6. Library of Congress Manuscript Division, William Yale, "Report in Detail of Interview in London (Sept. 27th 1919 to Oct. 14th 1919)," in Tasker H. Bliss Papers, Box 354, Arab State File. Quote on 3.

7. "The Arab Problem: Suggestions for a Settlement," *The Times*, October 8, 1919, 8.

8. Lieshout, *Britain and the Arab Middle East*, 376–78.

9. Pichon to Cambon, October 11, 1919, in Hokayem, *Documents diplomatiques*, 1: 705–6. The Paris negotiations are treated in detail in my Part V.

10. Allawi, *Faisal I*, 254; Picot to Pichon, October 9, 1919, and Cambon to Foreign Office, October 14, 1919, in Hokayem, *Documents diplomatiques*, 1: 702–3, 707–8.

11. Rida, "The Syrian Issue and the Parties."

12. Rida, "Second Syrian Trip (2)."

13. The Hotel d'Orient was run by the Khawwam brothers. One of the first hotels in Damascus, dating from the mid-nineteenth century, it was a traditional Damascene house with two courtyards. Weber, *Damascus*, II: 188.

14. Gelvin, *Divided Loyalties*, 89–90.

15. Gelvin, *Divided Loyalties*, 91–96.

16. Rashid Rida's diary, September 21–23, 1919, quoted in Ryad, "Like a Mill Donkey."

17. Muhammad Rashid Rida, "Second Syrian Trip (9)," *al-Manar* 23 (March 1922): 235–40. Rida's diary, September 26–28, 1919, quoted in Ryad, "Like a Mill Donkey."

18. Muhammad Rashid Rida, "Second Syrian Trip (5)," *al-Manar* 22 (April 1921): 390–96, and "Second Syrian Trip (6)," *al-Manar* 22 (September 1921): 617–23; Rida's diary, September 29–October 3, 1919, in Ryad, "Like a Mill Donkey." Rida published a speech by a women's activist, Anbara Salam, in the April 1921 issue of *al-Manar*.

19. Muhammad Rashid Rida, "Second Syrian Trip (7)," *al-Manar* 22 (October 1921): 768–85; Rida's diary, October 7, 1919, quoted in Ryad, "Like a Mill Donkey."

20. Rida's diary, October 12–13, 1919, quoted in Ryad, "Like a Mill Donkey"; Muhammad Rashid Rida, "Second Syrian Trip (3)," *al-Manar* 21 (August 1920): 498–99.

21. Rida, "Second Syrian Trip (7)"; Rida's diary, October 28–November 12, 1919, quoted in Ryad, "Like a Mill Donkey."

22. Rida's diary, November 21 and 25, 1919, in Ryad, "Like a Mill Donkey."

23. *Organization of the Higher National Committee in the Syrian Capital* [Nizam al-Lajna al-Wataniya al-'Ulya fi al-'Asima al-Suriya] (Damascus: Matba'a al-Taraqi, 1919).

24. Gelvin, *Divided Loyalties*, 184–86.

25. MAE-Nantes, "Le Premier Cri/First Cry to Diplomatic Traitors in the Civilized World," author's translation of a leaflet dated September 20, 1919, Carton 2372. The leaflet itself was a translation from Arabic.

26. The National Archives of the United Kingdom, London [hereafter TNA-London], Michel Lutfallah to Lloyd George, September 16, 1919, FO 371/4183, 346–51,

27. Hakim, *Suriya wa al-'Ahd al-Faysali*, 115; Shahrastan, *Mu'tamar al-Suri*, 78, 80.

28. Tauber, *Formation of Modern Syria*, 21. The speaker and author was Muhammad Shurayqi.

29. Arab Independence Party to Pichon, November 15, 1919, in Hokayem, *Documents diplomatiques*, I: 742–44.

30. Republic of France, Ministry of Foreign Affairs archive at La Courneuve [hereafter MAE-Courneuve], Petition signed by Azm and Darwazeh, October 28, 1919, in Serie Levant 1918–1940, Syria-Lebanon; Qadri, *Mudhakkirat*, 150; Allawi, *Faisal I*, 260; Gelvin, *Divided Loyalties*, 97–98.

31. "Syrians' Demonstration [Muthahirat al-Suriyin]," *al-Kawkab*, November 25, 1919.

32. Allawi, *Faisal I*, 260; Russell, *First Arab State*, 114.

33. Musa, *al-Murasalat al-tarikhiya*, 2: 236–37.

34. Musa, *al-Murasalat al-tarikhiya*, 2: 234–37.

35. Qadri, *Mudhakkirat*, 141. Clemenceau denied that the appointment of Gouraud had any political significance and promised that Syria would remain united. However, on the same day, Clemenceau wrote to Monsignor Hoyek assuring him that Lebanon would be independent: Hokayem, *Documents diplomatiques*, I: 738–39.

36. Julie d'Andurain, *Henri Gouraud: Photographies d'Afrique et d'Orient* (Paris: Éditions Pierre de Taillac, 2016), 158–61.

37. Russell, *First Arab State*, 110.
38. Allawi, *Faisal I*, 261; Hakim, *Suriya wa al-'Ahd al-Faysali*, 118–19; Shahrastan, *al-Mu'tamar al-Suri*, 80–81.
39. Russell, *First Arab State*, 109; GHQ Cairo to War Office, September 22, 1919, in Rush, *Records of the Hashemite Dynasties*, 10: 280.
40. Qadri, *Mudhakkirat*, 150; "The Arabs Are One People Speaking with One Voice [al-Arab insan wahid yantiqun bifam wahid]," *al-Mufid*, November 23, 1919.
41. Howard, *King-Crane Commission*, 262; Patrick, *America's Forgotten Middle East Initiative*, 178–79; KCDC, King to Crane, November 18, 1919, accessed September 11, 2018, at http://collections.oberlin.edu/cdm/singleitem/collection/kingcrane/id/1355/rec/1. King and Crane had promised Wilson not to speak publicly of the report until it was formally released. Secretary of State Robert Lansing, who had fallen out of favor with Wilson in Paris, failed to present the King-Crane case to Congress.
42. William E. Borah, "The League of Nations," November 19, 1919, in *The Senate: Classic Speeches 1830–1993*, vol. 3 (Washington, DC: Government Printing Office, 1994), 574.
43. Library of Congress Manuscript Division, Telegrams dated October 28 and November 7, 16, and 26, 1919, Mark L. Bristol Papers, Box 76 "Syria, General, 1919" file.
44. Shahrastan, *al-Mu'tamar al-Suri*, 80–82, 144; Allawi, *Faisal I*, 261; Hakim, *Suriya wa al-'Ahd Faysali*, 119; *al-Asima* [The Capital], November 27, 1919.
45. Shahrastan, *al-Mu'tamar al-Suri*, 145; *al-Asima*, December 4, 1919, 2.
46. Tauber, *Formation of Modern Syria*, 22; Russell, *First Arab State*, 111–12. Gouraud refused both Clemenceau's and Allenby's appeals to delay the occupation of the Bekaa. See notes from Gouraud to Pichon, November 25, 1919; Gouraud to Clemenceau, November 29, 1919; Clemenceau to Gouraud, November 30, 1919; and Gouraud to Clemenceau, December 5, 1919, in Hokayem, *Documents diplomatiques*, I: 750–51, 759–66.
47. Al-Hakim, *Suriya wa al-'Ahd al-Faysali*, 122; Russell, *First Arab State*, 114.
48. Al-Hakim, *Suriya wa al-'Ahd al-Faysali*, 123; Qadri, *Mudhakkirat*, 151–52; Tauber, *Formation of Modern Syria*, 23.
49. De Caix to Clemenceau, December 13, 1919; Gouraud to Clemenceau, December 17 and 29, 1919, in Hokayem, *Documents diplomatiques*, I: 770–71, 781–82. On Gouraud in West Africa and Morocco, see Andurain, *Henri Gouraud*, 21–131.

50. Khoury, *Tutelle coloniale*, 6–8, 41–52.

51. Grew, *Turbulent Era*, 1: 401–3.

52. Clemenceau to Gouraud, December 9, 1919, in *Correspondance Fayçal-Gouraud/Murasilat Faysal-Ghuru*, ed. George Adib Karam (Beirut: Publications de l'Université Libanaise, 2009), 50–51; Khoury, *Tutelle coloniale*, 29–32; Khoury, *La France et l'Orient arabe*, ix, 59–60, 286–88, 294. On the negotiations, see Hokayem, *Documents diplomatiques*, November 27–28, I: 752–59.

53. The negotiations are described in greater detail in Part V of this book. For the text of the accord, see Karam, *Correspondance Fayçal-Gouraud*, 53–61.

54. As protests continued, Zaid began to fear for his personal safety. He asked Druze chiefs south of Damascus to send cavalry to protect him: Tauber, *Formation of Modern Syria*, 23.

55. Faisal to Hussein, November 1919, in Musa, *al-Murasalat al-Tarikhiya*, Letter 138, 255–64.

Chapter 9: Revolution at the Quai d'Orsay

1. Khoury, *Tutelle coloniale*, 181.

2. Khoury, *Tutelle coloniale*, 182.

3. Graham to Curzon, July 27, 1919, in Woodward and Butler, *Documents on British Foreign Policy*, 4: 320; Khoury, *France et l'Orient arabe*, 266.

4. Andrew and Kanya-Forstner, *Climax of French Imperial Expansion*, 90, 100, 159, 166–71, 197, 201–2; de Caix to Gouraud, October 6, 1919, in PAAP 399, Carton 130, MAE-Courneuve; Haidar, *Mudhakkirat*, 486–89; Graham to Campbell, November 9, 1919, FO 800/153/240–41.

5. De Caix to his father, December 2, 1919, in Khoury, *Tutelle coloniale*, 179–80; Nevakivi, *Britain, France and the Arab Middle East*, 229; Andrew and Kanya-Forstner, *Climax of French Imperial Expansion*, 206.

6. MAE-Courneuve, Robert de Caix, undated handwritten memoir, "Mission au Levant," PAAP 353 de Caix/Vol. 4/Microfilm P 11204, 16; on the negotiations, see Nevakivi, *Britain, France, and the Arab Middle East*, 204–29, and Khoury, *France et l'Orient arabe*, 253–93; Allawi, *Faisal I*, 254–57. The British learned of the accord on January 7 from *Le Temps* and received an official text only on January 26. See Woodward and Butler, *Documents on British Foreign Policy*, nos. 4: 411, 412, 416, 421, 611–16, 624–27.

7. Khoury, *Tutelle coloniale,* 183.

8. Khoury, *Tutelle coloniale,* 55, 61–62, 70. I am in debt to the pioneering research on Robert de Caix by the late Gérard Khoury, whose two books cited here reveal the extent of this single man's influence on French policy.

9. Dallas, *At the Heart of a Tiger,* 584.

10. Duroselle, *Clemenceau,* 843–56; Hampden Jackson, *Clemenceau and the Third Republic* (London: Hodder and Stoughton, 1948), 221–22; Dallas, *At the Heart of a Tiger,* 465, 584.

11. Duroselle, *Clemenceau,* 857.

12. Georges Clemenceau, *Claude Monet: Les Nymphéas,* 2nd ed. (Paris: Bartillat, 2010), 133.

13. MAE-Courneuve, de Caix to Gouraud, January 22, 1920, in 399 PAAP, Gouraud Papers, Carton 142: Correspondance avec Robert de Caix.

14. L. Abrams and D. J. Miller, "Who Were the French Colonialists? A Reassessment of the *Parti Colonial,* 1890–1914," *Historical Journal* 19:3 (1976): 685–725; Martin Thomas, *The French Empire between the Wars* (Manchester: Manchester University Press, 2005), 30–35, 38; biographical information drawn from Khoury, *Tutelle coloniale,* 6–9.

15. MAE-Courneuve, "Mission au Levant," memoir dictated by Robert de Caix, likely in the 1960s, in PAAP 353, de Caix papers, microfilm P 11204, 288; Khoury, *Tutelle coloniale,* 16; Andrew and Kanya-Forstner, *Climax of French Imperial Expansion,* 207.

16. MAE-Courneuve, "Philippe Berthelot et l'émir," clip from unknown paper that mentions the February 17, 1920, article in *Bonsoir,* in PAAP 399 Carton 135.

17. Robert de Caix, "Note sur la politique de l'accord avec Faysal," in Khoury, *Tutelle coloniale,* 187–206.

18. Haidar, *Mudhakkirat,* 518–19, 528, 537.

19. Haidar, *Mudhakkirat,* 534, 541, 551–53, 561; Smith, *Sovereignty at the Paris Peace Conference,* 222–24.

20. Millerand to Beirut, Constantinople, London, and Rome, February 10, 1920, in Hokayem, *Documents diplomatiques,* I: 73–75. Quote on 74.

21. MAE-Courneuve, "Discourse prononcé par le Général Gouraud . . . le 21 Novembre 1919," in PAAP 399 Carton 151; Nevakivi, *Britain, France, and the Arab Middle East,* 213.

22. MAE-Courneuve, Père Chanteur, "Note sur la Syro-Palestine et la Turquie," August 1919, enclosed with a note from Père Jalabert on

October 16, 1919, and notes from a conversation with M. Huvelin, dated December 1919, in PAAP 399 Carton 130. See also MAE-Nantes, Paul Huvelin, "La Syrie au Lendemain de la Guerre," 27–29, Carton 2357.

23. MAE-Courneuve, "Note de R. de Caix sur la politique de l'accord avec Feysal," January 26, 1920, 51, in Série Levant 1914–1918 Syrie-Liban, vol. 22, microfilm P1311.

24. Gouraud to Millerand, January 25, 1920, and Gouraud to Foreign Affairs, February 2 and 6, 1920, in Hokayem, *Documents diplomatiques*, II: 34–37, 62–64, 66–67.

25. Vahram Shemmassian, "The Repatriation of Armenian Refugees from the Arab Middle East, 1918–1920," in Richard G. Hovannisian and Simon Payaslian, eds., *Armenian Cilicia* (Costa Mesa, CA: Mazda Publishers, 2008), 419–56; Susan P. Pattie, *The Armenian Legionnaires* (New York: I.B. Tauris, 2018), 231.

26. Stanley E. Kerr, *The Lions of Marash* (Albany: State University of New York Press, 1973), 95–99; Richard G. Hovannisian, "The Postwar Contest for Cilicia and the 'Marash Affair,'" in Hovanissian and Payaslien, *Armenian Cilicia*, 495–518.

27. Kerr, *Lions of Marash*, 172, 181, 193–96; Hovannisian, "Postwar Contest," 511.

28. Pattie, *Armenian Legionnaires*, 198–99.

29. Gouraud to Millerand, January 25, 1920; Moustafa Kemal to the population of Aintab, late January–early February 1920, in Hokayem, *Documents diplomatiques*, II: 34–37, 60–61.

30. Nadine Méouchy, "Le Mouvement des 'Isabat en Syrie du nord à travers le témoignage du Chaykh Youssef Saadoun (1919–1921)," in Nadine Méouchy and Peter Sluglett, eds., *The British and French Mandates in Comparative Perspectives* (Leiden: Brill, 2004), 651–71.

31. Meir Zamir, *The Formation of Modern Lebanon* (Ithaca, NY: Cornell University Press, 1985), 37–74.

32. Clemenceau to Hoyek, November 10, 1919, in Hokayem, *Documents diplomatiques*, I: 738–39. Also in Zamir, *Formation of Modern Lebanon*, 79–80.

33. Helmreich, *From Paris to Sèvres*, 242–73.

34. Lloyd George, *Memoirs of the Peace Conference*, II: 832. The telegram appears to have been published that day: "The Marash Massacres," *The Times*, March 6, 1920, 13. This was not the first news of the event; an earlier report was "Slaughter of Armenians," *The Times*, February 17, 1920.

35. TNA-London, "Les regrets de Lord Curzon," *Le Matin*, February 13, 1920, enclosed in note of same date from Graham to Curzon, alerting the foreign minister that high-ranking officials in Paris were upset at his lack of tact. FO 800/153, 248–50.

Chapter 10: The Prince, the Sheikh, and "the Day of Resurrection"

1. Hokayem, *Documents diplomatiques*, II: 21–26.
2. The following conversation is summarized in Muhammad Rashid Rida, "Lessons from King Faisal's Life (6)," *al-Manar* 34 (May 1934): 68–72. I have added detail from Rida's diary entries for January 14–20, 1920, as quoted in Ryad, "Like a Mill Donkey."
3. Chamber of Deputies minutes for December 27, 1918, and December 23, 1919, published in *Journal officiel de la République française. Débats parlementaires. Chambre des deputés* [hereafter *Journal officiel-Chambre*]. Accessed September 12, 2018, at https://gallica.bnf.fr/ark:/12148/bpt6k6465506k.texteBrut?download=1 and https://gallica.bnf.fr/ark:/12148/bpt6k6261828g.texteBrut?download=1.
4. "The Covenant of the League of Nations," Avalon Project, Yale Law School, accessed April 9, 2019, at http://avalon.law.yale.edu/20th_century/leagcov.asp#art22.
5. Quincy Wright, *Mandates under the League of Nations* (Chicago: University of Chicago Press, 1930), 458–61; Smith, *Sovereignty at the Paris Peace Conference*, 47–48, 167–68, 225–26, 250–52.
6. TNA-London, "Report on a Conversation in Cairo with Michel Bey Lotfullah on His Return from Syria August 5th 1919," FO 371/4182, 330–33.
7. Shahrastan, *al-Mu'tamar al-Suri*, 92.
8. Muhammad Rashid Rida, "Lessons from King Faisal's Life (3)," *al-Manar* 34 (December 1933): 633–34; and "Lessons from King Faisal's Life (6)."
9. "Mail from Syria," *al-Kawkab*, January 7, 1920, 10. Kamil al-Qassab, "A Demonstration in Damascus," and "Mail from Syria," *al-Kawkab*, January 27, 1920, 5–6 and 11; "Tract répandu dans Damas le jour de l'arrivée de l'Émir Fayçal" and other tracts collected by French intelligence, generously shared with the author by James Gelvin; Gelvin, *Divided Loyalties*, 141–42, 279, 281.
10. TNA-London, "Emir Faisal's Speech at the Arab Club at Damascus," translation from *al-Ahram*, February 1, 1920, in FO 371/5187, 13–15; Rimawi, *al-Hukm al-Hizbi fi Suriya*, 50–54.

11. Allawi, *Faisal I*, 265–66, 268–69; Russell, *First Arab State*, 123–24; Khoury, *Urban Notables and Arab Nationalism*, 89–90.

12. Qadri, *Mudhakkirat*, 161–69; quotes from 167; Gelvin, *Divided Loyalties*, 209–10.

13. Russell, *First Arab State*, 127. The first committee included Ahmad Qadri, Izzat Darwazeh, Shukri Quwwatli, Rafiq Tamimi, Ahmad Maryud, Said Haidar, and Tawfiq Natur. The second committee included Nasib al-Bakri, Rikabi, Khalid al-Hakim, Asad al-Hakim, Said Haidar, Jamil Mardam, and Muhammad al-Shurayqi.

14. Muhammad Rashid Rida, "Lessons from King Faisal's Life (8)," *al-Manar* 34:4 (August 1934): 316; "Lessons from King Faisal's Life (6)."

15. Rida published excerpts from his diary on this period in Muhammad Rashid Rida, "Lessons from King Faisal's Life (4)," *al-Manar* 33 (February 1934): 711–14; Russell confirms the snowstorm cut rail and telegraph connections to Damascus for three weeks: Russell, *First Arab State*, 131.

16. Rida, "Lessons from King Faisal's Life (4)," 714; confirmed in Rida's diary, February 12, 1920, as quoted in Ryad, "Like a Mill Donkey." On the February 9 meeting, see also Rimawi, *al-Hukm al-Hizbi*, 185–86.

17. Rida's diary, February 20, 1920, as quoted in Ryad, "Like a Mill Donkey."

18. Russell, *First Arab State*, 126; Allawi, *Faisal I*, 268; Cousse to Gouraud, February 9, 1920, in Hokayem, *Documents diplomatiques*, II: 71–72.

19. Gouraud to Millerand, February 7, 1920; Cousse to Gouraud, February 18, 1920; Gouraud to Ministry of Foreign Affairs, Paris, February 18, 1920; and Cambon to Millerand, February 25, 1920, in Hokayem, *Documents diplomatiques*, II: 69, 81–85, 94–95.

20. Gouraud to Faisal, March 2, 1920, in Hokayem, *Documents diplomatiques*, II: 99–100.

21. Rimawi, *al-Hukm al-Hizbi*, 188–91.

22. Muhammad Rashid Rida, "Lessons from King Faisal's Life (5)," *al-Manar* 33 (April 1934): 792–98.

23. Qadri, *Mudhakkirat*, 176–78; Rimawi, *al-Hukm al-Hizbi*, 190–93.

24. Abd al-Hadi, *Mudhakkirat*, 84–87; Rida's diary entry at the end of February 1920, as quoted in Ryad, "Like a Mill Donkey."

25. Rida's diary of February 29, 1920, as quoted in Ryad, "Like a Mill Donkey."

26. Allawi, *Faisal I*, 273–75, is typical in its description of Faisal cowed by Qassab's "mob." See also Allenby memo of March 7, 1920, No. EA 3004, and "Rapport Hebdomadaire du 2ème Bureau de l'Armée française

du Levant, Semaine du 2 au 8 mars 1920," in Hokayem, *Documents diplomatiques*, II: 119–20.

27. Darwazeh, *Mudhakkirat*, 2: 451.

28. Rida, "Lessons from King Faisal's Life (6)"; Darwazeh, *Mudhakkirat*, I: 448; Allawi, *Faisal I*, 271.

29. Rida's diary, as published in Rida, "Lessons from King Faisal's Life (6)," 68; and Muhammad Rashid Rida, "Second Syrian Trip (8)," *al-Manar* 22 (February 1922): 141–46.

30. Shahrastan, *al-Mu'tamar al-Suri*, 91–95.

31. The true date of Wilson's speech was July 4. Faisal paraphrased the original text, given here: "The settlement of every question, whether of territory, of sovereignty, of economic arrangement, or of political relationship, upon the basis of the free acceptance of that settlement by the people immediately concerned, and not upon the basis of the material interest or advantage of any other nation or people which may desire a different settlement for the sake of its own exterior influence or mastery." *Address of President Wilson Delivered at Mount Vernon July 4, 1918* (Washington DC: Government Printing Office, July 25, 1918), 4–5.

32. Appeals to Wilson's principles would soon ring hollow. Even as the Congress convened, the United States Senate was debating whether to sign the Versailles treaty, and would vote against it on March 19.

33. Amin Sa'id, *Al-Thawra al-Arabiya al-Kubra*, vol. 2, reprint of 1933 ed. (Damascus: Dar Rislan, 2015), 131–34; Russell, *First Arab State*, 133–34.

34. Russell, *First Arab State*, 133–34; Gelvin, *Divided Loyalties*, 193.

35. Rida, "Lessons from Faisal's Life (6)," 69; Arna'ut, *Dirasat hawla al-Hukuma*, 47.

36. The drafting committee also included Yusuf al-Hakim, a cabinet minister and former Ottoman official; Uthman Sultan of Tripoli; Saadallah Jabiri of Aleppo; and Wasfi Atassi of Homs. Darwazeh does not mention Rida, but Rida says he joined them in his diary. See Darwazeh, *97 Years*, 449; Shahrastan, *al-Mu'tamar al-Suri*, 96–99.

37. "Conversation avec S.M. Fayçal, roi de Syrie," *Le Petit Parisien*, March 29, 1920.

38. "The Official Program for Celebrations of March 8, 1920, Crowning Faisal I as King of Syria," *Syrian History.com*. Accessed June 14, 2017, at http://syrianhistory.com/en/photos/236?search=official+program +for+celebrations.

39. Abd al-Hadi, *Mudhakkirat*, 88.

40. Gelvin, *Divided Loyalties*, 246–48; "Feisal's Assumption of Kingship: Scene at Damascus," *The Times*, March 17, 1920, 15. The full list of deputies included Rashid Rida, Riad al-Solh, Amin Bayhum, and Tawfiq al-Bissar from the Lebanese coast; Dr. Ahmad Qadri, officially a deputy from Palestine; and Abd al-Qadir al-Khatib, Abd al-Rahman Yusuf, Teodor Antaki, Abd al-Qadir Kaylani, Ahmad al-`Iyashi, Saad al-Din al-`Iyashi, Mahmud Fa'ur, and Fath al-Mar'ashi from the Syrian interior.

41. "The Declaration of Independence and the Congress's Historic Resolution on It," *al-Manar* 21 (July 1920): 441–44. Translation by the author. An alternative English translation is found in Husri, *Day of Maysalun*, 138–40.

42. "Mubay`a al-Ruusa' al-Ruhin' [Oath of Spiritual Leaders]," *al-Asima* 108 (March 11, 1920): 3. The oath was signed by leaders of the Jewish, Armenian Catholic, Armenian Orthodox Syriac, Maronite, Greek Catholic, and Greek Orthodox communities. See also Darwazeh, *Mudhakkirat*, I: 450; Shahrastan, *al-Mu`tamar al-Suri*, 103–5.

43. Abd al-Rahman Shahbandar, "Faisal ibn al-Hussein," and "The Coronation of Prince Faisal as King," in Hasan al-Hakim, ed., *Abd al-Rahman al-Shahbandar: Hayatuhu wa Jihaduhu* (Beirut: Dar al-Mutahida lil-Nashr, 1985), 41–45, 123–29.

44. Gelvin, *Divided Loyalties*, 246–52; "The Crowning of Faisal I as King of Syria on March 8, 1920," *Syrian History.com*. Accessed June 11, 2019, at http://syrianhistory.com/en/photos/2738?search=crowning.

45. Cousse to High Commissioner, Report no. 204, March 9, 1920.

46. Sa`id Tali`, ed., *Dhikra fi al-Istiqlal al-Suri* (Damascus: Sioufi Brothers, May 8, 1919). Tali`was a Fatat member, deputy from Tripoli, and friend of Darwazeh. The volume was republished in Cairo in 1920 and reissued to honor Faisal after his death in 1933.

47. Shahrastan, *al-Mu'tamar al-Suri*, 135.

48. U.S. National Archives and Records Administration, Jackson (consul at Aleppo) to Secretary of State, March 13, 1920, RG59 890d.00/9, microfilm 722, roll 8; Postcard "Tatwij al-Amir Faisal Malikan `ala Suriya, Hama Da'ira al-Baladiya" [Coronation of Prince Faisal as King of Syria, Hama City Hall], accessed June 14, 2017, at www.alamy.com DRHR25; Gelvin, *Divided Loyalties*, 173; Library of Congress Prints and Photographs Division, "Arab Demonstration" and "Anti-Zionist Demonstration at Damascus Gate, March 8th, 1920," LC-M31- 13945,

Matson Photograph Collection, accessed September 13, 2018, at http://www.loc.gov/pictures/item/mpc2004000615/PP/.

49. Allawi, *Faisal I*, 275–77; Shahrastan, *al-Mu'tamar al-Suri*, 106; Brémond, *Le Hedjaz dans la Guerre Mondiale*, 340. Iraqi officials had made a side announcement of their own independence at the Syrian ceremony. Shahrastan claims that Hussein had heard about the declaration as early as March 9 and that he and his son Prince Abdullah objected to it.

50. Gouraud's congratulations were enclosed in note no. 43710 from Cousse to Faisal, March 10, 1920; Gouraud to Millerand, March 10, 1920, in Hokayem, *Documents diplomatiques*, II: 125–26.

51. Gouraud to Faisal, March 15, 1920, in Hokayem, *Documents diplomatiques*, II: 148–49. See also Shahrastan, *al-Mu'tamar al-Suri*, 109–10.

Chapter 11. Wilsonism Colonized at the San Remo

1. "Feisal's Assumption of Kingship," *The Times*, March 17, 1920, 15.

2. *The Times*: "Emir Feisal as King of Syria," "Indian Moslems' Protest," and "Coercion of the Turk," March 21, 1920, 16; "Arabs' Claim of Independence," March 16, 1920, 16; "Prime Minister on Caliphate: Indian Delegation's Case," March 22, 1920, 10.

3. "Constantinople: The Balance between East and West," *The Times*, February 25, 1920.

4. "Syria Proclaims Freedom and King," *The Times*, March 12, 1920, 1; "Christians in Syria Back Independence," March 14, 1920, 15; "Still a Friend, Feisal Says," March 18, 1920, 2.

5. Frederick Jones Bliss, "Basis of the Syrian Claims," *New York Times*, March 28, 1920, 1; Bliss to Wilson, March 24, 1920, *The Papers of Woodrow Wilson Digital Edition*, accessed June 4, 2018, at http://rotunda.upress.virginia.edu/founders/WILS-01-65-02-0128-0002 (original ed.: vol. 65).

6. "En Asie-Mineure," *L'Humanité*, March 14, 1920, 3. The article is signed "M.C." the initials of Marcel Cachin.

7. "L'Imbroglio Syrien," *Journal des Débats*, March 14, 1920; "Le Guêpier Syrien," *L'Homme libre*, March 14, 1920, 1; "L'émir Faiçal proclamé roi," *Le Temps*, March 14, 1920, 1.

8. Marcelle Hertzog-Cachin, *Regards sur la vie de Marcel Cachin* (Paris: Éditions Sociales, 1980), 7–8, 46–49, 67–79. Until 1969, the French socialist party was formally named the French Section of the Workers'

International (SFIO). Later in 1920 Cachin led a splinter movement that founded the French communist party.

9. *Journal officiel-Chambre,* December 27 and 29, 1918; December 23, 1919; February 5, 1920, accessed digitally through the French national library site Gallica on April 10, 2019, at https://gallica.bnf.fr/ark:/12148/bpt6k6465508d.texteBrut?download=1; https://gallica.bnf.fr/ark:/12148/bpt6k6261828g.texteBrut?download=1; and https://gallica.bnf.fr/ark:/12148/bpt6k6419728q.texteBrut?download=1.

10. Sylvie Brodziak and Jean-Noel Jeanneney, eds., *Georges Clemenceau: Correspondance 1858–1929* (Paris: Robert Laffont, Bibliothèque National de France, 2008), 542.

11. *Journal officiel-Chambre,* March 26, 1920, 739–40, accessed April 10, 2019, at https://gallica.bnf.fr/ark:/12148/bpt6k6419751z.texteBrut?download=1. Cachin was referring to Colonel Cousse, through whom General Gouraud sent his personal congratulations on March 10.

12. Haidar, *Mudhakkirat,* 588–600.

13. MAE-Courneuve, de Caix to Kammerer, March 23, 1920, PAAP 353 vol. 3/microfilm 11203, 211–14. Note: Khoury printed this letter mistakenly as addressed to Berthelot in *Tutelle coloniale,* 220–25. I found it in Paris in a folder labeled "Letters to Kammerer." On March 31, de Caix wrote again to Kammerer saying he didn't want to write a long letter to him because he wouldn't read it (Khoury, *Tutelle coloniale,* 226). Hokayem also lists the letter as to Kammerer, *Documents diplomatiques,* II: 164.

14. Khoury, *France et l'Orient arabe,* 330. On March 28, the leader of the colonial caucus drew furious applause in the Chamber for a speech claiming that Faisal "threatens to throw us into the sea!"

15. Robert Lansing, quoting a February 3, 1919, memo in his *Peace Negotiations,* 151–53. Like Curzon, Lansing was loath to recognize the sovereign authority of the Peace Conference or League of Nations. On advice to Wilson, see *The Papers of Woodrow Wilson Digital Edition,* November 12, 1919, accessed May 17, 2018, at http://rotunda.upress.virginia.edu/founders/WILS-01-64-02-0031-0001 [vol. 64, print version].

16. Smith, *Sovereignty at the Paris Peace Conference,* 47–52, 74–81, 222–26, 250–56. Quote on 47.

17. John Fisher, *Curzon and British Imperialism in the Middle East 1916–1919* (New York: Routledge, 1999), xi–xvi, 237; Harold Nicolson, *Curzon: Last Phase 1919–1925* (London: Constable, 1934), 6–8, 194–95, 201–2.

18. On God's divine will, see Nicolson, *Curzon: Last Phase,* 16.

19. Timothy J. Paris, *Britain, the Hashemites and Arab Rule 1920–1925* (London: Frank Cass, 2003), 70–71.

20. Young, *Independent Arab*, 304–6. Curzon said he first heard of the coronation on March 8: Curzon to Allenby, March 19, 1920, R. Butler, ed., *Documents on British Foreign Policy,* First Series, vol. 13 (London: Her Majesty's Stationery Office, 1963), 232.

21. Paris, *Britain, the Hashemites, and Arab Rule,* 70; Curzon to Allenby, March 19, 1920, in Butler, *Documents on British Foreign Policy,* 13: 231.

22. Paris, *Britain, the Hashemites, and Arab Rule,* 72.

23. No documentation of the roster of those present at the critical vote of March 7 survives. This estimate is based on analysis of the photos of deputies assembled at the moment of independence and published in the official commemoration of Independence Day: Sa`id Tali`, ed., *Dhikra Istiqlal Suriya* (Cairo: Matba`at Ibrahim wa Yusuf Berladi, 1920).

24. MAE-Courneuve, French translation of Faisal's letter to Wilson, April 1, 1920, and telegram received April 13 from Jusserand, Washington, in P1312 Levant 1918–1929, Syrie Liban, vol. 26: 89–91, 144–45.

25. Haidar, *Mudhakkirat,* 606.

26. Haidar, *Mudhakkirat,* 615–17.

27. American University of Beirut, Jafet Library, Special Collections, "Condolence Letters Received on the Death of Dr. Howard Bliss," file in Howard Bliss Collection 1902–1920, AA: 2.3.2.1.1.19.

28. MAE-Courneuve, "Weekly Report on Political Affairs," Beirut, April 20, 1920, Série E-Levant 1918–1929, vol. 28; Direction des Affaires Politiques et Commerciales, 15–27 mai 1920; Carton 313 Dossier 1/ Syrie-Liban-Cilicie/Dossier générale.

29. Garnett, *Letters of T. E. Lawrence,* 298–99.

30. Bodleian Libraries at Weston Library, Special Collections, Oxford [hereafter, Bodleian Library], Lawrence to Curzon, September 27, 1919, in MS.Eng.d.3327 Letters from T. E. Lawrence, 94–100, and Fareedah el Akle to Lawrence, March 30, 1920, in MS Eng.d.334, copies of the Letters of T. E. Lawrence, 467–71; Wilson, *Lawrence of Arabia,* 621–26, 631; Philip Knightley and Colin Simpson, *The Secret Lives of Lawrence of Arabia* (New York: McGraw-Hill, 1969), 153–57.

31. Quotation from the 1922 Oxford introduction to *Seven Pillars,* letter to S. F. Newcombe, February 16, 1920, and letter to F. N. Doubleday, March 20, 1920, in Garnett, *Letters of T. E. Lawrence,* 263, 298–99, 300–2; Wilson, *Lawrence of Arabia,* 630.

32. MAE-Courneuve, Cambon to MAE, March 23, 1920: 173, Levant 1918–1929 Syrie-Liban, vol. 25; Cambon to Millerand, March 30, 1920; Millerand to Cambon, March 31, 1920; Cambon to Millerand, April 1, 1920, in Hokayem, *Documents diplomatiques,* II: 177–78, 182–83; "Record by Earl Curzon of a Conversation with the French Ambassador on the Syrian Question," in Butler, *Documents on British Foreign Policy,* 13: 237–39.

33. De Caix to Kammerer, March 31, 1920, and April 11, 1920, in Khoury, *Tutelle coloniale,* 230–33.

34. Gouraud to Millerand, April 19, 1920, in Hokayem, *Documents diplomatiques,* II: 228–30.

35. Wilson to Colby, April 17, 1920, Link, *Papers of Woodrow Wilson,* vol. 65, accessed online May 17, 2018, at http://rotunda.upress.virginia.edu/founders/WILS-01-65-02-0205.

36. Meinertzhagen to Curzon, April 4, 1920; Allenby to Curzon, April 7, 1920; "Memorandum by the French Ambassador," April 8, 1920, in Butler, *Documents on British Foreign Policy,* 13: 246–48.

37. Lloyd George, *Memoirs of the Peace Conference,* II: 841, 848, 854–56; Department of State, *Papers Relating to the Foreign Relations of the United States,* 1920, vol. 3 (Washington, DC: Government Printing Office, 1936), 779–83 [hereafter, *FRUS 1920*]

38. Nevakivi, *Britain, France, and the Arab Middle East,* 245–46; Andrew and Kanya-Forstner, *Climax of French Imperial Expansion,* 216–17. The text of the oil agreement was accessed on June 14, 2018, at http://www.worldlii.org/int/other/LNTSer/1920/17.html.

39. Yergin, *The Prize,* 179.

40. Nevakivi, *Britain, France, and the Arab Middle East,* 246–48; Andrew and Kanya-Forstner, *Climax of French Imperial Expansion,* 217–18.

41. Nevakivi, *Britain, France, and the Arab Middle East,* 241–43.

42. "Minutes of the Meeting Held at San Remo 25 April 1920: Distribution of 'A' Mandates," in Hokayem, *Documents diplomatiques,* II: 239–43. Translation from French by the author.

43. Haidar, *Mudhakkirat,* 623–27.

44. Wilson, *Lawrence of Arabia,* 631–34.

45. Wise to President Wilson, May 5, 1920, Link, *Papers of Woodrow Wilson,* vol. 65, accessed online May 17, 2018, at http://rotunda.upress.virginia.edu/founders/WILS-01-65-02-0261.

46. Hijaz Delegation to Supreme Council, April 20, 1920, Hokayem, *Documents diplomatiques,* II: 261–62.

Chapter 12: The Sheikh versus the King—A Parliamentary Revolution

1. Shahrastan, *al-Mu'tamar al-Suri*, 229.
2. Darwazeh, *Mudhakkirat wa Tasjilat*, 2: 457–58.
3. Radwan Atassi, *Sagesse syrienne: Histoire de la Syrie à traverse la biographie de Hachem Atassi (1873–1960)* (Paris: L'Harmattan, 2013), 21–27.
4. The following dialogue translates and combines two accounts by Rida, from Muhammad Rashid Rida, "Second Syrian Trip (10b)," *al-Manar* 22 (May 1922): 390–96, and "Lessons from King Faisal's Life (7)," *al-Manar* (June 1934): 152–57. See also Shahrastan, *al-Mu'tamar al-Suri*, 104, 107–8. The exchange was witnessed by Faisal's chamberlain, Ihsan al-Jabiri, who confirmed Rida's account in a 1966 personal interview: Rimawi, *al-Hukm al-Hizbi fi Suriya*, 201–2.
5. The National Archives of the United Kingdom, London [hereafter, TNA-London], "General Organic Law of the Arab Empire," translation enclosed in Storrs to Clayton, "Note on Proposals Drawn Up by Sheikh Rashid Rida, for the Formation of an Arab Kingdom," December 9, 1915, in FO 882/15, 63–67; Eliezer Tauber, "Three Approaches, One Idea: Religion and State in the Thought of `Abd al-Rahman al-Kawakibi, Najib `Azuri and Rashid Rida," *British Journal of Middle Eastern Studies* 21:2 (1994): 190–98; Michelle Campos, *Ottoman Brothers* (Stanford: Stanford University Press, 2010), 46–51.
6. Muhammad Rashid Rida, "The Constitution, Freedom, and the Islamic Religion," *al-Manar* 12:8 (September 1909): 606–8; Elizabeth F. Thompson, *Justice Interrupted: The Struggle for Constitutional Government in the Middle East* (Cambridge, MA: Harvard University Press, 2013), 1–116; Zaman, *Modern Islamic Thought in a Radical Age*, 47–55; Haddad, "Arab Religious Nationalism in the Colonial Era; Charles Kurzman, "Introduction," in Charles Kurzman, ed., *Liberal Islam* (New York: Oxford University Press, 1998); Charles Kurzman, ed., *Modernist Islam 1840–1940* (New York: Oxford University Press, 2002).
7. Muhibb al-Din al-Khatib, "Teaching Independence and Democratic Principles," *al-Asima* 96:1 (January 26, 1920): 1.
8. Shahrastan, *Mu'tamar al-Suri*, 109–10. Members of the cabinet were drawn from all three zones, with some shifting of personnel since 1919. Minister of Interior Rida al-Solh was from the Lebanese coast. Foreign Minister Sa`id al-Husseini was from the Southern Zone, Palestine. The remainder came from within the Eastern Zone: Finance Minister

Faris al-Khoury (the only Christian); Education Minister Sati` al-Husri; War Minister Yusuf al-Azmeh; Minister of Commerce, Agriculture, and Public Works Yusuf al-Hakim; Justice Minister Jalal al-Din Zahdi; and Chief of the Advisory Council Alaa al-Din al-Durubi.

9. Erik J. Zürcher, *The Young Turk Legacy and Nation Building* (New York: I.B. Tauris, 2010), 221–28; Helmreich, *From Paris to Sèvres,* 308. English translation of the constitution adopted by the Grand National Assembly on January 20, 1921, accessed April 2, 2019, at http://genckaya .bilkent.edu.tr/1921C.html.

10. Zürcher, *Young Turk Legacy,* 110–50, 195–204, 221–28; Taner Akçam, *From Empire to Republic: Turkish Nationalism and the Armenian Genocide* (New York: Zed Books, 2004), 180–207.

11. TNA-London, "The Sentiments and Aspirations of the Nation," *Al-Difaa,* April 12, 1920, in FO 371/5188.

12. Atassi, *Sagesse syrienne,* 11–27.

13. Rida, "Lessons from King Faisal's Life (7)."

14. Shahrastan, *Al-Mu'tamar al-Suri,* 190.

15. Quoted in David, *Un Gouvernement arabe,* 48. Quote is from the newspaper *Al-Asima.* See also Fahrenthold, *Between the Ottomans and the Entente,* 45–47, on references to the American model at an earlier Arab congress in Paris in 1913.

16. Alan Taylor, *American Revolutions* (New York: W.W. Norton, 2016), 253–93.

17. Nathan J. Brown, "Reason, Interest, Rationality, and Passion in Constitution Drafting," *Perspectives in Politics* 6:4 (December 2008): 675–89.

18. The lawyers were Atassi's cousin Wasfi Atassi, also from Homs; Saadallah al-Jabiri of Aleppo; Sa`id Haidar of Baalbek; and Uthman Sultan from Tripoli (who taught at the new Damascus law school). The religious clerics were Shaykh Abd al-Qadir al-Kilani, a conservative former mayor of Hama; and Shaykh Abd al-Azim al-Trabulsi. Also on the committee were Ibrahim al-Qasim Abd al-Hadi, a friend of Darwazeh from Palestine; and Teodor Antaki, a Christian from Aleppo. There are some discrepancies on names. See Arna'ut, *Dirasat hawla al-Hukuma,* 86; Shahrastan, *al-Mu'tamar al-Suri,* 40, 179–83.

19. On the recommendation of the late Khairiyah Qasimiyah, I rely on the final version of the constitution, containing 147 (not 148) articles as published in the authoritative documentary compendium, Hasan al-Hakim, ed., *al-Watha'iq al-tarikhiya al-muta`alliqa bil-qadiya al-Suriya 1915–1946* (Beirut: Dar Sadir, 1974), 194–213. While Shahrastan also relied

on this text, she employed original article numbers used in debates before the omission of Article 3 in July.

20. Herbert F. Wright, ed., *The Constitutions of the States at War 1919* (Washington, DC: Government Printing Office, 1919), 590–91.

21. Shahrastan, *al-Mu'tamar al-Suri*, 46–50; Rimawi, *al-Hukm al-Hizbi*, 202–4. Gelvin, *Divided Loyalties*, 189, estimates that the Progress Party had 35 seats; the Moderate Liberals, 20; and the Democrats, 20.

22. "Second Syria Trip (10b)." Rida says he had "no other choice" on 395.

23. James L. Gelvin, "Post Hoc Ergo Propter Hoc? Reassessing the Lineages of Nationalism in Bilad al-Sham," in C. Philipp and T. Schumann, eds., *From the Syrian Land to the States of Syria and Lebanon* (Beirut, 2004), 127–42; Arna'ut, *Dirasat hawla al-Hukuma*, 37–50.

24. David Dean Commins, *Islamic Reform: Politics and Social Change in Late Ottoman Syria* (New York: Oxford University Press, 1990), 105–7, 129–31; Gelvin, *Divided Loyalties*, 109–10; Philip S. Khoury, *Syria and the French Mandate* (Princeton: Princeton University Press, 1987), 259.

25. Shahrastan, *Mu'tamar al-Suri*, 149–59, based on "The Government before the People: The Cabinet Answers Congress's Questions," *al-Difaa*, April 25–26, 1920.

Chapter 13: Women's Suffrage and the Limits of Islamic Law

1. This account of the suffrage debate is based on the report of the newspaper *al-Difaa'* of April 27, 1920, reproduced in Shahrastan, *al-Mu'tamar al-Suri*, 193–208. Unlike Shahrastan, I use the article's final number, 78, rather than 79. My account also incorporates the following sources: an edited version of the debate published in *al-Hawadith*, April 25, 1975, 47–53: Hanifa al-Khatib, *Tarikh Tatawwur al-Haraka al-Nisa'iya fi Lubnan* (Beirut: Dar al-Hadatha, 1984), 193–205; and Akram Khater, trans., "Women and the Vote in Syria," in Akram Fouad Khater, ed., *Sources in the History of the Modern Middle East*, 2nd ed. (Belmont, CA: Wadsworth, 2011), 169–77.

2. Anbara Salam Khalidi, *Memoirs of an Early Arab Feminist*, trans. Tarif Khalidi (London: Pluto Press, 2013), 44–45, 57–59, 71–75; Elizabeth Thompson, *Colonial Citizens* (New York: Columbia University Press, 2000), 94–95.

3. Rida, "Second Syrian Trip (5)."

4. Faisal had married Huzaima bint Nasser in 1904. While their son, Ghazi, participated in the coronation, Huzaima remained out of public view.

5. "Hurray for the Syrian Prince," al`Arus 6:1 (February 1920): 1.

6. Rosita Forbes, *Quest: The Story of Anne, Three Men, and Some Arabs* (London: Cassell, 1922); Baz, *Nazik Abid*, 10.

7. "Bismallah al-Rahman al-Rahim," *Nur al-Fayha'/Light of Damascus* 1:1 (February 1, 1920): 2.

8. Khalidi, *Memoirs of an Early Arab Feminist*, 98–99, 110.

9. Ibrahim Hasan al-Khatib, "The Rights of Women before and after Islam," *Nur al-Fayha'* 1:1 (February 1920): 7. Khatib represented the Sheheem district in the Khorroub province of the Chouf region southeast of Beirut.

10. Leila Ahmed, *Women and Gender in Islam* (New Haven: Yale University Press, 1992), 144–88; Beth Baron, *The Women's Awakening in Egypt* (New Haven: Yale University Press, 1994), 103–21; Thompson, *Colonial Citizens*, 94–100, 117–26.

11. al-Hakim, *Suriya wa al-`Ahd al-Faysali*, 95–96; Arna'ut, *Dirasat hawla al-Hukuma*, 37–46, 68.

12. Arna'ut, *Dirasat hawla al-Hukuma*, 50–51.

13. Gelvin, *Divided Loyalties*, 148–49, 214–15.

14. James L. Gelvin, "'Modernity,' 'Tradition,' and the Battleground of Gender in Early 20th-Century Damascus," *Die Welt des Islams* 52 (2012): 1–22; Ahmed, *Women and Gender in Islam*, 144–68.

15. Weismann, *Abd al-Rahman al-Kawakibi*; David Commins, "Religious Reformers and Arabists in Damascus, 1885–1914," *International Journal of Middle East Studies* 18 (1986): 405–25; Joseph H. Escovitz, "He Was the Muhammad `Abduh of Syria": A Study of Tahir al-Jaza'iri and His Influence," *International Journal of Middle East Studies* 18 (1986): 293–310.

16. My understanding of Rida's pivotal role began with reading the doctoral dissertation of Dyala Hamzah. I thank her for sharing a copy of it with me. Hamzah has published an English-language condensation of her argument as "From `Ilm to Sihafa or the Politics of the Public Interest (*Maslaha*): Muhammad Rashid Rida and His Journal *al-Manar* (1898–1935)," in Hamzah, *The Making of the Arab Intellectual*, 90–127. Based on Rida's record in 1919–20, I offer here a modification of Hamzah's view. Contrary to many previous Islamic scholars—and to his own later practice—in 1920 Rida used the concept of public interest (in Arabic, *al-maslaha al-`amma*) to limit the jurisdiction of religion, not to expand it. See Felicitas Opwis, *Maslaha and the Purpose of the Law* (Leiden: Brill, 2010). On the contrast to his later writings that expanded the jurisdiction of Islamic law, see Ahmad Dallal, "Appropriating

the Past: Twentieth-Century Reconstruction of Pre-Modern Islamic Thought," *Islamic Law and Society* 7:1 (2000): 326.

17. Eyewitness report by Asad al-Kawakibi in Al-Sayyid Youssef, *Rashid Rida and the Return to the Salafi Path* (Cairo: Merit, 2000), 10–11; Rida, "Syrian Trip," *al-Manar* 11 (January 1909); Arna'ut, *Dirasat hawla al-Hukuma,* 39–44; Commins, "Religious Reformers and Arabists in Damascu"; Gelvin, *Divided Loyalties*, 110.

18. Darwazeh, *Mudhakkirat*, I: 462.

19. Arna'ut, *Dirasat hawla al-Hukuma*, 47–48, 87.

20. Rashid Rida's diary, April 26, 1920, as published in "Lessons from King Faisal's Life (7)."

21. Gelvin, *Divided Loyalties,* 192. On Rida's worry that Europeans would exploit a rift in Congress, see his "Lessons from King Faisal's Life (7)."

22. Nazik al-ʿAbid, "Girl of the Nation, Where Are You?" *Nur al-Fayha* (May 31, 1920): 116. I thank Ceighley Cribb for sharing her research on *Nur al-Fayha* with me.

Chapter 14: A Democratic Consitiution for Christians and Muslims

1. Shahrastan, *al-Mu'tamar al-Suri,* 149–59, based on "The Government before the People: The Cabinet Answers Congress's Questions," *al-Difaa,* April 25–26, 1920; Hakim, *Suriya wa al-ʿAhd al-Faysali,* 156–57; Khoury, *Syria and the French Mandate,* 327.

2. Rashid Rida's diary, April 26, 1926, as published in Rida, "Lessons from King Faisal's Life (7)."

3. Hakim, *Suriya wa al-ʿAhd al-Faysali,* 144–45; Darwazeh, *Mudhakkirat,* I: 456, 467; Muhammad Rashid Rida, "Second Syrian Trip (10)," *al-Manar* 23:4 (April 1922): 313–16.

4. Rida, "Lessons from King Faisal's Life (7)."

5. Hakim, *Suriya wa al-ʿAhd al-Faysali,* 156–59; Darwazeh, *Mudhakkirat,* I: 467–68; Rida, "Lessons from King Faisal's Life (7)."

6. Sabbagh, *al-Mu'tamar al-Suri,* 197–98; Shahrastan, *al-Mu'tamar al-Suri,* 115.

7. Rashid Rida's diary, May 5–6, 1920, quoted in Ryad, "Like a Mill Donkey."

8. Arna'ut, *Dirasat hawla al-Hukuma*, 41–44.

9. Rimawi, *al-Hukm al-Hizbi,* 210–16; Sabbagh, *al-Mu'tamar al-Suri,* 200; Hakim, *Suriya wa al-ʿAhd al-Faysali,* 160–65.

10. Hakim, *Suriya wa al-ʿAhd al-Faysali,* 166.

11. Shahrastan, *al-Mu'tamar al-Suri*, 185–87.

12. Rashid Rida's diary, June 18, 1920, as published in Rida, "Lessons from King Faisal's Life (9)," *al-Manar* (October 1934): 393–94; Arna'ut, *Dirasat hawla al-Hukuma*, 68–69.

13. Darwazeh, *Mudhakkirat*, I: 353, 356–57; Rida, "Second Syrian Trip (10b)."

14. U.S. National Archives and Records Administration, College Park, MD, Jackson to Admiral Mark L. Bristol, Constantinople, May 1, 1920, RG 890d.00/16, microfilm M727, roll 8.

15. Ussama Makdisi, *The Culture of Sectarianism* (Berkeley: University of California Press, 2000); Engin Akarlı, *The Long Peace: Ottoman Lebanon, 1861–1920* (Berkeley: University of California Press, 1993).

16. Mustafa Aksakal, *The Ottoman Road to War in 1914* (New York: Cambridge University Press, 2010); Suny and Goçek, *A Question of Genocide.*

17. Carol Hakim, *The Origins of the Lebanese National Idea, 1840–1920* (Berkeley: University of California Press, 2013); Mark Farha, "From Anti-Imperial Dissent to National Consent: The First World War and the Formation of a Trans-Sectarian National Consciousness in Lebanon," Najwa al-Qattan, "Historicizing Hunger: The Famine in Wartime Lebanon and Syria," and Andrew Arsan, "The Patriarch, the Amir, and the Patriots: Civilisation and Self-Determination at the Paris Peace Conference," in T. G. Fraser, ed., *The First World War and Its Aftermath* (London: Gingko Library, 2015), 91–146.

18. Youssef Mouawad, *Maronites dans l'histoire* (Beirut: L'Orient des Livres, 2017), 143–65.

19. Memorandum by Hoyek to the Paris Peace Conference of October 25, 1919, reprinted in Zamir, *Formation of Modern Lebanon*, 269–78; Hakim, *Origins of the Lebanese National Idea*, 242–46; Carla Eddé, *Beyrouth: Naissance d'une capitale (1918–1924)* (Paris: Sindbad, 2010), 336–45.

20. Haidar, *Mudhakkirat*, 562, 569–71.

21. Clemenceau to Hoyek, November 10, 1919, in Hokayem, *Documents diplomatiques*, I: 738–39; Hoyek to Cambon, January 28, 1920, and Gouraud to Khoury, February 13, 1920, in Hokayem, *Documents diplomatiques*, II: 57–58, 76–77.

22. Khoury, *France et L'Orient arabe*, 329; Hakim, *Origins of the Lebanese National Idea*, 251–53; Zamir, *Formation of Modern Lebanon*, 78–79; Sami Salameh, ed., *The Mufakkira of Bishop Abdallah Khoury* (Zouk Mikael, Lebanon: Notre Dame University Press, 2001), 11–13, 22–33, 170–72.

23. Lebanese Delegation to Millerand, March 18, 1920, and Gouraud to Millerand, March 4 and 21, 1920, in Hokayem, *Documents diplomatiques*, II: 105–7, 156, 162–63.

24. Zamir, *Formation of Modern Lebanon*, 86–89; Gouraud to Millerand, March 4, 10, and 25, 1920, in Hokayem, *Documents diplomatiques*, II: 105–7, 123, 173–74.

25. Gouraud to Millerand, March 21, 1920, in Hokayem, *Documents diplomatiques*, II: 162.

26. Muhammad Jamil Barout, "The Syrian General Congress (1919–1920): The First Syrian Constitution, Context, Nature, Stages and Issues," *Tabayyun* 3 (January 2013): 23–48 [in Arabic]. The number of deputies in the Congress fluctuated over time. By my count, based on memoirs and Shahrastan, *al-Mu'tamar al-Suri*, there were 87 or 88 deputies in the spring of 1920. A Cairo Bureau intelligence report dated October 18, 1920, counted 88 deputies who served in the Congress between November 1919 and March 1920: TNA-London, FO 371/5040, 213–18.

27. Jordi Tejel, *Syria's Kurds: History, Politics, and Society* (New York: Routledge, 2009), 9–11; Stefan Winter, "The Other Nahdah: The Bedirxan, the Millis and the Tribal Roots of Kurdish Nationalism in Syria," *Oriente Moderno* 25: 3 (2006): 461–74.

28. Campos, *Ottoman Brothers*, 93; Matossian, *Shattered Dreams of Revolution*, 47, quoting *al-Muqattam*, August 22, 1908, 3; Anne-Laure Dupont, "Réforme et Revolution dans la Pensée Arabe après 1908," in F. Georgeon, ed., *L'ivresse de la liberté: La révolution de 1908 dans l'Empire ottoman* (Walpole, MA: Peeters, 2012), 425–27.

29. Umar Ryad, *Islamic Reformism and Christianity* (Leiden: Brill, 2009); Simon A. Wood, *Christian Criticisms, Islamic Proofs: Rashid Rida's Modernist Defense of Islam* (Oxford: Oneworld, 2010); Imad Eldin Shahin, *Through Muslim Eyes: M. Rashid Rida and the West* (Herndon, VA: International Institute of Islamic Thought, 1994).

30. Rida, "Second Syrian Trip (10)."

31. Rashid Rida's diary, Tuesday, April 13, 1920, as quoted in Ryad, "Like a Mill Donkey."

32. Rida, "Second Syrian Trip (6)."

33. Mari Ajamy, "Hail the Prince of Syria," *al-Arus* 6:1 (February 1920): 1; Thompson, *Colonial Citizens*, 95, 120–21; Michel Jeha, *Mary Ajami* (Beirut: Riyad al-Rayyis, 2001).

34. Husri, *Day of Maysalun*, 101–14. In Arabic, Faisal used the current term for minority, *al-aqaliya*, as opposed to majority, *al-akthariya*. See original Arabic texts of his speeches in Husri, *Yawm Maysalun*, 229, 231. On the history of "minoritization" after 1920, see Benjamin Thomas White, *The Emergence of Minorities in the Middle East* (Edinburgh: Edinburgh University Press, 2011); Laura Robson, ed., *Minorities and the Modern Arab World* (Syracuse, NY: Syracuse University Press, 2016); Jeffrey Culang, "Liberal Translations: Secular Concepts, Law and Religion in Colonial Egypt," PhD dissertation, City University of New York, 2017.

35. TNA-London, "Report on a Conversation in Cairo with Michel Bey Lotfallah on His Return from Syria, August 5th, 1919," FO 371/4182, 330–33; SUP to Rida, March 1, 1919, and "Fourteen Principles of the Syrian Union Party," dated Damascus, 1919. I thank Umar Ryad for sharing copies of these documents from his personal archive.

36. Gertrude Bell, "Syria in October 1919," 15–16, in L/P25/10/802, India Office Library and Records, British Library, London; Hakim, *Suriya wa al-`Ahd al-Faysali*, 141–42.

37. "Support for Harmony and Independence between Muslims and Christians," *al-Asima* 108 (March 11, 1920): 6.

38. Reports on Congress sessions addressing Articles 88, 89, 92, and 127–131 in *al-Asima*, June 1–14, 1920; Gouraud to Millerand, June 12, 1920, in Hokayem, *Documents diplomatiques*, II: 413–14; Russell, *First Arab State*, 149. These articles are numbered 87, 88, 91, and 126–130 in the final draft of the constitution reprinted in my Appendix C.

39. Shahrastan, *al-Mu'tamar al-Suri*, 147.

40. Shahrastan, *al-Mu'tamar al-Suri*, 187.

41. Barout, "Syrian General Congress," 36–40, 46; Shahrastan, *al-Mu'tamar al-Suri*, 331–32.

42. Hakim, *Suriya fi al-`Ahd al-Faysali*, 160, 164; Shahrastan, *al-Mu'tamar al-Suri*, 93.

43. Rida "Second Syrian Trip (10)"; *al-Muqattam*, August 31, 1908, 4, as quoted in Matossian, *Shattered Dreams of Revolution*, 1–2. The record of Rida's writings and constitutionalism in 1920 challenges older views that his Syrian-Arab nationalism was fundamentally Islamic at this time. See, for example, Asher Kaufman, *Reviving Phoenicia* (New York: I.B. Tauris, 2004), 7. As will be shown in my Epilogue, Rida's turn to political Islamism occurred later in the 1920s.

44. Shahrastan, *al-Mu'tamar al-Suri*, 38–41; Darwazeh, *Mudhakkirat*, I: 350–52; Pierre Fournié and Jean-Louis Riccioli, *La France et le Proche-Orient 1916–1946* (Tournai, Belgium: Casterman, 1996), 66–67. The proportions given are based on these sources, whose precise counts vary owing to the fluctuating membership of the Congress.

45. Rashid Rida's diary, July 5, 1920, quoted in Ryad, "Like a Mill Donkey."

46. Shahrastan, *Mu'tamar al-Suri*, 179–82, 229.

47. Hakim, *al-Watha'iq al-Tarikhiya*, 194.

48. "One People," June 1, 1920, and "Minority Rights," June 3, 1920, in *Lissan al-Hal*. General observations of press coverage are based on a survey of the following papers in 1919–20: *Lissan al-Hal, al-Haqiqa, al-Balagh, al-Baraq,* and *al-Bashir.* I thank Catherine Batruni for her research assistance.

49. Gouraud to Millerand, July 12, 1920, in Hokayem, *Documents diplomatiques,* II: 468–69; Zamir, *Formation of Modern Lebanon,* 89–90; Eddé, *Beyrouth,* 96–99; Seale, *Struggle for Arab Independence,* 150–52.

50. Hakim, *Suriya wa al-'Ahd Faysali,* 164–65.

Chapter 15: Battle Plans for Syria

1. De Caix to Berthelot, May 4, 1920, in Khoury, *Tutelle coloniale,* 239.

2. Andrew and Kanya-Forstner, *Climax of French Imperial Expansion,* 218.

3. Hokayem, *Documents diplomatiques,* II: 267.

4. Millerand to Gouraud, May 4, 1920; Gouraud to Millerand, May 11, 1920, 300–1; Millerand to ambassador in London and high commissioners in Constantinople and Beirut, May 11, 1920, in Hokayem, *Documents diplomatiques,* II: 272–74, 296–98.

5. Allenby to Curzon, April 27, 1920, in Butler, *Documents on British Foreign Policy,* 13: 252–53.

6. 'Abd al-Hadi, *Mudhakkirat,* 97.

7. Faisal to Millerand, enclosed in Faisal to Gouraud, May 14, 1920; Gouraud to Millerand, May 19, 1920, in Hokayem, *Documents diplomatiques,* II: 307, 328–30.

8. Shahbandar to Cousse, May 9, 1920, in Hokayem, *Documents diplomatiques,* II: 291–92; MAE-Courneuve, Gouraud to Millerand, May 25, 1920, 28, Série E-Levant 1918–1929, vol. 28; Direction des Affaires Politiques et Commerciales, 15–27 mai 1920, Carton 313 Dossier 1/Syrie-Liban-Cilicie/Dossier générale.

9. Curzon to Cambon, May 18, 1920; Millerand to Curzon, May 25, 1920; Millerand to Gouraud, May 26, 1920, in Hokayem, *Documents diplomatiques*, II: 320–23, 343–46, 351–53.

10. Millerand to ambassador to London and high commissioners of Constantinople and Beirut, May 11, 1920; Millerand to Gouraud, May 26, 1920; Millerand to Gouraud, July 23, 1920, in Hokayem, *Documents diplomatiques*, II: 296–98, 351–53, 525–26.

11. Curzon to Hardinge, April 26, 1920, in Butler, *Documents on British Foreign Policy*, 13: 251–52; MAE-Courneuve, "Declaration to Prince Faisal," "Response to Curzon on Accord," and "Paris to High Commissioner, Beirut," all May 26, 1920, vol. 28, Série E-Levant 1918–1929, 223–25.

12. Millerand to Gouraud, May 27, 1920 [with enclosure for Prince Faisal]; Millerand to Cambon, June 11, 1920, in Hokayem, *Documents diplomatiques*, II: 359–61, 409–11; MAE-Courneuve, Gouraud to Department, May 20, 1920, Série E-Levant, Carton 313, vol. 28, Dossier 1/Syrie-Liban-Cilicie/Dossier générale, Direction des Affaires Politiques et Commerciales, May 15–27, 1920.

13. Millerand to Gouraud, May 27, 1920, in Hokayem, *Documents diplomatiques*, II: 356–61.

14. `Abd al-Hadi, *Mudhakkirat*, 76, 83–84, 88, 92–93, 96–98.

15. Qadri, *Mudhakkirati `an al-Thawra al-`Arabiya al-Kubra*, 220–25.

16. Shahbandar to Cousse, June 2, 1920; Faisal to Millerand, enclosed in Gouraud to Millerand, June 10, 1920; Faisal to Gouraud, June 18, 1920, in Hokayem, *Documents diplomatiques*, II: 377–78, 402–3, 426.

17. MAE-Courneuve, de Caix to Kammerer, March 23, 1920, 211–14, in PAAP 353 Robert de Caix papers, microfilm 11203. Letters in Cousse's files suggest he was in sympathy with local officials who were not thrilled at the appointment of a "grand old colonial" as high commissioner. See also Republic of France, Ministry of Foreign Affairs archive at Nantes, Fonds Beyrouth [hereafter MAE-Nantes], HC/Beyrouth to Cousse, October 22, 1919, Carton 2430 Papiers Cousse.

18. Millerand to Cambon, June 11, 1920, and Millerand to French ambassador in London, June 12, 1920, in Hokayem, *Documents diplomatiques*, II: 409–11, 414–15; Khoury, *France et l'Orient arabe*, 342.

19. Millerand to Gouraud, June 12, 1920, in Hokayem, *Documents diplomatiques*, II: 416–17.

20. Handwritten notes of Millerand's conversation with de Caix on June 5, 1920, about moving against Damascus and Faisal with the aid of leaders

in the four hinterland cities and Bedouin tribes: MAE-Courneuve, Papiers Millerand, vol. 10, Questions coloniales, 120–21.

21. Memo preserved in Millerand's personal papers at the French national archive, reprinted in Khoury, *Tutelle coloniale*, 246–47. Khoury also makes the case for de Caix's influence on Millerand in *France et l'Orient arabe*, 340.

22. The correspondence is archived in the newly opened collection of General Gouraud's papers at MAE-Courneuve, PAAP 399/142, de Caix to Gouraud, June 8, 1920.

23. MAE-Courneuve, Gouraud to de Caix, undated response to de Caix's June 8 letter, PAAP 399/142.

24. Faisal to Millerand, enclosed in Gouraud to Millerand, June 10, 1920, in Hokayem, *Documents diplomatiques*, II: 402–3.

25. Faisal to Berthelot, enclosed in Gouraud to Berthelot, June 10, 1920, in Hokayem, *Documents diplomatiques*, II: 404–5.

26. Memo preserved in Millerand's personal papers at the French national archive, reprinted in Khoury, *Tutelle coloniale*, 246–47.

27. Gouraud to Millerand, June 12, 1920, in Hokayem, *Documents diplomatiques*, II: 413–14.

28. Millerand to Gouraud, May 27, 1920; Faisal to Gouraud, June 10, 1920, in Hokayem, *Documents diplomatiques*, II: 356–58, 399–400.

29. Khoury, *France et l'Orient arabe*, 350.

30. Salameh, *Mufakkira of Bishop Abdallah Khoury*, 59–63, 70.

31. "M. d'Estournelles de Constant proteste contre le Traité turc et la Campagne de Syrie," *L'Humanité*, June 17, 1920, 1; Jean-Michel Guieu, "La paix par la Société des Nations? Les évolutions du pacifism français dans les années 1920," in Stéphane Tison, ed., *Paul d'Estournelles de Constant: Cocilier les nations pour éviter la guerre (1878–1924)* (Rennes: Presses Universitaires de Rennes, 2015).

32. Paul Louis, "Les Affaires d'Orient," *L'Humanité*, June 18, 1920, 3.

33. Haidar, *Mudhakkirat Rustum Haidar*, 647–54.

34. Auguste Gauvain, "La Conférence de Boulogne," *Journal des Débats*, June 23, 1920, 1.

35. *Journal officiel de la République française. Débats parlementaires. Chambre des deputés* [hereafter *Journal officiel-Chambre*], June 25, 1920, accessed online, June 22, 2018, at https://gallica.bnf.fr/ark:/12148/bpt6k6331072j.item.

36. "Des Accords de 1916 au Moussoulisme," *L'Homme libre*, June 26, 1920, 1.

37. MAE-Courneuve, de Caix to Gouraud, July 7, 1920, PAAP 399/142.

38. *Journal officiel-Chambre*, June 25, 1920, 2430–37, 2443–45, 2447–52. Accessed online, June 22, 2018, at https://gallica.bnf.fr/ark:/12148/bpt6k6331073z .item.

39. *Journal officiel-Chambre*, June 16, 1920, 2464–65, 2471. Accessed online, June 22, 2018, at https://gallica.bnf.fr/ark:/12148/bpt6k6331074c.item.

40. MAE-Courneuve, de Caix to Gouraud, June 24, 1920, PAAP 399/142.

41. "Bulletin du jour," *Le Temps*, June 28, 1920, 1; "Nous sommes en Syrie. Nous y restons," *L'Homme libre*, June 27, 1920, 1; "C'en est fait," *L'Humanité*, June 27, 1920, 1.

42. Kurzman, *Democracy Denied*.

43. "Speech of Habib Lutfallah to Diplomatic and Financial Study Group of the French Senate," June 29, 1920, in Hokayem, *Documents diplomatiques*, II: 440–42.

44. Dan Eldar, "France in Syria: The Abolition of the Sharifian Government, April–July 1920," *Middle Eastern Studies* 29:3 (July 1993): 487–504. Reference to 494.

45. *Journal officiel de la République française. Débats parlementaires. Sénat. Compte rendu* [hereafter *Journal officiel-Senat*], July 28, 1920. Accessed online July 10, 2018, at https://gallica.bnf.fr/ark:/12148/bpt6k6463152t .item.r=Journal+officiel+de+la+République+françaisesenat+1920+ senat +1920.

46. Haidar, *Mudhakkirat*, 659–60.

Chapter 16: The French Ultimatum and Faisal's Dissolution of Congress

1. Haidar, *Mudhakkirat*, 659; Faisal to Allenby, June 19, 1920, in Rush, *Records of the Hashemite Dynasties*, 10: 367–68.

2. Allawi, *Faisal I*, 281; Rashid Rida's diary, June 20, 1920, as quoted in Ryad, "Like a Mill Donkey."

3. Rashid Rida's diary, end of June 1920, as quoted in Ryad, "Like a Mill Donkey."

4. Rashid Rida's diary, July 5, 1920, as quoted in Ryad, "Like a Mill Donkey."

5. Cousse to Gouraud, June 24, 1920, in Hokayem, *Documents diplomatiques*, II: 428–29.

6. Service Historique de l'Armée de Terre, Vincennes [hereafter SHAT-Vincennes], Cousse to HC, July 1, 1920, Renseignements 625,

SHD-GR4-H114-004; Cousse to HC Beirut, July 15, 1920. No. 696, SHD-GR4-H114-005.

7. SHAT-Vincennes, Cousse to HC, July 4, 1920. Renseignements 633, SHD-GR4-H114-004.

8. SHAT-Vincennes, Memo dated July 4, 1920, on meeting with Faisal and Cousse to HC, July 6, 1920, Renseignements 647, SHD-GR4-H114-004.

9. Gelvin, *Divided Loyalties*, 114–24; Tauber, *Formation of Modern Syria*, 177–78.

10. SHAT-Vincennes, Cousse to HC, July 8, 1920. Renseignements 662; Branet, Adjunct Liaison Damas to HC letter, July 10, 1920. Renseignements 671, SHDGR-GR-4-H–114-004; Gelvin, *Divided Loyalties*, 213.

11. Haidar, *Mudhakkirat*, 662–63.

12. MAE-Nantes, Prime Minister to President of the Syrian Congress, May 19, 1920, Carton 2358.

13. SHAT-Vincennes, Cousse to High Commissioner, July 7, 1920. Renseignements 654; Cousse to High Commissioner, July 9, 1920. Renseignements 665; Cousse to High Commissioner, July 10, 1920. Renseignements 673 in SHD-GR4-H114-004-0001.

14. SHAT-Vincennes, Liaison Français Damas, Renseignements No. 694, July 13, 1920, SHD-GR4-H114-004.

15. Sabbagh, *al-Mu'tamar al-Suri*, 290–95; SHAT-Vincennes, Cousse to Gouraud, July 13, 1920, Renseignements No. 691, SHD-GR4-H114-004; Husri, *The Day of Maysalun*, 61.

16. `Abd al-Hadi, *Mudhakkirat*, 99.; Haidar, *Mudhakkirat*, 99; Qadri, *Mudhakkirat*, 224, 237.

17. Rashid Rida's diary, July 13–14, 1920, quoted in Ryad, "Like a Mill Donkey."

18. Qadri, *Mudhakkirat*, 239.

19. MAE-Courneuve, de Caix to Gouraud, July 7, 1920, 399 PAAP/142.

20. Gouraud to Millerand, July 10, 1920, in Hokayem, *Documents diplomatiques*, II: 460–61.

21. Gouraud to Millerand, July 11, 1920; Gouraud to Millerand, July 12, 1920; Gouraud to Millerand, transmitting two telegrams from Lebanon, July 12, 1920; Gouraud to Hoyak, July 12, 1920, in Hokayem, *Documents diplomatiques*, II: 465, 468–71, 476–77.

22. Haidar, *Mudhakkirat*, 665–66; Paléologue to Millerand, July 12, 1920, in Hokayem, *Documents diplomatiques*, II: 470.

23. Haidar, *Mudhakkirat*, 666.

24. Millerand to Department, July 13, 1920, in Hokayem, *Documents diplomatiques,* II: 473–74.

25. Curzon to Allenby, July 12, 1920, in Hokayem, *Documents diplomatiques,* II: 472. France was believed to have proof of palace complicity, should it be needed to justify invasion. On July 9, Rashid Rida learned of the theft of royal treasury records containing the proof of expenditures on militias fighting in the Bekaa. Everyone assumed the records had been handed over to the French. See Rashid Rida's diary, July 9, 1920, in Ryad, "Like a Mill Donkey."

26. Olivier Bouzy, "Idéologie ou historiographie: Evolution de l'image politique de Jeanne d'Arc du XVIe au XXIe siècle," in *Connaissance de Jeanne d'Arc* 3 (2004): 25–45, accessed online July 12, 2018, at https://gallica.bnf.fr/ark:/12148/bpt6k5831710v/f27.image; Jay Winter, *Sites of Memory, Sites of Mourning* (New York: Cambridge University Press, 1995), 15–28.

27. Duroselle, *Clemenceau,* 867–68; Dallas, *At the Heart of a Tiger,* 585. For an exhibition on Clemenceau's passion for Buddhist philosophy and art, see http://www.guimet.fr/sites/clemenceau-asie/. Accessed July 11, 2018.

28. Haidar, *Mudhakkirat,* 670.

29. "Grave Situation en Syrie," *l'Asie arabe,* July 15, 1920, 1. Accessed online July 11, 2018, at https://gallica.bnf.fr/ark:/12148/bpt6k6273008v/f1.item.r=Faissal.zoom.

30. SHAT-Vincennes, Général M. Goybet, *De Beyrouth à Damas: Carnet de campagne du Général M. Goybet,* Savoie, 1922, SHAT-Vincennes, SHGDR-GR-4-H-246-009-0074 through -0125, 23. Photo of parade in Beirut accessed July 10, 2018, at https://www.granger.com/results.asp?image=0325170&itemw=0&itemf=0001&itemstep=1&itemx=1.

31. Goybet, *De Beyrouth à Damas,* 4–5.

32. SHAT-Vincennes, Cousse to HC Beirut, July 15, 1920, Renseignement 696, SHD-GR4-H114-005; MAE-Nantes, HC to Cousse, July 10, 1920, Carton 2372, dossier "Correspondance Cousse"; Brémond, *Le Hedjaz dans la Guerre Mondiale,* 332; Qadri, *Mudhakkirat,* 225.

33. Thomas, *The French Empire between the Wars,* 45, 56–57, 63.

34. Gouraud to Faisal, July 14, 1920, in Hokayem, *Documents diplomatiques,* II: 479–86. English translation in "The Case of Emir Feisal," *Current History* 13 (March 1921): 251–54.

35. Darwazeh, *Mudhakkirat,* I: 472.

36. Gelvin, *Divided Loyalties*, 280–81, quoting *al-Kinana*, July 15, 1920, 3; SHAT-Vincennes, in Zone West Cabinet Politique: No. 1270 Daily Bulletin, July 23, 1920, SHD-GR4-H60-001.

37. Muhammad Rashid Rida, "The Aftermath of the Great War," *al-Manar* 21 (April 1920): 337–44.

38. Darwazeh, *Mudhakkirat*, I: 474.

39. Qadri, *Mudhakkirat*, 238.

40. Cooper, *Breaking the Heart of the World*, 384–90.

41. League of Nations Archives in Geneva [hereafter LN-Geneva], Eric Drummond, memo on conversation with Mrs. Forbes, emissary of Prince [*sic*] Feisal, July 22, 1920, Série 4284 Events in Syria, Boxes R21–28; Dossier 3: Mandates for Arab Countries doc. 5690. Faisal's emissary at Geneva was Rosita Forbes, a British travel writer and journalist who had passed through Damascus in April. She met Rustum Haidar several times in Paris before traveling to the League of Nations in Geneva.

42. Sabbagh, *al-Mu'tamar al-Suri*, 297; Qadri, *Mudhakkirat*, 241–42.

43. Rashid Rida's diary, July 15, 1920, as quoted in Ryad, "Like a Mill Donkey."

44. SHAT-Vincennes, Cousse to HC Beirut, July 16, 1920, SHD-GR 4-H114-005; July 21 and 23, 1920: Zone West daily bulletins 1266 and 1270, SHD-GR4-H60-001 and SHD-GR4-H114-004; Qadri, *Mudhakkirat*, 242.

45. Darwazeh, *Mudhakkirat*, I: 475–76; Allawi, *Faisal I*, 286.

46. Qadri, *Mudhakkirat*, 239–41.

47. Husri, *Day of Maysalun*, 62–63.

48. Darwazeh, *Mudhakkirat*, I: 475–76; Allawi, *Faisal I*, 287; Rashid Rida's diary, July 17–19, 1920, in Ryad, "Like a Mill Donkey."

49. Qadri, *Mudhakkirat*, 242; Rida's diary, July 17, 1920, quoted in Ryad, "Like a Mill Donkey."

50. Muhammad Rashid Rida, "Clear Facts about the Arab Question: A Historical Essay," *al-Manar* 22 (June 1921): 442–79.

51. SHAT-Vincennes, Cousse to General Commandant en Chef Armée Levant, July 19, 1920, SHD-GR 4-H114-005.

52. SHAT-Vincennes, Zone West Cabinet Politique, No. 1275 Daily Bulletin, July 24, 1920, SHD-GR4-H114-004; Rida, "Clear Facts about the Arab Question," 466–68.

53. Rashid Rida's diary, July 19, 1920, quoted in Ryad, "Like a Mill Donkey"; Allawi, *Faisal I*, 288, quoting Qasimiyah, *al-Hukuma*, 202, note 1.

54. Darwazeh, *Mudhakkirat*, I: 475–76; Qadri, *Mudhakkirat*, 248; SHAT-Vincennes, Cousse to General Commandant en Chef Armée Levant, July 20, 1920, SHD-GR 4-H114-005.

55. Muhammad Rashid Rida, "Lessons from King Faisal's Life (10)," *al-Manar* 34:9 (April 1935): 710–12; Rida "Lessons from King Faisal's Life (7), (8), (9)."

56. Hokayem, *Documents diplomatiques*, II: 501–3.

57. Cousse to HC, July 20, 1920, in Hokayem, *Documents diplomatiques*, II: 504–7; SHAT-Vincennes, Zone West Cabinet Politique: No. 1268 Daily Bulletin, July 20, 1920, SHD-GR4-H60-001; and Cousse to "Mon Général," July 20, 1920, SHD-GR 4H-114-005-0116 and 0117; Rashid Rida's diary, July 20–21, 1920; Russell, *First Arab State*, 185. Note: Qadri used the Arabic word *fitna*, meaning civil war, in his memoirs.

58. Darwazeh, *Mudhakkirat*, I: 473.

59. Qadri, *Mudhakkirat*, 248–49.

60. Rida, "Clear Facts about the Arab Question," 469; Allawi, *Faisal I*, 288–89, quoting Taha al-Hashimi, *Mudhakkirat Taha al-Hashimi* (Beirut, 1967), 61–62; Tauber, *Formation of Modern Syria*, 78.

61. SHAT-Vincennes, Zone West Cabinet Politique: No. 1266 Daily Bulletin, July 21, 1920, SHD-GR4-H60-001.

Chapter 17: Maysalun—The Arab State's Last Stand

1. Husri, *Day of Maysalun*, 64.

2. Goybet, *De Beyrouth à Damas*, 23–24.

3. Husri, *Day of Maysalun*, 64–65.

4. Qadri, *Mudhakkirat*, 248.

5. SHAT-Vincennes, Cousse to Gouraud, Renseignements No. 690, July 12, 1920, SHD-GR4-H114-004.

6. SHAT-Vincennes, "Feissal" to Général Commandant en Chef Armée Levant, July 22, 1920, SHDGR 4-H114-005-0108.

7. Husri, *Day of Maysalun*, 65–76. Quote on 76.

8. T. E. Lawrence, "Letter to the Editor," *The Times*, July 22, 1920; Général de la Panouse to War Ministry, July 30, 1920, in Hokayem, *Documents diplomatiques*, II: 555–57.

9. Texts of Faisal's calls to war are reprinted in Sa`id, *al-Thawra al-`Arabiya al-Kubra*, 2: 191–93.

10. Rashid Rida's diary, July 23, 1920, in Ryad, "Like a Mill Donkey"; Rida, "Clear Facts about the Arab Question," 471.

11. Husri, *Day of Maysalun*, 77; Qadri, *Mudhakkirat*, 251.

12. Baz, *Nazik `Abid*, 10–11; Nadia Muhanna, "Behind the Legends, Naziq al-Abed," accessed April 21, 2019, at https://nadiamuhanna.wordpress .com/2011/04/29/behind-the-legends-naziq-al-abed/.

13. Goybet, *De Beyrouth à Damas*, 27; Gouraud to Millerand, July 24, 1920, in Hokayem, *Documents diplomatiques*, II: 529.

14. Goybet, *De Beyrouth à Damas*, 30–37.

15. Gouraud to Millerand, July 9, 1920, in Hokayem, *Documents diplomatiques*, II: 457–60; Général (CR) du Hays, *Les Armées françaises au Levant, 1919–1939*, vol. 2 (Paris: Ministère de la Défense, État-Major de l'Armée de Terre, Service Historique, 1978), 93–97.

16. I follow here Tauber's calculations based on a survey of estimates of troops and deaths, which vary greatly: Tauber, *Formation of Modern Syria*, 217–18.

17. Gouraud, "General Order no. 22," in Goybet, *De Beyrouth à Damas*, 48.

18. Qadri, *Mudhakkirat*, 263–64.

19. Husri, *Day of Maysalun*, 53–54; Russell, *First Arab State*, 189–90; Allawi, *Faisal I*, 291.

20. Darwazeh, *Mudhakkirat*, I: 480.

21. Darwazeh, *Mudhakkirat*, I: 481–82.

22. Qadri, *Mudhakkirat*, 265–66; Husri, *Day of Maysalun*, 79–80; Rashid Rida's diary, July 24, 1920, quoted in Ryad, "Like a Mill Donkey."

23. Darwazeh, *Mudhakkirat*, I: 481.

24. Husri, *Day of Maysalun*, 79–80; Allawi, *Faisal I*, 291–92.

25. `Abd al-Hadi, *Mudhakkirat*, 100.

26. Goybet, *De Beyrouth à Damas*, 40–45; SHAT-Vincennes, "État-Major, L'Occupation de Damas par l'Armée du Levant," SHDGR-$ -H246-009/ 0046-52.

27. Goybet, *De Beyrouth à Damas*, 45–46.

28. Instructions of General Gouraud for Colonel Toulat, July 26, 1920, in Hokayem, *Documents diplomatiques*, II: 538.

29. Qadri, *Mudhakkirat*, 273; Toulat to Gouraud, July 28, 1920, in Hokayem, *Documents diplomatiques*, II: 548–49.

30. Rashid Rida's diary, July 18, 1920, in Ryad, "Like a Mill Donkey"; Rida, "Clear Facts about the Arab Question," 470.

31. Toulat to Gouraud, July 30, 1920, in Hokayem, *Documents diplomatiques,* II: 558.
32. `Abd al-Hadi, *Mudhakkirat,* 100–1; MAE-Courneuve, Toulat to HC, Aley, and Faisal to General Gouraud, July 28, 1920, PAAP 399, Carton 134.
33. Allawi, *Faisal I,* 293.
34. Husri, *Day of Maysalun,* 82–83.
35. Allawi, *Faisal I,* 300.
36. Darwazeh, *Mudhakkirat,* I: 483; Allawi, *Faisal I,* 294.
37. MAE-Courneuve, de Caix to Gouraud, July 17/21, 1920, 399 PAAP/142.
38. MAE-Nantes, Millerand to Commandant Armée du Levant, July 29, 1920, Carton 2358; and "Directives," orders to Goybet, July 24, 1920, Carton 2371; Gouraud for Goybet, in Hokayem, *Documents diplomatiques,* II: 534; MAE-Courneuve, Gouraud to Toulat, July 29, 1920, PAAP 399 Carton 178, folder "Déroulement."
39. Gouraud to Department, July 29, 1920, and Gouraud to Millerand, July 29, 1920, in Hokayem, *Documents diplomatiques,* II: 552–54; Général Catroux, *Deux missions en Moyen Orient* (Paris: Plon, 1958), 30–34, 86–88.
40. Rashid Rida's diary, July 31 and August 2, 1920, in Ryad, "Like a Mill Donkey."
41. Gouraud to Millerand and Millerand to Gouraud, August 2, 1920; Gouraud to Millerand, August 3, 1920; Millerand to Gouraud, August 6, 1920; Gouraud to Millerand, August 7, 1920, in Hokayem, *Documents diplomatiques*, II: 567–69, 571–72, 574–76, 581–89; Khoury, *France et l'Orient arabe,* 395–96.
42. Eric Drummond, Secretary-General of the League of Nations, to Hussein, King of Hijaz, August 5, 1920, in Hokayem, *Documents diplomatiques,* II: 578–79; Pedersen, *The Guardians,* 46–55; Patrick, "Woodrow Wilson, the Ottomans, and World War I," 905.
43. Articles 27 and 94 of the Treaty of Sèvres set the Turkish-Syrian boundary and recognized Syria's provisional independence under the advice of a mandate. Accessed April 27, 2019, at https://wwi.lib.byu.edu/index.php/Section_I,_Articles_1_-_260. Text of Sharif Hussein–Drummond letters, in Hokayem, *Documents diplomatiques,* II: 561, 578–79.
44. David Lloyd George to Mr. President, August 5, 1920, *The Papers of Woodrow Wilson Digital Edition,* http://rotunda.upress.virginia.edu/founders/WILS-01-66-02-0050-002. Accessed May 17, 2018.

45. MAE-Courneuve, de Caix to Gouraud, August 9, 1920, 9 and 11, PAAP 399, Carton 142.

46. Khoury, *Syria and the French Mandate*, 97–99.

47. SHAT-Vincennes, Speech of General Gouraud at Damascus City Hall, August 7, 1920, SHDGR-GR 4-H-114-005-0055 to 0061; and Zone West Cabinet Politique, Daily Bulletin 1324, August 11, 1920, SHD-GR4-H60-001.

48. SHAT-Vincennes, Sermon by Monsignor Giannini at Damascus Latin Church, August 8, 1920, SHDGR-GR 4-H-114-005.

49. MAE-Courneuve, "Entrée du Général Gouraud à Damas le 7 août 1920," PAAP 399, Carton 178.

50. Michael Provence, *The Last Ottoman Generation and the Making of the Modern Middle East* (New York: Cambridge University Press, 2017), 3, quoting journalist Pierre La Mazière, *Partant pour la Syrie* (Paris: Audinière, 1928), 191; James Barr, *A Line in the Sand* (New York: W.W. Norton, 2012), 94. Barr later suggested General Goybet said it. See "Gen. Gouraud: 'We're Back!' Did He Really Say It?" *Syria Comment*. Accessed April 27, 2019, at https://www.joshualandis.com/blog/general-gouraud-saladin-back-really-say/.

51. Qadri, *Mudhakkirat*, 277–78; TNA-London, Easton, Untitled Cairo Bureau intelligence report, October 10, 1920, FO 371/5040, 213–18.

52. SHAT-Vincennes, Toulat to Général Commandant en Chef, August 21, 1920, Archives SHD-GR 4-H114-005; Tauber, *Formation of Modern Syria*, 37–38.

53. In the early twentieth century, the French used *apache* for violent street ruffians. See https://en.oxforddictionaries.com/definition/apache and https://www.larousse.fr/dictionnaires/francais/apache/4390?q=apache#4377, accessed July 23, 2018.

54. Qadri, *Mudhakkirat*, 237.

Chapter 18: Wilson's Ghost in Geneva

1. Muhammad Rashid Rida, "The European Trip," Part 1, *al-Manar* 23 (February 1922): 114–20.

2. Rida, "Clear Facts about the Arab Question," 478.

3. Pedersen, *The Guardians*, 7; Marie-Renée Mouton, "Le Congrès syrio-palestinien de Genève (1921)," *Relations Internationales* 19 (Autumn 1979): 313–38, reference to 320.

4. LN-Geneva, Series 4284 Box R21 Events in Syria, File 2, Doc. 6882, Habib Lotfallah to Drummond, September 17, 1920, and Drummond to Lotfallah, September 22, 1920.

5. Paul Hymans, president of the Assembly of the League of Nations, to President Wilson, November 16, 1920, *The Papers of Woodrow Wilson Digital Edition*, accessed July 24, 2018, at http://rotunda.upress.virginia.edu/founders/WILS-01-66-02-0485.

6. LN-Geneva, Series 4284 Box R21, File 5, Doc. 8876. Telegram from Rashid Rida arrived November 26, 1920.

7. LN-Geneva, Series 248/Box 6/Doc. 8654, 11496, 10779; Pedersen, *The Guardians*, 50–52; Friedhelm Hoffmann, *Die Syro-Palästinensische Delegation am Völkerbund und Šakīb Arslān in Genf, 1921–1936/46* (Berlin: Lit, 2007), 43–73. I am grateful to Rawan Zoubi for her translation.

8. LN-Geneva, Series 4284/Box R21/File 5. Handwritten memo dated November 29, 1920; File 8 /doc. 9053, telegram protesting death sentences; File 11/doc. 9954, from former Hejaz delegate, December 25, 1920; File 33/doc. 8666 Syrian Union protest, November 22, 1920.

9. LN-Geneva, Series 4284/Box R21/File 21/Doc. 11504.

10. LN-Geneva, Series 15122/Box 589/Doc. 11691, General Haddad Pasha to Drummond, 14 March 1921.

11. Allawi, *Faisal I*, 310–13, 334. Quote on 313.

12. Allawi, *Faisal I*, 319–36, 361–81.

13. Rida, "Clear Facts about the Arab Question," 478–79.

14. Pedersen, *The Guardians*, 45–55. Quote on 52.

15. Muhammad Rashid Rida, "The European Trip (4)," *al-Manar* 23 (June 1922): 441–59. Quotes on 442–43.

16. LN-Geneva, Congrès Syrio-Palestinien, *Appel adressé à la 2ème Assemblée Générale de la Société des Nations* (Geneva: Geneva Tribune Press, 1921), Series 4284/Box R21. I present here translations from the Arabic version that Rida published in "The European Trip (4)," 449–59.

17. Rida, "The European Trip (4)," 455.

18. Muhammad Rashid Rida, "The European Trip (5)," *al-Manar* 23 (July 1922): 553–60.

19. Muhammad Rashid Rida, "The European Trip (6)," *al-Manar* 23 (October 1922): 635–57.

20. Société des Nations, Commission Permanente des Mandats, *Procès Verbaux de la Première Session*, Geneva, October 4–8, 1921, 1–10.

Accessed June 12, 2019, at https://biblio-archive.unog.ch/Dateien/CouncilMSD/C-416-M-296-1921-VI_BI.pdf.

21. Mouton, "Le Congrès," 323–26.

22. Columbia University Rare Books and Manuscripts Library, Bakhmeteff Archive, "Memoirs of Charles R. Crane," 429–30, Papers of Charles R. Crane, Box 20. The speeches were published as *Wilson's Fourteen Points* (Cairo: Mokattam Press, 1925) and *Crane and Syria* (Cairo: Salafiya Press, 1927). The Salafiya Press was a religious press associated with Rida.

23. King-Crane Commission Digital Collection, Oberlin College Archives [hereafter KCDC], Donald Brodie, "Mr. Crane's Visit to Syria, April 1–9, 1922," accessed July 27, 2018, at http://dcollections.oberlin.edu/cdm/compoundobject/collection/kingcrane/id/1777/rec/1; and Abd al-Rahman Shahbandar, *Mudhakkirat wa Khutub*, ed. Muhammad Kamil al-Khatib (Damascus: Manshurat al-Wizara al-Thiqafiya, 1993), chapter titled "Crane in Syria," 9–68.

24. Khoury, *Syria and the French Mandate*, 122.

25. Brodie, "Mr. Crane's Visit to Syria," 8; "Memoirs of Charles R. Crane," 430–32; Philip S. Khoury, "'Abd al-Rahman Shahbandar: An Independence Leader of Interwar Syria," in C. Mansour and L. Fawaz, eds., *Transformed Landscapes* (New York: American University in Cairo Press, 2009), 31–60.

26. Khoury, *Syria and the French Mandate*, 121–25.

27. "Crane Sentenced by French in Syria but Free in Paris," *New York Times*, May 26, 1922, 1. Postcard of Shahbandar and two others sentenced, accessed July 27, 2018, at http://www.syrianhistory.com/en/photos/320?tag=Abdul+Rahman+Shahbandar.

28. KCDC, Shahbandar to Wilson, April 6, 1922. In apparent error, the archive dated the letter May 6, 1922. Accessed September 23, 2018, at http://dcollections.oberlin.edu/cdm/compoundobject/collection/kingcrane/id/1466/rec/1.

29. "French Military Court Sentences Charles R. Crane," *Sacramento Union*, May 26, 1922, reprinting a story published that day in the *Chicago Daily News*. See also "The Damascus Riots," *The Times*, May 26, 1922, 10; Catroux, *Deux missions*, 96–99.

30. "Syrians Threaten War on the French," *New York Times*, May 14, 1922: 3; "No Question at Paris of Bringing Crane to Account," *Boston Globe*, May 27, 1922: 7; and "Crane Again Jars French on Syria," *New York*

Times, May 27, 1922, 1. A search on Newspapers.com turned up 433 American newspaper articles mentioning Crane's name in May 1922.

31. "First Publication of the King-Crane Report on the Near East," *Editor and Publisher* 55:27 (December 2, 1922).

32. Secretary of State to Ambassador in France and Ambassador in France (Herrick) to Secretary of State, May 19 and June 30, 1922; Balfour to Hughes, January 13, 1922; Secretary of State to Balfour, January 27, 1922; Secretary of State to Ambassador in Great Britain (Harvey), April 3, 1922; Harvey to Secretary of State, May 1, 1922; Secretary of State to Harvey, May 8, 1922; British Chargé (Chilton) to Secretary of State, July 10, 1922; State Department, *Papers Relating to the Foreign Relations of the United States 1922*, vol. 2 (Washington, DC: Government Printing Office, 1938), 117–33, 268–300 [hereafter *FRUS 1922*].

33. Philippe Gouraud, *Le Général Henri Gouraud au Liban et en Syrie 1919–1923* (Paris: L'Harmattan, 1993), 147–49, 163–64; Comte R. de Gontaut-Biron, *Comment la France s'est installée en Syrie (1918–1919)* (Paris: Plon, 1922), 185–212; Alfred Fabre, *La crise des Alliances* (Paris: Société d'Études et d'Informations Économiques, 1922), 15–39, 51–61; Haut Commissariat de la République française, *La Syrie et le Liban en 1921* (Paris: Émile Larose, 1922), 242; David, *Gouvernement arabe à Damas*, 56–63, 73–79, 118–20; Auguste Gauvain, "Five Years of French Policy in the Near East," *Foreign Affairs* 3:2 (December 15, 1924): 277–92.

34. LN-Geneva, Annual report for 1922 in Series 4284/Box 22/File 1/Doc. 22042, 2–10. Quote from 10.

35. Amir Shakib Arslan, *A'mal al-Wafd al-Suri al-Filastini*, ed. Sawsan al-Najjar Nasr (al-Shouf, Lebanon: Dar al-Taqaddamiya, 2009), 50–54; Pedersen, *The Guardians*, 80–92, 107–11.

36. "A Mandates Approved," *The Times*, July 25, 1922, 9; Wright, *Mandates under the League of Nations*, 56–59.

37. Turkish Diplomatic Mission to Department of State, May 18, 1922, enclosed in Ambassador in France (Herrick) to Secretary of State, May 26, 1922, in *FRUS 1922*, 2: 280–81.

38. LN-Geneva League of Nations, "Mandate for Syria and the Lebanon," August 12, 1922, Series 4284, Box 22, Articles 2, 15, and 19. Published in English as "French Mandate for Syria and Lebanon," supplement to *American Journal of International Law* 17:3 (July 1923): 177–82.

39. Arslan, *A'mal al-Wafd al-Suri*, 120, 130–32.

40. MAE-Courneuve, "Independence Is Not Given," PAAP 399, Carton 130.

41. Muhammad Rashid Rida, "The European Trip," Part 7, *al-Manar* 23 (November 1922): 700–2.

42. MAE-Courneuve, Gouraud to Poincaré, August 17, 1922, and November 9, 1922, PAAP 399, Carton 130, File 2, "Officiel Départ"; *Journal officiel-Chambre*, 2ème séance du 23 juin 1922, 1971–84. Deputy Louis Chappedelaine was joined by Edouard Daladier and Léon Blum in proposing immediate budget cuts. They received general applause from the Chamber. On Chappedelaine's Verdun honors, see http:// www2.assembleenationale.fr/sycomore/fiche/(num_dept)/1648.

43. Priya Satia, *Spies in Arabia: The Great War and the Cultural Foundations of Britain's Covert Empire in the Middle East* (New York: Oxford University Press, 2008), 439–62.

44. Daniel Neep, *Occupying Syria under the French Mandate* (New York: Cambridge University Press, 2012), 50–57; Martin Thomas, *Empires of Intelligence: Security Services and Colonial Disorder after 1914* (Berkeley: University of California Press, 2007), 14–44.

45. Khoury, *Tutelle coloniale*, 66–70, 83–86.

46. Muhammad ʻIzzat Darwazeh, *Hawl al-Haraka al-ʻArabiya al-Haditha*, vol. 3 (Beirut: Manshurat al-Arabiya al-ʻAsiriya, 1959), 136, as quoted in Arna'ut, *Dirasat hawla al-Hukuma*, 95–96.

47. "Simplicity Marks Service in the Home," *New York Times*, February 7, 1924: 2; F. W. Brecher, "Charles R. Crane's Crusade for the Arabs, 1919–39," *Middle Eastern Studies* 24:1 (1988): 43.

48. "Memorial Services for Woodrow Wilson," *Congressional Record, House of Representatives*, December 15, 1924, 628–35; Rabitat Sharqiya, *The Democratic President Wilson* (Cairo: Mokattam Press, 1925).

49. Throntveit, *Power without Victory*, 299.

50. Pedersen, *The Guardians*, 45.

Epilogue: Parting of Ways

1. Hakim, *Abd al-Rahman al-Shahbandar*, 110.

2. Michael Provence, *The Great Syrian Revolt and the Rise of Arab Nationalism* (Austin: University of Texas Press, 2005), 81–83.

3. Provence, *Last Ottoman Generation*, 163–64.

4. Seale, *Struggle for Arab Independence*, 202–5; William L. Cleveland, *Islam against the West: Shakib Arslan and the Campaign for Islamic Nationalism* (London: Al Saqi, 1985), 52–55.

5. Columbia University Rare Books and Manuscripts Library [hereafter CURBML], "Memoirs of Charles R. Crane," 499–500, Bakhmeteff Archive, Papers of Charles R. Crane, Box 20.

6. Provence, *Last Ottoman Generation*, 170–75.

7. French Ministry of Foreign Affairs archive at Nantes, Fonds Beyrouth [hereafter MAE-Nantes], Robert de Caix, "L'organisation donnée à la Syrie et au Liban depuis 1919 et l'élaboration du Statut Organique," November 20, 1925, Carton 1359, Dossier 1 Statut Organique. After days of research, I have concluded that all mention of the 1920 constitution was erased from the archive.

8. Provence, *Last Ottoman Generation*, 175.

9. Thompson, *Justice Interrupted*.

10. Khoury, "'Abd al-Rahman Shahbandar," 38–42; Cleveland, *Islam against the West*, 56–58, 64–65.

11. The National Archives of the United Kingdom, London [hereafter TNA-London], Henderson to Chamberlain, November 7, 1927, FO 141/810/6; "Scission du comité syro-palestinien," *Le Temps*, December 3, 1927, 2.

12. Khoury, *Syria and the French Mandate*, 262–68, 346–54.

13. Weldon C. Matthews, *Confronting an Empire, Constructing a Nation: Arab Nationalists and Popular Politics in Mandate Palestine* (New York: I.B. Tauris, 2006), 44–74.

14. Noah Haiduc-Dale, *Arab Christians in British Mandate Palestine* (Edinburgh: Edinburgh University Press, 2013), 97–120.

15. Darwazeh, *Hawl al-Haraka al-'Arabiya al-Haditha*, 3: 82. Accessed August 11, 2018, at https://archive.org/stream/al.haraka.al.arabya/al.haraka.al.arabya.03#page/n87/mode/2up.

16. Charles W. Anderson, "From Petition to Confrontation: The Palestinian National Movement and the Rise of Mass Politics, 1929–1939," PhD dissertation (New York University, 2013), 127–35, 149–56, 182–200.

17. Muhammad Rashid Rida, "The General Islamic Congress in Jerusalem," Parts 2 and 3, *al-Manar* 32 (March 1932): 192–208 and (April 1932): 284–92; Basheer M. Nafi, "The General Islamic Congress of Jerusalem Reconsidered," *Muslim World* 86:3–4 (1996): 243–72.

18. Darwazeh, *Hawl al-Haraka al-'Arabiya*, 3: 86–89. Includes text of December 13, 1931, resolution.

19. Allawi, *Faisal I*, 489–533.

20. Allawi, *Faisal I*, 431, 467–68, 489.

21. Tawfiq al-Suwaydi, *My Memoirs: Half a Century of the History of Iraq and the Arab Cause*, trans. Nancy Roberts (Boulder: Lynne Reinner, 2013), 122.

22. Allawi, *Faisal I*, 434–49, 508–16; Charles Tripp, *A History of Iraq*, 3rd ed. (Cambridge: Cambridge University Press, 2000), 44–74; Samira Haj, *The Making of Iraq 1900–1963* (Albany: State University of New York Press, 1997), 28–31.

23. Allawi, *Faisal I*, 542–47, 552–53; Darwazeh, *Hawl al-Haraka al-ʿArabiya*, 3: 86–89; Basheer M. Nafi, "King Faysal, the British, and the Project for a Pan-Arab Congress, 1931–33," *Islamic Studies* 37:4 (1998): 479–503.

24. Allawi, *Faisal I*, xx–xxii, 553–60.

25. Hakim, *Abd al-Rahman al-Shahbandar*, 52–54.

26. "Amity with Britain Is Pledged by Iraq," and "100,000 Arabs Pay Homage to Feisal," *New York Times*, September 12, 1933, 4, and September 15, 1933, 12. Allawi estimates only 30,000 turned out in Haifa: Allawi, *Faisal I*, xxiii–xxvii.

27. Darwazeh, *Mudhakkirat*, I: 834–35.

28. Tripp, *History of Iraq*, 77–91; Peter Wien, *Iraqi Arab Nationalism* (New York: Routledge, 2006), 34–42.

29. "Feisal, Twice King, Dreamt of Empire," and "King Feisal," *New York Times*, September 9 and 12, 1933.

30. "Feisal of Iraq," and "King Feisal," *The Times*, September 9 and 11, 1933.

31. "Morte Subite du Roi Fayçal," *Le Temps*, September 9, 1933, 1.

32. French Ministry of Foreign Affairs archive at La Courneuve [hereafter MAE-Courneuve], Gouraud to Senator Fernand David, November 4, 1933, PAAP 399, Carton 178.

33. MAE-Courneuve, Gouraud to General Huntzinger, October 30, 1937, and Huntzinger to Gouraud, November 25, 1937, PAAP 399, Carton 178.

34. MAE-Courneuve, "Le Retour de Fayçal à Damas," n.d. (likely 1925), PAAP 202, vol. 63, Syrie I; Peter A. Shambrook, *French Imperialism in Syria 1927–1936* (Reading, UK: Ithaca Press, 1998), 47–51, 55–60, 254–55; Khoury, *Syria and the French Mandate*, 353–54.

35. Rashid Rida, "al-Malik Faisal al-Husseini al-Hashimi," *al-Manar* 33:5 (September 1933): 387.

36. Muhammad Rashid Rida, "Lessons from King Faisal's Life (1) and (2)," *al-Manar* 33:6 (October 1933): 457–61 and 33:7 (November 1933): 555–60. The following summary of the series draws on parts 2–10.

37. Eliezer Tauber, "Rashid Rida's Political Attitudes during World War I," *Muslim World* 85:1–2 (1995): 118–19. See also Umar Ryad, "Islamic

Reformism and Great Britain: Rashid Rida's Image as Reflected in the Journal *Al-Manar* in Cairo," *Islam and Christian-Muslim Relations* 21:3 (July 2010): 263–85.

38. Muhammad Rashid Rida, *al-Khilafa* (Cairo: Hindawi, 2013), 109–10.

39. Israel Gershoni and James P. Jankowski, *Egypt, Islam, and the Arabs* (New York: Oxford University Press, 1986), 60–63, 264–67; Reinhard Schulze, *A Modern History of the Islamic World*, trans. Azizah Azodi (New York: I.B. Tauris, 2000), 65–74.

40. Muhammad Rashid Rida, *The Muhammadan Revelation*, trans. Yusuf Talal DeLorenzo (Alexandria, VA: Al-Saadawi Publications, 1996), 116. The original 1934 publication was titled *al-Wahy al-Muhammadi*.

41. Rida, *Muhammadan Revelation*, 136.

42. Rida, *Muhammadan Revelation*, 121.

43. Muhammad Rashid Rida, "A Generous American Publishes *The Muhammadan Revelation* in the East," *al-Manar* 34:9 (March 1935): 718–19.

44. "Charles R. Crane," *New York Times*, February 16, 1939, 16; CURBML, Crane Memoirs, 609–10.

45. Ahmad al-Sharabasi, *Rashid Rida sahib al-Manar* (Cairo: Matabi` al-Ahram at-Tijariyyah, 1970), 207–13. Quote on 213.

46. Muhi al-Din Rida, "The Late Muhammad Rashid Rida (1)," *al-Manar* 35 (April 1936): 215–21.

47. "Rashid Rida Dies," *New York Times*, August 24, 1935, 15.

48. "Speech of Dr. `Abd al-Rahman Shahbandar at the Memorial," *al-Manar* 35 (April 1936): 234–36.

49. "Speech of Mr. Habib Jamati," *al-Manar* 35 (April 1936): 208–10.

50. Personal interviews with Sami Moubayed and Amr Mallah, May 2019.

51. David Commins, "Hasan al-Banna (1906–1949)," in Ali Rahnema, ed., *Pioneers of Islamic Revival* (Atlantic Highlands, NJ: Zed Books, 1994), 125–33; Richard P. Mitchell, *The Society of Muslim Brothers* (New York: Oxford University Press, 1993), 322.

52. Brynyar Lia, *The Society of the Muslim Brothers in Egypt: The Rise of an Islamic Mass Movement 1928–1942* (Reading, UK: Ithaca Press, 1998), 53–76, 94.

53. Mitchell, *Society of Muslim Brothers*, 15; Commins, "Hasan al-Banna," 132. The Muslim Brotherhood published a later version of this essay with the claim that Banna submitted it (again?) to Farouk in 1947. The Arabic original and English translation were accessed August 17, 2018,

at http://www.ikhwanweb.com/article.php?id=802. It was translated into English by Charles Wendell, who repeated the Brotherhood's dating error. I use Wendell's translation here: Charles Wendell, trans., *Five Tracts of Hasan al-Banna (1906–1949)* (Berkeley: University of California Press, 1978), 103–32.

54. Lia, *Society of Muslim Brothers*, 202.

55. Hasan al-Banna, "In the Public Square Again," *al-Manar* 35:5 (July 1939): 3–7. Quote on 5.

56. Khoury, *Syria and the French Mandate*, 327–45.

57. Khoury, *Syria and the French Mandate*, 464–71.

58. Hakim, *Abd al-Rahman al-Shahbandar*, 123–29.

59. Thompson, *Colonial Citizens*, 152–53.

60. Khoury, *Syria and the French Mandate*, 584–89; Khoury, "'Abd al-Rahman Shahbandar," 31–60; Moubayed, *Steel and Silk*, 329–30; Hakim, *Abd al-Rahman al-Shahbandar*, 231–32.

61. "The Constitution of Syria of September 5, 1950," in Helen Miller Davis, *Constitutions, Electoral Laws, Treaties of States in the Near and Middle East* (Durham, NC: Duke University Press, 1953), 402–33.

Appendix A: Members of Congress in March 1920

1. In addition to the text of the poster, I have relied principally on the list of Congress delegates in Shahrastan, *al-Mu'tamar all-Suri*, 38–41. Additional sources include Muhammad `Izzat Darwarzeh, *Hawl al-Haraka al-'Arabiya*, 97–100, and BNA, FO 5040/162744, note 1171, Ernest Scott, acting high commissioner, Ramleh, to Lord Curzon, October 18, 1920, enclosure from Col. G. L. Easton, 215–17; and on the Arabic Wikipedia page for the Syrian National Congress, https://ar.wikipedia.org/wiki/المؤتمر_السوري_العام.

2. A slightly different version of the Congress poster may be found on the al-Solh family website, under the time line for Afaf al-Solh. Accessed October 28, 1919, at http://el-solh.com/timelines/afif-el-solh/.

Appendix B: The Syrian Declaration of Independence

1. Yusuf Suyufi, *Dhikra Istiqlal Suriya: 17 jumada al-thania 1338 al-muwafiq 8 maris sanat 1920* (Cairo: Suyufi Ikhwan, Matba`at Taha Ibrahim wa

Yusuf Barladi, 1920); "Text of the Resolution on the Independence of Syria Passed by the General Syrian Congress," in Husri, *Day of Maysalun,* 138–40.

Appendix C: The Syrian Constitution of July 19, 1920

1. Hakim, *al-Watha'iq al-tarikhiya al-muta'alliqa bi al-qadiya al-Suriya,* 194–213.
2. David, *Un Gouvernement arabe,* 135–53.
3. David, *Un Gouvernement arabe,* 135.
4. David, *Un Gouvernement arabe,* 101, 118–20, 130–32.
5. Shahrastan, *al-Mu'tamar al-Suri,* 193.
6. Shahrastan, *al-Mu'tamar al-Suri,* 188. The draft constitution published in Shahrastan contains minor differences but the same Article 1. See 245–62.
7. Majid Khadduri, "Constitutional Development in Syria," *Middle East Journal* 5:2 (Spring 1951): 137–60. See also Khadduri's section on the 1920 Syrian Constitution in a key reference book, *Dustur: A Survey of the Constitutions of the Arab and Muslim States of Islam* (Leiden: E. J. Brill, 1966), 65–70.
8. Angus M. Mundy, "The Arab Government in Syria from the Capture of Damascus to the Battle of Meisalun," master's thesis (American University of Beirut, 1965), 144–68. Mundy was an American government official posted in Damascus.

Acknowledgments

1. Samer S. Shehata, "In Egypt, Democrats vs. Liberals," *New York Times,* July 2, 2013, op-ed page.

Index